D0754264

Teacher Training and Effective Pedagogy in the Context of Student Diversity

Volume 1
Research in Bilingual Education Series

Editor: Liliana Minaya-Rowe
University of Connecticut

Teacher Training and Effective Pedagogy in the Context of Student Diversity

Edited by

Liliana Minaya-Rowe

INFORMATION AGE
PUBLISHING

80 Mason Street • Greenwich, Connecticut 06830 • www.infoagepub.com

Library of Congress Cataloging-in-Publication Data

Teacher training and effective pedagogy in the context of student
diversity / edited by Liliana Minaya-Rowe.
    p. cm. – (Research in bilingual education ; v. 1)
Includes bibliographical references and index.
 ISBN 1-930608-79-9 – ISBN 1-930608-78-0 (pbk.)
 1. Education, Bilingual–United States. 2. Teachers–Training
of–United States. 3. Multicultural education–United States. I.
Minaya-Rowe, Liliana. II. Series.
 LC3728 .T43 2002
 370'.71'1–dc21

                             2002004356

ISBN: 1-930608-78-0 (paper); 1-930608-79-9 (cloth)

Printed in the United States of America

for Maria Luz

CONTENTS

FOREWORD

The linguistically and culturally diverse student population of the United States represents a tremendous resource that we must nurture, develop, and educate well. In too many discussions, students who speak a language other than English at home are cast in the role of "problem," even liability. It is time to move from that deficit model to one that accepts and values the diversity of students and provides the high quality education that every student deserves.

How might this be accomplished? From a research perspective, there is considerable consensus on how to change learning environments in order to improve the education of English language learners. This is not to say that we have all the answers. We certainly do not. Moreover, it would be a mistake to think that we could ever have all the answers, because the students and the contexts for learning are always changing.

However, research has pointed to some key features for high quality education for our diverse student population. August and Hakuta (1997), for example, synthesize attributes of effective schools from the research. Two of the most important attributes are knowledgeable *instructional personnel* and ongoing *staff development.* Teachers and other instructional leaders need to know how to customize the learning environment for their students, adapting pedagogy to the local context and the needs of students. In addition, ongoing, appropriate and effective professional development is critical for those instructional personnel—both for specialist teachers (bilingual and ESL) and for all teachers who work with English language learners. It comes as no surprise that teachers and administrators play a key role in effective schools.

Unfortunately, these attributes are not widely apparent in schools serving students from diverse language and culture backgrounds. We do not have an adequate supply of teachers with preparation as specialists in language and culture. The National Commission on Teaching and America's Future (1996) reported significant shortages of teachers qualified to teach students with limited English proficiency and of bilingual teachers trained to teach in another language. Further, our teacher preparation programs by and large do not ensure that all teacher candidates learn strategies for teaching linguistically and culturally diverse students. Every new set of demographic information that is released points to increasing numbers of students from non-English language backgrounds, meaning that more and more teachers have such students in their classrooms. Snow and Wong Fillmore (2002) argue, for example, that *all* teachers need specific knowledge about language in order to work effectively with students from diverse language backgrounds, including basic understanding of the processes of language and literacy development, second language learning, and academic language growth. Programs that attend to these topics are rare.

Why is there not more attention to teachers' needs for such preparation? One issue is that of mindset. There is a widely held perception that English language learners need only to learn English, and once they do that, they are just like all the other students (the "problem" is "fixed"). As a result, some schools and policy makers place a singular focus on English proficiency, often without understanding the connections between language development and academic learning. (This is not to minimize the importance of developing high levels of proficiency in English for all students. Well-prepared English language teachers are essential, and all teachers should be prepared to support English language development.)

In order to provide high quality education to our entire student population, we must develop a cadre of educators with the "knowledge, skills, and dispositions" to work effectively with English language learners (González & Darling-Hammond, 1997).

Achieving this calls for improved teacher/administrator preparation programs and appropriate, coherent professional development for practicing educators. ALL teachers must be prepared to foster language development and shelter content instruction to create the best possible environment for English language learners. They must understand the full range of factors that may put diverse students at risk and be able to perceive and appreciate the diverse strengths the students bring with them. School personnel need to understand the whole student, not just the English language learner part. That said, it is also extremely important to provide qualified bilingual teachers and adult bilingual models, as well as English language teachers, in the schools.

The present collection helps us respond to the challenge of improving the preparation of teachers to work with our multilingual and multicultural student population. The editor has assembled reports of research that deal with both the form and content of teacher education as related to diverse students. From studies of pre-service teacher beliefs and knowledge to investigations of specific models for teacher development, the chapters offer research-based discussions that can inform teacher preparation practice. The editor and authors are to be congratulated for preparing a set of articles grounded in research that can help us see what can be done to improve teacher education and that can inspire further research on this important topic. We should act now to apply their findings and to extend them through further research.

—Donna Christian

REFERENCES

August, D., & Hakuta, K. (1997). *Improving schooling for language-minority children: A research agenda.* Washington, DC: National Academy Press.

Gonzalez, J., & Darling-Hammond, L. (1997). *New concepts for new challenges, Professional development for teachers of immigrant youth.* McHenry, IL: Delta Systems Co., Inc. and Center for Applied Linguistics.

National Commission on Teaching and America's Future. (1996). *What matters most: Teaching for America's future.* New York: Columbia University, Teachers College.

Snow, C., & Wong Fillmore, L. (2002). What teachers need to know about language. In C. Adger, C. Snow, & D. Christian (Eds.), *What teachers need to know about language.* McHenry, IL: Delta Systems, Co., Inc. and Center for Applied Linguistics.

INTRODUCTION

Liliana Minaya-Rowe

The central question in this edited book is how to train teachers of an increasing multilingual and multicultural American school population. Six million American children—one in eight—live in homes where a language other than English is spoken and more than 150 different languages are spoken by English language learners (ELLs) today (Wagonner, 1999). Since the numbers of ELLs will continue to rise steadily, schools require instructional programs to prepare them not only to learn English but also to compete academically. The provision of effective programs for ELLs is one of the most important challenges confronting teacher education today. Although teacher training has lagged behind new and effective pedagogy, this increase creates a wider gap between what teachers have been trained to do and the skills they need to teach our nation's ELLs (Riley, 2000). ELLs' opportunities to succeed academically depend upon teachers' knowledge of effective pedagogy to address their linguistic and academic needs.

The professional development of teachers of ELLs is one of the most unexamined and overlooked areas of pre-service and in-service teacher education in the United States. This predicament can no longer continue, especially since most of these students do not succeed in the American school system and one-half of them drop out of school (Secada, Chávez, Garcia, Muñoz, Oakes, Santiago-Santiago, & Slavin, 1998). As the presence of ELLs is felt in schools nationwide, school staff are increasingly under pressure to examine their assumptions concerning the students in their classes and their own instructional practices. Most do not receive the preparation before entering the workforce, however, and they have limited opportunities to update their knowledge and skills on an ongoing basis throughout their careers.

PURPOSE OF THE BOOK

The purpose of this volume is twofold. First, the book attempts to initiate a research-based dialogue from a variety of perspectives specifically about teacher training and teaching in the context of student linguistic and cultural diversity, and, second, to cast a wide net over three major areas of professional development that have the potential to impact on teacher quality and on the educational services provided to ELLs at all levels of instruction. This book represents a first attempt to a quiet revolution going on in teacher education (Johnson, 2000). It allows the reader to uncover research activities and experiences that constitute individual teacher education program initiatives. A revolution, because it is stirring the very essence of what stands at the core of teacher education, a core that has long been based more on training to teach monolingual English-speaking students and less on teaching ELLs, their first and second language development, using their bilingualism to teach academics, and on the process of becoming an effective teacher of ELLs.

This state-of-the-art review brings together research on effective pedagogy and teacher training. The nine feature chapters are directly concerned with effective new structures and practices for professional development and are presented in a framework that considers a wide spectrum of topics to address issues such as: what teachers need to understand about English language learners, what kind of professional experiences are likely to facilitate those understandings, and what kinds of teacher education programs and school settings are able to support their ongoing learning. The authors also discuss the implications of their work for helping English language learners connect and benefit from school from the points of view of (1) school reform, (2) teachers' bilingual proficiencies, (3) teachers' knowledge and beliefs, and (4) teacher training programming and sustainability.

BUILDING A FOUNDATION

This volume is an effort to bring together research of teacher education and effective teaching to add to other current and future studies in order to draw, compare, contrast and revise. While research on teacher training in the field of bilingual education is scarce, this lack of information provides fertile ground for future studies (Weiner, 2000). The present volume represents an effort to understand effective teacher training in the context of student linguistic and cultural diversity. In addition, previous research reviews have been comprehensive focusing on bilingual education with a chapter or two on teacher education, but none have tried to extrapolate how ELLs are taught and the required professional development to teach them.

There is much to study and write about best ways to train teachers of ELLs and this volume attempts to stimulate more research and writing. If we do not address issues of immediate training needs of teachers in classroom with ELLs, teacher training institutions and school systems not making the effort to address those needs, benefit by our silence (Faltis, 1999). They can both ignore the educational needs of ELLs and continue maintaining the status quo and ignoring the needs for professional development and teacher training and, consequently, reflecting the inadequacy of their training services. Universities and school systems do not need to change core curriculum in professional development and teacher education for ELLs' educational needs when no one is raising issues or asking questions about them. Short-term multicultural components in most in service programs at the district level usually consist of a few hours of training. Furthermore, teacher training institutions can get away with little or no courses, curriculum and comprehensive programs that meet needs of teachers and teachers to be in the context of schooling of ELLs. Then, colleges of education continue to offer fewer and inferior academic offerings, usually taught by adjunct or non-tenured faculty who do not have the voice and the opportunity to have an impact on university policies, curriculum and structural changes, reinforcing the image that the education of ELLs is of compensatory nature.

The majority of the chapters represent long-term sustained engagement of the authors with their universities, schools or communities and evidence collaboration among researchers, practitioners and school communities. Their research was conducted mostly in school districts across the US with large numbers of ELLs. Their research methodologies are appropriate for the study designs and situate the book solidly within the linguistically and culturally diverse student population. The authors have followed basic principles in their research:

1. They have used the methodological approaches and the complementary roles played between qualitative (e.g., ethnographic) research and quantitative (e.g., the more empirically driven). They have designed research that includes the observation of general patterns and trends in teacher education as well as minute details of teaching language and academic development, one-to-one, in various settings. In this way, their research does not only apply to the particular teachers or teacher-to-be, but that higher-order generali-

zations could be made with the data obtained (Denzin & Lincoln, 2000; Minaya-Rowe, 1992).

2.   They have researched teacher training based on a diversity of disciplinary involvement. Volume contributors have relied on several disciplines, each with their characteristic methods and theories, and include education, linguistics, psychology, anthropology as well as sociology. However, sociocultural theory has provided the *lingua franca* for this volume and the possibility of drawing all the chapters into a coherent whole, an important attempt for transforming the study into practice, action and policy recommendations (Tharp, Estrada, Dalton, & Yamauchi, 2000). Sociocultural theory lends itself to teacher education and teachers because we must concentrate on development and explain that learner and teacher are participants in sociocultural activity (Rogoff, 1990).

3.   Their main goal has been to examine the cumulative experiences of teacher training and effective pedagogy within the case study research framework reflected in the latest trends with the potential of covering important areas of teacher education and teaching (Cummins, 1999). The accumulation of such case studies allows researchers to present a rich and robust picture of teacher education and pedagogy in the context of linguistically and culturally diverse students.

ORGANIZATION OF THE BOOK

The book includes nine chapters written by researchers, teacher trainers and educators, the quiet revolutionaries, who have dedicated great part of their professional lives to understanding and improving teacher preparation programs to teach in linguistically and culturally diverse contexts. Chapters within each of the three main sections draw mainly from what actually happens in teacher training. Although this volume is research-based, all authors discuss the implications of their work for improving the conditions of schooling of ELLs. In this book we focus attention on teaching and teacher training practices, teacher training and school reform, and effective teacher training models, three areas with the potential to make a difference in the quality of education ELLs receive. Additionally, the terminology used by the authors to refer to students served—ELLs, bilingual, ESL, language minority, linguistically and culturally diverse, and so forth— has been kept as they are interchangeably used in the literature of bilingual schooling. In the same context, teacher education, professional development and staff development have also been kept to represent teacher training at the pre-service and in-service levels.

The nine chapters collected in this volume address factors influencing teacher education and teaching practices at the pre-service and in-service levels, teachers' beliefs about second language learning, learning their students' first language in order to teach them, and teachers acquiring and using professional knowledge. They also address school and district reform efforts in staff development, and implementation of a responsive learning community program and a resiliency program. They also include descriptions of teacher training models. All the chapters draw mainly from what actually happens in teacher training and are research-based. However, all chapters discuss implications of their work for improving the conditions of schooling of ELLs. A brief preview of the organization of the book and the various chapters follows.

Part I. Effective Practices in Teacher Training

The first part focuses on teaching in classrooms with ELLs and training teachers to teach them, professional knowledge and beliefs of teachers. The chapters in this part all start with the assumption that the traditional characterization of teachers in a homogeneous English monolingual and mainstream classroom setting rather than a culturally and linguistically diverse one is misguided. In their chapter, Hersh Waxman and Yolanda Padrón show ways to enhance the education of ELLs in traditional classrooms by improving the quality of classroom instruction. To back up their claims, they draw on five teaching practices—culturally responsive teaching, cooperative learning, instructional conversations, cognitively-guided instruction, and technology-enriched instruction. They pose a perspective on effective teaching practice which emphasizes models of teaching and learning that incorporate more active student learning and changing the teachers' role from that of delivering knowledge to one of facilitating learning, thus setting the stage for the ensuing chapters in the section. The authors examine implications for teacher education and professional development and school reform models, long-term professional development that enhances and expands teachers' current repertoire of instructional strategies rather than radically altering them, and to disseminate the research conducted in the field as opportunities. They proclaim the need for a change of policy to empower teachers with the authority to implement changes and to be sufficiently supported and valued.

In the next chapter, Toni Griego Jones reviews the beliefs of pre-service teachers about second language learning and how these beliefs relate to prior experiences working with language minority students. From an analysis of a survey, she shows the importance of addressing beliefs about second language learning, how beliefs influence what and how pre-service teachers learn, and beliefs as the process of change in teacher education. She embeds the complexity of patterns and the differences between pre-service teachers who had experiences with second language learners with those who did not with agreement, or lack of, key concepts in bilingual education and English as a second language, although they often misunderstand the language acquisition process.

In the following chapter, Liliana Minaya-Rowe and Ana María Olezza examine a teacher training graduate course taught in Spanish to meet mainstream, bilingual and ESL teachers' language proficiency and professional development needs to teach English to ELLs using the standards-based content curriculum. Using the context of socioconstructivism, theories of second language acquisition and sheltered instruction methodology, the five standards for effective pedagogy, and the language across the curriculum movement, the authors argue for a professional development approach that is both interactive and exploratory, that requires an understanding of both social and school factors that influence second language acquisition and academic learning. From an examination of reflective and interactive journals, questionnaires and surveys, end-of-course evaluation, and a survey administered a year after the course, the authors demonstrate how participants have benefitted from the course and how they are applying the sheltered instruction approach to develop ELLs' weaker language during subject matter instruction.

The final chapter of this section deals with features of pre-service teachers' emerging professional knowledge as demonstrated in the earliest lesson teaching experiences. Stephanie Stoll Dalton and Roland Tharp contribute to the notion of professional teaching knowledge and its utilization form in relation to pre-service teachers' prior experience and knowledge and the treatment available in their teacher education program. The authors draw on a detailed study and examine both quantitative and qualitative data of pre-service teachers. They describe professional knowledge as a function of two meaning systems, professional education lexicon and professional contextual structures, acquisition and utilization of the meaning systems for productive teaching practice, and a framework for judging the appropriacy of instructional activities and their effect. Specific attention is given to the relationship between the two meaning systems for developing teachers' professional knowledge with examples of professional lexicon, conceptual structures and standards of pedagogy.

Part II. Teacher Training and School Reform

Part II of the volume focuses on teacher training and school reform. Linking to the previous section describing teacher education and effective pedagogy to school reform, the first chapter by Margarita Calderón presents staff development practices in a variety of school and district contexts. Taking the level of commitment, or lack of, to the ongoing professional development of teachers working with language minority students, Calderón reports on a survey from a five-year national study on beliefs, experiences and professional needs of teachers on the job. She examines five themes: type of staff development experiences and their value to the teachers; teachers use, confidence, and appropriation of linguistic and cross-cultural skills for bilingual instruction; teachers' knowledge of research-based instruction; the status of primary language and bilingual program at their school; and, the type of collegial practices, relationships, and support systems at the school or district levels. The results show a range of professional development opportunities and their perceived value, and that comprehensive school reform models, two-way whole-school programs, and trainer of trainers' institutes provide more comprehensive approaches and follow-up support systems to help teachers transfer new knowledge and skills into the classroom.

The next chapter deals with aspects of the Responsive Learning Communities (RLC) Project, a multi-year school reform effort with the collaboration of teachers, school district personnel and university researchers. Eugene Garcia, Marco Bravo, Laurie Dickey, Katherine Chun, and Xiaoqin Sun-Irminger articulate the importance of developing and implementing a more responsive pedagogy and establishing a RLC with particular attention to authentic assessment of literacy for multilingual and multicultural student populations. They start with an overview of theoretical perspectives as a conceptual framework, its principles and implementation, for the RLC. This framework recognizes the primary linguistic assets that each child brings to the schooling process and utilizes those assets in constructing instruction. Their research methodology and findings focus on students' bilingual writing development in English, Spanish, and Chinese. Finally, the authors illustrate that the language of the student can be developed and assessed utilizing a set of important principles which provide for the authentic assessment of the effects of that assessment within well-articulated primary language and English literacy standards, and utilizing those assessments on an ongoing basis to modify instruction to benefit student learning.

In the subsequent chapter, Yolanda Padrón, Hersh Waxman, Robert Powers and Ann Brown examine the effectiveness of a teacher training resiliency program for teachers to improve their classroom instruction, students' resiliency behaviors, and students' academic achievement. They report the results of the Pedagogy for Improving Resiliency Program (PIRP) implemented in 4th and 5th grades in an urban school setting serving mostly Hispanic ELLs. The authors define the dimensions of educational resilience as the likelihood of success despite adversities. They focus on predictors of academic success rather than on academic failure and identify factors that are alterable and that distinguish resilient and non-resilient students. They claim that their findings are both promising and discouraging. They are promising because teachers in the treatment classes taught better—gave more explanations, more encouragement and focus on the task processes and their students had higher reading achievement gains than respective teachers and students in the comparison classrooms. They are discouraging because treatment teachers and their schools raised the concern of how the PIRP program would impact the students' achievement on the state wide assessment test.

Part III. Effective Teacher Training Models

The final section of this volume focuses on two chapters on effective teacher training models, varying foci on teacher development, and on extracting from them their implications for policy. Josefina Villamil Tinajero and Dee Ann Spencer open this section with a profile of two complementary teacher preparation programs: a pre-service program for paraprofessionals and other undergraduate students interested in bilingual teacher certification and an in-service program for bilingual teachers. The authors review the district needs and new structures and practices for professional development inherent in the two projects. They also examine a participant's survey in terms of program sustainability. The authors offer practical advice to educational professionals and conclude with a discussion of a number of interconnected factors to which the sustainability of the two projects can be attributed.

In the final chapter, Jack Levy, Lynn Shafer and Kristy Dunlap propose the Language Minority Teacher Induction Project (LMTIP) to increase achievement of bilingual students through a mentoring system for beginning teachers that features reflective practice and action research. This chapter clearly exemplifies how action research contributes to the academic achievement of and the improvement of instruction for bilingual students and how mentoring, reflective practice and the formation of teacher support groups contribute to successful action research in multilingual settings. According to the authors, the LMTIP has resulted in many examples of improved academic achievement and instruction for bilingual students and contributed to the confidence and resiliency of the project's beginning teachers.

REFERENCES

Cummins, J. (1999). Alternative paradigms in bilingual education research: Does theory have a place? *Educational Researcher, 28*(7), 26–32, 41.

Cummins, J., & Fillmore, L.W. (2000). *Language and education: What every teacher (and administrator) needs to know.* (Casette Recording No. NABE00-FS10A). Dallas, TX: CopyCats.

Denzin, N.K., & Lincoln, Y.S. (Eds.). (2000). *Handbook of qualitative research* (2nd ed.). Thousand Oaks, CA: Sage.

Faltis, C.J. (1999). Creating a new history. In C.J. Faltis & P. Wolfe (Eds.). *So much to say: Adolescents, bilingualism, and ESL in the secondary school* (pp. 1–9). New York: Teachers College Press.

Gonzalez, J.M., & Darling-Hammond, L. (1997). *New concepts for new challenges: Professional development for teachers of immigrant youth.* McHenry, IL: Delta Systems Co.

Hakuta, K. (2001, April). *The education of language minority students.* Testimony to the U.S. Commission on Civil Rights. [Online]. Available: http//www.stanford.edu/~hakuta/Docs/Civil-RightsCommission.htm

Johnson, K.E. (2000). Innovations in TESOL teacher education: A quiet revolution. In K.E. Johnson (Ed.), *Teacher Education* (pp. 1–7). Alexandria, VA: Teachers of English to Speakers of Other Languages, Inc.

Laturnau, J. (2001). *Standards-based instruction for English language learners.* Honolulu: Pacific Resources for Education and Learning.

Menken, K., & Antunez, B. (2001). *An overview of the preparation and certification of teachers working with low English proficiency students.* Washington, DC: Educational Resources Information Center.

Minaya-Rowe, L. (1992). Bilingual education: An action research agenda for the nineties. *The Journal of Educational Issues of Language Minority Students, 11,* 45–61.

Riley, R.W. (2000). *Remarks as prepared for delivery by the U.S. Secretary of Education: Web-Based Education Commission.* [On-line]. Available: http://www.ed.gov/Speeches/02-2000/20000202.html

Rogoff, B. (1990). *Apprenticeships in thinking: Cognitive development in social context.* New York: Oxford University Press.

Secada, W., Chavez-Chavez, R., Carcia, E., Muñoz, C., Oakes, J., Santiago-Santiago, I., & Slavin, R. (1998). *No more excuses. The final report of the Hispanic Dropout Project.* Washington, DC: U.S. Department of Education.

Tharp, R.G. (1999). *Proofs and evidence: Effectiveness of the standards for effective pedagogy.* [On line] http://www.crede.ucsc.edu/HomePage/Standards/Effectiveness.html

Tharp, R.G., Estrada, P., Dalton, S.S., & Yamauchi, L.A. (2000). *Teaching transformed: Achieving excellence, fairness, inclusion, and harmony.* Boulder, CO: Westview Press.

Weiner, L. (2000). Research in the 90s: Implications for urban teacher preparation. *Review of Educational Research, 70*(3), 369–406.

Part I

EFFECTIVE PRACTICES IN TEACHER TRAINING

CHAPTER 1

RESEARCH-BASED TEACHING PRACTICES THAT IMPROVE THE EDUCATION OF ENGLISH LANGUAGE LEARNERS

Hersh C. Waxman and Yolanda N. Padrón

ABSTRACT

This chapter describes how we can enhance the education of English language learners (ELLs) in traditional classrooms by improving the quality of classroom instruction. First, we discuss several critical problems associated with the education of ELLs: (a) instructional programs that have not been effective in meeting educational needs, (b) the shortage of adequately qualified teachers, (c) teacher expectations, and (d) teaching practices that predominantly consist of a basic skills, mastery orientation which leads to student compliance and passivity. Second, in response to the concerns of current instructional practices used with ELLs, many educators have advocated that alternative teaching practices be used that emphasize more active student learning and teachers becoming facilitators of learning. Five teaching practices are described in the chapter: (a) culturally responsive teaching, (b) cooperative learning, (c) instructional conversation, (d) cognitively-guided instruction, and (e) technology-enriched instruction. These research-based, instructional practices all stress a student-centered model of classroom instruction and they have also been found to be beneficial for ELLs. The final sections focus on implications for teacher education, teachers' professional development, and research.

INTRODUCTION

One of our greatest educational challenges is improving the education of English language learners (ELLs) or students whose first language is not English and they are either beginning to learn English, or have demonstrated some proficiency in English. There are more than 3.5 million ELL students in U.S. schools and these numbers have increased dramatically during the past few decades. Hispanic students constitute the largest group of ELLs, but they have the lowest levels of education and the highest dropout rate (U.S. Department of Education, 2000). Hispanic students' educational aspirations and academic performance in science, mathematics, and reading are significantly lower than white students (U.S. Department of Education, 1999, 2000). In addition, approximately 40% of Hispanic students are one grade or more below expected achievement levels by the eighth grade and only about 50% graduate "on time" (U.S. Department of Education, 1999). These facts and reports are especially problematic, given that Hispanic children primarily reside in urban cities and are immersed in neighborhoods of concentrated poverty where the most serious dropout problems exist (García, 1999). Hispanic students are more than twice as likely to experience poverty than white students (U.S. Department of Education, 1994). Furthermore, Hispanic children start elementary school with less preschool experiences than white children and this gap has widened over time (Smith, 1995; U.S. Department of Education, 1999, 2000).

Presently, about 56% of all public school teachers in the United States have at least one ELL student in their class, but less than 20% of the teachers who serve ELLs are certified ESL or bilingual teachers (Alexander, Heaviside, & Farris, 1999). Furthermore, in a recent profile of the quality of our nation's teachers, The National Center for Education Statistics (Lewis et al., 1999) found that most teachers who taught ELLs or other culturally diverse students did not feel that they were well prepared to meet the needs of their students. In another recent national survey of classroom teachers, 57% of all teachers responded that they either "very much needed" or "somewhat needed" more information on helping students with limited English proficiency achieve high standards (Alexander, Heaviside, & Farris, 1999).

Several different alternatives are often proposed to address these educational challenges. Often special language programs (e.g., bilingual education, transitional bilingual, ESL programs) are implemented to address these educational concerns, but recently many of these programs have been eliminated because of political ideologies rather than research-based, objective decisions. Consequently, most ELLs attend typical, mainstreamed classrooms for most of their elementary and secondary schooling.

The purpose of this chapter is to describe how we can improve the education of ELLs in traditional classrooms. We argue that improving the quality of classroom instruction will enhance the educational outcomes of ELLs. First, we discuss several critical problems associated with the education of English language learners (ELLs): (a) instructional programs that have not been effective in meeting educational needs, (b) the shortage of adequately qualified teachers, (c) teacher expectations, and (d) teaching practices that predominantly consist of a basic skills, mastery orientation which leads to student compliance and passivity. Second, in response to the concerns of current instructional practices used with ELLs, many educators have advocated that alternative teaching practices be used that emphasize more active student learning and teachers becoming facilitators of learning. Five teaching practices are described in the chapter: (a) cognitively-guided instruction, (b) culturally responsive teaching, (c) technology-enriched instruction, (d) cooperative learning, and (e) instructional conversation. These research-based, instructional practices all stress a student-centered model of classroom instruction and they have also been found to be beneficial for ELLs. The final sections of the chapter focus on implications for teacher education, teachers' professional development, and research.

PROBLEMS ASSOCIATED WITH THE UNDERACHIEVEMENT OF ELLS

Several critical problems have been associated with the underachievement of ELLs. Although some educators argue that the most serious concerns are basic funding or political beliefs that influence decisions (Melendez, 1993), several educational problems are "alterable," possibly pointing the way to educational improvements for ELLs. One of these critical problems is that an increasing proportion of ELLs with limited proficiency in English (nearly 25%) are not being served by appropriate instructional programs (U.S. Department of Education, 1992). Furthermore, many of the current instructional programs that ELLs are enrolled in have not been effective in meeting their educational needs (Faltis, 1993). One explanation why these programs have not been effective is that there have been many implicit assumptions that curricular or instructional innovations that improve the education of English-monolingual students will work equally well for ELLs (Le Celle-Peterson & Rivera, 1994).

—

A second serious problem associated with the failure of ELLs involves the shortage of adequately qualified teachers of ELLs and the preparation of credentialed teachers for ELLs (García, 1994; Gersten & Jiménez, 1998). Teachers of ELLs have to address the "double demands" of ELLs which include acquiring a second language while learning traditional academic content (Gersten & Jiménez, 1998). Estimates indicate that nearly half of the teachers assigned to teach ELLs have not received any preparation in methods to teach ELLs (García, 1994). Furthermore, the number of teachers prepared to teach ELLs falls short of the tremendous need for teachers of ELLs. In addition, the majority of classroom teachers and school administrators are white, while the proportion of nonwhite and Hispanic students are increasing rapidly (U.S. Department of Education, 1997). In a recent profile showing the quality of our nation's teachers, for example, the National Center for Education Statistics (Lewis et al., 1999) found that most teachers educating ELLs or other culturally diverse students did not feel that they were well prepared to meet the needs of their students. Alternative forms of teacher preparation and teacher staff development are being implemented by local school districts to meet the needs of ELLs, but they have generally not been effective in training qualified teachers of ELLs.

A third critical problem has to do with teacher expectations of ELLs. Many teachers simply view ELLs as low-performing native English-speaking children (Yates & Ortiz, 1991). Some teachers also believe that the academic failure of ELLs is primarily a function of language difficulties (Irvine & York, 1993), and that students must develop English oral proficiency before they can be taught to read and write (Díaz-Rico & Weed, 1995). In addition, several studies and reviews of research have found that schools serving ELLs and other minority students often devote less time and emphasis to higher-order thinking skills than do schools serving white students (Coley & Hoffman, 1990; Losey, 1995; Moll, 1986; Padrón & Knight, 1989; Padrón & Waxman, 1993). ELLs and other minority students have often been denied the opportunity to learn higher-level thinking skills because it has been believed that they must demonstrate the ability to learn the basics or lower levels of knowledge before they can be taught higher-level skills (Rivera & Zehler, 1991; Waxman, Padrón, & Knight, 1991). Furthermore, many teachers generally emphasize remediation for ELLs and other low-achieving students, which has resulted in teachers' lower expectations for these students and an overemphasis on repetition of content through drill-and-practice (Knapp & Shields, 1990; Lehr & Harris, 1988). The result of these practices may lead students to adopting behaviors of "learned helplessness" and having a passive orientation to schooling (Coley & Hoffman, 1990). Another prevalent expectation for ELLs is that there needs to be a heavy emphasis on learning English at the expense of learning content (Cummins, 1986; Gersten & Jiménez, 1998).

Finally, a fourth critical problem has to do with the current teaching practices that are prevalent in most classrooms serving ELLs. The most common instructional approach found in schools that serve ELLs is the direct instructional model, where teachers typically teach to the whole class at the same time and control all of the classroom discussion and decision making (Brookhart & Rusnak, 1993; Haberman, 1991; Padrón, & Waxman, 1993). This teacher-directed instructional model emphasizes lecture, drill-and-practice, remediation, and student seatwork consisting mainly of work-sheets (Stephen, Varble, & Taitt, 1993). Haberman (1991) argues that this over reliance on direct instruction in schools serving minority students constitutes a "pedagogy of poverty." He maintains that this teacher-directed, instructional style leads to student compliance, passive resentment, and teacher burnout. Furthermore, he criticizes this orientation because teachers are generally held accountable for "making" students learn, while students usually assume a passive role with low engagement in tasks or activities that are generally not authentic. Cummins and Sayers (1990) similarly argue that this instructional approach creates compliant students who cannot think critically, creatively, or solve problems.

Several recent studies have examined classroom instruction for ELLs and found that this "pedagogy of poverty" orientation exists in many class-rooms with ELLs (Padrón & Waxman, 1993; Waxman, Huang, & Padrón, 1995). In a large-scale study examining the classroom instruction of 90 teachers from 16 inner-city middle level schools serving predominantly ELLs, Waxman, Huang, and Padrón (1995) found that students were typically involved in whole-class instruction and not interacting with either their teacher or other students. About two-thirds of the time, for example, students were not involved in verbal interaction with either their teacher or other students. There were very few small group activities and very few interactions with other students. Students rarely selected their own instructional activities, and they were generally very passive in the classroom, often just watching or listening to the teacher, even though they were found to be on task about 94% of the time. In these classrooms, teachers typically focused on the content of the task or assignment, responded to students' signals, communicated the task's procedures, and checked students' work. Teachers were observed spending very little time interacting with students regarding personal issues, encouraging students to succeed, showing personal regard for students, and showing interest in students' work. They also spent more time explaining things to students rather than questioning, cueing, or prompting students to respond.

In another study examining middle-school instruction in mathematics and science inner-city classrooms serving ELLs, Padrón and Waxman (1993) found that science teachers spent about 93% of the time in whole-class instruction, while mathematics teachers spent about 55% of the time in whole-group instruction. Students in mathematics classes worked independently about 45% of the time, while there was no independent work observed in science classes. In the mathematics classes, there was no small group work observed, and students only worked in small groups in science classes about 7% of the time. Questions about complex issues were not raised by any of the mathematics and science teachers. Furthermore, teachers seldom (4%) posed open-ended questions for students in science classes and they never posed these questions in mathematics classes.

The results of these studies illustrate that classroom instruction in schools serving predominantly ELLs often tends to be whole-class instruction with students working in teacher-assigned activities, generally in a passive manner (i.e., watching or listening). Students are on task most of the time, but about two-thirds of the time there is no verbal interaction with either their teacher or other students. There are very few small group activities and very few interactions with other students. Teachers were observed keeping students on task most of the time, focusing on the task, communicating the tasks' procedures, praising students' performance, checking students' work, and responding to students' signals (e.g., raising their hands). Teachers also spent more time explaining things to students than questioning, cueing, or prompting students to respond. Teachers were not frequently observed encouraging extended student responses or encouraging students to help themselves or help each other.

In summary, the increasing number of students from culturally and linguistically backgrounds, the large number of students dropping out, the lower achievement levels of culturally and linguistically different students, and ineffective instructional programs and classroom instruction constitutes critical educational problems for ELLs. Unfortunately, the pedagogically-induced learning problems or instructional inadequacies previously described, may also account for students' poor academic achievement and low motivation (Fletcher & Cardona-Morales, 1990). These problems also have created severe inequities in our schools that contradict our democratic policies entitling all children to the right to learn (Darling-Hammond, 1997).

Educators need to focus on research-based instructional practices that have been found to be effective for ELLs. Although there have been many programs and school-based interventions that have been found to be beneficial for some types of students at risk of failure, these programs and interventions may not necessarily be effective for ELLs. Educational practices need to specifically address the concerns of ELLs who come from different cultures and who are trying to learn a new language.

EFFECTIVE TEACHING PRACTICES FOR ELLS

Many educators maintain that the best way to improve the education of ELLs is to provide them with better teachers and classroom instruction (Padrón & Waxman, 1999). Educators need to focus on research-based instructional practices that have been found to be effective for ELLs. While the term "research" often evokes negative connotations for educational practitioners and policymakers (Goodlad, 2001), it is the best criteria we have for determining effective practices in education. Although there have been many programs and school-based interventions that have been found to be beneficial for some types of students at risk of failure, these programs and interventions may not necessarily be effective for ELLs. Teaching practices need to specifically address the concerns of ELLs who come from different cultures and who are trying to learn a new language.

The following sections review five teaching practices that have been successfully used with ELLs. Our perspective on effective teaching practices emphasizes models of teaching and learning that incorporate more active student learning and changing the teachers' role from that of delivering knowledge to one of facilitating learning (Padrón & Waxman, 1999; Waxman & Padrón, 1995; Waxman, Padrón, & Arnold, 2001). The following five teaching practices all stress this changing model of classroom instruction and they all have been found to be previously successful for ELLs. These research-based instructional practices are: (a) culturally responsive teaching, (b) cooperative learning, (c) instructional conversation, (d) cognitively-guided instruction, and (e) technology-enriched instruction. The following sections briefly describe each of these practices and explain why they are beneficial for ELLs.

Culturally Responsive Instruction

One of the major education problems of schools serving diverse student populations is that the curriculum and teaching practices have not reflected the diversity within the population (Padrón & Waxman, 1999; Waxman & Padrón, 1995). The culture in which many ELLs live often prevents them from acquiring the middle-class cultural patterns on which most school curriculum and instructional materials are based. This phenomenon is often viewed as a mismatch between the culture of the home and the school culture, or a discrepancy between what schools are about and the needs and concerns of students (Au & Kawakami, 1994; Gordon & Yowell, 1994). Many classroom teachers need assistance in acquiring the knowledge and skills necessary to bridge the gap between the culture of the school and the home culture of students.

Culturally responsive instruction is often viewed as a process that addresses these previously mentioned concerns (Erickson, 1987). It emphasizes the serious miscommunication problems that can occur in classrooms when teachers do not understand their students' social and cultural milieu (Lucas & Schecter, 1992). Culturally responsive instruction focuses on the students' needs and culture and tries to create conditions that support the empowerment of students (Darder, 1993). This type of pedagogy is sometimes called: (a) culturally-sensitive instruction (Boyer, 1993), (b) culturally-relevant teaching (Ladson-Billings, 1992, 1995), (c) culturally compatible instruction (Jordan, 1985), (d) culturally sensitive scaffolding (Lee, 1992), (e) culturally responsible pedagogy (Pewewardy, 1994), (f) equity pedagogy (McGee Banks & Banks, 1995), or (g) multicultural instruction (Saldana & Waxman, 1996, 1997).

Culturally responsive instruction emphasizes the everyday concerns of students and tries to incorporate these concerns into the curriculum. Culturally responsive instruction, however, is more than merely including aspects of the students' culture into the curriculum, textbooks, and learning activities. It also focuses on the critical family and community issues that students encounter daily. Culturally responsive instruction helps students prepare themselves for meaningful social roles by emphasizing both social responsibility and academic responsibility. Furthermore, it addresses the promotion of racial, ethnic, and linguistic equality as well as the appreciation of diversity (Boyer, 1993).

Culturally responsive instruction requires a learner-centered instructional approach, where teachers assume the role of a facilitator rather than the source of all knowledge (Branch, Goodwin, & Gualtieri, 1993). In this approach, teachers use students' prior knowledge or existing cultural knowledge as a foundation or scaffold to guide students in instructional tasks (Lee, 1992). Some of the benefits of culturally responsive instruction for ELLs are that it: (a) improves the acquisition and retention of new knowledge by working from students' existing knowledge base, (b) improves self-confidence and self-esteem by emphasizing existing knowledge, (c) increases the transfer of school-taught knowledge to real-life situations, and (d) exposes students to knowledge about other individuals or cultural groups (Rivera & Zehler, 1991). When teachers develop learning activities based on familiar concepts, it helps facilitate literacy and content learning and helps ELLs feel more comfortable and confident with their work (Peregoy & Boyle, 2000).

A large body of research has found a significant relation between culturally responsive instruction and students' academic success (Au & Jordan, 1981; Erickson, 1987; Tharp & Gallimore, 1988). There have only been a few studies, however, that have specifically examined culturally responsive instruction for ELLs. One such study (Darder, 1993) found that

Latino teachers who engaged in responsive instruction were more likely to recognize and address the academic and social needs of their students. Darder (1993) also found that other successful strategies for ELLs included collaborative group work, cooperative grouping, and more opportunities for student dialogue. These are other effective teaching practices that will be discussed later in this chapter. Furthermore, students had more responsibility for their own learning and students were more involved in the development of curriculum activities and decisions about classroom activities. Darder (1993) further found that the key difference between effective Latino and white teachers was that Latino teachers were more likely to reinforce and perpetuate students' cultural values. McCollum's (1989) study comparing whole class lessons taught in third grade by a Spanish-speaking Puerto Rican teacher and an English-speaking white teacher found similar results.

This research provides evidence that instructional practices that address the cultural and linguistic needs of students are effective methods for preparing students to compete in mainstream society. Cummins (1986) argues that students can either be "empowered" or "disabled" by providing instruction that adds a second language and culture or subtracting the students' language and culture. He adds that this empowerment is necessary for successful learning to occur (Cummins, 1986). The knowledge that students gain from instruction that is culturally relevant to their experiences can empower them to be successful in mainstream society (Osborne, 1996). Unfortunately, there is also evidence that the culture-related instruction is often not implemented in classrooms (Padrón & Knight, 1989; Saldana & Waxman, 1996, 1997).

Cooperative Learning

McLaughlin and McLeod (1996) described cooperative learning as an effective instructional approach that stimulates learning and helps students come to complex understandings by discussing and defending their ideas with others. One commonly accepted definition is that "cooperative learning is the instructional use of small groups so that students work together to maximize their own and each other's learning" (Johnson & Johnson, 1991, p. 292). The traditional roles of teacher and student are altered in cooperative learning settings. Instead of lecturing and transmitting material, teachers facilitate the learning process by encouraging cooperation among students (Bejarano, 1987). This teaching practice is student-centered and creates an interdependence among students and teachers (Rivera & Zehler, 1991).

Research studies and syntheses of research have found that cooperative learning structures, such as working together in small cooperative groups, promote improved cognitive and affective student outcomes. More specifically, several reviews of the research have found that cooperative learning improves student outcomes such as: (a) attitudes toward school and motivation toward learning, (b) social skills, (c) classroom discipline, (d) achievement, retention, and critical thinking, (e) decision making, (f) higher-level thinking skills, and (g) self-esteem (Johnson & Johnson, 1984, 1991; Johnson, Maruyama, Johnson, Nelson, & Skon, 1981; Slavin, 1990, 1991).

Cooperative learning has been widely used in classrooms for several decades, but only recently has it gained support an as effective teaching practice for ELLs. As an instructional practice, cooperative grouping impacts ELLs in several different ways. Cooperative grouping: (a) provides opportunities for students to communicate with each other, (b) enhances instructional conversations, (c) decreases anxiety, (d) develops social, academic, and communication skills, (e) enhances self-confidence and self-esteem through individual contributions and achievement of group goals, (f) improves individual and group relations by learning to clarify, assist, and challenge each other's ideas, and (g) develops proficiency in English by providing students with rich language experiences that integrate speaking, listening, reading, and writing (Calderón, 1990, 1991; Christian, 1995; García, 1994; Rivera & Zehler, 1991). Furthermore, cooperative learning activities provide ELLs with "the skills that are necessary to function in real-life situations such as the utilization of context for meaning, the seeking of support from others, and the comparing of nonverbal and verbal cues" (Alcala, 2000, p. 4).

Cooperative learning is particularly beneficial for ELLs who are learning a second language because it requires students to engage in meaningful communication about the task at hand which is the ideal context for language learning. It is especially effective for students, who are less fluent in English, when they are grouped with students who are more fluent. Such cooperative learning situations are effective, since students often are required to negotiate roles using linguistic and social strategies (McLaughlin & McLeod, 1996). In other words, ELLs do better in cooperative situations because they can make sense of and talk through what they are learning with other students.

Many Hispanic ELLs tend to prefer cooperative rather than competitive learning situations because they mirror the cooperative attitudes characteristic of work patterns in their home and communities (Charbonneau & John-Steiner, 1988; Rivera & Zehler, 1991). De Avila (1988), for example, used peer cooperation to enable Hispanic ELLs to successfully acquire mathematical concepts. Students had access to materials both in their home and in second languages and were able to use their teacher as a resource as well. The program was successful because ELLs not only seemed to learn more in a cooperative environment working with peers, but they also enjoyed working individually with the teacher. Other research has similarly found that cooperative learning is a successful instructional practice for ELLs (García, 1994; Moll, 1988).

García (1988, 1990, 1992, 1994) has been involved in several studies and reviews of research that examined effective instruction for ELLs, and has found that cooperative or collaborative learning is an effective teaching practice. He found that when teachers organized instruction so that students were required to interact with others, these student-student interactions often occurred at higher-cognitive levels. In these classroom settings, students often sought and received help from other students. August and Hakuta's (1998) review of research on ELLs also found that cooperative learning and collaborative inquiry were attributes of effective schools and classrooms.

Cooperative learning is one instructional practice that relates to several other of the effective practices described in this chapter. For example, cooperative learning can be considered a culturally-relevant strategy for ELLs because it ties into the interaction patterns used in their homes. The instructional discourse that often occurs in these student groups is also highly related to instructional conversation which will be discussed in the following section.

Instructional Conversation

As previously pointed out, classroom instruction for ELLs typically is teacher-centered, dominanted by teacher talk and student passivity. The teachers typically dominant classroom discussion and interaction, control all knowledge, and merely pass knowledge onto the students (Gallimore & Goldenberg, 1992). In addition, teachers generally are unresponsive to students' utterances and create very few meaningful interactions that promote language and literacy development (Gallimore & Goldenberg, 1992). While direct instruction practices may be suited to some knowledge and skill domains that are hierarchically organized in a linear sequence, these practices are not as effective for ill-structured domains or areas that are not hierarchically organized (Gallimore & Goldenberg, 1992). Basic or critical thinking skills are most effectively developed through instructional conversations or dialogue, which is the process of questioning and sharing ideas and knowledge (Tharp, 1997). The teaching practice of instructional conversation addresses the need for a cognitively challenging curriculum and moves teachers and students away from the typical recitation patterns that currently exist in schools.

Instructional conversation is a teaching practice or instructional strategy that provides students with opportunities for extended dialogue in areas that have educational value as well as relevance for students (August & Hakuta, 1998). Teachers and students relate the formal school content to the student's individual, community, and family knowledge, and teachers are able to contextualize instruction to fit the knowledge, skills, values, and culture of the learner (Tharp, 1997). This instructional approach is similar to culturally responsive teaching in that it focuses on the students' cultural knowledge, but it goes beyond that teaching practice because it also explicitly focuses on the processes of forming, expressing, and sharing ideas and knowledge. Furthermore, in instructional conversations, the classroom changes from the direct instructional orientation to dialogic teaching where teachers construct lessons based on students' experience and ideas and the classroom becomes a "community of learners."

Some important features of instructional conversation involve teachers in: (a) activating and using students' prior knowledge, (b) promoting complex language and expression, (c) minimizing factual questions, (d) responding to and using students' contributions, (e) using connected discourse, and (f) creating a challenging and nonthreatening atmosphere (Gallimore & Goldenberg, 1992). In instructional conversations, teachers also: (a) draw students into conversations, (b) create conversational purposes for children to say something, and (c) intentionally create and sustain a conversation that is a means to an instructional end (Gallimore & Goldenberg, 1992).

Instructional conversations are purposeful extended discourse with a teacher and other students that are typically initiated by students when the need arises (Tharp, 1995). As McLaughlin and McLeod (1996) describe it, "instructional conversation is an approach in which a teacher guides students toward discovering a deeper understanding of material through a discussion that incorporates students' ideas and backgrounds. The teacher and students become conversation partners and the whole group participates in constructing a personally meaningful and relevant intellectual creation" (p. 7).

August and Hakuta's (1998) comprehensive review of research found effective teachers of ELLs provide students with opportunities for extended dialogue. Much of the theoretical and research base for instructional conversation has been summarized by Tharp and Gallimore (1988) based on their work with the Kamehameha Early Education Project (KEEP). Tharp, Gallimore, and their colleagues developed and researched a successful reading program for native Hawaiian students that included instructional conversation as one of its major components. Saunders and Goldenberg (1992) have also substantiated the beneficial effects of an instructional conversation lesson on children's understanding of a complex concept. García's (1990) study of effective teachers of ELLs also lends support to the benefits of instructional conversation. He found that effective teachers of ELLs generally elicited student responses at a low cognitive and linguistic level, but then let students take control of the lesson which resulted in more advanced cognitive and linguistic discussion. In other words, effective teachers of ELLs used instructional conversation as a teaching practice in their classrooms.

Rather than limiting expectations for ELLs by avoiding use of language and discussion during instruction, instructional conversations emphasize the use of oral language through dialogues with teachers and classmates (Durán, Dugan, & Weffer, 1997). Because ELLs often do not have control of the English language, they generally do not participate in classroom discussions. Thus, one of the major benefits of the use of instructional conversation for ELLs is that it is a practice that is designed to provide extended discourse, which is an important principle of second language learning (Christian, 1995).

Instructional conversation also helps ELLs create meaning in the social context of the classroom. As Gardner (1985) describes it, we justify knowledge through a social process by engaging in extended conversations. Joint activity and discourse between teachers and students create a common context of experience within the classroom (Tharp, 1997). Furthermore, since instructional conversations reveal the knowledge, skills, and values of the learner, it thus allows the teacher to contextualize teaching to fit the needs of each student. This is especially critical for teachers of ELLs, because many of their students come from very diverse backgrounds.

Cognitively-Guided Instruction

Influenced by theory and research from the field of cognitive psychology, many educators have adopted an information-processing view of teaching and learning (Knight & Waxman, 1991; Shuell, 1993; Waxman, Padrón, & Knight, 1991). From this perspective, learning is viewed as an active process and teaching is a means of facilitating active student mental processing (Gagne, 1985). This cognitive approach also suggests that students need to apply cognitive strategies in order to learn (Winne, 1985). Therefore, cognitively-guided instruction emphasizes the development of students' cognitive learning strategies and the direct teaching and modeling of cognitive learning strategies as well as techniques and approaches that foster students' metacognition and cognitive monitoring of their own learning (Pressley & Ghatala, 1990; Waxman, Padrón, & Knight, 1991). In other words, this instructional practice encourages teachers to emphasize students' psychological processing as well as what is taught and how it is presented (Shuell,

1993). Furthermore, teachers are encouraged to focus on affective, motivational, metacognitive, developmental, and social factors that influence students since they all occur simultaneously and are all critical to students' learning (Presidential Task Force on Psychology in Education, 1993).

From the cognitive perspective, effective instruction (a) activates or assesses students' prior knowledge of content, (b) models or illustrates appropriate learning strategies, and (c) connects both prior knowledge and learning strategies to the new learning objectives (Jones & Friedman, 1988). Another goal of effective instruction is to shift the responsibility of learning from the teacher to the student. This perspective also assumes that individuals have prior knowledge differences and differ in the frequency and types of strategies they bring to the learning context (Jones & Friedman, 1988; Padrón, 1997). Effective teachers are aware of student differences and try to specifically help students who use weak or ineffective strategies or bring in less relevant information to the learning task. For ELLs and other students at risk of failure, strategy instruction may also need to include techniques which address students' affective needs (Coley & Hoffman, 1990). If students, for example, have developed a passive orientation to learning, then the strategy instruction would need to include an affective dimension so that students can perceive themselves as able learners. Strategy instruction for students who view themselves as unsuccessful at reading may need to focus on affective needs of students (Coley & Hoffman, 1990).

Strategy instruction focuses on explicitly teaching students what strategies to use and how they should use them. This instructional approach can be very beneficial for the large number of ELLs who are not doing well in school because once students learn how to effectively use cognitive strategies, some of the individual barriers to academic success faced by this group may be removed. Explicit instruction in strategies and modeling comprise only the initial steps of successful strategy instruction models (Jones, 1986). The scaffolding approach, which gradually relinquishes control of classroom dialogue and control of strategy use to students, is another important component of successful strategy training programs such as Reciprocal Teaching (Brown, Palincsar, & Purcell, 1986; Palincsar, 1986; Palincsar & Brown, 1984) and Question Answer Relationship (QAR) (Raphael, 1984, 1987). Reciprocal teaching takes place in a cooperative instructional environment where the teacher and students engage in dialogue. Students are instructed in four specific comprehension monitoring strategies: (a) summarizing, (b) self-questioning, (c) clarifying, and (d) predicting. Studies using reciprocal teaching have found that these strategies can successfully be taught to low-achieving students and ELLs and that the use of these strategies increases reading achievement (Padrón, 1992; Palincsar & Brown, 1984; Pressley & Harris, 1990).

There is a growing understanding that effective teaching practices for ELLs should include cognitive strategy instruction (Chamot, Dale, O'Malley, & Spanos, 1993; Gersten & Jiménez, 1998; O'Malley & Chamot, 1990; Padrón, 1992, 1993). August and Hakuta's (1998) comprehensive review of research also found that effective teachers of ELLs teach metacognitive strategies to students. There have been several studies conducted with ELLs that have focused on their cognitive reading strategies. Padrón, Knight, and Waxman (1986), for example, compared strategies used by bilingual and English-monolingual students using a think-aloud protocol. Students read a passage and stopped at predetermined intervals to explain the strategies that they were using in order to comprehend the passage. The results indicated that bilingual and monolingual third and fifth grade students were not using the same number of the cognitive reading strategies. Monolingual students indicated using significantly more strategies than bilingual students. That is, English-monolingual students, on the average, used about twice as many strategies as bilingual students. In another study investigating the relationship between students' perceptions of cognitive reading strategies and gains in reading achievement, Padrón and Waxman (1988) found that certain strategies predict students' gain in reading comprehension.

Cognitive strategy training programs may be an effective means of improving cognitive outcomes of ELLs (Chamot & O'Malley, 1987; O'Malley & Chamot, 1990; Padrón, 1992; Padrón & Knight, 1989). Padrón (1992), for example, found that explicit training of reading strategies significantly improved the reading achievement of ELLs. Padrón (1992) randomly assigned 87 third, fourth, and fifth grade Hispanic bilingual students to four instructional groups. Group One was taught using Reciprocal Teaching (see, e.g., Palincsar & Brown, 1984). Group Two was instructed using the Question Answer Relationships (see, e.g., Raphael, 1984; Raphael & Pearson, 1985). Two control groups were used to determine whether it was the strategy training or the additional instruction that increased students' reading achievement. Group Three, therefore, read passages and answered questions, while students in the fourth group remained in their regular classroom and received instruction from their teacher on a subject other than reading. Students who participated in either the Reciprocal Teaching or the Question Answer Relationship groups scored significantly higher on a standardized reading achievement test than students who participated in the control groups.

Chamot and O'Malley (1987) have also developed an effective instructional program for limited English proficient students that specifically focuses on strategy instruction. Overall, their research indicates that when strategies are modeled for the student and they have an opportunity to practice the strategy, learning outcomes improve. Their work also highlights the importance of ELLs being able to use effective learning strategies.

Technology-Enriched Instruction

Another instructional practice that can improve the teaching and learning of ELLs is the use of technology in the classroom (Padrón & Waxman, 1996). Several studies and reviews of research specifically focusing on ELLs have found that technology is effective for ELLs (Chavez, 1990; Cummins & Sayers, 1990; De Villar, 1990; Merino, Legarreta, Coughran, & Hoskins, 1990; Padrón & Waxman, 1996; Walker de Felix, Johnson, & Shick, 1990). Chavez (1990), for example, examined first and second grade students who were instructed to use the "Write to Read" (WTR) Program to develop English writing and reading skills. He found that the use of the WTR Program provided a risk-free environment for ELLs which made the students feel comfortable about expressing their ideas.

Students' story writing also showed improvement in sentence structure and the breadth of the content. Merino, Legarreta, Coughran, and Hoskins (1990) found that pairing a limited English proficient (LEP) student with a fluent English proficient (EP) student was effective in producing on-task behavior, equitable turn taking, and cooperative exchanges during computer-based science activities. Dixon's (1995) study also demonstrated the benefits of LEP students working collaboratively with EP students at a computer during mathematics. She found that both LEP and EP students who worked in a computer-based, dynamic instructional environment significantly outperformed students who worked in traditional instructional environments on measures of reflection and rotation concepts and two-dimensional visualization ability.

Research evidence also indicates that multimedia use with ELLs can produce positive effects. Walker de Felix, Johnson, and Schick (1990), for example, developed two interactive videodisc lessons that were tested with fourth-grade English as a second language (ESL), inner-city students. Their findings provide evidence of the advantages of contextually-rich learning environments for ELLs. Web-based picture libraries also can promote ELLs' comprehension in content classrooms (Smolkin, 2000). Furthermore, some types of technology like multimedia are effective for ELLs and students at risk because they help students connect images, sound, and symbols (Kozma & Croninger, 1992; Poirot & Canales, 1993–94). Multimedia can also connect student learning in the classroom to real life situations and authentic learning situations (Means & Olson, 1994). In addition, multimedia technology can be especially helpful for ELLs because it can facilitate auditory skill development by integrating visual presentations with sound and animation (Bermúdez & Palumbo, 1994; Mielke & Flores, 1992–93). Digitized books are now available and allow ELLs to request pronunciations of unknown words, request translations of sections, and ask questions (Jiménez & Barrera, 2000).

Another area that holds promise for improving the teaching and learning of ELLs is the use of computer networks and telecommunications. ELLs can communicate with authentic audiences through the Internet and other technologies (García, 2000). Cummins and Sayers (1990) work with computer-mediated learning networks for ELLs exemplifies research in this area. They describe a partnership between classes from North and South America where teachers and students work jointly on curricular projects through extensive computer networks. They found that this networking project improved students' academic achievement and also promoted other important outcomes like students' cultural understanding.

Several conceptual articles and research studies have examined the specific ways technology impacts students at risk and ELLs. Instructional technology has been found to be beneficial for students at risk of failure and ELLs in the following ways: (a) it is motivational, (b) it is nonjudgmental, (c) it can individualize learning and tailor the instructional sequence to meet students' needs and rate of learning, (d) it allows for more autonomy, (e) it can give prompt feedback, (f) it provides the students with a sense of personal responsibility and control, (g) it can be less intimidating to students, (h) it gives the students a rich linguistic environment, (i) it diminishes the authoritarian role of the teacher, and (j) it decreases situations where students could be embarrassed in class for not knowing answers (Cantrell, 1993; Mielke & Flores, 1992–1993, Poirot & Canales, 1993–94). Technology also allows ELLs to (a) work in collaborative inquiry projects, (b) access online resources in several languages, and (c) click onto video, audio, and literacy aids in two languages (García, 2000).

De Villar and Faltis (1991) specifically discuss the effectiveness of technology for ELLs by describing how computer-integrated instruction facilitates social integration, communication, and cooperation for ELLs. All of these characteristics of technology are especially beneficial for ELLs because they are often disengaged from schools and have generally experienced more failure than success in learning situations.

In addition, there is evidence to show that Latino students are more kinesthetic learners and learn better through hands-on activities and in small group and individualized instruction than through whole-class or direct instruction approaches (Poirot & Canales, 1993–94). Computers also provide students the opportunity for hands-on learning and working collaboratively in pairs or small groups. Several of the studies previously described (Dixon, 1995; Merino, Legarreta, Coughran, & Hoskins, 1990) illustrate the value of ELLs working collaboratively with English proficient students. Such pairings have been found to improve students' cognitive outcomes, and they can also benefit the psychosocial development of ELLs.

Another important outcome of technology-enriched classrooms is that it can help reduce or eliminate the teacher dominated, whole-class, direct instructional approach that exists in most classrooms with ELLs (Cummins & Sayers, 1990; De Villar & Faltis, 1991). Swan and Mitrani (1993), for example, compared the classroom interactions between high school students and teachers involved in (a) computer-based instruction and (b) traditional instruction. They found that student-teacher interactions were more student-centered and individualized during computer-based teaching and learning than traditional teaching and learning.

In another study that examined changes in classroom instruction as a result of technology, Sandholtz, Ringstaff, and Dwyer (1992) found that high access to computers enabled teachers to individualize instruction more. In a national study, Worthen, Van Dusen, and Sailor (1994) found that students using a computerized integrated learning system (ILS) in both laboratory and classroom settings were more actively engaged in learning tasks than students in the non-ILS classrooms. In another study that included many ELLs, Waxman and Huang (1996–97) found that instruction in classroom settings where technology was not often used tended to be whole-class approaches, where students generally listened or watched the teacher. Instruction in classroom settings where technology was moderately used had much less whole-class instruction and much more independent work.

The preceding studies all support the notion that technology use in classrooms may change teaching from the traditional, teacher-centered model to a more student-centered, instructional approach. Technology changes the nature of classroom interactions because it alters the ways that information can be obtained, manipulated, and displayed (Waxman & Bright, 1993).

DISCUSSION

The five instructional practices that are described in this chapter have all been found to be effective for teaching ELLs and there are several benefits of incorporating these approaches in schools serving ELLs. In a classroom with many ELLs, instruction becomes extremely complex. Not only does the teacher have to deal with students' language and knowledge-base differences, but he or she also must interpret content presented in textbooks from a cultural perspective different from that of the student (Padrón, 1991). Instructional conversation and culturally responsive instruction, however, are two practices that can help mechanisms for contextualizing instruction.

The implementation of cognitively-guided instruction also has several positive components that can improve the education of ELLs. In reciprocal teaching, for example, the text may either be read by the students or the teacher may read the text aloud to students. This technique can be very useful when teaching ELLs who may experience a great deal of difficulty with the language. The teacher reading the text provides the students with the opportunity to learn the four comprehension strategies presented in reciprocal teaching, without having to wait until they learn to decode (Padrón, 1991).

Technology-enriched instruction also has the potential for deepening classroom instruction, making it more meaningful, and assisting the learning of higher-order thinking skills (Niemiec & Walberg, 1992). When technology is used this way as an instructional tool, it can eliminate the total reliance on direct instructional approaches and empower all students with the thinking skills that will help them help themselves. Technology-enriched environments, however, include new and different instruction approaches than those to which teachers have been exposed to in their teacher education programs. Teachers, for the most part, have been trained with direct instructional models, while technology-enriched instruction requires a student-oriented approach that requires the teacher to assume a facilitator or coaching role. Technology-enriched instruction also requires some knowledge about technology that needs to be provided on an ongoing basis by the school or district.

The teaching practices reported in this chapter are not meant to be presented as dichotomous, coherent instructional programs, but rather as different practices or strategies that can be implemented simultaneously into the classroom. All the instructional approaches are deeply integrative and interwoven. The principles and conditions of culturally responsive instruction (e.g., respect for diversity), for example, can be taught and applied through cooperative learning (Le Blanc & Skaruppa, 1997). From a cognitively-guided teaching perspective, some methods such as reciprocal teaching are explicitly designed for students to construct knowledge through the social process of cooperative learning. Other aspects of cooperative learning techniques such as discussion, debate, negotiation, and compromise reflect aspects of instructional conversation. Similarly, students' language development can be enhanced by having them work in small groups while using technology (Chisholm, 1994; DeVillar, 1989, 1990; DeVillar & Faltis, 1991). The search for the "one best method" or approach to classroom instruction for ELLs may be futile, but the practices described in this chapter indicate that there are several effective teaching practices for ELLs.

Implications for Teacher Education

One of the major challenges for teacher educators is to disseminate the research that has been conducted in this field to pre-service and classroom teachers (Boyle-Baise & Grant, 1992; Olmedo, 1992). Teacher education programs at both the in-service and pre-service levels should ensure that teachers are provided with appropriate knowledge and training of effective instructional practices for teaching ELLs. Prospective teachers, in particular, need to have field experiences and student teaching opportunities in culturally-diverse settings. Teacher education programs should also develop teachers who can recognize and change the pedagogy of poverty (Brookhart & Rusnak, 1993). School administrators should similarly recognize the dangers of existing instructional practices and encourage teachers to change their current practices. The implementation of these instructional approaches must be carefully orchestrated. It will require a strong commitment from teachers because these approaches are quite different from those that they have been typically exposed to in their teacher preparation programs.

In preparing teachers for these new instruction approaches, teacher education programs should: (a) provide the knowledge base about the cognitive and affective processes that influence learning, (b) include information about general and domain-specific metacognitive strategies and how they can be effectively taught to students of differing abilities and backgrounds, (c) encourage pre-service teachers to "think aloud" during explanations so that they can model metacognitive thinking for their students, and (d) focus on learner-centered instructional approaches (Presidential Task Force on Psychology in Education, 1993). This will call for a change in policy that will need to empower teachers with the authority to implement such changes as well as support so that they will feel sufficiently supported and valued (Presidential Task Force on Psychology in Education, 1993). In order to carry out such changes, teachers need to be given more opportunity to restructure their classroom environment. Furthermore, teachers should be included as active participants and collaborators in the training process (Gallimore & Goldenberg, 1992).

Several other factors related to teacher preparation must be addressed in implementing these instruction approaches. Teachers may need to receive more information on how to address the cultural and linguistic differences represented in their classrooms. Boyer (1993), for example, argues that culturally responsive teaching requires ethnic literacy development of all those who teach. Staff development procedures become crucial to the implementation of these instructional interventions because many teachers have not been exposed to strategy training procedures, instructional technology, instructional conversation, or ways to incorporate cultural pluralism into their instruction. Furthermore, because many teachers do not believe that these practices are beneficial, particularly for ELLs, teacher training may need to specifically address issues related to teachers' attitudes and perceptions of ELLs.

Teachers of ELLs are presented with complex classroom situations. They must diagnose students' needs in terms of the knowledge, language, and learning strategies that they know, those that they do not know, or do know but do not use. In addition, teachers in these classrooms must also deal with different cultural backgrounds, and in many instances, with different levels of language proficiency. The variety of languages found in many classrooms today and the difficulty in assessing the students' levels of proficiency make diagnosis difficult. Therefore, teacher education programs must help teachers readily diagnose students' background knowledge and learn how to address student differences in the classroom. University faculty may also need to change their repertoire of teaching patterns in order to meet the challenge of preparing teachers to use these instructional approaches (Le Blanc & Skaruppa, 1997). Finally, teacher education faculty should model these teaching practices and provide opportunities for pre-service and in-service teachers to engage in such practices (Le Blanc & Skaruppa, 1997).

To increase the potential of technology in schools, teachers of ELLs need training in the use of technology (Mielke & Flores, 1992–1993). This is important because recent studies have found that the longer that pre-service and in-service teachers are exposed to computers and the greater variety of computers that they have experience with, the more comfortable they feel in using computers (Liao, 1993; Padrón, 1993).

Teacher training institutions should also be involved in changing the teachers' role from that of delivering knowledge to one of facilitating learning in a technology-rich environment. Chisholm (1993) and Hunt (1994), for example, suggested that teacher preparation programs need to include several aspects if technology is to be incorporated into elementary to high school classrooms, including: (a) address classroom management issues; (b) expose prospective teachers to classrooms where a variety of technologies are being used; (c) demonstrate various types of software and instructional methods that can be utilized with a diverse student population; (d) model teaching and learning strategies by university faculty using computer-related technologies; and (e) train teachers in the evaluation of software. The evaluation of software must include more that just being able to determine whether a particular program is of high quality or whether it is easy to use. For teachers of ELLs, the evaluation of software must also include being able to determine whether the software is culturally appropriate and whether it can be utilized by students with various learning styles (Chisholm, 1993). Policymakers should target such teacher training efforts specifically for high-poverty schools serving ELLs because there is evidence that those teachers receive less professional development in areas like instructional technology than teachers from more economically-advantaged schools (Wenglinsky, 1998).

Implications for Teachers' Professional Development

In recent years, many school districts across the United States have adopted and implemented comprehensive reform models for their schools. These models are designed to help alleviate teachers' decision making in the classroom by explicitly telling them "what" to teach and "how" to teach it. While there is some evidence to support some of these models, there is also quite a bit of controversy involving their use. Some educators argue that adopting such models represents an "act of desperation on the part of educators because they do not believe that the school can reform and succeed on its own" (Becker, 2000). Others are critical of school reform models because these generic models assume that students, teachers, and schools throughout the United States are similar. As Jackson and Davis (2000) put it, "ultimately, no one size educational program can possibly fully capitalize on the diversity of student and faculty interests and talents, and community resources, that define each and every ... school" (p. 225). We also agree with Jackson and Davis (2000) that teachers need to adapt and tailor effective teaching practices that build on students' and educators' diversity and strengths.

The professional development of teachers needs to be seriously addressed in order to improve the education of ELLs (Jiménez & Barrera, 2000). Whereas most teacher professional development lasts one day or less (i.e., < 8 hours), many teachers report that they need long-term professional development (i.e., > 8 hours) in order to: (a) use new methods of classroom instruction like cooperative grouping, (b) integrate educational technology in the subject they teach; and (c) address the needs of ELLs and other students from diverse cultural backgrounds (Lewis et al., 1999). Classroom teachers want more time for training and planning, as well as more opportunities to collaborate and learn from other teachers.

Research shows that professional development approaches are more successful when they try to enhance and expand a teacher's current repertoire of instruction strategies rather than radically altering them (Gersten & Woodward, 1992; Richardson, 1990; Smylie, 1988). Reforms that simply add work to an already crowded teaching schedule, and that are not perceived by teachers as helping them to meet their teaching goals, will be rejected by those teachers (Mehan, 1991). This underscores the importance of teachers' knowledge and the way teachers organize their teaching day when considering a change in education. Creamer and Creamer (1988) suggest that major innovations require that the individuals involved perceive the change as both necessary and useful and that the changes be compatible with other programs and goals. For change to occur, Creamer and Creamer (1988) conclude that (a) adequate personnel and resources must be provided and sustained throughout all planning and implementation phases; (b) top-level leadership must exhibit a firm commitment to the project; (c) project leaders must emerge to champion the cause; and (d) the outcomes of the project must be apparent.

Rather than radically altering teachers' classroom instruction, these teaching practices should be presented as opportunities for teachers to expand their current repertoire of instructional strategies (Gersten & Jiménez, 1994). Teachers also must receive extensive modeling and time to practice before expecting to see significant change. Additionally, time for collaborative feedback among the teachers and adequate resources and materials are critical to successful change. Darling-Hammond (1996) found that those teachers who have access to teacher networks, enriched professional roles, and collegial work feel more efficacious in gaining the knowledge they need to meet the needs of their students. Teachers should be provided with opportunities to interact and have conversations around standards, theory, and practical classroom implementation. Furthermore, these processes must be implemented in an atmosphere of instructional leadership and trust, where teachers' professionalism is both valued and rewarded.

Implications for Research

Although research on effective teaching for students for ELLs has made significant progress over the past decade, there are still additional areas that need further investigation. To capture all the processes and nuances that occur in classrooms attended by students at risk of failure, triangulation procedures are needed to collect data from multiple perspectives (Evertson & Green, 1986). Collecting multiple measures or indicators of classroom processes may provide us with a more comprehensive picture of the quality of classroom instruction provided to ELLs as well as what practices are most effective for them and why they are effective. Further classroom research focusing on instruction for ELLs should also examine the social context surrounding instruction because it provides important information on how instructional aspects such as classroom interaction differ according to settings, topics, situations, activities, and purposes (Losey, 1995).

Our nation faces very serious challenges in serving ELLs. Progress has been made in isolated areas, but to sustain this progress and to extend it to much larger numbers of schools, a more solid research base must be provided for the many suspected connections between instructional processes and student outcomes, and for the level of effectiveness of various promising programs in diverse contexts (Rossi & Stringfield, 1995). More studies are needed to examine why some ELLs overcome diversity and are succeeding in our schools. These students, often called resilient learners, often face enormous adversity in their lives but nevertheless succeed. Although threatened by a variety of risks, they overcome apparently insurmountable odds to build promising futures (Masten, 1994). Through the study of resilience, educators can identify factors that provide protection and support for some ELLs and then apply them to similar students from disadvantaged backgrounds who have not done well in school (Padrón, Waxman, & Huang, 1999; Waxman, Huang, & Padrón, 1997).

Additionally, further correlational, longitudinal, and especially experimental research is needed to examine the effects on students' cognitive, affective, and behavioral outcomes of the instructional practices detailed in this chapter. In particular, we need to examine the extent that these practices enhance students' higher-level thinking, motivation, and educational aspirations. Since these approaches have not been incorporated into an integrated program for improving teaching and student learning, evaluative research studies will need to examine the impact of such interventions. Other research questions that still need to be investigated in this area include examining (a) the ideal or optimum levels that these practices should be used, (b) how teachers' beliefs, attitudes, and expectations influence their verbal interactions and classroom instruction and how they can be improved, and (c) what other district- or school-level factors (e.g., district policies, school organization or climate) influence the teaching practices used with ELLs. More studies also are needed to examine how schools and teachers can improve their classroom instruction. These and similar issues still need to be examined so that we can continue to understand and improve the education of ELLs.

SUMMARY

Although most of the teaching practices summarized in this chapter are based on theoretical and conceptual frameworks, there are still concerns related to whether too little attention has been placed on the development of general instructional theory for ELLs. There have been only a few conceptual models of instructional effectiveness (Cremmers, 1994), and these models have not explicitly focused on instructional practices for ELLs. Classroom settings for ELLs are quite complex, however, and a general instructional theory for ELLs may not sufficiently help teachers understand how to improve their teaching practices. Educational reformers typically have searched for "simplistic answers" to our wide array of educational problems (Good, 1988). Reformers generally have focused on solving educational problems without taking into account the growing diversity of students in the nation's schools. Instruction improvements should focus on the needs of students.

The most important issue related to effective classroom instruction is not the form (e.g., simple characteristics of instruction such as large- or small-group teaching) it takes, but the quality of the instruction (Good, 1988). All the teaching practices described in this chapter need to be taught well. Furthermore, there is an affective component associated with all of these practices that needs to be considered as well. Given the problems associated with low expectations of ELLs, teachers' high expectations for these students must be ensured. They must provide ELLs with academic tasks that are complex and challenging (Rivera & Zehler, 1991). Teachers also need to create warm, positive classroom environments and be supportive of all students. They should create a classroom and instructional learning environment that is supportive of students and alternative cultural perspectives (Branch, Goodwin, & Gualtieri, 1993).

ELLs and other students at risk of academic failure prefer a classroom learning environment where the teacher is responsive to their needs (Richardson, Casanova, Placier, & Guifoyle, 1989). One most important factor for establishing an effective school and classroom learning environment is having a teacher who is positive and supportive, and who cares about students (Phelan, Davidson, & Cao, 1992; Waxman, 1992). As Trueba and Bartolomé (1997) put it, "teachers must convey in their daily work the conviction that they are committed to humanizing the educational experience of students by eliminating hostility, and replacing messages of distrust or disdain with respect for all" (p. 3). This is especially critical for ELLs.

In addition to these issues, there are other pertinent areas and specific content that teachers of ELLs need to be aware of. Of utmost concern is that teachers of ELLs must be knowledgeable about language development and language acquisition. Another area that teachers need to address are methods for motivating ELLs. Meyer (2000), for example, argues that the "yearning goad" or the passion and pursuit of interesting topics is an approach for motivating ELLs. Yet few activities in the school curriculum are based on student-generated topics. Furthermore, few teachers exhibit "personal passions" in their instruction that generate student interest (Meyer, 2000).

Other aspects of schools and classrooms are similarly important in order to improve the education of ELLs. Systemative student assessment, staff development, opportunities for student-directed activities, home and parent involvement, explicit skills instruction, balanced curriculum, supportive school-wide climate, school leadership, customized learning environments, articulation and coordination within and between schools, and use of native language and culture are other factors that have been found to be attributes of effective schools and classrooms (August & Hakuta, 1998).

This chapter has not focused on other theoretical frameworks of effective teaching like Cummins' (2000) transformative pedagogy, where effective instruction is viewed as a collaborative process or critical inquiry that enables students to relate the curriculum to their own lives and analyze broader social issues. While transformative pedagogy includes some teaching practices previously described like culturally-relevant instruction and instructional conversation, its primary focus is to encourage students to critically examine social issues that affect their lives (e.g., discrimination, racism) and challenge the societal, status quo. While there is some empirical evidence that supports this teaching practice for ELLs (e.g., Delgado-Gaitan & Trueba, 1991; Trueba, 1988), presently there is not a substantive body of research that validates its effectiveness. One explanation for this may be that few teachers employ this teaching strategy because it is seldom emphasized in in-service and pre-service teacher education programs.

In conclusion, the five research-based, instructional practices described in this chapter have all been found to improve the education of ELLs. These instructional practices are not necessarily recent developments in education, but they can be considered new because they have not been widely used in teaching ELLs. Although the focus in this chapter is on instruction for ELLs, these practices should not be limited to them. The research base suggests that they are effective for most students. In terms of practice, it may be that teachers need to follow the knowledge base from the paradigm of research that they believe most adequately describes their philosophy of education or situational knowledge. Once teachers begin to examine their existing teaching practices critically, they may acknowledge the value of more student-centered practices such as those described in this chapter. When that occurs, teachers may begin to tailor and adapt these practices to their own classroom needs.

ACKNOWLEDGMENT

This chapter was supported in part by U.S. Department of Education, Office of Educational Research and Improvement grants from the National Center for Research on Education, Diversity, and Excellence and Mid-Atlantic Regional Laboratory for Student Success. The opinions expressed in this article do not necessarily reflect the position, policy, or endorsement of the granting agency.

Address all correspondence to Dr. Hersh C. Waxman, College of Education, University of Houston, Houston, TX 77204-5872; Fax 713 743-9870; E-mail: Hwaxman@uh.edu

REFERENCES

Alcala, A. (2000). A framework for developing an effective instructional program for limited English proficient students with limited formal schools. *Practical Assessment, Research & Evaluation, 7*(9). Available online: http://ericae.net/pare/getvn.asp?v=7&n=9.

Alexander, D., Heaviside, S., & Farris, E. (1999). *Status of education reform in public elementary and secondary schools: Teachers' perspectives.* Washington, DC: U.S. Department of Education, National Center for Education Statistics.

Au, K., & Jordan, C. (1981). Teaching reading to Hawaiian children: Finding a culturally appropriate solution. In H. Trueba, G. Guthrie, & K. Au (Eds.), *Culture and the bilingual classroom: Studies in classroom ethnography* (p. 139–152). Rowley, MA: Newbury House.

Au, K.H., & Kawakami, A. J. (1994). Cultural congruence in instruction. In E.R. Hollins, J.E. King, & W.C. Hayman (Eds.), *Teaching diverse populations: Formulating a knowledge base* (pp. 5–23). Albany: State University of New York Press.

August, D., & Hakuta, K. (Eds.). (1998). *Educating language-minority children.* Washington, DC: National Academy Press.

Becker, A. (2000, June). *International perspectives in language diversity and teacher training.* Paper presented at the Teaching English Language Learners: Effective Programs and Practices Conference, Storrs, CT.

Bejarano, Y. (1987). A cooperative small-group methodology in the language classroom. *TESOL Quarterly, 21,* 483–504.

Bermúdez, A.B., & Palumbo, D. (1994). Bridging the gap between literacy and technology: Hypermedia as a learning tool for limited English proficient students. *The Journal of Educational Issues of Language Minority Students, 14,* 165–184.

Boyer, J.B. (1993). Culturally-sensitive instruction: An essential component of education for diversity. *Catalyst for Change, 22*(3), 5–8.

Boyle-Baise, M., & Grant, C. (1992). Multicultural teacher education: A proposal for change. In H.C. Waxman, J. Walker de Felix, J.E. Anderson, & H.P. Baptiste, Jr. (Eds.), *Students at risk in at-risk schools: Improving environments for learning* (pp. 174–193). Newbury Park, CA: Corwin.

Branch, R.C., Goodwin, Y., & Gualtieri, J. (1993). Making classroom instruction culturally pluralistic. *The Educational Forum, 58,* 57–70.

Brookhart, S.M., & Rusnak, T.G (1993). A pedagogy of enrichment, not poverty: Successful lessons of exemplary urban teachers. *Journal of Teacher Education, 44*(1), 17–26.

Brown, A.L., Palincsar, A.S., & Purcell, L. (1986). Poor readers: Teach don't label. In U. Neisser (Ed.), *The school achievement of minority children: New perspectives* (pp. 105–143). Hillsdale, NJ: Erlbaum.

Calderón, M. (1990). *Cooperative learning for limited English proficient students.* Baltimore, MD: Center for Research on Effective Schooling.

Calderón, M. (1991). Benefits of cooperative learning for Hispanic students. *Texas Research Journal, 2,* 39–57.

Cantrell, J. (1993). Technology's promise for at-risk students. *Thrust for Educational Leadership, 23*(2), 22–25.

Chamot, A.U., Dale, M., O'Malley, J.M., & Spanos, G.A. (1993). Learning and problem solving strategies of ESL students. *Bilingual Research Journal, 16*(3 & 4), 1–34.

Chamot, A.U., & O'Malley, J.M. (1987). The cognitive academic language learning approach: A bridge to the mainstream. *TESOL Quarterly, 21,* 227–249.

Charbonneau, M.P., & John-Steiner, V. (1988). Patterns of experience and the language of mathematics. In R.R. Cocking & J.P. Mestre (Eds.), *Linguistic and cultural influences on learning mathematics* (pp. 91–100). Hillsdale, NJ: Lawrence Erlbaum.

Chavez, R.C. (1990). The development of story writing within an IBM Writing to Read Program Lab among language minority students: Preliminary findings of a naturalistic study. *Computers in the Schools, 7*(1/2), 121–144.

Chisholm, I.M. (1994). Culture and technology: Implications for multicultural teacher education. *Journal of Information Technology and Teacher Education, 2,* 213–228.

Christian, D. (1995). Two-way bilingual education. In C.L. Montone (Ed.), *Teaching linguistically and culturally diverse learners: Effective programs and practices* (pp. 8–11). Santa Cruz, CA: National Center for Research on Cultural Diversity and Second Language Learning.

Coley, J.D., & Hoffman, D.M. (1990). Overcoming learned helplessness in at risk readers. *Journal of Reading, 33,* 497–502.

Creamer, E.G., & Creamer, D.G. (1988). Predicting successful organizational change: Case studies. *Journal of College Student Development, 29,* 4–11.

Creemers, B.P.M. (1994). *The effective classroom.* London: Cassell.

Cummins, J. (1986). Empowering minority students: A framework for interventions. *Harvard Educational Review, 56,* 18–36.

Cummins, J. (2000). *Language, power, and pedagogy.* Clevendon, UK: Multilingual Matters.

Cummins, J., & Sayers, D. (1990). Education 2001: Learning networks and educational reform. *Computers in the Schools, 7*(1/2), 1–29.

Darling-Hammond, L. (1996). The quiet revolution: Rethinking teacher devlopment. *Educational Leadership, 53*(6), 4–10.

Darling-Hammond, L. (1997). *The right to learn: A blueprint for creating schools that work.* San Francisco: Jossey-Bass.

Darder, A. (1993). How does the culture of the teacher shape the classroom experience of Latino students?: The unexamined question in critical pedagogy. In S.W. Rothstein (Ed.), *Handbook of schooling in urban America* (pp. 195–221). Westport, CT: Greenwood.

Delgado-Gaitan, C., & Trueba, H.T. (1991). *Crossing cultural borders: Education for immigrant families in America.* London: Falmer.

De Avila, E.A. (1988). Bilingualism, cognitive function, and language minority group membership. In C.B. McCormick, G.E. Miller, & M. Pressley (Eds.), *Cognitive strategy research: From basic research to educational applications* (pp. 104–121). New York: Springer-Verlag.

De Villar, R.A. (1989). Computers, software and cooperative learning: Working together to the benefit of the language minority student. In J.H. Collins, N. Estes, W.D. Gattis, & D. Walker (Eds.), *The Sixth International Conference on Technology and Education* (Vol. 1, pp. 367–370). Edinburgh, UK: CEP Consultants.

De Villar, R.A. (1990). Second language use within the non-traditional classroom: Computers, cooperative learning, and bilingualism. In R. Jacobson & C. Faltis (Eds.), *Language distribution issues in bilingual schooling* (pp. 133–159). Clevedon, UK: Multilingual Matters.

De Villar, R.A., & Faltis, C.J. (1991). *Computers and cultural diversity: Restructuring for school success.* Albany: State University of New York Press.

Díaz-Rico, L.T., & Weed, K.Z. (1995). *The crosscultural, language, and academic development handbook.* Needham Heights, MA: Allyn & Bacon.

Dixon, J.K. (1995). Limited English proficiency and spatial visualization in middle school students' construction of the concepts of reflection and rotation. *Bilingual Research Journal, 19,* 221–247.

Durán, B.J., Dugan, T., & Weffer, R.E. (1997). Increasing teacher effectiveness with language minority students. *The High School Journal, 84,* 238–246.

Erickson, F. (1987). Transformation and school success: The politics and culture of educational achievement. *Anthropology and Education Quarterly, 18,* 335–356.

Evertson, C., & Green, J. (1986). Observation as inquiry and method. In M.C. Wittrock (Ed.), *Handbook of research on teaching* (3rd ed., pp. 162–207). New York: Macmillan.

Faltis, C.J. (1993). Programmatic and curricular options for secondary schools serving limited English proficient students. *The High School Journal, 76,* 171–181.

Fletcher, T.V., & Cardona-Morales, C. (1990). Implementing effective instructional interventions for minority students. In A. Barona & E.E. García (Eds.), *Children at risk: Poverty, minority status, and other issues in educational equity* (pp. 151–170). Washington, DC: National Association of School Psychologists.

Gagne, E. (1985). *The cognitive psychology of school learning.* Boston: Little Brown.

Gallimore, R., & Goldenberg, C.N. (1992). Tracking the developmental path of teachers and learners: A Vygotskian perspective. In F.K. Oser, A. Dick, & J-L. Patry (Eds.), *Effective and responsible teaching: The new synthesis* (pp. 203–221). San Francisco: Jossey-Bass.

García, E.E. (1988). Attributes of effective schools for language minority students. *Education and Urban Society, 20,* 387–398.

García, E.E. (1990). Instructional discourse in "effective" Hispanic classrooms. In R. Jacobson & C. Faltis (Ed.), *Language distribution issues in bilingual schooling* (pp. 104–117). Clevedon, UK: Multilingual Matters.

García, E.E. (1992). Effective instruction for language minority students: The teacher. *Journal of Education, 173*(2), 130–141.

García, E. (1994). *Understanding and meeting the challenge of student cultural diversity.* Boston: Houghton Mifflin.

García, G.N. (2000). *The factors that place Latino children and youth at risk of educational failure.* Paper presented at the annual meeting of the American Educational Research Association, New Orleans, LA.

Gardner, H. (1985). *The mind's new science: A history of the cognitive revolution.* New York: Basic Books.

Gersten, R., & Jiménez, R.T. (1994). A delicate balance: Enhancing literature instruction for students of English as a second language. *The Reading Teacher, 47,* 438–449.

Gersten, R., & Jiménez, R. (1998). Modulating instruction for language minority students. In E.J. Kameenui & D.W. Carnine (Eds.), *Effective teaching strategies that accommodate diverse learners.* Columbus, OH: Merrill.

Gersten, R., & Woodward, J. (1992). The quest to translate research into classroom practice: Strategies for assisting classroom teachers' work with "at-risk" students and students with disabilities. In D. Carnine & E. Kameenui (Eds.), *Higher cognitive functioning for all students* (pp. 201–218). Austin, TX: Pro-Ed.

Good, T.L. (1988). Observational research . . . grounding theory in classrooms. *Educational Psychologist, 25,* 375–379.

Goodlad, J. (2001, April). *What would John Dewey say about education today?* Paper presented at the annual meeting of the American Educational Research Association, Seattle, WA.

Gordon, E.W., & Yowell, C. (1994). Cultural dissonance as a risk factor in the development of students. In R.J. Rossi (Ed.), *Schools and students at risk* (pp. 51–69). New York: Teachers College Press.

Haberman, M. (1991). Pedagogy of poverty versus good teaching. *Phi Delta Kappan, 73,* 290–294.

Hunt, N.P. (1994). Intentions and Implementations: The impact of technology coursework in elementary classrooms. In J. Willis, B. Robins, & D.A. Willis, (Eds.), *Technology and teacher education annual* (pp. 38–41). Charlottesville, VA: Association for the Advancement of Computing in Education.

Irvine, J.J., & York, D.E. (1993). Teacher perspectives: Why do African-American, Hispanic, and Vietnamese students fail? In S.W. Rothstein (Ed.), *Handbook of schooling in urban America* (pp. 162–173). Westport, CT: Greenwood.

Jiménez, R.T., & Barrera, R. (2000). How will bilingual/ESL programs in literacy change in the next millennium? *Reading Research Quarterly, 35,* 522–523.

Johnson, D.W., & Johnson, R. (1984). *Circles of learning.* Alexandria, VA: Association for Supervision and Curriculum Development.

Johnson, D.W., & Johnson, R.T. (1991). Classroom instruction and cooperative grouping. In H.C. Waxman & H.J. Walberg (Eds.), *Effective teaching: Current research* (pp. 277–293). Berkeley, CA: McCutchan.

Johnson, D.W., Maruyama, G., Johnson, R., Nelson, D., & Skon, L. (1981). Effects of cooperative, competitive, and individualistic goal structures on achievement: A meta-analysis. *Psychological Bulletin, 89,* 47–62.

Jones, B.F. (1986). Quality and equality through cognitive instruction. *Educational Leadership, 43*(7), 4–11.

Jones, B.F., & Friedman, L.B. (1988). Active instruction for students at risk: Remarks on merging process-outcome and cognitive perspectives. *Educational Psychologist, 23,* 299–308.

Jordan, C. (1985). Translating culture: From ethnographic information to educational program. *Anthropology and Education Quarterly, 16*, 105–123.

Knapp, M.S., & Shields, P.M. (1990). Reconceiving academic instruction for the children of poverty. *Phi Delta Kappan, 71*, 753–758.

Knight, S.L., & Waxman, H.C (1991). Students' cognition and classroom instruction. In H.C. Waxman & H.J. Walberg (Eds.), *Effective teaching: Current research* (pp. 239–255). Berkeley, CA: McCutchan.

Kozma, R.B., & Croninger, R.G. (1992). Technology and the fate of at-risk students. *Education and Urban Society, 24*, 440–453.

Ladson-Billings, G. (1992). Culturally relevant teaching: The key to making multicultural education work. In C.A. Grant (Ed.), *Research and multicultural education: From the margins to the mainstreams* (pp. 106–121). London: Falmer.

Ladson-Billings, G. (1995). But that's just good teaching! The case for culturally relevant pedagogy. *Theory into Practice, 34*, 158–165.

LeBlanc, P.R., & Skaruppa, C. (1997). Support for democratic schooling: Classroom level change via cooperative learning. *Action in Teacher Education, 19*(1), 28–38.

Le Celle-Peterson, M. & Rivera, C. (1994). Is it real for all kids? A framework for equitable assessment policies for English language learners. *Harvard Educational Review, 64*, 55–75.

Lee, C.D. (1992). Literacy, cultural diversity, and instruction. *Education and Urban Society, 24*, 279–291.

Lehr, J.B., & Harris, H.W. (1988). *At risk, low-achieving students in the classroom.* Washington, DC: National Education Association.

Lewis, L., Parsad, B., Carey, N., Bartfai, N., Farris, E., & Smerdon, B. (1999). *Teacher quality: A report on the preparation and qualifications of public school teachers.* Washington, DC: U.S. Department of Education, Office of Educational Research and Improvement, National Center for Education Statistics.

Liao, Y.K. (1993). Effects of computer experience on computer attitudes among preservice, inservice, and postulant teachers. In D. Carey, R. Carey, D.A. Willis & J. Willis (Eds.), *Technology and teacher education annual* (pp. 498–505). Charlottesville, VA: Association for the Advancement of Computing in Education.

Losey, K.M. (1995). Mexican American students and classroom interaction: An overview and critique. *Review of Educational Research, 65*, 283–318.

Lucas, T., & Schecter, S.R. (1992). Literacy education and diversity: Toward equity in the teaching of reading and writing. *The Urban Review, 24*, 85–103.

Masten, A.S. (1994). Resilience in individual development: Successful adaptation despite risk and adversity. In M.C. Wang & E.W. Gordon (Eds.), *Educational resilience in inner-city America: Challenges and prospects* (pp. 3–25). Hillsdale, NJ: Lawrence Erlbaum.

McCollum, P. (1989). Turn-allocation in lessons with North American and Puerto Rican students: A comparative study. *Anthropology and Education Quarterly, 20*, 133–158.

McGee Banks, C.A., & Banks, J.A. (1995). Equity pedagogy: An essential component of multicultural education. *Theory into Practice, 34*, 152–158.

McLaughlin, B., & McLeod, B. (1996). *Educating all our students: Improving education for children from culturally and linguistically diverse backgrounds* (Vol. 1). Santa

34   H.C. WAXMAN and Y.N. PADRÓN

Cruz, CA: National Center for Research on Cultural Diversity and Second Language Learning.

Means, B., & Olson, K. (1994). The link between technology and authentic learning. *Educational Leadership, 51*(7), 15–18.

Mehan, H. (1991). *Sociological foundations supporting the study of cultural diversity* (Research Report #1). Santa Cruz, CA: National Center for Research on Cultural Diversity and Second Language Learning.

Melendez, M. (1993). Bilingual education in California: A Status report. *Thrust for Educational Leadership, 22*(6), 35–38.

Merino, B.J., Legarreta, D., Coughran, C.C., & Hoskins, J. (1990). Interaction at the computer by language minority boys and girls paired with fluent English proficient peers. *Computers in the Schools, 7*(1/2), 109–119.

Meyer, L.M. (2000). Barriers to meaningful instruction for English learners. *Theory into Practice, 39*, 228–236.

Mielke, A., & Flores, C. (1992–1993). Bilingual technology equalizes opportunities in elementary classrooms. In L.M. Malave (Ed.), *Annual conference journal: NABE '92–'93* (pp. 81–92). Washington, DC: National Association for Bilingual Education.

Moll, L.C. (1986). Writing as communication: Creating strategic learning environments for students. *Theory into Practice, 25*(2), 102–107.

Moll, L. (1988). Educating Latino students. *Language Arts, 64*, 315–324.

Niemiec, R.P., & Walberg, H.J. (1992). The effects of computers on learning. *International Journal of Educational Research, 17*, 99–108.

Olmedo, I.M. (1992). Teacher expectations and the bilingual child. *Action in Teacher Education, 14*(2), 1–8.

O'Malley, J.M., & Chamot, A.U. (1990). *Learning strategies in second language acquisition.* Cambridge: Cambridge University Press.

Osborne, A.B. (1996). Practice into theory into practice: Culturally relevant pedagogy for students we have marginalized and normalized. *Anthropology & Education Quarterly, 27*, 285–314.

Padrón, Y.N. (1991). Commentary on dialogues promoting reading comprehension. In B. Means, C. Chelemer, & M.S. Knapp (Eds.), *Teaching advanced skills to at-risk students: Views from research and practice* (pp. 131–140). San Francisco: Jossey-Bass.

Padrón, Y.N. (1992). Strategy training in reading for bilingual students. *Southwest Journal of Educational Research into Practice, 4*, 59–62.

Padrón, Y.N. (1993). The effect of strategy instruction on bilingual students' cognitive strategy use in reading. *Bilingual Research Quarterly Journal, 16*(3 & 4), 35–51.

Padrón, Y.N. (1997). Latino students and reading: Understanding these English language learners' needs. In K. Beers & B. Samuels (Eds.), *Into Focus: Understanding and creating middle school readers* (pp. 105–124). Norwood, MA: Christopher-Gordon.

Padrón, Y.N., & Knight, S.L. (1989). Linguistic and cultural influences on classroom instruction. In H.P. Baptiste, J. Anderson, J. Walker de Felix, & H.C. Waxman (Eds.), *Leadership, equity, and school effectiveness* (pp. 173–185). Newbury Park, CA: Sage.

Padrón, Y.N., Knight, S.L., & Waxman, H.C. (1986). Analyzing bilingual and monolingual students' perceptions of their reading strategies. *The Reading Teacher, 39*, 430–433.

Padrón, Y.N., & Waxman, H.C. (1988). The effect of students' perceptions of their cognitive strategies on reading achievement. *TESOL Quarterly, 22*, 146–150.

Padrón, Y.N., & Waxman, H.C. (1993). Teaching and learning risks associated with limited cognitive mastery in science and mathematics for limited-English proficient students. In Office of Bilingual Education and Minority Language Affairs (Eds.), *Proceedings of the Third National Research Symposium on Limited English Proficient Students: Focus on middle and high school issues* (Vol. 2, pp. 511–547). Washington, DC: National Clearinghouse for Bilingual Education.

Padrón, Y.N., & Waxman, H.C. (1996). Improving the teaching and learning of English language learners through instructional technology. *International Journal of Instructional Media, 23*(4), 341–354.

Padrón, Y.N., & Waxman, H.C. (1999). Effective instructional practices for English language learners. In H.C. Waxman & H.J. Walberg (Eds.), *New directions for teaching practice and research* (pp, 171–203). Berkeley, CA: McCutchan.

Palincsar, A.S. (1986). The role of dialogue in providing scaffolded instruction. *Educational Psychologist, 21*(1/2), 73–98.

Palincsar, A., & Brown, A. (1984). Reciprocal teaching of comprehension-fostering and comprehension-monitoring activities. *Cognition and Instruction, 1*, 117–175.

Peregoy, S.F., & Boyle, O.F. (2000). English learners reading English: What we know what we need to know. *Theory into Practice, 39*, 237–247.

Pewewardy, C.D. (1994). Culturally responsible pedagogy in action: An American Indian magnet school. In E.R. Hollins, J.E. King, & W.C. Hayman (Eds.), *Teaching diverse populations: Formulating a knowledge base* (pp. 77–92). Albany: State University of New York Press.

Phelan, P., Davidson, A.L., & Cao, H.T. (1992). Speaking Up: Students' perceptions on School. *Phi Delta Kappan, 73*, 695–704.

Poirot, J.L., & Canales, J. (1993–94). Technology and the at-risk: An overview. *The Computing Teacher, 21*(4), 25–26, 55.

Presidential Task Force on Psychology in Education. (1993). *Learner-centered psychological principles: Guidelines for school redesign and reform.* Washington, DC American Psychological Association.

Pressley, M., & Ghatala, E.S. (1990). Self-regulated learning: Monitoring learning from text. *Educational Psychologist, 25*, 19–33.

Pressley, M., & Harris, K.R. (1990). What we really know about strategy instruction. *Educational Leadership, 48*(1), 31–34.

Raphael, T. (1984). Teaching learners about sources of information for answering questions. *Journal of Reading, 27*, 303–311.

Raphael, T. (1987). Research on reading: But what can I teach on Monday? In V. Richardson-Koehler (Ed.), *Educators' handbook: A research perspective* (pp. 26–49). New York: Longman.

Raphael, T., & Pearson, P.D. (1985). Increasing students' awareness of sources of information for answering questions. *American Educational Research Journal, 22*, 217–235.

Richardson, V. (1990). Significant and worthwhile change in teacher practice. *Educational Researcher, 19* (7), 10–18.

Richardson, V., Casanova, U., Placier, P., & Guilfoyle, K. (1989). *School children at risk.* London: Falmer.

Rivera, C., & Zehler, A.M. (1991). Assuring the academic success of language minority students: Collaboration in teaching and learning. *Journal of Education, 173*(2), 52–77.

Rossi, R.J., & Stringfield, S.C. (1995). What must we do for students placed at risk. *Phi Delta Kappan, 77,* 73–76.

Saldana, D.C., & Waxman, H.C. (1996). The integration of multicultural education in urban middle level schools. *Issues in Middle Level Education, 5*(2), 9–29.

Saldana, D.C., & Waxman, H.C. (1997). An observational study of multicultural teaching in urban elementary schools. *Equity and Excellence in Education, 30*(1), 40–46.

Sandholtz, J.H., Ringstaff, C., & Dwyer, D.C. (1992). Teaching in high-tech environments: Classroom management revisited. *Journal of Educational Computing Research, 8,* 479–505.

Saunders, W., & Goldenberg, C. (1992, April). *Effects of instructional conversations on transition students' concepts of friendship: An experimental study.* Paper presented at the annual meeting of the American Educational Research Association, San Francisco.

Shuell, T.J. (1993). Toward an integrated theory of teaching and learning. *Educational Psychologist, 28,* 291–311.

Slavin, R.E. (1990). Research on cooperative learning: Consensus and controversy. *Educational Leadership, 47*(4), 52–55.

Slavin, R.E. (1991). Synthesis of the research on cooperative learning. *Phi Delta Kappan, 48*(5), 71–82.

Smylie, M.A. (1988). The enhancement function of staff development: Organization and psychological antecedents to individual teacher change. *American Educational Research Journal, 25,* 1–30.

Smith, T.M. (1995). *The educational progress of Hispanic students.* Washington, DC: U.S. Department of Education, National Center for Educational Statistics.

Smolkin, L. (2000). How will diversity affect literacy in the next millennium? *Reading Research Quarterly, 35,* 549–550.

Stephen, V.P., Varble, M.E., & Taitt, H. (1993). Instructional strategies for minority youth. *The Clearing House, 67,* 116–120.

Swan, K., & Mitrani, M. (1993). The changing nature of teaching and learning in computer-based classrooms. *Journal of Research on Computing in Education, 26,* 40–54.

Tharp, R.G. (1995). Instructional conversations in Zuni classrooms. In C.L. Montone (Ed.), *Teaching linguistically and culturally diverse learners: Effective programs and practices* (pp. 12–13). Santa Cruz, CA: National Center for Research on Cultural Diversity and Second Language Learning.

Tharp, R.G. (1997). *From at-risk to excellence: Research, theory, and principles for practice.* Santa Cruz, CA: Center for Research on Education, Diversity and Excellence.

Tharp, R.G., & Gallimore, R. (1988). *Rousing minds to life: Teaching, learning, and schooling in social context.* Cambridge: Cambridge University Press.

Trueba, H.T. (1988). Culturally-based explanations of minority students' academic achievement. *Anthropology of Education Quarterly, 19,* 270–287.

Trueba, E.T., & Bartolomé, L.I. (1997). *The education of latino students: Is school reform enough?* (Digest No. EDO-UD-97-4). New York: ERIC Clearinghouse on Urban Education, Teachers College, Columbia University.

U.S. Department of Education. (1992). *The condition of bilingual education in the nation: A report to the Congress and the President.* Washington, DC: Author.

U.S. Department of Education. (1997). *The condition of education 1997.* Washington, DC: U.S. Department of Education, National Center for Education Statistics.

U.S. Department of Education. (1999). *The condition of education 1999.* Washington, DC: U.S. Department of Education, National Center for Education Statistics.

U.S. Department of Education (2000). *Key indicators of Hispanic student achievement: National goals and benchmarks for the next decade.* Washington, DC: U.S. Department of Education, National Center for Education Statistics.

Walker de Felix, J., Johnson, R.T., & Shick, J.E. (1990). Socio- and psycholinguistic considerations in interactive video instruction for limited English proficient students. *Computers in the Schools, 7*(1/2), 173–190.

Waxman, H.C. (1992). Reversing the cycle of educational failure for students in at-risk school environments. In H.C. Waxman, J. Walker de Felix, J. Anderson, & H.P. Baptiste (Eds.), *Students at risk in at-risk schools: Improving environments for learning* (pp. 1–9). Newbury Park, CA: Sage.

Waxman, H.C., & Bright, G.W. (1993). Research methods and paradigms in technology and teacher education. In H.C. Waxman & G.W. Bright (Eds.). *Approaches to research in teacher education and technology* (pp. 1–9). Charlottesville, VA: Association for the Advancement of Computers and Education.

Waxman, H.C., & Huang, S.L. (1995). An observational study of technology integration in urban elementary and middle schools. *International Journal of Instructional Media, 22*(4), 329–339.

Waxman, H.C., & Huang, S.L. (1996–97). Classroom instruction differences by level of technology use in middle school mathematics. *Journal of Educational Computing Research, 14*(2), 147–159.

Waxman, H.C., Huang, S.L., & Padrón, Y.N. (1995). Investigating the pedagogy of poverty in inner-city middle level schools. *Research in Middle Level Education, 18*(2), 1–22.

Waxman, H.C., Huang, S.L., & Padrón, Y.N. (1997). Motivation and learning environment differences between resilient and non-resilient Latino middle school students. *Hispanic Journal of Behavioral Sciences, 19,* 137–155.

Waxman, H.C., & Padrón, Y.P. (1995). Improving the quality of classroom instruction for students at risk of failure in urban schools. *Peabody Journal of Education, 70*(2), 44–65.

Waxman, H.C., Padrón, Y.N., & Arnold, K.A. (2001). Effective instructional practices for students placed at risk of failure. In G.D. Borman, S.C. Stringfield, & R.E. Slavin (Eds.), *Title I: Compensatory education at the crossroads* (pp. 137–170). Mahwah, NJ: Lawrence Erlbaum.

Waxman, H.C., Padrón, Y.N., & Knight, S.L. (1991). Risks associated with students' limited cognitive mastery. In M.C. Wang, M.C. Reynolds, & H.J. Walberg

(Eds.), *Handbook of special education: Emerging programs* (Vol. 4, pp. 235–254). Oxford: Pergamon.

Wenglinsky, H. (1998). *Does it compute? The relationship between educational technology and student achievement in mathematics.* Princeton, NJ: Educational Testing Service Policy Information Center.

Winne, P. (1985). Steps toward promoting cognitive achievements. *The Elementary School Journal, 85,* 673–693.

Worthen, B.R., Van Dusen, L.M., & Sailor, P.J. (1994). A comparative study of the impact of integrated learning systems on students' time-on-task. *International Journal of Educational Research, 21,* 25–37.

Yates, J.R., & Ortiz, A.A. (1991). Professional development needs of teachers who serve exceptional language minorities in today's schools. *Teacher Education and Special Education, 14*(1), 11–18.

CHAPTER 2

RELATIONSHIP BETWEEN PRE-SERVICE TEACHERS' BELIEFS ABOUT SECOND LANGUAGE LEARNING AND PRIOR EXPERIENCES WITH NON-ENGLISH SPEAKERS

Toni Griego Jones

ABSTRACT

This chapter reports on a study of 91 pre-service teachers' beliefs about second language learning and how their beliefs related to prior experiences working with language minority students. The chapter first addresses the need to prepare all pre-service teachers, not just bilingual and ESL teachers, for teaching language minority students in K-12 schools, and provides an update on the current state of readiness and preparation of teacher candidates who are in regular teacher preparation programs. Secondly, the research on the importance of addressing beliefs, specifically beliefs about second language learning, as the focus of change in teacher preparation is presented. The chapter then describes the pre-service study, including data collection methods and analysis, and ends with a discussion of the significance and implications of findings for teacher preparation programs. Key findings were that pre-service teachers with or without prior experiences with

L2 learners generally agreed with key concepts in bilingual/ESL education although those with prior experiences held stronger beliefs. Further, they seemed to learn from experiences but often misunderstood the language acquisition process. The chapter ends with a discussion of how teacher preparation programs can be revised to better prepare all pre-service teachers for second language learners.

THE CHALLENGE

Since the late eighties, I have been engaged in teacher preparation in large state Universities with bilingual teacher certification programs as well as "regular" elementary and secondary programs. I have had the good fortune of working with pre-service teachers in both bilingual (Spanish/English) and monolingual (English) programs, and although we were basically preparing all teacher candidates for positions in the same public schools, it often felt that I was wading in two distinct streams because of the radically different expectations and views of the bilingual certification and regular certification pre-service students. Granted that the pre-service teachers were preparing to teach in different programs within the public schools, but their visions of the children they would eventually teach were so dissimilar that it seemed we were preparing teachers for children in different countries. The teacher candidates in bilingual certification were focused exclusively on children who, for the most part, were Spanish speakers and those in non-bilingual programs envisioned their children to be monolingual English speakers. The "regular" pre-service teachers in fact, rarely thought about the possibility that they would be expected to teach children from culturally diverse backgrounds, even less those with different languages. Having spent many years as a classroom teacher in bilingual and regular classrooms in public schools, I knew that both groups' expectations reflected some reality, but I also knew that both groups were in for some surprises. Those who were headed for bilingual classrooms probably would teach mostly Spanish (or some other language) dominant children, but because of the need to desegregate schools and the increasing popularity of dual language schools, they would likely teach monolingual English speakers as well. The monolingual teacher candidates on the other hand, were very likely to have non-English speaking children in their classrooms although they did not anticipate it.

Further, my monolingual students, like most teacher candidates, believed that they would someday teach in schools like those they attended. Like most pre-service teachers, these monolingual students were primarily White, middle class, mostly females who had received a very segregated education and had little personal experience with children learning English as a second language. When I talked about teaching in culturally and linguistically diverse classrooms, I experienced some resistance in my classes, sometimes open, sometimes subtle, from my monolingual pre-service teachers. While we debated this eventuality in my education foundations courses, students could still keep the idea of teaching children who did not speak English at arms' length. However, the reality of the K-12 student demographics hit when they went out to do supervised fieldwork, particularly student teaching.

Pre-service teachers' disbelief about teaching children from non-English backgrounds was something I encountered wherever I taught as I moved from one part of the country to another. The disbelief and sometimes intimidating encounters between monolingual pre-service teachers and English as a Second Language learners seemed to be happening across the country. In the Midwest, I remember supervising elementary student teachers who were studying for bilingual certification and others who were in "regular" non-bilingual programs. Those who intended to be bilingual teachers were very focused on learning about second language acquisition and how they could meet the needs of second language learners. The non-bilingual teacher candidates, on the other hand, did not know about second language learners, nor did they assume they would someday have responsibility for teaching them. Once, I recall supervising a student teacher who happened to have a newly arrived Chinese speaker in her elementary classroom. When I first observed the student teacher, I noticed that the Chinese child was sitting off by herself coloring. When I asked the student teacher about her, she said that the child had to do that because she did not speak English. The student teacher did not seem to believe that the child was her responsibility and that she could teach her English or any of the other subjects she was teaching the other children. Instead, the student teacher took the position that she couldn't be expected to teach the school's curriculum to someone who did not know English. In spite of my efforts to explain that all children are the responsibility of the teacher and my assistance with ESL strategies, the teacher candidate absolutely refused to take ownership for the Chinese child, believing that until the child learned English, she could not and didn't have to teach her. I do not know where or how she expected the child to learn English, but I began to ponder the strength of this college student's belief that it wasn't her responsibility to teach the non-English speaking child. Was the teacher candidate overwhelmed because she did not know what to do to teach the child? Or, was there something else keeping her from accepting responsibility for teaching English (certainly a subject she knew, but not from the perspective of a second language)? Her belief that it was not her responsibility, that it was unreasonable to expect her to teach the child English and all the other subjects was so strong that she resisted her supervisor's assistance and criticism. Unfortunately, the cooperating classroom teacher reinforced the student teacher's belief that it was not her responsibility to teach the child. She informed me that they were waiting for the Bilingual/ESL Office in the District to do something with the child. Meanwhile, they sat the child in the corner to color and incidentally pick up whatever she was able to in English and other content areas. When I moved West to a region where there are many more language minority school children, I expected a greater awareness of responsibility for second language learners. However, my monolingual teacher candidates still seemed to have much of the same disbelief and tendency to let ESL students be someone else's responsibility.

EVERYONE'S RESPONSIBILITY

After the *Lau v. Nichols* court ruling in 1974 and subsequent federal and state legislation, more and more children were provided with Bilingual or ESL services in public schools. However, the notion that *all* English language learners (ELLs) are served by bilingual and/or ESL programs is false. The fact is that many children who are from other language backgrounds are *not* in bilingual classrooms or English as a Second Language programs. Many are in English only classrooms staffed by monolingual English-speaking teachers with very little training for teaching second language learners. Estimates are that over half of the children identified as needing special language instruction, that is, those identified as limited English proficient, do not receive instruction from certified bilingual or ESL teachers (Abramson, Pritchard, & Garcia, 1993). Looked at another way, most regular classroom teachers, up to 66%, have second language learners in their classrooms (Fleischman & Hopstock, 1993). However we look at services for ELLs, the fact is that the majority of children who are in the process of learning English as a Second Language are actually in regular, mainstream, English only classrooms taught by monolingual classroom teachers, teachers who have not received any preparation for teaching English as a Second Language. This situation was exacerbated in the 1990s with the national move toward deleting or diminishing bilingual programs in states like California and Arizona. For example, with the passage of Proposition 227 in 1998 in California (the state with the largest percentage of non-English speaking students at 1.5 million), there are even more "limited English proficient" students in non-bilingual classrooms with teachers who have not been trained or oriented toward responsibility for English language learners (Mora, 2000). According to Mora, one year after the passage of the Proposition, the percentage of students receiving instruction in bilingual classrooms fell from 30% to 12% (Mora, 2000). Children who had previously been in bilingual classrooms are now in regular classrooms.

Looking at this from a program perspective, the intense political debates in the national media during the 1990s gave the impression that bilingual programs were pervasive in the country's schools, but according to a national survey conducted by the U.S. Department of Education, the percentage of public schools that provide bilingual or ESL programs is relatively small and doesn't reach all children identified as needing special language services. This national survey reported that approximately 33% of central city schools had bilingual and/or ESL programs, 22% of urban fringe or large towns, and about 12% of rural and small towns provided bilingual and/or ESL programs in 1993–94 (National Center for Education Statistics, 1997). This means that most of the schools in all areas did not have bilingual or ESL programs. Clearly, my monolingual teacher candidates' assumptions that bilingual and ESL teachers would teach all the children whose first language was not English, and that *they* would not teach second language learners was false. At the end of the 1990s even schools that hadn't needed bilingual and ESL programs in the 70s and 80s began to experience the pressures of immigrant populations and subsequent demand for programs for second language learners. The result of the burgeoning language minority populations and declining number of bilingual and ESL programs at the beginning of the new millennium was that teacher educators were left scrambling to learn what it means to teach children from other language backgrounds and trying to figure out how to prepare prospective teachers for them.

COLLEGE OF EDUCATION RESPONSIBILITY

Awareness of the need to prepare *all* pre-service and in-service teachers is on the rise in teacher preparation programs across the country, even though they are far from adequately addressing the need for teachers who are prepared for the cultural and linguistic diversity in schools. The two factors mentioned above in particular are putting pressure on teacher preparation programs to open up and include knowledge about teaching second language learners. First, the burgeoning population of language minority students and second, the political move to curtail bilingual programs exert pressure on teacher preparation programs to expand training beyond bilingual and ESL certification programs and educate all prospective teachers about the needs of second language learners.

Most states have standards that attempt to address diversity in teacher preparation, but only one state, California, has offered certification in the area of teaching culturally diverse students for *all* teachers. This has been in place since 1992 but only 32% of the monolingual teaching force held this cross-cultural certification at the time of the passage of Proposition 227

(Mora, 2000). Another indicator of the importance of addressing preparation for cultural and linguistic diversity is the National Council for Accreditation of Teacher Education (NCATE, 2001) inclusion of a Standard for Diversity among the six Standards used to review and approve teacher preparation programs. Most Colleges of Education have a required multicultural course in their teacher preparation programs, but the country still has a long way to go in preparing all teachers for teaching linguistically diverse student populations.

According to many who study cultural diversity, the challenge for Colleges of Education to prepare the predominantly White middle-class preservice teachers with limited or no experience with children from racial/ethnic, cultural, and social class backgrounds different from their own is growing more urgent by the day (Banks, 1991; Nieto, 1997; Sleeter, 2001). Learning about cultural differences can be difficult enough even when teachers and students speak the same language. Add to that the fact that teachers need to learn how to deal with *language* differences, with not speaking or understanding the same communication code of their students. Understanding what it means to communicate with children in an entirely different language takes cultural sensitivity to a new level.

Colleges of Education need to take up the challenge of preparing prospective teachers for linguistic diversity as it is the incoming teachers who will have to stem the tide of language minority students' failure in K-12 schools. Those who are already teaching in the nation's schools do not feel prepared for limited English proficient students and their district in-service training does not appear to be addressing their professional development needs. According to a report on teacher quality analyzing results from a survey conducted by the National Center for Education Statistics, 54% of teachers report they teach limited English proficient students, but relatively few of these teachers (only 20%) felt very well prepared to teach their children (National Center for Education Statistics, 1999).

WHAT EDUCATORS NEED TO KNOW

Where do teacher preparation programs start? What should be included in teacher preparation programs to prepare teachers for teaching English Language Learners (ELLs) can be sorted into two categories: (1) what they need to know about second language learning and learners and (2) what pre-service teachers need to know and understand about themselves. There is a research-based body of knowledge that is accepted as good practice in teaching English language learners (August & Hakuta, 1997; Carrasquillo & Rodriguez, 1996; Cummins, 1999; Krashen, 1999; Wong-Fillmore & Valadez, 1986). These practices are based on the assumption that there is an interdependent relationship between language development and cognitive development (Mora, 2000). Some key concepts for second language acquisition are: (1) proficiency in the native language enhances learning in content areas and in a second language, (2) learning a second language depends on the amount of comprehensible input in that language, (3) there is a common underlying proficiency for both language systems so that one supports the other in learning content, and (4) there are differences in the levels of proficiency needed to succeed at various tasks, from interpersonal communications to working at academic subjects. In spite of the knowledge base, though, some teacher educators contend that teachers do not receive enough training in teacher preparation programs to understand the structure, purposes, and patterns of language to teach all children in their native language, much less in a second language learners (Wong-Fillmore & Snow, 2000). They point out that when speakers of languages other than English are not learning efficiently in bilingual or non-bilingual classrooms, they are not being *taught* effectively.

Wong-Fillmore and Snow (2000) also believe there is a real need to ensure that knowledge about language teaching and learning is widely shared with policy makers as well as teachers (Wong-Fillmore & Snow). Events such as the passage of Proposition 227 in California and Proposition 203 in Arizona revealed a "dismaying lack of understanding about the facts of second language learning and the nature of bilingual education" (p. 10). I would add that the knowledge base on second language acquisition theory and effective practices for second language learning is something that principals, central administrators, and all who are responsible for implementing policy decisions should know and utilize. Research on change and program implementation indicates that *all* relevant personnel must take ownership for a new orientation or practice in order for the change to take place (Griego Jones, 1995). In this case, everyone in the key implementation positions in districts as well as all classroom teachers must take ownership for effectively educating language minority students.

Most important, all of what we know about teaching language minority students must be used in preparing new, incoming educators, particularly teachers, as they are the front line for the children. To do this, we need to understand what pre-service teachers already know and believe about second language learners and learning. As extensive as it is, the body of knowledge about effective practices for second language learners is useless if it doesn't connect with the pre-service teacher's beliefs about second language learning. There has to be some readiness within the pre-service teachers themselves to receive the knowledge and do something with it. Therefore, in order to begin preparing teachers for the linguistic diversity found in today's schools, it is important to know what pre-service teachers believe about goals for the schooling of children from non-English backgrounds, what they believe about the process of learning a second language, and how they feel about languages other than English being used for instruction. The rest of this chapter reports on selected findings from a study that assessed a range of pre-service teachers' beliefs about second language learning and teaching language minority students. The findings reported here are about how pre-service teacher beliefs related to prior experiences working with language minority students.

THEORETICAL FRAMEWORK

The framework for this study is provided by research on why beliefs are important in pre-service teacher education in general, and specifically, why beliefs are important in learning to teach linguistically diverse students. Richardson (1996) summarizes the literature on the importance and function of beliefs in teacher education by stating that: (1) beliefs strongly influence what and how pre-service teachers learn, and (2) beliefs are the focus of change in the process of educating teachers. Theories that view learning as an active, constructive process acknowledge that existing knowledge and beliefs strongly influence individuals as they approach a learning task (Brookhart & Freeman, 1992; Fang, 1996; Nespor, 1987; Pajares, 1992). When students enter pre-service teacher education programs, they bring beliefs about teaching, learning, and subject matter, they have acquired during many years of being students. These existing beliefs determine what prospective teachers build upon, what they can accept or reject in teacher education.

Where Beliefs Come From

To understand why pre-service teachers are not all prepared to understand needs of English language learners (ELLS), we need to review where teacher candidates' beliefs come from. For most subject areas, pre-service teachers have some prior experience. They have all taken mathematics, science, social studies, and English language arts, but when it comes to second language learning, the majority of teacher candidates have very little experience to draw upon. For most, the closest experience they have had to learning a second language will have been studying a foreign language in high school. Most pre-service teachers do not have proficiency in more than one language because they come from monolingual homes and unfortunately, American students do not develop high levels of proficiency in foreign languages when they study them in school. There is some hope, however, that may change in the 2000s as foreign languages are now recognized as part of the core curriculum in *Goals 2000: Educate America Act* and foreign language instruction is more prevalent now in elementary schools. Foreign language instruction increased by nearly 10 percent in elementary schools and remained stable at the secondary level between 1987 and 1997 (Center for Applied Linguistics, 2001) so there may be reason to expect that more prospective teachers will have more exposure to languages other than English. Coincidently, the most popular language to study in elementary and secondary schools is Spanish (Center for Applied Linguistics, 2001) and this is a direct match with the most common home language other than English in U.S. K-12 public schools. Currently, most Colleges of Education do not require foreign language study, so prospective teachers do not have the opportunity to learn a second language as part of teacher preparation and have had no reason to perceive second language learning as part of teacher preparation programs.

The lack of experience with learning a second language is an important consideration in preparing prospective teachers for today's schools because researchers of teacher knowledge, beliefs, and behavior believe that pre-service teachers' own schooling experience is one of the most powerful predictors of how they themselves will teach (Richardson, 1996). Since prospective teachers get their knowledge and their beliefs about teaching from their own schooling experience as well as from teacher preparation programs, they can hardly be expected to understand cultural diversity and its implications for teaching from their own experience. If they have not experienced learning a second language themselves or if they have not witnessed the process in others, what do they have to build upon in their teacher preparation programs?

Even if teacher candidates don't know a second language, they could learn about cultural differences in using language and develop some understanding of the needs of second language learners if they at least had opportunities to learn about cultural backgrounds other than their own. However, significantly, for the preparation of teachers for culturally and linguistically diverse students, research indicates that the majority of White pre-service teachers have had very little contact with minorities prior to entering teacher education programs (Sleeter, 2001; Zimpher & Ashburn, 1992). They have not generally experienced cultures and languages other than their own and this has resulted in lack of knowledge and parochial beliefs about minority children. Gomez and Tabachnick (1992) even suggest that views of prospective teachers could actually limit minority children's opportunities to benefit from schooling because of the parochialism inherent in pre-service teachers' beliefs.

Cultural Match or Mismatch

When educators first became concerned about the condition of schooling for minority children, one of the first "solutions" to the problem was to find more teachers like the students themselves. In the 80s much of the literature in teacher education implied that the needs of culturally and linguistically diverse student populations would be met by recruiting more racial and ethnic minorities into teaching. Recruitment and retention of minorities (and of bilingual candidates) was given as a solution to the problem of ineffective schooling for minority children and in fact, some gains were made after the Civil Rights Movement in recruiting underrepresented minorities into teaching. Those gains are reversing though, and the population of pre-service teachers is expected to be even more homogeneous in the early 2000s (Gay, 2000).

Although more teachers from minority backgrounds and teachers with bilingual skills are absolutely needed in the profession, they alone cannot provide for the education of the massive numbers of language minority children. Further, we can't make the assumption that all minority teachers automatically understand the educational needs of minority children, particularly the linguistic needs. According to research, whether prospective teachers come from majority or minority backgrounds, most are from monocultural backgrounds and thus wouldn't have any personal experiences to draw upon for *cross-cultural* understanding (Aaronshohn, Carter, & Howell, 1995; Causey, Thomas, & Armento, 1999). Because of the segregated nature of public schools, most pre-service students of any racial and ethnic background probably attended schools with others of their own race and ethnicity and do not have a great deal of experience with people from another group (Gay, 2000). If prospective teachers don't have opportunities to learn about the variety of cultural differences in this country, they are even at a greater disadvantage when it comes to understanding what it means to learn a second language. Would prior contact with second language learners inform their beliefs about second language learning? Would the type of contact make a difference? These are some of the questions explored in the study reported here.

METHODOLOGY/DATA COLLECTION

The sample for this study was a group of 91 pre-service teachers beginning their teacher preparation program at a large southwestern university where the majority of graduates teach in schools with high percentages of Spanish speakers and Native Americans. A survey was given early in the fall of 1996 to students taking an Educational Foundations course, one of the first in the professional sequence. The students were in two on-campus sections and one off-campus cohort of "non-traditional" students who had completed their first two years at a local community college. Students in the off-campus groups were all participants in an alternative bilingual certification program while about 10% of the on-campus group were in some sort of bilingual certification program. The majority of respondents had junior and senior (65%) status and the remainder were Post Baccalaureate students. Seventy percent were female; ethnic/racial breakdown was 47% white non-Hispanic, 41% Hispanic, African American, American Indian, and Asian students accounted for less than 1% each and the rest did not respond to this query. Sixty-three percent claimed they were proficient in a second language and the majority (72%) of those gave Spanish as their other language. This is a much higher percentage than most national figures would indicate (Zimpher & Ashburn, 1992).

Students were asked to voluntarily complete a two-page Likert scale questionnaire that asked them to rate their agreement on a scale of 1–5 (strongly agree to strongly disagree) with 30 statements related to non-English speakers and learning a second language. Respondents were also asked if their university program so far had included information about bilingualism, Bilingual Education, and English as a Second Language, and if so, what courses. Finally, they were asked if they had any kind of experience working with non-English speaking children prior to entering the College of Education and to describe any such experiences.

The statements they were asked to react to reflected language acquisition principles that are commonly accepted in the fields of Bilingual Education and ESL or they were commonly held beliefs by the general public. The cornerstone of bilingual education is the development of and the use of a child's native language in instruction (Krashen & Biber, 1988) so some statements were about the importance of developing a child's native language and using the native language for classroom instruction. Developing a child's native language, whatever it is, helps in cognitive development and the development of literacy. Research strongly supports the value of not only maintaining, but developing the first language of a child. Those children who are literate in their native language have a great advantage in learning a second (Hakuta, 1986; Krashen, 1993). All research on biliteracy demonstrates the importance of developing a child's main line of communication for literacy and for teaching the entire curriculum.

Other statements addressed the relationship between first and second languages. An accepted tenet of bilingual education is that it is not only possible for children to grow up bilingual and biliterate, but the interplay of two languages actually helps each language to develop. There was a time in the seventies when researchers worried that the first language sometimes interfered with learning a second. Since then, however, more researchers believe that knowing the rules and structure of one language helps children understand the purpose and structure of a second, and that, in fact, children who are bilingual have a cognitive advantage in learning all aspects of the curriculum (Hakuta, 1986). Research also tells us that spending more time in English only environments does not necessarily result in learning more English (Cummins, 1999; Hakuta, 1986; Krashen, 1993).

All statements were grounded in language acquisition research, but they also reflected assumptions commonly held by the public about second language learning. The assumption that using two languages is confusing to children or that spending more time in English automatically results in learning more English are pervasive in media debates about bilingual education. For most citizens of the United States, the media is a primary source of their "information" about second language learning, bilingualism, and bilingual education. Statements in the survey were clustered into the following categories: Belief statements about the (1) importance of maintaining and developing native language, (2) importance of using native language for instruction in school, and (3) statements about the relationship between L1 and L2 in classroom settings.

DATA ANALYSIS

Responses were analyzed to determine agreement/disagreement with statements using SPSS to determine relationships between agree/disagree responses and variables such as pre-service teacher proficiency in a second language, race/ethnicity, gender, course work dealing with bilingualism, Bilingual Education, and/or ESL, and prior experience working with non-English speakers. A qualitative analysis of prior experiences looked at duration, amount of oversight from cooperating teachers, and type of experience. Classroom experiences were further broken down into categories (observation in bilingual and non-bilingual classrooms, tutoring individuals or small groups, bilingual or non-bilingual classroom) The following describes prior experiences and Chart 1 illustrates how pre-service teachers in each category of prior experience responded to six key language acquisition statements.

Statements related to the native language asked about the importance of maintaining or developing the native language in general, and specifically developing it and using it for instruction in schools. Other statements were about how children acquire a second language and the relationship between the native language and a second language. There were sixteen statements, with several asking the same question in different wording to ensure reliable responses to key ideas. Six key statements were selected from the questionnaire as representative of key concepts in the question-

Chart 1. Type of Prior Experiences of Pre-service Teachers

	Observations in Bilingual Classrooms	Observations in Regular Classrooms	Employed in Alternative Programs	Volunteer Programs	ESL Tutoring	None
# 1	70%	83%	80%	69%	66%	67%
# 2	40% M	60% M	40% M	62%	100% M	41% M
# 3	80%	70%	90%	62%	83%	50%
# 4	60%	67%	90%	54%	83%	45%
# 5	60% M	63%	70%	38%	100%	36% M
# 6	70%	50%	80%	69%	100%	36% D.K.

The largest percentage is recorded (Slightly + Strongly). In some cases, the Don't Know category was the largest.

1. It is important to develop a child's native language in school.
2. It is important that children from non-English home backgrounds speak English at home.
3. It is important to use a child's native language to teach him/her in school.
4. Using more than one language in schools is confusing to children.
5. Children learn more English if they are taught only in English.
6. Using a child's native language (not English) in school will keep him/her from learning English.

naire. Chart 1 illustrates the types of experiences pre-service teachers had and compares them with agreement/disagreement responses to the representative statements.

When the majority of students agreed or disagreed with statements supported by research, they were considered to be in alignment with the statements accepted in the field of Bilingual/ESL education. When pre-service teachers agreed with statements that would be considered "false" in the field, the percentages were coded as misalignment (M). The largest percentages (agreed, disagreed, don't know) were recorded in Chart 1 with DK indicating that the largest percentage response for a given statement was the category of Don't Know.

FINDINGS

A significant percentage of all students (76%) claimed some prior experience working with non-English speaking children, mostly through classroom observation in public schools, volunteer work in youth programs outside of the classroom and one to one tutoring. Most of these experiences were within the few years before entering the College of Education. Analysis of descriptions of experiences indicated that the reason for the high percentage of prior experiences for on-campus students (72 of the 91) was that applicants to the College of Education were required to submit documented experience in educational settings as part of their application. Applicants are asked to document their experiences working with children in schools or other settings. When teacher candidates apply, their experiences in schools working with teachers "count" more than volunteering in day care centers, after-school programs, or alternative programs in their applications. Consequently, pre-education majors regularly arrange to observe and volunteer in local schools or educational settings in anticipation of applying to the College of Education. The pre-service teacher contact with language minority children in this sample, therefore, was much greater than in the general population of pre-service teachers and made this a particularly interesting sample to study.

Only twenty-two students said they did not have prior experiences working with non-English speaking children, even though they may have had experiences with other children in schools. For those who did report some experience with children learning a second language, their prior experiences fell into the following categories:

1.   Observation/helping in bilingual classrooms in public schools (10 students).

2. Observation/helping in "regular" classrooms in public schools (30 students).
3. Employment in school programs such as alternative programs, preschool, after-school programs, summer school (10 students).
4. Volunteer work in summer day camps in the United States and Mexico (13 students).
5. Tutoring ESL one-to-one in formal settings (6 students).
6. No prior experience (22 students).

The duration of time spent in these experiences varied widely from several months to three years, but not everyone reported how long they had spent working with non-English speakers so it was not useful to compare this variable with agreement/disagreement statements. Neither did enough of the sample describe the kind or amount of supervision they had while doing their work with non-English speakers. The few descriptions that alluded to supervision indicated that pre-service students were on their own when they had their interactions with children learning a second language. The questionnaire did not have written directions asking pre-service teachers to talk about duration and supervision. Instead, they were given oral directions and this could account for the fact that not much was reported on these two variables. On the other hand, it could be that the pre-service students just did not have much supervision during their volunteer experience. In terms of time, their experiences could have been one shot events or part of an experience with a bigger group of children and so were difficult for pre-service teachers to report.

DISCUSSION

There were no consistent patterns, although there were some differences between pre-service teachers who had experiences with second language learners and those who did not, depending on the statement. The following describes differences or similarities for each statement. For Statement 1, about the importance of developing a child's native language in school, there was agreement across all categories. All groups of pre-service teachers, those with prior experiences and those with none, agreed with this statement by significant percentages. These responses are in alignment with what research and practice accept as true regarding the importance of developing the native language of children. Maintaining a child's native language, in fact, is a key principle of bilingual/ESL education. The percentage of agreement was particularly high across all categories of pre-service students with prior experiences, ranging from 66% to 83%. Pre-service teachers with no experience with second language learners also reported a high percentage of agreement at 67%. For this statement, there was no difference between those with prior experience and those without. The high level of agreement indicates pre-service teachers believed in the importance of developing the native language of children.

In the case of Statement 2, that it is important that children from non-English home backgrounds speak English at home, pre-service teachers from all prior experience categories except one agreed with the statement. This statement would be regarded as false in the Bilingual/ESL fields so the response percentages were coded as M, misalignment. Researchers support the idea that children should communicate with their parents and caregivers in their *native* languages so that they develop the high levels of native language proficiency necessary for the acquisition of literacy and cognitive functioning (Wong-Fillmore, 1991). Practicing English should be left to situations where children have English role models to practice with. When children use English and parents don't know English, they can't communicate with each other and this has had devastating effects on parent/child relationships. The loss of ability to communicate with parents has been detrimental to the emotional as well as cognitive well being of language minority children over the years. Therefore, knowledgeable bilingual and ESL teachers do not encourage children to use English as home. Instead, they encourage children and parents to speak and practice literacy skills in their native language, knowing that the development of native language will automatically assist the learning of English as a second language in school. This statement can be important because one of the most common "errors" classroom teachers make in dealing with language minority parents is to exhort parents and children to "speak English at home." For this statement, there was no particular difference between pre-service teachers with prior experiences and those without as the pre-service teachers with no experience also had a 41% agreement with this false statement, almost the same as those who observed/volunteered in bilingual classrooms where native language and English were part of the instructional day. It is unlikely that pre-service teachers would observe anything in their prior experiences that could enlighten them on this point, but if left unchecked they would join others in their well meaning, but counterproductive advice to parents.

Statement 3 is also about the native language, but it asks about the use of a child's native language for *instruction* in schools. It puts the role of teacher and the teacher's use of languages other than English into the picture. Pre-service teachers with prior experiences again had very high levels of agreement with this statement, with percentages ranging from 62% to 90%. Those without prior experiences, however, only agreed at 50%. Both Statement 3 and Statement 1 contain the very core of bilingual education, the use of a child's native language for instruction is the distinguishing characteristic of bilingual programs. All bilingual programs in this country, Transitional, Developmental, or Dual Language, use the native language for instruction in subjects and literacy development in addition to teaching English as a Second Language. The high level of agreement with Statement 3 infers a belief in the inherent usefulness of communicating with children in the most efficient way. However, the difference between those with prior experiences and those with none when asked about the use of languages other than English indicates hesitancy on the part of those who have not directly confronted the situation of communicating with children who don't understand English.

In Statement 4, the idea that using more than one language in schools is confusing to children is a commonly held belief in the general public and is an assumption that is often used as an argument against bilingual instruction. The statement is not however, substantiated by research in second language learning. On the contrary, research demonstrates that using a child's first language can be helpful in learning a second (Brown, 1987; Krashen, 1993). For this statement, pre-service teachers needed to disagree in order to be in alignment with accepted research and practice in second language acquisition—and they did disagree. Across all categories except those with no experience, disagreement with the statement ranged from 54% to 90%. Those with no experience also disagreed, but were the only group with less than 50% disagreement at 45%.

Statement 5, indicating that children learn more English if they are taught only in English, is also a common misconception. It seems counter intuitive to say that using more English will not necessarily, nor even usually, result in learning more English. But, in fact, research (Collier, 1995; Krashen, 1999) does not support the "sink or swim" approach of immersing children in English. Research supports the practice of structuring and phasing in the second language as children continue to develop their *first* language, that is, of providing meaningful, comprehensible input. This is especially true for language minority children from less enriched educational backgrounds who are also struggling to learn subjects as well as English. The most effective bilingual programs have a very carefully planned phasing in of content areas to correspond with developing proficiency in the second language (Krashen & Biber, 1988).

Pre-service teachers with prior experiences with L2 learners were mostly in alignment with accepted practice and research as they disagreed with this statement about learning more English is only taught in English, with percentages ranging from 38% to 100%, with one notable exception— those who observed in bilingual classrooms. Although the group that taught in volunteer programs had a rather low percentage of agreement, 38%, this was still the largest percentage in that group for that statement, with 31% agreeing and 31% saying they didn't know. Those pre-service teachers who had observed in bilingual programs *agreed* (60%) with the statement. The percentage of misalignment (60%) of those who had observed in bilingual programs was surprising and could be a cause for concern. This statement is completely against principle and practice in bilingual education. The agreement of pre-service teachers who observed in bilingual classrooms indicates that something about bilingual instruction needs to be explained. The other pre-service teachers who observed in non-bilingual classrooms or other settings disagreed and therefore were more in line with accepted practice in second language acquisition. This is surprising because we might expect that students observing in bilingual classrooms would pick up more about second language acquisition. However, since we don't know what kind of bilingual classrooms students observed, whether transitional, dual language, or developmental, we do not really know what they observed about learning English. The only constant throughout bilingual classrooms is some use of the native language of the children for instruction. Perhaps these pre-service teachers didn't see the learning of English if they observed when the native language was being used and made no assumptions about children's learning of English. A relatively low percentage, 36% of pre-service teachers with no prior experience *also agreed* with the statement, putting them at odds with accepted research and practice.

Statement 6, using a child's native language (not English) in school will keep him/her from learning English also reflects a commonly held fear among educators and parents that children won't learn English if they have access to their native language as a "crutch." Again, the majority of pre-service teachers with prior experiences disagreed with this statement. This aligned them with research and practice in second language learning which says that when children have native language support they learn English efficiently and less traumatically. In my experience as a classroom teacher, children's motivation to learn English is generally so strong that, children do learn English, given comprehensible input in English. Percentages of disagreement ranged from 50 to 100% for those with prior experiences. There was a difference between pre-service teachers with prior experience and those without for this statement. Students reporting no prior experiences split into thirds in their responses to this statement with the largest percentage, 36%, saying they didn't know. Pre-service teachers with no preparation or experience dealing with second language learners would have no way of knowing the importance of native language in the development of literacy and in comprehension of content matter so it is heartening that pre-service teachers are open to the use of both languages for educating language minority children.

Experiences in K-12 Classrooms

An analysis of the categories of pre-service teachers produced some interesting findings. Two of the groups of pre-service teachers, those who observed in bilingual and non-bilingual classrooms, gained their experiences with non-English speakers by observing/helping in public school classrooms very much like the classrooms they will someday be teaching in. These two groups represented the bulk of respondents with prior experiences (41 of 70 or 59%). Presumably, some of their inferred beliefs about second language learning came from working in the most common schooling contexts for second language learning. Even without reflection or guidance (at best with minimal guidance since few reported anything about their supervision) on what they were observing, they tended to believe what generally parallels best practice in second language teaching. There were only a few instances of Misalignment across all categories of pre-service teachers. Only two statements produced Misalignments, the statement about the importance of using English at home and the one about children learning more English if they are taught only in English. For the statement about learning more English if taught only in English, only two groups (observers in bilingual classrooms and those with no prior experiences) were misaligned with accepted principles in the field.

Pre-service teachers who observed/volunteered in "regular" non-bilingual classrooms were in complete alignment with accepted practice and research except in the case of Statement 2 about the use of English at home. They observed in classrooms where non-English speakers would have been mixed with native English speakers and would not necessarily have been given any specialized instruction. Many pre-service teachers in regular classrooms reported "helping" language minority children in these classrooms, primarily by translating or otherwise helping children understand the classroom curriculum. Some commented that they felt good knowing enough of the child's native language (Spanish in all cases) to translate and explain curriculum.

Pre-service teachers whose experiences had been observing and volunteering in regular (non-bilingual) classrooms gave the most detailed descriptions of their experiences. They wrote more in answer to the query that asked them to describe their prior experiences with non-English speakers than any other group. Pre-service teachers in the other four groups with prior experience tended to just list the settings or give brief sentences or phrases about where and how they worked with non-English speakers.

Aside from their misalignment with Statement 5 and Statement 2, the group that observed in bilingual classrooms was also strongly aligned with accepted practice and research. Their responses to the other statements were *very* strongly in alignment. Overall, this group seemed to hold the strongest beliefs with high percentages of agreement and disagreement. However, their misalignments (by 60%) that children learn more English if they are taught only in English could be of concern to bilingual teachers as it was a high percentage that came away with an "erroneous" belief about the learning of English. The differences between those who observed in bilingual and non-bilingual classrooms were not strong enough or consistent enough to say that pre-service teachers who observed in one setting as opposed to the other were in closer alignment with accepted practice and research, although the two cases of misalignment in the group that observed in bilingual classrooms could be cause for concern to local bilingual teachers.

Alternative and Volunteer Settings

A total of 29 pre-service teachers with prior experience had their experiences in settings that are not the common context for schooling for L2 learners. Their experience was in alternative settings such as after-school programs, day-care, volunteer tutoring in groups or one-on-one. Even so, they were all engaged in some very direct way with second language learners as opposed to just observing or helping a teacher. They did more than observe and help out with individuals in classrooms, they were responsible for teaching something to the children, either in groups or individually. These pre-service teachers did not report any training or preparation for the jobs they had dealing with second language learners, but it is possible that they had minimal training for what they were doing.

Not surprisingly, those who were actually employed to work with L2 learners had the second highest percentages of alignment with selected statements and the lowest percentage of misalignment with Statement 2. This group had been employed in some way in school programs targeting minority children and even though the programs were not necessarily targeting second language learners, they apparently often had these students in them. Employees in alternative instructional settings had the second highest overall alignment with principles and practice in second language acquisition. The pre-service teachers who were *most* closely aligned with the statements was the group with experience in tutoring one-to-one even though they also had the highest misalignment percentage on Statement 2 (100%). This could be an indication that direct involvement and responsibility for teaching ESL or teaching other subjects to English language learners by using native language or ESL is a most powerful and productive experience in developing beliefs about second language learning and learners.

The category of volunteers in alternative settings had the greatest variety of experiences within the category and their responses were also the most varied. They differed from all the other groups in that they agreed with Statement 2 and their alignment responses with statements about how English is learned were not as strongly held as in other prior experience groups. Percentages of agreement or disagreement was lower than the other groups with prior experience and was generally more in line with the group that didn't have prior experiences.

Themes

The main themes that emerged from the pre-service teachers' descriptions dealt with: (1) the time it takes to learn a second language, (2) the concept of levels of proficiency needed for various activities (for example, social, interpersonal interactions vs. academic tasks), and (3) comments on the academic achievement of language minority students. Some of the teacher candidates' comments appear to be misconceptions or misunderstandings about the time it takes to become proficient in a second language and about the level of proficiency needed for academic work. For example, there were a number of comments on how quickly and easily children learn English, illustrated by the comment made by one that children "started to understand English within a week and to speak within a month or two." In a dual language classroom where English speakers were learning Spanish, another observed that children were "forced to listen" to teachers using Spanish and thought that was "criminal." There didn't seem to be an understanding that children have to hear a language in order to learn it. This is a first and very necessary "stage" in learning a language. A strong theme was the recognition that children learning English as a Second Language were "behind" their peers in achieving the goals of the school that even though children learned English quickly, their "understanding still was not as good as children born speaking English."

A key finding from the descriptions was that pre-service teachers *learned* from their interactions with children, even though they might have misinterpreted some of what they observed. Some stated they had learned from the children who were acquiring ESL, but did not elaborate on *what* they had learned from the children. Most said they had enjoyed their experience helping children, usually by translating, and they felt good when they could help children understand.

Implications/Significance

The first significant implication for teacher preparation is that pre-service teachers with or without prior experiences with second language learners are open to developing children's native languages even when the language is not English. The majority were not in bilingual or ESL certification programs, but they were not in opposition to accepted principles in the bilingual education field. In fact, they generally agreed with key concepts important in bilingual/ESL education even though those without prior experiences did not express themselves as strongly (in the high percentages) that those with prior experience did. Those without prior experiences tended more toward the 50% mark, while those with experiences generally had higher percentages of alignment or misalignment. There were no significant differences between pre-service teachers with or without prior experiences in the statements about the *importance* of the native language. However, for the statements that dealt with the *use of the native language in the classroom,* there was some difference. For these statements, those with prior experiences agreed more strongly with accepted principles of bilingual/ESL education while those without again tended toward the middle, around 50% or less. The stronger (higher percentages) agreement of those with experiences might be an indication that they felt they "knew" something. It could be then, that prior experiences with language minority children make a difference in what they believe about second language learning, at least in that those with experience had stronger opinions. The experiences directly teaching ESL or using what they knew of a child's native language to communicate with them may have been especially useful in forming beliefs. The small group that specifically tutored English language learners as opposed to observing and "helping" children in classrooms or programs expressed the strongest opinions. A word of caution is that the sample of pre-service teachers in this study was relatively small compared to the population of pre-service teachers and beliefs are always inferred, but the study provided useful information for adjusting the teacher preparation program.

The teacher preparation program for the university students who were not in the bilingual certification program needed to consciously connect course work and field experiences to the "incidental" second language learners encountered in the schools. First, course work needs to incorporate theory and pedagogy in the field of second language learning, and second, all students need to have specific assignments/experiences with second language learners in public schools. Encounters with children who are learning English as a second language cannot be left to chance. Results suggested that providing assignments for course field work, experiences that directly give them responsibility for communicating and/or teaching

ESL or content to L2 learners would be helpful to understanding how second language acquisition takes place. The experience of struggling to get something across when languages are not common has potential to help prospective teachers gain insight to second language acquisition. However, the experience alone does not explain what is happening with children. From descriptions in this study, it is clear that pre-service teachers need guidance and time to reflect on what children are going through. As pre-service teachers observe and "help" children who are learning English as a Second Language, they are making judgments about what is going on with the children. *Guided* reflection could be most effective in communicating concepts about the relationship of L1 and L2 and how native language proficiency helps second language acquisition. In the field experiences that are part of course work and practical, students could describe what they see children doing and discuss these observations with faculty who are knowledgeable about second language acquisition. This would involve collaboration between university faculty in "regular" and bilingual certification programs and that in itself would be a learning experience for all pre service teachers. Since experience and interactions with children seems to be key to pre service teacher learning, field work assignments could ask them to collect and reflect on children's oral and written samples in English and their native languages at various stages and to conduct case studies of children from non-English backgrounds. Pre-service teachers could be asked to help children write autobiographies of second language learners and write their own autobiographies about how they themselves learned their native language or any second language. The guidance and explanations of bilingual and ESL faculty in the "regular" teacher preparation program is crucial to maximizing the learning experiences for pre-service teachers. They can help pre-service teachers to see connections between second language acquisition theory and what they are observing in children's behavior.

There is a growing body of research showing the effectiveness of identifying and modifying pre-service teachers' beliefs about minority children as part of teacher preparation, with the goal of changing beliefs and behaviors (Cabello & Burnstein, 1995; Pajares, 1993; Zeichner, Melnick, & Gomez, 1996). In this study, identifying pre-service teachers' beliefs was the first step to understanding their teacher preparation needs relative to language minority children. The qualitative descriptions of "prior experiences" gave insight to pre-service teachers' ideas of what working with children meant to them and suggested how supervised field experiences with non-English speakers can be structured to maximize learning about children's needs and how to meet them. The next step is to study how addressing their beliefs affected their learning to teach as they progress through the teacher preparation program.

Most of the pre-service students (75%) in this sample did not intend to teach in bilingual or ESL programs, but the reality is they will have children from non-English backgrounds in their classrooms. Since these teacher candidates seemed open and supportive of native language maintenance and development, perhaps my student teacher of years ago and those who debated with me in my foundations classes are not typical of those going into teaching. They may have been more memorable because of their vocal resistance to the idea of teaching children who were different from them in language and cultural background. The results from this small study were encouraging and the job of preparing them for language minority students may not be as impossible as the demographic mismatch of teachers and children suggests.

REFERENCES

Aaronshohn, E., Carter, C., & Howell, M. (1995). Preparing monocultural teachers for a multicultural world. *Equity & excellence in education, 29*(1), 5–9.

Abramson, S., Pritchard, R., & Garcia, R. (Summer, 1993). Teacher Education and limited-English-proficient students: Are we meeting the challenge? *Teacher Education Quarterly,* 53–65.

August, D., & Hakuta, K. (Eds.). (1997). *Improving schooling for language minority children: A research agenda.* Washington, DC: National Academy Press.

Branaman, L., & Rhodes, N. (1998). *Foreign language instruction in the United States: A national survey of elementary and secondary schools.* (Executive Summary). Washington,DC: Center for Applied Linguistics.

Brookhart, S.M., & Freeman, D.J. (1992). Characteristics of entering teacher candidates. *Review of Educational Research, 62,* 37–60.

Brown, H.D. (1987). *Principles of language learning and teaching.* Englewood Cliffs, NJ: Prentice-Hall.

Cabello,B., & Burnstein, N. (1995). Examining teachers' beliefs about teaching culturally diverse classrooms. *Journal of teacher education, 46*(4), 285–294.

Causey, V.E., Thomas, C.D., & Armento, B.J. (1999). Cultural diversity is basically a foreign term to me: The challenges of diversity for preservice teacher education. *Teaching and teacher education, 16*(1), 33–45.

Cummins, J. (1999). Alternative paradigms in bilingual education research: Does theory have a place? *Educational Researcher, 28*(7), 26–34.

Collier, V.P. (1995). *Promoting academic success for ESL students.* Jersey City: New Jersey Teachers of English to Speakers of Other Languages-Bilingual Education.

Enright, D.S., & McCloskey, M.L. (1988). *Integrating English: Developing English language and literacy in the multicultural classroom.* New York: Addison-Wesley Publishing Company.

Fang, Z. (1996). A review of research on teacher beliefs and practices. *Educational research, 38*(1), 47–65.

Fleischman, H.L., & Hopstock, P.J. (1993). *Descriptive study of services to limited English proficient students, Vol. 1: Summary of findings and conclusions.* Arlington, VA: Development Associates, Inc.

Gay, G. (2000). Multicultural teacher education for the 21st century. *The teacher educator, 36*(1), 1–16.

Gomez, M.L., & Tabachnick, B.R. (1992). Telling teaching stories. *Teaching Education, 4*(2), 129–138.

Griego Jones, T. (Spring, 1995). *Implementing bilingual programs is everybody's business.* (FOCUS Occasional Papers in Bilingual Education, No. 11). Washington, DC: National Clearinghouse for Bilingual Education.

Hakuta, K. (1986). *Mirror of language.* New York: Basic Books, Inc.

Krashen, S. (1993). *Principles and practices in second language acquisition.* New York: Prentice-Hall.

Krashen, S., & Biber, D. (1988). *On course.* Sacramento: California Association for Bilingual Education.

Mora, J. (2000). Staying the course in times of change. Preparing teachers for language minority education. *Journal of teacher education, 51*(5), 345–357.

National Council for Accreditation of Teacher Education. (2001). *Professional standards for the accreditation of schools, colleges, and departments of education.* Washington, DC: National Council for Accreditation of Teacher Education.

National Center for Education Statistics. (1997). *Schools and staffing survey, 1987–88 and 1993–94 (school questionnaire).* Washington, DC: U.S. Department of Education.

National Center for Education Statistics. (1999). *Teacher quality: A report on the preparation and qualifications of public school teachers* (Statistical Analysis Report January 1999). Washington, DC: U.S. Department of Education.

National Center for Education Statistics. (1997). *Schools and staffing survey.* Washington, DC: U.S. Department of Education, Office of Educational Research and Improvement.

Nespor, J. (1987). The role of beliefs in the practice of teaching. *Journal of Curriculum Studies, 19*(4), 317–328.

Nieto, S. (1997). What do teachers need to know? In J. Paul, M. Churton, H. Rosselli-Koston, W. Morse, K. Marfu, C. Lavely, & D. Thomas (Eds.), *Foundations of special education* (pp.187–201). Pacific Grove, CA: Brooks/Cole Publishing Co.

Pajares, M. (1992). Teachers' beliefs and educational research: Cleaning up a messy construct. *Review of Educational Research, 62*(3), 307–332.

Richardson, V. (1996). The role of attitudes and beliefs in learning to teach. In J. Sikula (Ed.). *Handbook of research on teacher education* (2nd edi., pp. 102–119). New York: Macmillan.

Sleeter, C.E. (2001). Preparing teachers for culturally diverse schools: Research and the overwhelming presence of whiteness. *Journal of Teacher Education, 52*(2), 94–106.

Wong-Fillmore, L. (1991). When learning a second language means losing the first. *Early Childhood Research Quarterly, 6,* 323–346.

Wong-Fillmore, L., & Valadez, C. (1986). Teaching bilingual learners. In M.C. Wittrock (Ed.). *Handbook of research on teaching* (3rd ed., pp. 648–683). Upper Saddle River, NJ: Merrill/Prentice-Hall.

Wong-Fillmore, L., & Snow, C.E. (2000). *What teachers need to know about language.* (Paper prepared for the Center for Applied Linguistics). Washington, DC: U.S. Department of Education, Office of Educational Research and Improvement.

Zeichner, K., Melnick, S., & Gomez, M. (Eds.). (1996). *Currents of reform in pre-service teacher education.* New York: Teachers College Press.

Zimpher, N., & Ashburn, E. (1992). Countering parochialism in teacher candidates. In M. Dilworth (Ed.), *Diversity in teacher education: New expectations* (pp. 40–62). San Francisco: Jossey-Bass.

CHAPTER 3

SHELTERED SPANISH INSTRUCTION:

TEACHERS OF ENGLISH LANGUAGE LEARNERS LEARNING IN THEIR STUDENTS' FIRST LANGUAGE

Liliana Minaya-Rowe and Ana María Olezza

ABSTRACT

This chapter examines a graduate teacher training course designed to meet both the Spanish language proficiency needs of mainstream, bilingual and English as a second language (ESL) teachers, and their common professional development needs to implement second language teaching in the standards-based curriculum. The overarching goal of the course is to encourage teachers of English language learners (ELLs) to analyze the constraints and opportunities they perceive in teaching ELLs. Real life experience takes the place of simulation, since teachers experiment first hand the difficulties and challenges faced by their own students when having to attend to new language and content at the same time. For most course participants the language of instruction (Spanish) is their second language (L2) and the biweekly course meetings are conducted almost exclusively in this language guided by the theoretical framework for learning both language and content through the Sheltered Instruction Observation Protocol (SIOP). Course participants benefitted from the course and demonstrated (a) command of the second language to the extent that they could function in relatively fixed linguistic exchanges (e.g., at school, with their students and their students' parents), (b) awareness of the teaching and learning process, and (c) applied the SIOP strategies to promote linguistic and academic success for their students. The chapter discusses the role of a course of this nature as a useful addition in pre-service and in-service efforts and how teacher training institutions can use it to prepare teachers in the context of linguistic and cultural diversity.

INTRODUCTION

Public school enrollments are being transformed by an increase in the number of ELLs who bring the richness of linguistic and cultural diversity with them to school (Garcia, 2000). Education reforms have raised the bar so that all students in the United States must finish school and participate in the economic and social world of the new century. These reforms place tremendous pressure on schools across the nation who are continuously challenged to meet the needs of a widely diverse population (Marcos, 1998).

The U.S. population grew at a rate of 17% from 1980 to 2000. Hispanics are the fastest growing group and represented 11.7% of the U.S. population in 2000 and are projected to double to 24.3% by 2050 (NCBE, 2000). Asia, Latin America, and Africa have replaced Europe as the main source of newcomers (Ovando & Collier, 1998). The educational significance of this demographic shift is that many immigrants are children, or are adults who give birth to children, who enter schools speaking little or no English. An estimated 9.9 million of the total 45 million school-aged children live in households in which languages other than English are spoken (NCES, 1997). Since the numbers of ELLs continue to rise steadily, schools will require instructional programs to prepare them not only to learn English but to compete academically.

This tremendous growth of ELLs in the nation's schools has also added to the need for teacher development. While the school enrollment across the nation grew by 13.6% from 1989 to 2000, ELLs' enrollment increased by 104.3% during the same period (NCBE, 2000). This increase creates a greater gap between teacher training and the skills needed to teach ELLs across the nation (Riley, 2000). Most educators do not receive the preparation to teach this population before entering the workforce and they have limited opportunities to update their knowledge and skills in an ongoing basis throughout their careers (Faltis, 1999; Gottlieb, 1999).

ELLs' opportunities to succeed academically depend on teachers' knowledge and applications of effective pedagogy in the classroom. To date, much of the staff development in schools on language and academic needs of ELLs has been addressed to bilingual and/or ESL teachers (González & Darling-Hammond, 1997; Milk, 1990). Universities have developed undergraduate and graduate programs with curricula and courses to prepare these professionals. In turn, school systems have addressed staff development programs for furthering the continuing education of in-service teachers (Calderón, 2000). However, comparatively little attention has been focused on mainstream teachers who have or will have ELLs in their classrooms (Menken & Antúnez, 2001). This is a cause for concern if we consider that the numbers of ELLs in the regular classroom are increasing, and will continue to increase at a very rapid pace, if demographic projections hold true (Wagonner, 1999).

Current legislation (e.g., Proposition 227 in California, Proposition 203 in Arizona, Connecticut's PA 99-211) have pushed ELLs into mainstream classes at the beginning or at earlier stages of their L2 acquisition development. Even with emphasis on hiring and retaining bilingual teachers, the rank of teachers continues to fill with white, female, middle class, monolingual teachers who have had limited interracial and intercultural experiences (Hamayan, 1990; Melnick & Zeichner, 1997). In general, pre-service teacher preparation programs have not offered sufficient opportunities for learning to teach ELLs. Therefore, much of this learning takes place on the job (Clair, 2000).

A number of professional organizations have set forth teaching standards to improve the student academic achievement (Robles-Rivas, 2001). For example, the National Council of Teachers of Mathematics' Standards describe the foundation of mathematical ideas and applications for all levels of education (Romberg & Wilson, 1995). Similarly, the National Science Education Standards (NSES) outline what students need to know, understand, and be able to do to be scientifically literate at different grade levels (NSES, 1994). By the same token, the standards proposed by the Teachers of English to Speakers of Other Languages (TESOL) pose that ELLs need to become proficient in English to have unrestricted access to grade-appropriate instruction in academically challenging subjects. TESOL advocates L2 development for ELLs across grade levels "promoting English language development as well as reinforcement of subject matter being taught" (Peregoy & Boyle, 2001, p. 24). The need to integrate language and content area standards calls for the design and implementation of common teacher training experiences to serve all ELLs, whether they are in bilingual, ESL, maintream, foreign language or special education classrooms (Lightbown & Spada, 1999; Orr, 2001).

BACKGROUND

The theoretical groundwork for this chapter is based on socioconstructivism, current theories on L2 methodology, the five standards for effective pedagogy, and the Language Across the Curriculum (LAC) movement. L2 pedagogy emphasizes language and content instruction, fostering personally and academically meaningful language development (Collier & Thomas, 2001). The four language modes—listening, speaking, reading and writing—are taught as an integrated whole, lessons are learner-centered and meaningful to the students, and social interaction and collaborative learning are emphasized (Krashen, Candin, & Terrell, 1996). Furthermore, the philosophy of learning movement calls for a reduction in the amount of teacher talk in order to expose students to more opportunities for using language in creative, useful and motivating ways (Schifini, 2000).

SOCIOCONSTRUCTIVISM

Research on learning processes in social contexts, e.g., schooling and professional development, has provided an explanation of how interaction impacts cognition. According to Shotter (1997), the learning process involves self and others in an exchange of ideas to deepen individual understanding. Vygotsky (1986) contends that learning is a sociocultural practice and that language gives and receives meaning from social activity. In other words, thought develops from undergoing changes produced by interactions. Vygotsky's theory assumes that cognitive development arises as a result of social interactions between individuals and that learning is a dynamic social process in which dialogue between the novice and the expert leads to the development of higher cognitive levels. His "zone of proximal development" (ZPD) is defined as the distance between the actual developmental level as determined by individual problem solving and the level of potential development as determined through problem solving in collaboration with more capable peers. It is the level of performance at which a learner is capable of functioning when there is support from interaction with a more capable individual. Interactions in the "zone" are those that use speech, visual representations such as modeling and feedback.

Although the writings of Vygotsky were not directly related to L2 learning, the relationship drawn between learning and cognitive development offers valuable insights into the role of social interaction in language acquisition. Vygotsky (1978) reiterates that "...language and consciousness are both lodged within a matrix of social activity, and that this activity system, rather than the isolated individual, should be the primary focus of study" (p. 21). Krashen's Input Hypothesis is reminiscent of Vygotsky's ZPD (Richard-Amato,

1996). According to Krashen (1985, 1989) comprehensible input is a key factor in acquiring an L2. Acquisition occurs when learners understand language that is slightly beyond their current level of competence through input that is made comprehensible by the context or a simplified linguistic message in a way that is meaningful. Krashen (1989) states that learners "...move from *i* (their current level), to + *1* (the next level along the natural order), by understanding input containing *i* + *1*" (p. 2) as illustrated in Figure 1.

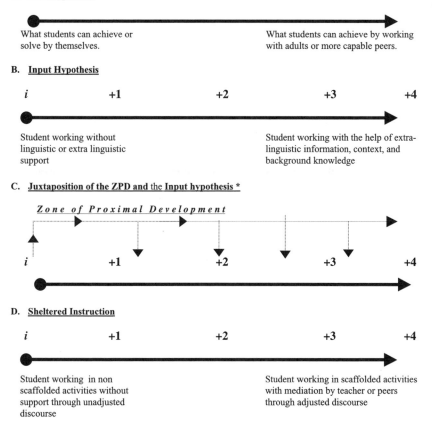

A. **ZPD Hypothesis**

What students can achieve or solve by themselves.

What students can achieve by working with adults or more capable peers.

B. **Input Hypothesis**

i   +1   +2   +3   +4

Student working without linguistic or extra linguistic support

Student working with the help of extra-linguistic information, context, and background knowledge

C. **Juxtaposition of the ZPD and the Input hypothesis ***

Zone of Proximal Development

i   +1   +2   +3   +4

D. **Sheltered Instruction**

i   +1   +2   +3   +4

Student working in non scaffolded activities without support through unadjusted discourse

Student working in scaffolded activities with mediation by teacher or peers through adjusted discourse

Note: * There is a basis for comparison between Vygotsky's ZPD (dotted line) and Krashen's (*i*+1) theories (solid line). Both emphasize the distance between what a child does by himself/herself and what he/she can achieve by working in collaboration with an adult or more capable peer. In addition, sheltered instruction merges both concepts into a representation that describes properties that portray teacher behavior in the planning and delivery of effective lessons for second language learner.

Figure 1.   The input hypothesis and the zone of proximal development.

THEORIES OF L2 ACQUISITION AND METHODOLOGY

Language teaching methodologies have undergone a radical shift from the behaviorist methods of the 1960s to an interactive instructional approach in which the student takes an active (intrinsic) role (Gravelle, 2000). The process of developing L2 proficiency is an essential part of both learning and instruction (Tharp, Estrada, Dalton, & Yamauchi, 2000). L2 learning depends on access to and participation in legitimate social activities in which students use multiple forms and functions of language with the goal of understanding and using new discourse appropriately to accomplish their purposes (Faltis & Hudelson, 1998). Thomas and Collier (1997) pose a model with four major components to explain the process of L2 learning in the classroom: (1) Sociocultural, students learn the L2 in situations that occur in their everyday lives; (2) language development, the subconscious and conscious aspects of language learning; (3) academic development, academic knowledge and conceptual development in all content areas of the curriculum; and, (4) cognitive development, the subconscious natural process that occurs developmentally from birth to schooling and beyond.

The Sheltered Instruction (SI) methodology provides L2 learners with a medium to develop the academic and linguistic demands in their L2 (Shaw, Echevarria, & Short, 1999; Short, 1999). The key components of SI are lesson preparation, comprehensibility, lesson delivery, and interaction (Echevarria, Vogt, & Short, 2000). SI is scaffolded and mediated to provide refuge from the linguistic demands of L2 discourse which is beyond the current level of comprehension of the students. The theoretical underpinning of the model is that L2 acquisition is enhanced through meaningful use and interaction. SI can be described as a melding of elements of L2 principles and elements of quality teaching (Echevarria & Graves, 1998). It is also influenced by sociocultural theory because it occurs within social and cultural contexts. This approach facilitates a high level of student involvement and interaction in the classroom. Teachers present material in patterns related to their students' language and culture as well as that of the school. Through this approach, students learn new material through the lens of their own language and culture (Valdes, 1996).

THE FIVE STANDARDS FOR EFFECTIVE PEDAGOGY

Researchers from the Center for Research in Education, Diversity and Excellence (CREDE) have proposed five standards to provide teachers with tools to enact best teaching practices (Dalton, 1998). They are: (1) Joint productive Activity, when experts and novices work together for a common product or goal; (2) Language Development, fostered best through meaningful use and purposeful conversation between teachers and students; (3) Contextualization, which utilizes students' knowledge and skills as a foundation for new knowledge; (4) Challenging Activity, ELLs are not often challenged academically on the erroneous assumption that they are of limited ability; and (5) Instructional Conversation, promoted through dialogue, by questioning and sharing ideas and knowledge. CREDE's researchers pose that these five standards have the potential to give all students the opportunity to obtain the language and the content necessary to succeed in school (Padron & Waxman, 1999). The standards have been designed to generate activity patterns of collaboration, reflection, and activity involvement of teachers and students during classroom instruction (Tharp et al., 2000). These five principles went through a consensus defining process where researchers, teachers, parents, administrators and policy makers had the opportunity to alter them when necessary. Tharp (1999) suggests that these standards "...are recommendations on which literature is in agreement, across all cultural, racial, and linguistic groups in the United States, at all age levels, and in all subject matters. Even for mainstream students, the standards describe the ideal conditions for instruction; but for students at-risk of educational failure, effective classroom implementation of the standards is vital" (p. 5). Furthermore, Rueda (1998) poses that the five standards can also be applied to professional development. He states that "...the principles that describe effective teaching and learning for students in classrooms should not differ from those of adults in general and teachers in particular" (p. 1).

THE LANGUAGE ACROSS THE CURRICULUM (LAC) MOVEMENT

The LAC movement follows the example set by SI which seeks to use content as the central learning tool in L2 classes. LAC has emerged as a means to improve cross-cultural knowledge and purpose-specific multilingual and intercultural skills of post secondary students. Rather than relegating content instruction to subject matter instruction, LAC works with university and/or college faculty to identify the specific vocabulary and genres students need in order to function effectively in another language in their respective disciplines (Straight, 1998). LAC aims to facilitate the use of languages in a variety of meaningful contexts and to motivate and reward students for using their multilingual skills in every class they take at each level in the university curriculum (Stryker & Leaver, 1997). In short, students who learn languages for a purpose, learn it better (Fichera & Straight, 1997).

METHODS

Participants. The participants for this study were a group of fifteen master's degree students who worked as teachers (bilingual, ESL, or mainstream) of Hispanic students at all levels of instruction in various school districts throughout the state. They were enrolled in the University of Connecticut's Program of Specialization in Bilingual Bicultural Education with the objective of enhancing teaching skills and completing degree and bilingual and/or ESL certification requirements. More specific program objectives included: (1) Increasing the number of qualified teachers of ELLs in the state; (2) Improving teachers' first and L2 proficiency and competence; and, (3) Broadening career opportunities for teachers of ELLs. Their training program included course work in literacy and biliteracy, assessment of bilingualism, bilingual program evaluation, ESL teaching methods and curriculum design, legal aspects and foundations of bilingual and bicultural education, linguistics, anthropology and other courses meant to develop expertise in bilingual and bicultural education. As a result of their training, teachers received a Master of Arts Degree in Education with Emphasis on Bilingual Bicultural Education. In addition, they received the Bilingual/ESL certification endorsement from the state's Department of Education.

A Spanish Sheltered Instruction Course. The three-credit graduate course is listed in the University of Connecticut Graduate School Catalog as "EDCI 313 Bilingual Education and Biliteracy" and is part of the Department of Curriculum and Instruction (EDCI) regular offerings. EDCI 313 was offered in the summer of 2000 for $4\frac{1}{2}$ hours twice a week during the 6-week summer session. Out of the fifteen students registered, eight were ESL teachers, two were bilingual teachers and five were mainstream teachers. Their level of Spanish language proficiency was assessed using informal measures and ranged from advanced beginner (2), to intermediate (7), to advanced (6). Consequently, EDCI 313 was designed to meet the participants' varied language proficiency needs in addition to the SI pedagogy needed of teachers who would be implementing literacy and content for ELLs.

The language objectives differed for course participants. For bilingual students (native speakers of Spanish, most raised in Puerto Rico or the US and schooled in English), the language objective was to improve facets of their Spanish proficiency, e.g., academic writing, and to increase vocabulary range in standards-based content areas. For ESL and mainstream teachers (nonnative speakers of Spanish with some high school or college Spanish training), the language objective was to increase their command of the L2 to the extent that they could function in relatively fixed linguistic exchanges (e.g., at school, with their students, and their students' parents).

The pedagogical objectives related to SI and to the notion of reflection. Participants examined the myriad of factors that shape what they do in their classrooms in order to become effective practitioners. They were encouraged to analyze the constraints and opportunities they perceive in teaching ELLs. What perhaps was uncommon in this approach was the means utilized to foster reflection and sensitization concerning the dynamic SI classroom context that they needed to create. Real life experience took the place of simulation, since participants experimented first hand the difficulties and challenges faced by ELLs when having to attend to new language and content at the same time. For most course participants the language of instruction (Spanish) was their L2 and the biweekly course meetings were conducted almost exclusively in this language using the SI approach. Figure 2 presents a descriptive summary of the course, the language, cultural and academic goals, participants background and requirements.

The Sheltered Instruction Observation Protocol (SIOP) proposed by Echevarria, Vogt, and Short (2000) provided a framework for EDCI 313, its content selection and lesson preparation. The SIOP is based on the premise that L2 acquisition is enhanced through meaningful use and interaction. Through the study of content, students interacted in Spanish with meaningful material that was relevant to their training. Since language processes, such as listening, speaking, reading, and writing, develop independently, SI Spanish lessons incorporated activities that integrated those skills. These lessons mirrored high quality non-sheltered teaching for native Spanish speakers and careful attention was paid to the students distinctive L2 development needs.

Essential in this process was the articulation of different levels of Spanish used with and by the participants and the provision of comprehensible input through the use of realia and meaningful activities such as visual aids, modeling, demonstrations, graphic organizers, vocabulary previews, predictions, adapted texts, joint productive activities, peer tutoring, instructional conversations and first language support. The goal was to create a nonthreatening environment where participants felt comfortable taking risks with language. However, lesson activities were linguistically and academically challenging. Our objective was to make specific connections between the content being taught and students' experiences or prior knowledge while expanding their language base. Through joint productive activity, we attempted to promote a high level of student engagement and interaction with the teacher, with one another and with text in order to promote elaborate discourse. Students were also explicitly taught functional language skills such as how to negotiate meaning, ask for clarification, confirm information, argue, persuade, and disagree. When requested, exercises on grammar points (e.g., identification and discussion

Goals	Activities
1. Language Goals	• Academic Vocabulary • Noun Phrase • Reading "Leyendas" • Merienda
2. Cultural Goals	• Music, Dancing, Folklore • Poetry • Cooking • Integrative, understandings, values and beliefs (Puerto Rican, Anglo, African American, Others)
3. Academic Goals	• Bilingual Education and Biliteracy. Same as official syllabus
4. Student Characteristics	• Mixed (limited, intermediate and advanced speakers of Spanish)
5. College Level	• Graduate, undergraduate students & teachers
6. Entry Level	• Some knowledge of Spanish
7. Length of Student Participation	• Summer course; follow-up during the fall
8. Participation of Mainstream, Bilingual and ESL Teachers	• Mainstream teachers with special training
9. Teacher Qualifications	• Certified ESL • Bilingual certification • Multicultural training • Mainstream working with large numbers of ELLS
10. Instructional Materials, Texts, Visual Aids, Handouts	• Spanish with adaptations as needed visuals, realia, culturally appropriate readings, tapes

Source: Adapted from Genesee (1999).

Figure 2.   Descriptive summary of sheltered Spanish instruction.

of noun phrases in Spanish in a poem) were practiced. Through instructional conversations and meaningful activities, students practiced and applied their knowledge of Spanish as well as their content knowledge. Diverse supplementary materials were used to support the academic texts. These included an interactive audiotape home assignment with selected readings and related questions prepared by the instructors, models and other realia.

The SIOP Lesson Planning Guide's thirty items grouped into three main sections—Preparation, Instruction, and Review/Assessment—were used to enhance our instructional practices. We used the Preparation items to determine the language and content objectives, the use of supplementary materials, and the relevance of the activities in our lessons. We used the Instruction items to build background, provide comprehensible input, encourage interaction, use strategies, and deliver the SI lesson. We used the Review/Assessment section to review the key vocabulary and content concepts, assess student learning, and provide feedback to students on their output. The course also stressed interactive small-group learning activities or learning centers and attended to the participants' diverse language proficiency levels. We encouraged heterogeneous groupings based on differences in Spanish proficiency (i.e., deliberate mixing of high proficiency with low proficiency students within learning groups) to maximize learning possibilities. Students with lower levels of Spanish would benefit from the input provided by more proficient classmates, and students with higher proficiency levels would benefit from the need to explain cognitively demanding tasks in Spanish to their "limited Spanish proficient" classmates.

Two textbooks were chosen for use in the course: *La enseñanza de la lectura y la escritura en español en el aula bilingüe (The teaching of reading and writing in Spanish in the bilingual classroom.* Freeman & Freeman, 1998) and *Leyendas de Puerto Rico (Puerto Rican Legends.* Muckley & Martínez-Santiago, 1999). At the beginning of each lesson, students engaged in sharing sessions (*Compartiendo con los amigos*). This was followed by a review of key vocabulary of a specific portion or reading (e.g., *Repaso del vocabulario de "Compadre Conejillo"*). Students often acted out a legend from Puerto Rico (e.g., *Representación de la leyenda por los estudiantes de la clase*), or rewrote different sections using SI strategies and formats. A presentation and demonstration of a language or literacy methodology or strategy followed (e.g., *Dos enfoques para la enseñanza de la lectura*). The class developed a study guide (Guía de estudio) with specific steps to follow when working with a chapter or reading passage. This activity was often followed by a cooperative learning group activity, a jigsaw. The students were also in charge of the morning break (*Merienda*) at midpoint of the lesson. Those who had signed up to lead the activity on a given day prepared a snack or dish in front of the group. They would provide their classmates with specific explanations (as they modeled the preparation of the dish) and the printed recipe in Spanish (e.g., how to prepare *Fondú de chocolate con frutas*). Finally, everybody enjoyed the delicacies prepared in a relaxed social moment. After the break, the formal SI lesson would continue with a grammar exercise (e.g., *Continuación de la frase nominal*). This would be followed by group or subgroup comments on the reading assignment (*Comentarios sobre la lec-*

tura del apéndice. Los taínos). The final portion of the lesson included music, culture and poetry (e.g., the song *Agüeybana* sung by the entire group, the game *Veo, veo*, dancing *la salsa*, and so forth). The reflection (*Reflexión*) focused on oral and written comments on the day's activities and the assignment would include specific directions to follow (e.g., *Continuar diario de las palabras*).

INSTRUMENTS

In this study, the goal was to better understand the teaching-learning process of the L2, Spanish, through "rich descriptions" and multiple data sources (Bernard, 2000). We investigated how teachers moved from surface engagement with theory to an engagement that promoted reflective commitment to become more effecttive teachers of ELLs. The constructs of instructional and social interaction were examined as cultural phenomena reflecting the interactive process of the construction of meaning and the language of the learning process. Ethnographic techniques such as journals, questionnaires, and surveys were used; specifically, a written survey of teachers' self perception regarding the features of SI implemented in the course, an interactive journal used to guide teachers' reflections and the course content, an end of course evaluation, and a survey administered a year later. The rationale for the selection of techniques was based on the need to capture the insider's or "emic" point of view (Lincoln & Guba, 2000). The researchers' intent was to explain behavior on the basis of the participants' ideational and cognitive categories (Miles & Huberman, 1994). It is possible to identify and describe the set of understandings and specific knowledge in the participants' heads that are shared among them and that guide their behavior in the specific context under consideration (Glanz, 1998). Participants set the language and content goals for themselves (Denzin & Lincoln, 2000).

Language Proficiency Background Data.   A survey of 14 questions completed at the beginning of the course investigated the participants' previous efforts at learning Spanish and their level of confidence in their knowledge of their students' cultural background. The results are presented in Table 1.

Most of the participants studied Spanish at school or in college for 1–6 years with a native Spanish speaker. Reading was the easiest language skill followed closely by understanding. The most commonly used method by their Spanish instructor was identified as grammar based. Most expressed that they felt comfortable speaking Spanish to students and their parents and that learning Spanish was a positive experience overall. Most were satisfied with the results obtained although they were not confident when they had to speak or write in Spanish. Some were open to learn the culture of their ELLs and others stated they understood their students' cultural, social and linguistic "funds of knowledge."

Table 1. Language Proficiency Background Data

1. *Where did you learn Spanish?*	
Elementary/High School	9
College	6
Home	2
Puerto Rico	1
Television	1
Reading	2
Tapes	2
2. *How long did you study Spanish?*	
1 semester	1
1 to 5 years	6
More than 5 years	2
3. *Where did you study Spanish?*	
Wethersfield High School	1
St. Joseph's College	1
University of Puerto Rico	1
Public School and College	2
Central Connecticut State University	1
Home	1
Catholic University of Puerto Rico	1
University of Hartford	1
New London High School	1
Ecuador	1
4. *Did you study Spanish with a Spanish native speaker?*	
Yes	8
No	3
Not until college	1
A little bit	1

Table 1.   Language Proficiency Background Data (Cont.)

5.	*Which do you find easier: speaking, reading, writing or understanding something that is said?*	
	Speaking + writing	1
	Reading	6
	All of them	2
	Writing	2
	Reading + listening	1
	Understanding	3
	Speaking	1
6.	*What method or approach did your teacher use? (e.g. whole language, translation, grammar based)*	
	Grammar based	9
	Whole language	4
	Translation	1
	Dictation	1
	Conversation	1
7.	*Are you comfortable speaking Spanish to your students and their parents? Why? Why not?*	
	Yes	7
	No	3
	Somewhat comfortable	1
	Nervous (in front of people other than students)	1
8.	*Was learning Spanish a positive or a negative experience?*	
	Positive	7
	Negative	3
	Fearful	1
	Stressful	1
9.	*Which aspects of your learning experience did you find most useful or beneficial?*	

- Living with a Spanish family
- Traveling to Spain
- Making friends
- Retaining vocabulary and grammar structures
- Conversation, songs
- Practice in talking
- Using Spanish with children
- Speaking to native speakers
- Learning from students

Table 1.   Language Proficiency Background Data (Cont.)

10.	*Which activities or strategies were the least helpful?*	
	• Repeating lists of words	
	• Correcting pronunciation of isolated words	
	• Grammar translation	
	• Memorizing and conjugating verbs	
	• Tapes	

11.	*Are you satisfied with the results you obtained?*	
	Yes	6
	No	4
	Somewhat	2

12.	*How confident are you when you have to speak or write in Spanish?*	
	Very confident (in class)	4
	Not confident	6
	A little confident	1
	Depending on the audience	1

13.	*How familiar are you with the culture of your Hispanic students?*	
	• Pretty open to learn	
	• Fairly familiar	
	• Very familiar (Puerto Rican)	
	• Not familiar	
	• Somewhat familiar	

14.	*Do you feel you understand their cultural background and their social and linguistic "funds of knowledge"?*	
	To a certain extent	1
	Yes	6
	Not very well	1
	Getting their background	3
	Somewhat	1

Questionnaire.   At the end of the course, participants were asked to voluntary and anonymously complete a 10-item questionnaire and rate their agreement on a five-point Likert scale (5 = strongly agree to strongly disagree = 0) with statements related to three specific areas: (a) learning a L2, (b) motivation, and (c) course activities. Summary results from the Questionnaire are presented in Table 2. Interpretation is simple: Students were pleased with the course and the nature of their instruction in the course. In their view, instruction in this course met their needs in the following areas (1) L2 methodology, (2) students' culture, and (3) classroom activities. These results coincide closely with SI course goals, which focused on Spanish language communication related to ELLs.

Table 2.   End of Course Questionnaire (n=14)

	Strongly Agree	Agree	Undecided	Disagree	Strongly Disagree	Totals
1	11	3				14
2	9	5				14
3	13	1				14
4	11	3				14
5	7	4	2	1		14
6	11	2	1			14
7	8	4	2			14
8	13	1				14
9	8	3	3			14
10	14					14
Total Response	105	26	8	1	0	140

1. This course will have a positive influence on my teaching.

2. The methodology used facilitated Spanish language acquisition.

3. I can incorporate the methodology utilized to my teaching practice.

4. This course was highly motivating.

5. This course increased my confidence to speak Spanish.

6. This course deepened my understanding of my students' culture.

7. The course strategies and classroom activities contributed to lowering my affective filter.

8. The course strategies and classroom activities made the lesson clear and meaningful.

9. I feel more confident to interact/communicate with the parents at my school.

10. I would re commend this course to other colleagues.

Another interpretation of these data results is presented in Chart 1. Almost three-fourths (105 responses) of the respondents strongly agreed with the 10 items related to a specific area of the course syllabus. A total of 93% either strongly agreed or agreed with the items. The results obtained for all items in the *Questionnaire* seem to suggest that the course may have led to important theoretical and practical insights related to effective pedagogy.

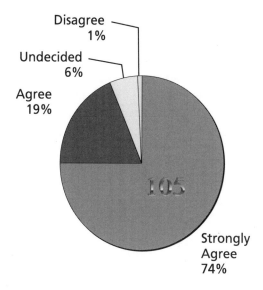

Disagree
1%

Undecided
6%

Agree
19%

Strongly
Agree
74%

Chart 1.   End of course questionnaire.

The University of Connecticut Survey of Courses and Teaching contains 11 general rating items. They are: (1) Presented course material in a clear and effective manner, (2) Overall organization, (3) Made the objectives of the course clear, (4) Fulfilled course objectives, (5) Clarified work assignments and student responsibilities, (6) Stimulated interest, (7) Graded fairly and impartially, (8) Used exam items that stressed important aspects of the course, (9) Accessibility to students both in and out of class, (10) Instructor's interest and concern for students, and (11) Preparation for each class. A 10-point response scale is used, ranging from 1 (UNACCEPTABLE) to 10 (OUTSTANDING) for students' ratings of their courses and instructors. There is ample evidence about the reliability of such ratings. However, researchers have argued about the uses and validity of student ratings of instruction. For the goals of this course evaluation, it is safest to regard student ratings as indicators of their *satisfaction* with *instruction,* and not as measures of teacher effectiveness. Since these 15 students were the immediate consumers of instructor services, they have the rights of consumers to evaluate those services. The results should thus be interpreted as consumers' perceptions about the worth of such services. Since all 15 students rated their instructors anonymously with a 10 (outstanding), we felt we did not need a table to tally their course ratings. Students were clearly satisfied with the nature of their course instruction. In their view, instruction in this course could not get appreciably better.

The *Survey* also allows students to comment on positive aspects of the course, and to make recommendations for course improvement. These comments are returned to instructors after the end of the semester. The student remarks for question 1 (What was the most positive aspect of the way in which this instructor taught this course?) shows concordance with their numerical ratings. Responses included: Teaching styles and methodologies; students involved in class activities and projects; interaction; application of the theory; good organization, preparation, and motivation; use of examples; approach with clear objectives, varied information; and, multiple opportunities for feedback. Although responses to question 2 (What can this instructor do to improve teaching effectiveness in the classroom?) do give occasional suggestions for change, most students had no recommendation whatsoever, which would be expected given the very high numerical ratings. Suggestions included: Breaking into level groups; and, focus on grammar.

Additional information on the impact of the Spanish SI experience on course participants was obtained from the *Survey* in the evaluation entitled *Comment Page for the Instructor Only*. The responses are so rich as to merit separate treatment elsewhere, but a few insights make possible a fuller understanding of the data presented. Students wrote about specific aspects of the course and/or portions of it. They expressed their satisfaction as presented in the following verbatim (uncorrected) statements.

First, participants valued the SI methodology and classroom activities employed.

> *The professors made a 4-1/2 hour class exciting. They put so much of themselves into each day's lesson. Our group really looked forward to what the professors had in store for us each day. They are really fabulous teachers and special women.*

> *This type of course should be offered to all educators. This is the way to learn a second language.*

> *This has been one of the best and most effective courses that I have taken in while at Storrs. The course was very successful at showing us how to make content comprehensible.*

Second, the participants' feelings surrounding the Spanish SI experience in their desire to continue having exposure to the L2 in other courses of their graduate program.

> *The professors were very enthusiastic and obviously enjoyed what they were doing. They made me feel very comfortable in a class where the language was*

unknown to me. I have come away with a great understanding of the Spanish language.

This was the BEST Spanish course I ever took. (I took 5 classes prior!). The methods used were excellent. The instructors made me very comfortable.

Very interactive. The instructors modeled best practices. The class was excellent. I was able to improve on my Spanish and learn theory and the application of the theory.

Third, the expansions in the participants' thinking and conceptualization of their training program, relations with peers and instructors, minority-majority relations and cultural identity.

All instructors were extremely positive. Much time and effort was put into the development of this class. Personal relationships were developed between instructors and students—this created outstanding products.

It has been a pleasant experience. My thought about graduate school @ UCONN improved greatly. I will travel the distance for these classes any time. These professors really care.

Continúen haciendo su labor como lo han hecho hasta ahora. Entre compañeros americanos e hispanos se han hecho comentarios muy positivos de ustedes. ¡Ustedes son un orgullo hispano! ¡Felicitaciones! (Continue doing your job as you have done up to now. Among American and Hispanic classmates, very positive comments have been made about you. You are a Hispanic pride! Congratulations!)

The Teaching Through a Sheltered Instruction Approach Survey was administered a year after participants took EDCI 313. The survey consists of 15 statements to investigate whether participants have incorporated elements of the SIOP when teaching ELLs in their lesson preparation, instruction and review. A summary of the responses is presented in Table 3.

All the participants strongly agreed or agreed that the SI Spanish course they took a year ago was very useful in the planning and delivery of their daily lessons to meet their ELLs' needs during the school year. They have incorporated the SIOP to integrate concept and language opportunities. They still consider comprehensible input as an important lesson component and adjust their speech to their ELLs' proficiency levels. They also use scaffolding techniques, group work to support the language and content objectives of their SI lessons, and provide a review of key concepts throughout the lesson. Furthermore, the participants also wrote additional comments with regards to specific aspects of EDCI 313, the instructors, the SIOP or portions of it. They wrote their continued satisfaction with the course they took a year ago as presented in the following statements.

Table 3.   Teaching through a Sheltered Instruction Approach Survey (n = 11)

I am :	Bilingual Teacher	ESL Teacher	Mainstream Teacher	Other	Totals	
	2	2	4	3	11	
	Strongly Agree	Agree	Undecided	Disagree	Strongly Disagree	Totals
1	7	4				11
2	6	2	3			11
3		2		3	6	11
4	8	3				11
5	11					11
6	1				10	11
7	11					11
8	8	3				11
9	7	3	1			11
10				2	9	11
11	10	1				11
12	8	3				11
13			3	5	3	11
14	9	2				11
15			3	1	6	10 (NA = 1)
Total Response	86	23	10	11	34	164

1. The Sheltered Spanish course I took in the summer of 2000 has proved to be very useful in the planning and delivery of my lessons.

2. Since receiving training I have incorporated the SIOP in the planning and delivery of my lessons.

3. I do not incorporate content and language objectives in all my lessons for English language learners (ELLs).

4. My SI lesson activities integrate concepts with language practice opportunities.

5. ELLs learn concepts when these are linked to their own experiences.

6. I do not present and reinforce (e.g. write, repeat, highlight) key vocabulary in my SI class.

7. Comprehensible input is an important component of the SI classroom.

8. I adjust my speech to my ELLs' proficiency level so that they understand me.

**Table 3.   Teaching through a Sheltered Instruction Approach Survey
(n = 11) (Cont.)**

9. I use scaffolding techniques throughout my SI lessons.

10. In my SI classroom ELLs have very few opportunities to interact with me and with their peers.

11. Group work supports language and content objectives in the SI lessons I teach.

12. I use hands-on materials and activities for ELLs to apply content and language knowledge.

13. I have used only some elements of the SIOP in my lesson planning and delivery.

14. I regularly provide a review of key concepts throughout the lesson.

15. I have used the SIOP for professional development in my district.

16. Additional comments.

Many of the strategies that were modeled in the SI class were used in my classroom. In fact, many other teachers in the school have been using strategies and techniques that I was exposed to during that class. The use of task cards, having students rewrite endings, and the variety of presenting work are just some of the things that are evident in my classroom after taking the course.

I have implemented many of the strategies I learned throughout the year. My next challenge will be to incorporate all I have learned into my own 4th grade classroom ... next year I will have my own mainstream classroom with all levels of ELLs in with mainstream! I am very excited about this new opportunity, but I will never forget the joys of being an ESL teacher. My new role will still allow me to use all the ESL strategies, just with a more varied group of students ... Thank you again for enabling me to become a more sensitive, creative, and child-centered teacher...

RESULTS

In this Spanish SI course, participants used their L2 to talk and write about their own experiences and notions about L2 learning and to voice their changing perspectives. The experience of having to deal with academic demands in the L2 can provide valuable insights into the world as viewed by ELLs. Through carefully planned experiences in which intellectual activity was coupled with interactive participation, the course instructors practiced a pedagogical approach that might help design more effective teacher education programs and facilitate the development of in-service and pre-service teachers of ELLs. Traditionally, SI has been part of an ESL program, a bilingual program, a dual language program, a newcomer's program, or a foreign language program. Our goal was to extend its role to the implementation of a graduate level university course with the purpose of developing a strong foundation in SI and a common knowledge base related to the understanding of language and to sociocultural issues underlying effective instructional practices for all teachers of ELLs (Tharp, 1997).

The SIOP proved to be a highly useful professional tool to aid in the planning of training units for teacher preparation sessions. Participants appeared to have benefitted from this course since their L2 achievement improved. Instructors also evaluated teacher change of attitude toward L2 teaching. Participants spoke highly of the benefits of classroom collaboration and interaction in increasing their ability to speak Spanish, and sensitizing them to their students' learning process. They found the lessons interesting and comprehensible. They enjoyed the class because they felt relaxed and confident. They reiterated that their vocabulary was increasing. Sometimes they felt nervous when they had to speak to the whole class and always were comfortable when they worked in groups. They stressed that they were going to use the techniques and routines introduced during the course in their own classrooms. The statement *Las horas de clase pasan rápido* (The class hours go by very fast) was often made. A year after they took EDCI 313, participants strongly agreed or agreed that the course was very useful in the planning and delivery of their daily lessons to meet their ELLs' needs. They incorporated the SIOP as an important lesson component to integrate concept and language opportunities to teach their ELLs.

Overall, this study provided strong support for a number of key characteristics which professional development initiatives need to adopt in order to respond effectively to the needs of teachers of ELLs. Effective teaching requires an understanding of both social and school factors that influence L2 acquisition and academic learning (Freeman & Freeman, 2001; Tharp & Gallimore, 1988). We have proposed an approach to staff development that is both interactive and exploratory (Milk, 1990; Scribner, 1999). Although the number of course participants was too small to make generalizations, the possibilities exhibited by this course appear to be promising. This course became a bridge between the theoretical content and the practical reality of the L2 classroom. We do not claim that this course is the answer to the problems posed by teacher education in these challenging times, but our experience leads us to believe that a course of this nature has a valuable role to play in pre-service and in-service efforts.

DISCUSSION

Professional development for teachers is complex and multifaceted (Short & Echevarria, 1999). Teachers currently joining the workforce face the challenge of teaching students who are ELLs (Calderon, 1999). When they enter teacher education programs, teaching students tend to see diversity as a problem to be overcome rather than as an asset in promoting discourse and learning (Zeichner, 1993). Furthermore, when teachers are not familiar with their students' culture they may have negative expectations or misinterpret their interaction patterns (Darling-Hammond & Sykes, 1999; Ladson-Billings, 1999). To equip all teachers to work successfully with a growing ELL student population requires continuing renewal and extension of the skills, knowledge, and awareness needed to remain effective in a culturally dynamic environment (Joyce & Showers, 1995). New and experienced teachers are likely to have had little or no formal instruction on L2 acquisition and L2 teaching methodology and need to integrate these perspectives into the content and structure of their lessons to ensure their successful teaching of ELLs (Cummins & Fillmore, 2000).

An important group of professionals who are responsible for the success of ELLs, as well as that of language majority groups in school, is the growing numbers of English monolingual teachers who are or will be part of dual language or enriched education programs. These educators need to become familiar with the principles of additive bilingualism, SI, and language–rich environments (Cloud et al., 2000). A working knowledge of the minority language can also prove to be an invaluable asset in these settings (Fillmore, 2001). Since ELLs' production in the L2 may lag behind their comprehension in the initial stages of language acquisition, they may occasionally fall back into their L1 for communicative purposes (Echevarria & Graves, 1998). If teachers have some information about their students' L1 and the role it plays in L2 learning, they may be able to use it as an opportunity to a more successful schooling (Faltis, 1999).

The current structure of university courses and of district-led professional development provide relatively few teachers or teachers-to-be with the opportunity to reflect and analyze the needs of students going through the L2 acquisition process to the degree that has been accomplished in this course (Milk, 1990; Rueda, 1998). There is rarely any occasion when teachers come together and collaborate on the teaching and learning process, certainly none that we know of that use the participants' L2 as the language of instruction in a sustained way (Clair & Adger, 1999). The teachers who participated in this course created learning communities in which they could explore their beliefs about their students and increased their repertoire of culturally relevant pedagogy (Calderón, 2000). These results can contribute to a better understanding of professional development needs of teachers of ELLs as they take on the task of preparing for the diversity they are sure to encounter in their classrooms (Crowther, 1998).

ACKNOWLEDGMENT

A previous version of this chapter was presented at the annual meeting of the American Educational Research Association, April 2001, Seattle, WA.

REFERENCES

Bernard, H.R. (2000). *Social research methods: Qualitative and quantitative approaches.* Lanhan, MD: Rowman & Littlefield Publication Group.

Calderón, M. (2000). Curricula and methodologies used to teach Spanish-speaking limited English proficient students to read English. In R.E. Slavin & M. Calderón (Eds.), *Effective programs for Latino students* (pp. 251–305). Mahwah, NJ: Lawrence Erlbaum Associates, Inc.

Calderón, M. (1999, March). *Success for Latino students and their teachers.* Keynote speech delivered at the annual meeting of the Teachers of English to Speakers of Other Languages, New York.

Clair, N. (2000). *Teaching educators about language: Principles, structures, and challenges.* [On-line]. Available: http://www.cal.org/ericcll/digest/0008teaching.html

Clair, N., & Adger, C.T. (1999). *Professional development for teachers in culturally diverse schools.* (ERIC Digest). [On line]. Available: http://www.cal.org/ericcll/

Cloud, N., Genesee, F., & Hamayan, E. (2000). *Dual language instruction: A handbook for enriched education.* Boston: Heinle & Heinle.

Collier, V.P. (1998). Language. In C.J. Ovando & V.P. Collier (Eds.), *Bilingual and ESL classrooms: Teaching in multicultural contexts* (2nd ed., pp. 86–134). New York: McGraw Hill.

Collier, V., & Thomas, W. (2001, February). *Reforming schools for English language learners: Achievement gap closure.* Feature speech delivered at the annual meeting of the National Association for Bilingual Education, Phoenix, AZ.

Crowther, S. (1998). Secrets of staff development support. *Educational Leadership, 55*(5), 75–76.

Cummins, J. (1996). *Negotiating identities: Education for empowerment in a diverse society.* Ontario: California Association for Bilingual Education.

Cummins, J., & Fillmore, L.W. (2000). *Language and education: What every teacher (and administrator) needs to know.* (Casette Recording No. NABE00-FS10A). Dallas, TX: CopyCats.

Dalton, S.S. (1998). *Pedagogy matters: Standards for effective teaching practice.* Santa Cruz, CA: Center for Research on Education, Diversity and Excellence.

Darling-Hammond, L. (1999). *Solving the dilemmas of teacher supply, demand and standards: How we can ensure a competent, caring, and qualified teacher for every child.* [On line]. Available: http://www.tc.columbia.edu/~teachcomm/CONFERENCE-99/SOLVING/

Darling-Hammond, L., & Sykes, G. (Eds.). (1999). *Teaching as the learning profession: Handbook of policy and practice.* San Francisco: Jossey-Bass.

Denzin, N.K., & Lincoln, Y.S. (Eds.). (2000). *Handbook of qualitative research* (2nd ed.). Thousand Oaks, CA: Sage.

Echevarria, J., & Graves, M. (1998). *Sheltered content instruction: Teaching English language learners with diverse abilities.* Needham Heights, MA: Allyn & Bacon.

Echevarria, J., & Short D. J. (2001, April) *The Sheltered Instruction Observation Protocol (SIOP) and the achievement of English language learners.* Paper presented at the annual meeting of the American Educational Research Association, Seattle, WA.

Echevarria, J., Vogt, M.E., & Short, D.J. (2000). *Making content comprehensible for English language learners: The SIOP model.* Needham Heights, MA: Allyn & Bacon.

Faltis, C.J. (1999). Creating a new history. In C.J. Faltis & P. Wolfe (Eds.), *So much to say: Adolescents, bilingualism & ESL in the secondary school* (pp. 1–9). New York: Teachers College Press.

Faltis, C.J., & Hudelson, S.J. (1998). *Bilingual education in elementary and secondary school communities.* Needham Heights, MA: Allyn & Bacon.

Fichera, V.M., & Straight, H.S. (Eds.). (1997). *Using languages across the curriculum: Diverse disciplinary perspectives.* Binghamton: State University of New York.

Fillmore, L.W. (1982). Language minority students and school participation: What kind of English is needed. *Journal of Education, 164,* 143–156.

Freeman, Y.S., & Freeman, D.E. (1998). *La enseñanza de la lectura y la escritura en español en el aula bilingüe.* Portsmouth, NH: Heinemann.

Garcia, E. (1999). *Student cultural diversity: Understanding and meeting the challenge* (2nd ed.). Boston: Houghton Mifflin.

Genesee, F. (1999). *Program alternatives for linguistically diverse students.* Santa Cruz, CA: Center for Research in Education, Diversity, & Excellence.

Genesee, F. (1994). *Integrating language and content: Lessons from immersion.* Santa Cruz, CA: National Center for Research on National Diversity and Second Language Learning.

Glanz, J. (1998). *Action research: An educational leader's guide to school improvement.* Norwood, MA: Christopher-Gordon Publishers.

Gonzalez, J.M., & Darling-Hammond, L. (1997). *New concepts for new challenges: Professional development for teachers of immigrant youth.* McHenry, IL: Delta Systems Co.

Gottlieb, M. (1999). Assessing ESOL adolescents: Balancing accessibility to learn with accountability for learning. In C.J. Faltis & P. Wolfe (Eds.), *So much to say: Adolescents, bilingualism & ESL in the secondary school* (pp. 176–201). New York: Teachers College Press.

Gravelle, M. (2000). *Planning for bilingual learners. An inclusive curriculum.* Arlington, VA: Stylus Publishing.

Guba, E., & Lincoln, Y.S. (2000). Paradigmatic controversies, contradictions and emerging confluences. In N.K. Denzin & Y.S. Lincoln (Eds.), *Handbook of qualitative research* (2nd ed., pp. 163–188). Thousand Oaks, CA: Sage.

Hakuta, K. (2001, April). *The education of language minority students.* Testimony to the U.S. Commission of Civil Rights. [On line]. Available: http://www.stanford.edu/~hakuta/Docs/CivilRightsCommission.htm

Hamayan, E.V. (1990). Preparing mainstream classroom teachers to teach potentially English proficient students. In Office of Bilingual Education and Minority Languages Affairs (Ed.), *Proceedings of the first research symposium of limited English proficient students' issues* (pp. 1–22). Washington, DC: U.S. Department of Education.

Hawley, W.D., & Valli, L. (1999). The essentials of professional development: A new consensus. In L. Darling-Hammond & G. Sykes (Eds.), *Teaching as the learning profession: Handbook of policy and practice* (pp. 127–150). San Francisco: Jossey-Bass.

Irujo, S. (Ed.). (2000). *Integrating the ESL standards into classroom practice: Grades 6–8.* Alexandria, VA: TESOL.

Joyce, B., & Showers, B. (1995). *Student achievement through staff development* (2nd ed.). White Plains, NY: Longman.

Kendall, J., & Marzano, R. (1996). *Content knowledge: A compendium of standards and benchmarks for K-12 education.* Aurora, CO: Mid-Continent Regional Education Laboratory.

Krashen, S.D. (2000). What does it take to acquire language? *ESL Magazine 3*(3), 22–23.

Krashen, S.D. (1989). We acquire vocabulary and spelling by reading: Additional evidence for the Input Hypothesis. *Modern Language Journal 73,* 440–464.

Krashen, S.D. (1985). *The Input Hypothesis: Issues and implications.* New York: Longman.

Krashen, S.D. (1981). *Second language acquisition and second language learning.* New York: Prentice Hall.

Krashen, S.D. (1982). *Principles and practices in second language acquisition.* Oxford: Pergamon Press.

Krashen, S.D., Candin, C.N., & Terrell, T.D. (1996). *The natural approach: Language acquisition in the classroom.* New York: Simon & Schuster International Group.

Ladson-Billings, G. (1999). Preparing teachers for diverse student populations: A critical race theory perspective. In A. Iran-Nejad & D.P. Pearson (Eds.), *Review of Research in Education 24,* 211–247. Washington, DC: American Educational Research Association.

Laturnau, J. (2001). *Standards-based instruction for English language learners.* Honolulu: Pacific Resources for Education and Learning.

Lightbown, P.M., & Spada, N. (1999). *How languages are learned* (rev. ed.). New York: Oxford University Press.

Marcos, K. (1998). *The benefits of early language learning.* ERIC Clearinghouse on Language and Linguistics. Resource Guides. [On-line]. Available: http://www.cal.org/ericell/fafs/rgos/benes.html

Menken, K., & Antúnez, B. (2001). *An overview of the preparation and certification of teachers working with low English proficiency students.* Washington, DC: National Clearinghouse for Bilingual Education.

Miles, M.B., & Huberman, A.M. (1994). *An expanded sourcebook: Qualitative data analysis.* Thousand Oaks, CA: Sage.

Milk, R.D. (1990). Preparing ESL and bilingual teachers for changing roles: Immersion for teachers of LEP children. *TESOL Quarterly 24*(3), 407–426.

Muckley, R.L., & Martínez-Santiago, A. (1999). *Legends from Puerto Rico. Leyendas de Puerto Rico.* Lincolnwood, IL: National Textbook Company.

National Council of Teachers of Mathematics. (1991). *Professional standards for school mathematics.* Reston, VA: Author.

National Center for Education Statistics. (1997). *1993–94 Schools and staffing survey: A profile of policies and practices for limited English proficient students. Screening meth-*

ods, program support, and teacher training. Washington, DC: US Department of Education, Office of Educational Research and Improvement.

National Clearinghouse for Bilingual Education. (1999). *The growing numbers of limited English proficient students.* Washington, DC: Author.

National Committee on Science Education Standards and Assessment. (1994). *National science education standards.* Washington, DC: Author.

Orr, J. (2001). Standards for bilingual and dual language classrooms. *Nabe News* 24(6), 4–7.

Padrón, Y.N., & Waxman, H.C. (1999). Classroom observations of the Five Standards for Effective Teaching in urban classrooms with ELLs. *Teaching and Change, 7,* 79–100.

Peregoy, S.F., & Boyle, O.F. (2001). *Reading, writing, and learning in ESL* (3rd ed.). New York: Longman.

Richard-Amato, P.A. (1996). *Making it happen: Interaction in the second language classroom.* White Plains, NY: Longman.

Riley, R.W. (2000). *Remarks as prepared for delivery by the U.S. Secretary of Education: Web-Based Education Commission.* [On-line]. Available: http://www.ed.gov/Speeches/02-2000/20000202.html

Robles-Rivas, E. (2001). *An examination of standards for effective pedagogy in a high school bilingual setting.* Unpublished doctoral dissertation, University of Connecticut, Storrs.

Romberg, T., & Wilson, L. (1995). Issues related to the development of an authentic assessment system for school mathematics. In T. Romberg (Ed.), *Reforming in school mathematics and authentic assessment* (pp. 1–18). Albany: State University of New York Press.

Rueda, R. (1998). *Standards for professional development: A sociocultural perspective.* Santa Cruz, CA: Center for Research in Education, Diversity, & Excellence.

Schifini, A. (2000). *Second language learning at its best. The stages of language acquisition.* Carmel, CA: Hampton Brown Publishers.

Scribner, J.P. (1999). Professional development: Untangling the influence of work context on teacher learning. *Educational Administration Quarterly, 35*(2), 238–266.

Shaw, J.M., Echevarria, J., & Short, D.J. (1999, April). *Sheltered instruction: Bridging diverse cultures for academic success.* Paper presented at the annual meeting of the American Educational Research Association, Montreal.

Short, D.J. (1999). Integrating language and content for effective sheltered instruction programs. In C. Faltis & P. Wolfe (Eds.), *So much to say: Adolescents, bilingualism, and ESL in secondary schools* (pp. 105–137). New York: Teachers College Press.

Short, D.J. (1991). *How to integrate language and content instruction. A training manual* (2nd ed.). Washington, DC: Center for Applied Linguistics.

Short, D.J., & Echevarria, J. (1999). *The Sheltered Instruction Observation Protocol: A tool for teacher–research collaboration and professional development.* Long Beach, CA: Center for Applied Linguistics.

Shotter, J. (1997). *Talk of saying, showing, gesturing, and feeling in Wittgenstein and Vygotsky.* [On-line]. Available: http://www.massey.sc.nz/~Alock/virtual/wittvyg.htm

Straight, H.S. (1998). *Languages across the curriculum.* ERIC Digest. [On-line]. Available: http://www.cal.org/ericcll/digest/lacdigest.html

Stryker, S.B., & Leaver, B.L. (Eds.). (1997). *Content-based instruction for the foreign language classroom: Models and methods.* Washington, DC: Georgetown University Press.

Teachers of English to Speakers of Other Languages. (1997). *ESL standards for pre-K-12 students.* Alexandria, VA: Author.

Tharp, R.G. (1999). *Proofs and evidence: Effectiveness of the five standards for effective teaching.* Santa Cruz, CA: Center for Research in Education, Diversity, & Excellence.

Tharp, R.G. (1997). *From at-risk to excellence. Research theory and principles for practice.* Santa Cruz, CA: Center for Research in Education, Diversity, & Excellence.

Tharp, R.G., Estrada, P., Dalton, S.S., & Yamauchi, L.A. (2000). *Teaching transformed: Achieving excellence, fairness, inclusion, and harmony.* Boulder, CO: Westview Press.

Tharp, R.G., & Gallimore, R. (1998). *Rousing minds to life: Teaching, learning, and schooling in social context.* New York: Cambridge University Press.

Thomas, W.P., & Collier, V. (1997). *School effectiveness for language minority students.* Washington, DC: National Clearinghouse for Bilingual Education.

Tomlinson, C. (2001). Standards and the art of teaching: Crafting high quality classrooms. *NASSP Bulletin 85*(622), 38–47.

Valdes, G. (1996). *Con respeto: Bridging the distances between culturally diverse families and schools. An ethnographic portrait.* New York: Teachers College Press.

Vygotsky, L.S. (1986). *Thought and language.* Cambridge, MA: MIT Press.

Vygotsky, L.S. (1978). *Mind in society: The development of higher psychological processes.* Cambridge, MA: Harvard University Press.

Wagonner, D. (1999). Who are secondary new comers and linguistically different youth? In C.J. Faltis & P. Wolfe (Eds.), *So much to say: Adolescents, bilingualism & ESL in the secondary school* (pp. 13–41). New York: Teachers College Press.

Zeichner, K. (1993). *Educating teachers for cultural diversity.* East Lansing: Michigan State University, National Center for Research on Teacher Learning.

## CHAPTER 4

HOW DO PRE-SERVICE TEACHERS ACQUIRE AND USE PROFESSIONAL KNOWLEDGE?

Stephanie Stoll Dalton and Roland G. Tharp

ABSTRACT

This chapter reports on a study of pre-service teachers' professional knowledge as enacted in early lesson teaching experiences in the mid-course of a teacher preparation program focusing on meeting the needs of at-risk minority K-6 students. During early teaching of mathematics lessons, pre-service teachers' professional knowledge and knowledge utilization were analyzed using video stimulated recall interviews to identify surface indicators and understand developing structures. In addition to questions about the role of pre-service teachers' every day, practical knowledge in the acquisition of professional knowledge, sources of influence available in the teacher education program as an academic, field-based experience which was learning community oriented were examined.

INTRODUCTION

Preparing to teach is more exacting and daunting than novices expect or teacher educators convey. Early experience in classrooms readily baffles novices who soon realize how disappointingly insufficient are their own experiences and even content area expertise for productive classroom teaching. Effective application of content expertise during early teaching experience is rarely reported, and the role of practical, everyday knowledge for effective teaching, particularly early teaching, remains largely unexplained. Carter (1990) points to the learning-to-teach problem as one more concerned with knowledge translation than unpacking the meaning of complex experiences. The nature of teacher learning itself is a new topic of research (Bransford, Brown, & Cocking, 1999). Even so, there is broad consensus that three areas of study, general education, content area knowledge, and professional or pedagogical knowledge properly comprise teachers' education, although reform continues to cycle through assertions about priority for one or another, such as basic skills or content area expertise (Dalton, 1998; Tom & Valli, 1990).

In fact, the notion of professional teaching knowledge is recent as are claims that there is a teaching knowledge base described in the literature of teacher education research (Fenstermacher, 1994; Wittrock, 1986). A number of reports define teaching expertise and outline frameworks and typologies (Cochran-Smith & Little, 1999; Grimmet & McKinnon, 1992; Kennedy, 1987; Shulman, 1987). Shulman (1987) delineated pedagogical content knowledge which is based on the ways teachers relate content and pedagogical knowledge. Studies of differences between teacher experts and novices suggest that experts have formed elaborate knowledge structures for understanding and interpreting teaching activity and because this knowledge is often tacit and interpretive, it is not readily transmissible to novices (Carter, 1990). Feiman-Nemser and Buchman (1986) studied student teachers' pedagogical thinking to examine their progress from focusing on control issues to assisting student learning. They concluded that the student teachers made little progress in understanding appropriate selection and presentation of student learning activities. They also found, like Zeichner and Tabachnick (1985), that pre-service teacher knowledge acquisition was differentially and, sometimes negatively, influenced by teacher education program and field experience. Studies of teacher preparation, particularly for linguistically and culturally diverse students, reveal programs' highly traditional organization, often atheoretic orientations, and content restrictions, particularly for language development, literacy instruction and diversity preparation (Fillmore & Snow, 2000; Ladson-Billings, 1999). Reports of best approaches for preparing teachers to teach diverse students range from a disbelief in the transportability of specific effective practices to recommendations of standards of pedagogy for all students (Cochran-Smith, 1997; Dalton, 1998; Tharp, Estrada, Dalton, & Yamauchi, 2000). Common understandings about theory, pedagogical principles, or pre-service teacher learning rarely characterize teacher preparation programs.

In many respects, the recent shift in understanding about the nature of knowledge and learning from an emphasis on individuals' learning to knowledge development that is socially influenced offers a coherent framework for teaching and teacher education (Cobb & Bowers, 1999; Putnam & Borko, 2000; Tharp & Gallimore, 1988). Research evidence clearly supports the role of collaborative, productive activity in learning, and the feature that assures knowledge acquisition is its application in action and interaction with other participants (Bransford, Brown, & Cocking, 1999; Tharp & Gallimore, 1988; Vygotsky, 1978; Webb, Troper, & Fall, 1995). In a socially situated view, participation in a particular setting constitutes what individuals learn. When community-centered preparation programs establish norms for teachers' joint involvement in planning and decision making teacher collaboration over successes and failures with pedagogy and other aspects of teaching reveals the importance of shared experiences and discourse for making meaning and problem solving teaching challenges (Bransford, Brown, & Cocking, 1999; Tharp et al., 2000). Vygotsky (1978) wrote that higher-order functions develop out of social interaction, and cannot be fully understood by study of the individual. What is known about participation and social interaction that influences learning has been reported in the literature of education, psychology, and anthropology and can be expressed as general pedagogical principles guiding learning for K-12 teaching as well as teacher preparation. The principles which claim a high degree of consensus are presented as pedagogy standards for teaching and learning (Dalton, 1998; Dalton & Tharp, 2000; Dalton & Youpa, 1998; Tharp et al., 2000). These standards are applied to the teacher education context and described in the following sections and listed in Table 5.

After situating the study in the framework of the program, we describe the study's theoretical perspective and research methodology. We then examine pre-service teachers' knowledge as a function of two meaning systems, professional education lexicon and professional conceptual structures, and their use of them in teaching, as discovered in stimulated recall interviews. The implications of the relationship between the two meaning systems for developing teachers' professional knowledge and other relationships among the variables are discussed. Finally, the role of the teacher education program in promoting acquisition and utilization of the meaning systems is discussed using the pedagogy standards as a framework for weighing evidence and program capacity.

SITUATING THE STUDY

Nine pre-service teachers participated in a teacher education program characterized by intellectually rigorous academic and research-based professional content, integrated with a variety of field placements in K-6 classrooms serving at-risk, diverse students. From 1986–8, the first cohort of pre-service teachers entered Pre-service Education for Teachers of Minorities (PETOM) in the College of Education at the University of Hawaii at Manoa—a program that continues. This alternative teacher education program was designed using the conceptual framework and research-based practices of the Kamehameha Elementary Education Program (KEEP) in-service teacher consulting model (Tharp, 1982).

The teacher education program, like its in-service counterpart, defined teacher expertise from a sociocultural perspective that promoted culturally responsive teaching through participation in the social processes of meaningful activity and interaction. In its two-year, field-based curriculum, there were courses in oral language development, culture, cognition, reading, educational foundations and psychology (including focus on motivation theory and management) along with generic methods coursework in mathematics, science, social studies, art, and physical education. The program provided field placements in schools serving urban and rural at-risk K-6 students beginning in the first semester of coursework. Students were recruited who were committed to improving the school experience for at-risk students, and each class was organized as a cohort.

A cross-institutional faculty was assembled with expertise in language development, literacy, numeracy, and cultural and ethnic issues. Faculty participated with the understanding that communication was a critical program feature requiring frequent meetings (weekly at least) to discuss program development, implementation, and student issues. Program evaluation was conducted each year. Faculty described the program saying, "Traditional instruction for pre-service teachers is scattered among different faculty members who rarely talk with one another. No single group is responsible for seeing the pre-service teachers through their entire program. As (others have) pointed out, university faculties may be even more isolated than elementary classroom teachers. Teacher educators rarely know what the other is teaching and rarely, if ever, observe one another teach. PETOM has provided an opportunity to break down this isolation" (Picard & Young, 1990, p.31).

THEORETICAL PERSPECTIVE

When teaching and learning are viewed as social ventures, joint activity and mutual exchanges of experience form teachers' knowledge, skills, and interpretive frameworks including caring and ideology (Cochran-Smith, 1997; Putnam & Borko, 2000; Tharp et al., 2000). In a socially situated view of teaching and teacher preparation, teacher-student interactions and activities are core elements of the learning process. Study is needed at the level of formative exchanges between teachers and students, teacher educators and pre-service teachers to understand and intensify the course of teacher learning and teacher education programs' capacity to influence it (Cohen, 1994; Goldstein, 1999; Ladson-Billings, 1999; Tharp et al., 2000; Zeichner, 1999). Vygotsky's (1978) concept of the zone of proximal development (ZPD) provides a tool for educators to examine the course of development from interpersonal to personal knowledge. Learners' reports about their functioning are informative about what knowledge has formed and how it is used, and the variety of developmental patterns that learners display even among those who begin at similar levels. According to Vygotsky, the social context of the individual is worth examining because cognitive and communicative skill appears "twice, or in two planes. First it appears on the social plane, and then on the psychological plane. First it appears between people as an interpsychological category and then within the child as an intrapsychological category" (Vygotsky, 1978, p. 163). The ZPD is "the difference between the actual developmental level as determined by independent problem solving and the level of potential development as determined through problem solving under … guidance or collaboration with more capable peers" (Vygotsky, 1978, p. 86).

Drawing on the notion that knowledge is distributed in materials and cultural tools and signs, in representational systems such as speech, literacy, mathematics, technology, and others, pre-service teachers need to acquire these resources for teaching (Cobb & Bowers, 1999; Moll, 1990; Putnam & Borko, 2000). This study investigates pre-service teachers' professional knowledge acquisition and application by focusing on the development of two meaning systems: (1) professional content and pedagogy-related lexicon and (2) professional conceptual structures. It then explores the activity of the teacher education program for its capacity to influence knowledge acquisition using a program framework based on the pedagogy standards.

LEXICON

The vocabulary of a language is its lexicon. Acquiring vocabulary means knowing something of a word's basic meaning, but words rarely have single, simple meanings especially as they relate to technical or professional domains. Lexicon refers to the specialized verbal codes of disciplines such as science, mathematics, and education, not unnecessary jargon (Rueda, 1998). As lexicon, words differ from informal communication in their degree of decontextualization. When words have formal and scientific or professional applications they represent the shared knowledge of the profession through an expanded meaning that goes beyond original social and concrete referents. Learners encounter professional lexicon in formal or academic discourse structures of coursework and other instructional activity where it is modeled and presented. Lexicon acquisition draws on the foundation of learners' everyday knowledge of language conventions, syntax, understanding, interpretation; acquisition depends on sufficient expressive opportunities which vary by individual (Fillmore & Snow, 2000; Tharp & Gallimore, 1998). Lexicon use signals the operation of meaning systems such as categorical knowledge for conveying a profession's theory, conceptual knowledge, history, and resources, and forms a basis for professional concept development. Examination of pre-service teachers' professional lexicon invokes the first research question: What education lexicon do pre-service teachers use to describe their teaching?

CONCEPT DEVELOPMENT

Teachers bring considerable knowledge and experience to their professional preparation referred to as practical knowledge, everyday knowledge, and spontaneous knowledge. The operation of practical knowledge for teaching has been studied to understand how professionals, such as teachers, work in action. Everyday knowledge like spontaneous knowledge is developed from experience and reflection upon it. It is immediate in the sense that it is bounded by the situation of its occurrence and does not involve labeling or verbalization (Fenstermacher, 1994). This directly contrasts with the nature of participation in school and instructional activity which provides learning experiences that differ from practical, situational thinking of everyday experience and involve language. The acquisition and expansion of word meaning is a form of abstraction that alters context bound and everyday thinking to become categorical and conceptual. Through abstraction, aspects of objects, situations are generalized in order to place them under specific categories of thought or abstract concepts like size, shape, color, theme, etc. Conceptual thinking, then, is expanded by and expands the power of words so that words gain function as concepts producing abstractions and generalizations. Even though spontaneous or everyday concepts are distinctively different from professional concepts, they are the foundation upon which conceptual learning depends (Panofsky, John-Steiner, & Blackwell, 1990; Vygotsky, 1978). Panofsky et al. (1990) explains how spontaneously learned native language mediates thinking that supports the learning of a second language and, similarly, everyday concepts comprise the basis on which professional concepts depend for their development (Ponofsky et al., 1990). Ideally, everyday and professional concepts interact and development is reciprocal and complementary with both concept levels eventually becoming useful in similar ways. In reality, the enormous variety of individuals' experiences develops some concepts more than others. For example, an individual may have proficiency with a verbal task involving complex material but little understanding of its practical function at the everyday level or high practical understanding but minimal professional awareness of a concept (Luria, 1976; Ponofsky et al., 1990). The process of pre-service teachers' concept development invokes the second research question: Does pre-service teachers' discussion of their teaching in stimulated recall interviews disclose their teaching concept knowledge and application capacity?

PEDAGOGY STANDARDS

The five standards for pedagogy presented in this chapter constitute a synthesis of research findings, primarily from the literature on effective teaching and learning for students at-risk due to cultural and/or linguistic diversity, race, poverty, or geographical isolation (Dalton, 1998; Dalton & Tharp, 2000; Dalton & Youpa, 1998; Tharp et al., 2000). These research-based findings when stated as pedagogy standards turn out to be as relevant to the majority of learners as they are to those on the educational margins because of the procedural guidance they offer. The pedagogy standards describe effective practice as ongoing participation in activities organized to increase experiences and discourse around shared texts, student learning and encourage the formation of interative learning communities (Bransford, Brown, & Cocking, 1999). The first standard (1) Joint Productive Activity (JPA) increases participants' opportunity to participate and interact to accomplish a cooperative product. JPA facilitates the four other standards comprising the set. (2) Language Development (LD) promotes individual speech and dialogue occasions with more expert others. (3) Making Meaning (MM) assures contextualization and incorporation of local knowledge and values. (4) Cognitive Challenge (CC) promotes differentiated activities that scaffold learning for deep knowledge. (5) Teaching through Dialog, especially the Instructional Conversation (IC), uses professional lexicon and other academic and professional tools and materials. Pedagogy standards when applied to participation in a learning community such as teacher education provide a framework for analyzing quality and impact of teaching and learning. This prompts the study's third research question: How are pre-service teachers guided by the teacher education program to form lexicon knowledge and transform everyday concepts to professional structures?

RESEARCH METHODOLOGY

The focus of this analysis is not on the individuals' acquisition of skills and knowledge as demonstrated in coursework and exams, but as participants in teaching activity with students in real classrooms. Videotape provided a visual and aural reference to stimulate pre-service teachers' reflection that includes interpretations and explanations of their practice in the terms and professional language they have acquired. We examined the quality of pre-service teachers' participation in activity through analysis of transcripts of pre-service teachers' stimulated recall interviews (while viewing a video of their teaching). Analysis searched out evidence of professional knowledge and its application in terms of pre-service teachers' lexicon and concept use, and the critical linkages within the community of practice that influenced performance reflecting professional knowledge. The stimulated recall interviews reported here were conducted between the first and second year, the midpoint, of the first PETOM cohort's experience in the program.

Research Questions

1. What education lexicon do pre-service teachers use to describe their teaching in stimulated recall interviews?
2. Does pre-service teachers' discussion of their teaching in stimulated recall interviews disclose their teaching concept knowledge and application capacity?
3. How are pre-service teachers guided by the teacher education program to form lexicon knowledge and transform everyday concepts into professional concepts?

Population of the Study

Our subjects were all nine members of a cohort of PETOM. These pre-service teachers were education degree-seeking undergraduates (B.Ed.), classified as juniors; or graduate Professional Diploma (P.D.) students who were female ranging in age from 20.6 to 35.1 years. Three of the students considered themselves nontraditional in that they were switching from a career line outside of education or returning to school from full-time homemaking.

Procedures

The qualitative method of data collection employed in this study was open-ended, stimulated recall interviews to elicit pre-service teachers' perspectives as fully as possible about their earliest experience of teaching. The focus of the interview was a videotape of each pre-service teacher teaching a math lesson, taught near the end of the second semester of Field Experience referred to in this program as Observation and Participation (OP). The lessons on the videotapes were taught in pre-service teachers' assigned OP classrooms for the second semester where they had formed relationships with the classroom teachers, their mentors, referred to here as host teachers. The videotaped lessons were among the earliest that the pre-service teachers had taught. The characteristics of the lessons are presented in Table 1.

Table 1.   Pre-service Teachers' Lesson Characteristics

Teacher	Grade/Topic	Group #/Ability	Length
Jane/1st lesson	K/Addition	6/Lowest	20 minutes
Nancy/1st lesson	K/Count, Add, Subt	4/Average	60 minutes
Mary/2nd lesson	1st/Graphing	8/Lowest	40 minutes
Helen/2nd lesson	3rd/Rounding, Estimating	5/Average	20 minutes
Tina/1st lesson	3rd/Multiplication	6/Lowest	40 minutes
Rachel/2nd lesson	4th/Decimals, Fractions	5/Highest	20 minutes
Debra/1st lesson	5th/Measure/Estimate	8/Low	30 minutes
Claudia/1st lesson	6th/Percent	18/Mixed	60 minutes
Linda/1st lesson	6th/Measure, Convert	25/Mixed	60 minutes

The Stimulated Recall Interview

The purpose of the stimulated recall, semi-structured interview was to elicit pre-service teachers' recall and report of their thinking during inter-active teaching. As a method, stimulated recall interviewing was used origi-nally by Bloom (1954) and consists of replaying a videotape or audiotape of a teaching episode to enable the viewer to recollect and report on his or her thoughts and decisions during the teaching episode. During the hour-long interview, the videotaped lesson was played back in the presence of the pre-service teacher and the inquirer. The playback and the inquirer's questions "stimulated" the pre-service teachers to recall and report aspects of their thinking while they were in the act of teaching their lesson. The teachers' reports and comments about their thoughts while teaching were audiotaped, subsequently transcribed and subjected to content analysis. The interviewer was the first author, who was also the coordinator of the program and familiar to the pre-service teachers. Questions were open-ended, allowing the subjects to extend or expand their discussion at will. In this process, the researcher poses questions on the basis of previous knowl-edge and theory, but modifies, refines or revises the research questions on the basis of emerging data and advancing understanding.

ANALYSIS: LEXICON USE

Each stimulated recall interview transcript was examined for word use that has technical or content meaning in professional teaching. Each use was tallied. These terms were compiled in a frequency count and in sentence context with referents to the original interview protocol. The following list presents three sample entries in the lexicon record of pre-service teachers' statements (with tags to the full interviews).

Ability/Ability Level/Ability Levels

- But she went more on ability, she thought they were average, but not on behavior. N8
- Shane is hard of hearing, has a hearing aide on one side and because of that and also because of his ability level he tends to focus in, focus out. H3
- I think I experienced mainly the difficulty of having different ability levels in one group. That was hard. H12

Desist

- And if it continues then I have to go on to another step and that would probably be, "Martin, stop it" or just a warning, a warning or a desist. M5
- So, this time I issue a little more warnings and desists which are appropriate I think for this phase. M6

Float/Floated

- Yea, oh, and I think I expected that during this part while they were sitting down doing the work sheet, that I would float around help whoever was doing what, you know. L5

Manipulative/s

- ...the lesson was on addition and in order to help them conceptualize addition, I used manipulatives, plastic Easter eggs, to help in that. J3

ANALYSIS: CONCEPT KNOWLEDGE

A logical system for classification and analysis of concept level was constructed to identify pre-service teachers' level of discourse as everyday or professionally conceptual. Quotive data representing concept use by pre-service teachers was marked in the interviews, concept by concept, for analysis. The quotive data was coded for distinguishing features that indicated everyday or professional concept use. In this method, there are no guarantees of logic, only a potentially critical contribution to the explanatory strength of the final account (Moll, 1990; Vygotsky, 1987).

FINDINGS

This discussion presents the study's findings about pre-service teachers' knowledge through the lenses of two representational systems of language and thought, use of professional lexicon and professional concepts. The analysis used pre-service teachers' descriptions of their experience anchored in videotape playback of their lessons. Lexicon reflecting content and pedagogy knowledge was counted. Lexicon was a marker signaling the possible presence of a concept, but other criteria were applied through coding to conclude the presence of a professional concept. The absence of a lexicon marker did not remove the possibility that a concept was functional although use of the appropriate label to frame or explain a situation was highly confirmatory of a concept structure. The research questions and their findings follow.

1. *What education lexicon do pre-service teachers use to describe their teaching in stimulated recall interviews?*

A frequency count of pre-service teacher lexicon use displayed in Table 3 showed that total terms used by all including multiple uses and repetitions was 1,108. The use of terms ranged from a low of 56 terms to a high of 244. The mean number of terms used was 123. The spread was more interesting than the mean which was influenced by one high count, 244. This was 98 terms more than the next highest total count, 146. The other differences in ranks ranged from 2 to 23. The difference between the highest ranked user of lexicon and the lowest was188 terms. Clearly, the pre-service teachers' frequency of professional lexicon use is highly differentiated.

The high use lexicon that clustered at more than twelve are presented in Table 2. The frequency of lexicon use by all the pre-service teachers ranged up to 163 for one term. The lexicon, Lesson Plan/s/ing or Planning in one form or another, was stated 113 times more than all the other terms. The high use terms are listed in Table 2.

Table 2.   High Use Lexicon

Lexicon	Total Use	Mean
Lesson/s/Plan/s/ing	163	18.0
Group/s/ed	50	5.5
Behavior	49	5.4
Focus/ed/ing	31	3.4
Attention	19	2.1
Experience/s	19	2.1
Worksheet/s	16	1.7
Praise/ing	13	1.4
Abstract	13	1.4

Common themes of early teaching are reflected in the pre-service teachers' list of lexicon use. While a mean does not indicate that every pre-service teacher used every term, the high use of the first three terms suggests a high level of appropriation of those terms and their application to practice. The enormous use of "Lesson Plan" indicates pre-service teachers' concern, perhaps preoccupation, about conveying a sense of purpose for the activities they present. They quickly learn that planning and preparation enable teachers to proceed through lessons smoothly without having to interrupt activity to consult manuals or guides about what to say or how to question or to locate an item needed for modeling or demonstration. The frequent use of "Group" indicates pre-service teacher focus on classroom organization and the advantages of arranging students in various ways to work productively together for the lesson goals the pre-service teachers set. 'Behavior, Focus, and Attention' can be considered to cluster to suggest pre-service teacher concern with classroom management and motivation for learning where novices usually struggle for proficiency. Although the frequency of use is very low for the remaining terms, they offer some information about pre-service teacher learning and application. "Experience" suggests an interest in students' prior knowledge and experience as a basis for new learning, an emphasis in the teacher education program. "Worksheets" suggests an effort to attend to task development and student success with tasks pre-service teachers' assign. "Praising" reflects the program's strong emphasis on building a positive classroom climate and developing a community. "Abstract" reflects a desire to deliver lessons that move students to a higher level of understanding of a topic, an emphasis in the program's methods coursework. The frequent use of these lexicon imply a focus on the part of the pre-service teachers that is beneficial to their emerging practice, and represents some of the foci of the teacher education program coursework.

2. *Does pre-service teachers' discussion of their teaching in stimulated recall interviews disclose their professional concept knowledge and application capacity?*

Analysis revealed that the pre-service teachers described and, in some cases, used a total of 40 professional concepts during stimulated recall. Table 3 presents number of professional concepts coded for each pre-service teacher.

Table 3.   Preservice Teachers' Professional Lexicon and Concept Frequency

Pre-service Teacher	Lexicon	Concept Use
Mary	244	9
Jane	146	1
Rachel	136	7
Tina	133	4
Helen	113	8
Linda	111	2
Nancy	96	3
Claudia	73	5
Debra	56	1
TOTALS	1,108	40

The range of professional concepts identified was from 1 to 9 indicating a spread in the capacity of these teachers to use concept knowledge to process new information encountered in the teaching situation. To discern if those who use more concepts have correspondingly high lexicon use the pre-service teachers were ranked in both strands for comparison in Table 4, Rank Order for Lexicon and Concept Use. A Spearman Rank-Order Correlation Coefficient for tied ranks was calculated with the result at .4125. This coefficient reveals some strength in the relationship of the variables suggesting that gains in lexicon are associated with gains in professional concept use.

Table 4.   Rank Order of Pre-service Teachers' Lexicon & Concept Use

Name	Lexicon	Concept
Mary	1	1
Jane	2	8
Rachel	3	3
Tina	4	5
Helen	5	2
Linda	6	7
Nancy	7	6
Claudia	8	4
Debra	9	8

In Table 4, six pre-service teachers are ranked similarly, that is, at the same level or within one rank on both measures, and three, Jane, Helen, and Claudia, have low corresponding rankings with Jane's being the most disparate. The highest ranked on lexicon use, Mary, was the highest ranked for professional concept use and the lowest ranked on lexicon use, Debra, ties for the lowest rank for concept application. Six rankings were commensurate across the two strands indicating corresponding development in the two strands of inquiry, lexicon and professional concept use. The trend was that those who are more advanced in appropriating lexicon described their teaching using professional concepts. Mary said "Right there what I'm doing, is I'm trying to model for the students. I'm gonna write that, they might not be there, they might not be hearing what I'm saying, so if they're seeing me do it, I hope in their minds they're thinking, 'Oh, teacher's doing something and I should be doing something too. What is the teacher doing?'" When Rachel was asked why she moved from using manipulatives in her lesson to blackboard use she said, "Cause I thought if they could see, cause I tried saying this is 10 and this is 10 in the hundreds and then if you multiplied that, then it would become ... cause I wanted them to see in another way I guess numerically or pictorally, in the more abstract way. So I thought they might connect with that better than with the cubes." Rachel made a deliberate shift from one level, concrete and manipulative, to another, visual and abstract, based on her in-flight assessment of her students' understanding and her own grasp of the material she was teaching. She was able to adapt her approach during teaching to provide additional assistance in response to circumstances.

In contrast, those who describe their teaching with everyday concepts were hesitant and troubled when planned strategies deteriorated. Claudia described her practical approaches in the following excerpt:

P: Yea, was okay. I think I like doing both, walking around and checking on their problems. But Bill (her host teacher) was telling me it was easier to do it that way and then you're sure to get everybody, when you have them up at the board.

I: Um, hum.

P: Then you can just stand there, "Okay," you know. So, either way I guess was okay.

I: So, by either way, you're talking about either having them up at the board or you're floating around checking the work?

P: Um, hum. But Bill's style I think was more, he'd rather have them up at the board.

I: Have you thought about what your style is?

P: No. I think I have to do it more often to try and figure out which is better for me. I need to watch more math, that's my problem. I'm gonna go into the (my own) kids' class and ask the teacher if I can come in when she teaches math.

Claudia's rationale for assuring her students' work quality was loosely formed and more an accommodation to her host teacher's model. When questioned about how to proceed she preferred a trial and error approach and to increase her observational learning time rather than examine her performance through the lens of the verbal and professional knowledge she was acquiring. Pre-service teachers who have fewer lexicon and fewer professional concepts are less able to frame and interpret teaching situations or take immediate action to maneuver lesson activity toward teaching goals.

Helen's descriptions of her lesson revealed an emerging professional concept, cueing. When she described praising a student for getting settled quickly she said, "Tia is very slow moving. Thank you Tia!" When she was asked to explain what she did Helen responded, "Well, it's cueing, right?

That I think is becoming pretty automatic now. When you see something happening, tune into it and get it taken care of." In fact, cueing is somewhat different from what Helen described making her definition partially correct. It is the giving of specific praise to student/s who are behaving for the purpose of informing a misbehaving student/s about appropriate behavior. Helen was praising a student for appropriate behavior not to provide a model for a misbehaving student. She continued to use the lexicon to label her actions, describing and applying it as an everyday concept three times and as a professional concept on the fourth occasion as follows.

1.   Throughout the tape I think there will be several times that I'm gonna cue in on Shane here. Shane is hard of hearing,...
2.   Yea, they're positive, they were real involved. I had everyone's attention and I, by glancing at them I felt that they were cued into what we were going to talk about.
3.   The two boys at the end, ... And I found it very easy to cue into, for me to cue into what they were saying. You know, because it carried along my objective real well.
4.   Well, in one sense you could say it served as a cue for the other kids, but I don't think that was it in this situation. (laughter) I was really aware of their meeting my objective and moving along quite well with these two.

In the case of those rankings outside the trend for closely matched lexicon and concept levels, Helen, Claudia, and Jane were the oldest and most experienced members of the cohort. Two were returning to school from homemaking and one was entering education after working in another professional area. School as a highly verbal context that promotes abstract learning contrasts sharply with learning and acting to solve practical problems in the everyday world. This difference suggests that transiting contexts is a factor to address in assisting intending teachers' verbal and conceptual learning.

Analysis disclosed trends in the relationships between the rankings but not direct correspondence. Professional lexicon and concept usage levels were ranked similarly for two-thirds of the pre-service teachers which suggests a relationship between lexicon and concept acquisition processes. High rates of lexicon use accompanied high concept use except for Jane who presented a very high lexicon and very low concept ranking and Claudia who presented a low lexicon rank and a high concept rank. Debra was ranked lowest for both.

3.   *How are pre-service teachers guided by the teacher education program to form lexicon knowledge and transform everyday concepts to professional concepts?*

During the stimulated recall interviews, pre-service teachers were asked to identify what sources of influence in the teacher education program community affected their understandings about teaching and what they did during teaching. All the pre-service teachers reported knowledge of teaching from their own experience through observational and experiential learning, but in the interview they were encouraged to cite influences from the entire community of practice for the teacher education program which included the university-based academic community and the K-12 school communities. This information provided by seven of the teachers was coded.

Of the 40 professional concept applications discussed by the pre-service teachers in stimulated recall, 20 were reported as influenced by the experience of fundamentally different and unexpected conditions arising during the activity of teaching. For example, Tina discussed how the manipulatives students were using were distracting students from the lesson goals. She said, "I think, at that time, I was thinking about, "What can I say now?" Or what can I do so that won't happen again?" When Tina's students would not remain in their seats for her lesson she applied a professional concept in the lesson activity saying, "Yea, I knew I had to say something. I didn't want to say, 'Oh what should we do?' So I figured maybe if I praise, cause they were always throughout the whole game, always sitting nicely and working together.... Yea, and then they sat down."

Twelve reports cited the use of conscious verbal and conceptual learning. For example, Mary described how she consciously used a verbal strategy to apply a professional concept, visual display, for management and academic purposes saying, "There, that's something I hadn't planned. They're asking to go back to the other room because they've been in the lesson and it's maybe about, yea, we started it. It's about when they would be changing. So, they finished their paper and they're like, 'Okay, we're finished, now it's time to go to our next one.' And they're thinking they're going to the games. But here I have to be the one who says, 'No we're gonna do something else.' So, right there what I said was, 'Oh, actually I have something special planned for you.' And I'm hoping that will help change their mind, you know. Something special and that's the key word that I hope they'll latch onto. So, it was like, 'Oh, here's something that's good.' There I briefly lifted up the visual aide. 'Remember, we're doing graphs?' So, that's trying to get them back on the focus."

The pre-service teachers reported thirteen occurrences of interpersonal influence through participation in the community of practice citing social interaction with peers, instructors, and host teachers. Debra discussed modeling after her math methods instructor. She said, "Birch did it with us, had us write it that way or he wrote it up when we gave him our measurements. He didn't take like fractions or whatever. So I looked at the board and I saw fractions, you know, like ten and a half (Ina.) And that's what I looked at. There's a pause already and I looked and I looked and I went, I think I want to work with whole numbers. I say it aloud, I'm thinking and I said it out loud. That's when I go over and I change it. And I ask them, which are you close to, ten or eleven? And change it to a whole number." Jane reported conferring often with her mentor teacher about the lesson she would be teaching which was influenced by her math methods instructor. She said, "So, I took that idea from the methods class and then a lot of that helped me. We (Jane and her host teacher, Billy) discussed what I wanted to do, or what she was doing with the children and what I might want to do. And, she said that she was going into, that would be next, addition with the children. So I thought, yea, I'd like to try addition ... She gave me advice and hints on what I could do and help, you know, tell me what I could do, what I could add and things like that."

The data suggest that professional concepts develop based on individuals' conscious use of lexicon, experience in teaching activity, and learning community participation. Lexicon frequency counts were total counts and did not reflect accuracy of word use, but they did indicate individuals' willingness to practice and take risks with new information and tools. High lexicon use accompanied low concept use in only a single case, Jane. Interviews revealed pre-service teachers' using lexicon to label and frame teaching situations, rehearsing lexicon, and experimenting with concept applications. In Jane's and Debra's cases, practice and risk-taking opportunities to acquire concept structures may have been lower than their peers or the program may not have provided adequate scaffolding and other supports. Pre-service teachers described drawing on relationships with instructors and host teachers through collaborations for planning and enacting their teaching. Their reliance on relationships in the community of practice to expand their knowledge base and guide their teaching applications suggests the operation of the ZPD where interaction influences the formation of individuals' thinking categories.

DISCUSSION

We apply the pedagogy standards to teacher education program teaching and learning to organize discussion of the findings for all three research questions. A list of the pedagogy standards as program or community standards is presented on the left in Table 5. The related outcomes listed on the right indicate teacher education program enactment of each standard.

Table 5. Pedagogy Standards for Teacher Education Program Analysis

Program Standard	Program Product
I. Joint Productive Activity (JPA)	Teacher educators and preservice teachers collaborating for common goals
II. Developing Language (DL)	Professional lexicon expansion and use in teaching and reflection
III. Making Meaning (MM)	Building on preservice teachers everyday concepts and experience
IV. Teaching Complex Thinking (CC)	Developing professional and content concepts and applications
V. Teaching Through Dialogue (IC)	Professional lexicon/concept use in dialogue and written text

The first standard as displayed in Table 5, Joint Productive Activity (JPA), increases opportunities for learners to engage and interact to accomplish a cooperative product. The common motivation provided by a joint goal inclines all participants to offer and receive assistance, since it is in everyone's best interest that the goal is reached. One-half of the 40 professional concepts identified by pre-service teachers were reported to arise from the activity of teaching. In other words, when pre-service teachers worked together with their students for a common instructional goal they learned even as they assisted students to learn. In the same way, teacher educators work together with pre-service teachers for a common goal which is pre-service teachers' teaching, the ultimate joint product of all effort in the community of practice. Although program assistors/instructors/mentors are not always physically present for pre-service teaching, their influence is continuously available through meaning systems such as lexicon and professional concepts, texts, and other materials of instruction. Pre-service teachers said they could often hear their instructors or mentor teachers talking to them "in their heads" while they were teaching. This reflects the program's distinguishing feature that teaching and learning are social, not products of solely individual effort (Rueda, 1998).

As learners speak, read, and write within the dilemmas of simulated and real practice, their language understanding and lexicon learning grow and are stimulated to interact. This process helps pre-service teachers use language to frame problems in fresh ways. The second program standard, Developing Language, encourages professional lexicon learning for teaching. In the formal instruction of program coursework, professional lexicon captures an event with more precision and organizes new knowledge in more useful or accessible ways (Rueda, 1998). Eight of the nine pre-service teachers ranked at the same level or higher for lexicon use than they did for concept use. In other words, all demonstrated a degree of facility in learning lexicon and using it to discuss teaching. A learning community with goals to develop quality teachers encourages professional expression as a fundamental activity providing safety for mistakes and praise for success. Mary explains how the program influenced her teaching when she says, "We had discussed these types of situations and what you would do in behavior modification or behavior management classes. And also the prompting I was doing in that case, I had learned in my methods class as well. We had done some reading (in our textbook). And we learned about 'prompt' there and also I had seen it modeled in my Observation-Participation class and with my host teacher. A couple of times I'd hear her say, the children were trying to guess, like the word was habitat. And they were going (saying), 'home,' and she's going (saying), 'Close, that's a good idea it starts with the same letter.' Then she says, 'It's the same type of meaning, it's another word we had learned before.' And so those are the same types of things you'll hear me saying there too. So there I'm giving them praise. So, I want them to keep on participating." Helen, as another example, expressed a degree of uncertainty in using lexicon appropriately when she said, "Well, in one sense you could say it served as a cue for the other kids, but I don't think that was it in this situation. (laughter) I was really aware of their meeting my objective and moving along quite well with these two." Nevertheless, she felt comfortable taking the risk and strengthened her hold on the concept.

The third program standard, Making Meaning means pointing out connections between pre-service teachers' everyday understandings and professional concepts that show how the knowledge they are gaining can be used productively in a range of situations. Valuing knowledge from personal and family experiences, community life, as well as school supports learning of professional concepts. The low correspondence of Jane, Helen, and Claudia's rankings reveals the strength of practical knowledge and the need to specifically address its influence in professional learning. Helen provides an example when she says, "Yea, I think so, I really think it's one of those things that it's almost a natural. I think one of the differences, though, is that, like for instance, when Desiree gave me hers and she had a step missing, you know, that final (step), I think prior to some of the things I learned this year, I may have given it back and said, 'You're missing something, go back and finish it up.' But, it kind of lent itself at that time to say, 'Come on, Desiree, I know you can do this, just do it in your head, tell me what it is.' So it became a positive thing for her although she had left out one of my steps I had given her to do, you know. I knew and she knew that she could complete it without any embarrassment to her either." Helen initially described assisting the student through coaching and questioning as "natural," demonstrating the value she places on everyday learning, a value that schools do not share. Even though she gradually increased the precision of her analysis in her discussion, she continued to interpret the event using everyday concepts. In this example, the preservice teacher's everyday concepts provided adequate meaning for her to practice. To expand meaning beyond the constraints of everyday understanding the teacher education program endeavored to build professional knowledge on everyday knowledge. The strengths of everyday concepts for transforming thinking were realized when they were recognized, expressed, and scaffolded into professional concepts through program participation that expanded individuals' verbal and conceptual resources for understanding and expressing meaning.

Helen's example anticipates the fourth program standard, Teaching Complex Thinking. Her comments revealed that, in fact, she drew on more than her "natural" or spontaneous knowledge to relate to her student when she cited "some of the things I learned this year." When preservice teachers are called upon to frame and solve practical teaching and learning problems, everyday knowledge interfaces with professional concepts like cueing, praising, planning, ability, and others. Program activities that focus on these interactions promote acquisition of the profession's knowledge as professional concepts. Even though Helen ranked near the high lexicon and high concept users, she did not shift from everyday to professional concepts as facilely as her peers. Although analysis found a slightly positive Spearman Rank-Order Correlation Coefficient for tied ranks calculated at .4125, the relationship among lexicon and concepts could be stronger if made more conscious. For example, pre-service teachers know "praise" and "punishment" from everyday experience developed on the basis of everyday meaning and action. But in teaching, pre-service teachers must become less dependent on any specific meaning and more guided by their increasing understandings of the words as professional lexicon with expanded meanings. For example, Tina's host teacher provided her feedback that helped her consciously attend to a concept, explaining, Tina said, "Yes, every time I did a lesson with a large group, she'd give me feedback after about how I did and one thing I really had to work on was explaining. Being clear on what I say and making it concrete or using words they know instead of using words they know but don't really understand too well. So, (I'm) just making my instructions clear and easy for them to understand and going step by step slowly." Assuring pre-service teachers develop professional concepts is an opportunity for community members to seek and provide responsive assistance for one another. This also enacts the first standard, JPA, when development activities are the responsibility of all members of the community.

The fifth is Teaching Through Dialogue. In Instructional Conversation (IC), participants are guided to construct more complex understandings of a topic, text, problem, or other activity through professional discourse. IC occurred in many program venues with instructors and peers, peers alone, host/mentor teachers, in field placement cadres, grade levels and other arrangements. The conversational hook of IC is a tool for linking pre-service teachers' everyday concepts to more professional structures. It is an opportunity to engage academic discourse that models and encourages professional lexicon, and generates group norms of expression. IC is also about standards and values, work habits, and the meanings of the things we make and the way we make them. This means that not only content is learned in joint activity, but producing together teaches language, meaning, and values, in the context of immediate issues. In this way, communities invent and educate themselves in relation to their goals. Program coursework and field experience seminars characterized by IC can strengthen the effects of program on pre-service teachers.

Although the small sample size of this study limits the generalizability of its findings, the claims made based on the evidence discovered in the transcript analysis are relevant to the knowledge issues of preparing teachers, credible in terms of a systematic analysis, and have inferential force. The pedagogy standards provide a framework for examining this program's activities to determine if they are activity-based, dialogic, meaningful, and productive for acquiring professional lexicon and concepts. The study's findings reveal how formative are the effects of membership in this community of practice on the transformation of pre-service teachers' knowledge from everyday to professional structures that are applicable in teaching.

CONCLUSION

Teacher education is an agent not a catalyst for teacher preparation by providing the intellectual, academic, and practical knowledge and experiences necessary for professionally informed teaching. The findings of this study affirm that the relational and activity-based processes of teacher preparation that produce professionally knowledgeable, quality teachers depend on congruence in what the program teaches with what happens in K-12 classrooms. Pre-service teachers engage, enact, and reflect the context of their preparation through formal learning, but also through critical collegial relationships with a variety of mentors in the community of practice.

Too little is known about the verbal and cognitive effects of participation in teacher education, particularly as it is applied in teaching at the level of teacher education and in K-12 classrooms. If transition from everyday to professional concepts is a key feature of teacher preparation as discussed here, the trajectory of this process is important to study. Because the formation and use of professional concepts are conscious acts and subject to deliberate use, their acquisition can be accessed through self-report and reflective techniques. Although this study's findings suggested relationships in pre-service teachers lexicon and professional concept acquisition, each pre-service teacher displayed an idiosyncratic pattern of struggle and growth to transit from thinking based on personal and practical experience to understandings based on professional knowledge. Their advance toward professional thinking skills was not a uniform march. Rather, concepts developed irregularly and one by one according to the specific practical, social, and professional experiences of the individuals. Individuals' development is never uniform or responsive equally to similar social influences. Even in the small sample of this study one pre-service teacher was operating almost entirely on everyday concepts and practical experience. Others were striving to use professional concepts and even to reorganize them into thinking structures while another was an active architect and user of her own categorical systems of professional knowledge.

These findings describe how a community of practice scaffolds everyday knowledge to become professional knowledge. Analysis during acquisition, as Vygotsky's developmental theory suggests, reveals growth, struggle, assimilation, and frustration. Novices deserve adequate assistance that will avoid the experience of defeat and produce success from the outset, but if defeat occurs, it is a learning opportunity for individuals and the community of practice. A guiding framework such as the program standards applied in this discussion represents an ideal, not a template, that strives to fit local circumstances and respects unique features of individuals, schools, and communities. It is a structure for rousing teacher education to produce quality teachers for a nation in need of their professional service.

AUTHOR NOTE

This article was written by Stephanie Stoll Dalton in her private capacity. No official support or endorsement by the U. S. Department of Education is intended or should be inferred.

REFERENCES

Bransford, J.D., Brown, A.L., & Cocking, R.R. (Eds.). (1999). *How people learn: Brain, mind, experience, and school.* Washington, DC: National Academy Press.

Carter, K. (1990). Teachers' knowledge and learning to teach. In W. Houston (Ed.), *Handbook of research on teacher education* (pp. 291–310). New York: Macmillan.

Cobb, P., & Bowers, J. (1999, March). Cognitive and situated learning perspectives in theory and practice. *Educational Researcher, 28*(2), pp. 4–15.

Cochran-Smith, M. (1997). Knowledge, skills, and experience for teaching culturally diverse learners: A perspective for practicing teachers. In J.J. Irvine (Ed.), *Critical knowledge for diverse teachers and learners* (pp. 27–87). Washington, DC: AACTE Publications.

Cochran-Smith, M., & Lytle, S.L. (1999). Relationships of knowledge and practice: Teacher learning in communities. In *Review of research in education* (pp. 249–305). Washington, DC: American Educational Researchers Association.

Dalton, S.S. (1998). *Pedagogy matters* (Research Report #4). Santa Cruz, CA: Center for Research on Education, Diversity, and Excellence, University of California, Santa Cruz.

Dalton, S.S. (1989). *A multi-case comparative study of nine preservice teachers' thinking at the midpoint of their program of study.* Dissertation Information Service. Ann Arbor: University of Michigan.

Dalton, S.S., & Youpa, D.G. (1998, April). Standards-based teaching reform in Zuni Pueblo middle and high schools. *Equity and Excellence in Education,* 55–68.

Darling-Hammond, L. (1997). *Doing what matters most: Investing in quality teaching.* Report of the National Commission on Teaching & America's Future (NCTAF). New York: Teachers College, Columbia University.

Fenstermacher, G.D. (1994). The knower and the known: The nature of knowledge in research on teaching. In Review of research in education (Vol. 20, pp. 3–55). Washington, DC: American Educational Researchers Association.

Feinman-Nemser, S., & Buchmann, M. (1986). *When is student teaching teacher education?* Research Series No. 178. East Lansing: Michigan State University, Institute of Research on Teaching.

Fillmore, L.W., & Snow, C.E. (2000). *What teachers need to know about language.* Paper prepared for Center for Applied Linguistics (CAL), Washington, DC with funding from OERI, USDOED.

Grimmet, P.P., & Mackinnon, A.M. (1992). Craft knowledge and the education of teachers. In G. Grant (Ed.), *Review of research in education* (pp. 385–456). Washington, DC: American Educational Researchers Association.

Kennedy, M.M. (1987). Inexact science: Professional education and the development of expertise. In *Review of research in education* (Vol. 14, pp. 133–167). Washington, DC: American Educational Researchers Association.

Ladson-Billings, G.J. (1999). Preparing teachers for diverse student populatons: A critical race theory perspective. In *Review of research in education* (Vol. 24, pp. 211–247). Washington, DC: American Educational Researchers Association.

McLaughlin, M.W., & Shepard, L.A. (1995). *Improving education through standards-based reform.* A report by the National Academy of Education Panel on Standards-Based Education Reform. Palo Alto, CA: Stanford University.

Moll, L.C. (Ed). (1990). *Vygotsky and education: Instructional implications and applications of sociohistorical psychology.* New York: Cambridge University Press.

Panofsky, C.P., John-Steiner, V., & Blackwell, P.J. (1990). The development of scientific concepts and discourse. In L. Moll (Ed.), *Vygotsky and education: Instructional implications and applications of sociohistorical psychology* (pp. 251–267). New York: Cambridge University Press.

Picard, A.J., & Young, D.B. (1990, September). Methods: Teaching and learning principles. *The Kamehameha Journal of Education, 1,* 12–23.

Putnam, R.T., & Borko, H. (2000, January-February). What do new views of knowledge and thinking have to say about research on teacher learning? *Educational Researcher*, 4–15.

Rueda, R. (1998). *Standards for professional development: A sociocultural perspective* (Research Brief #2). Santa Cruz: Center for Research on Education, Diversity, and Excellence, University of California, Santa Cruz.

Shulman, L.S. (1987). Knowledge and teaching: Foundations of the new reform. *Harvard Educational Review, 57*, 114–135.

Tharp, R.G. (1982). The effective instruction of comprehension: Results and description of the Kamehameha Early Education Program. *Reading Research Quarterly, 17*(4), 503–527.

Tharp, R.G., Estrada, P., Dalton, S.S., & Yamauchi, L. (2000). *Teaching transformed: Achieving excellence, fairness, inclusion, harmony.* Denver, CO: Westview Press.

Tharp, R.G., & Gallimore, R. (1988). *Rousing minds to life: Teaching, learning, schooling in social context.* New York: Cambridge University Press.

Tom, A., & Valli, L. (1990). Professional knowledge for teachers. In W. Houston (Ed.), *Handbook of research on teacher education* (pp. 373–392). New York: Macmillan.

Vygotsky, L. (1978). *Mind in society.* Cambridge, MA: Harvard University Press.

Webb, N.M., Troper, J.D., & Fall, R. (1995). Constructive activity and learning in collaborative small groups. *Journal of Educational Psychology, 87* (3), 406–423.

Wertsch, J.V. (1985). *Culture, communication, and cognition: Vygotskian perspectives.* New York: Cambridge University Press.

Wittrock, M.C. (Ed.). (1986). *Handbook of research on teaching* (3rd ed.). New York: Macmillan.

Wong-Fillmore, L.W., & Snow, C.E. (2000). *What teachers need to know about language.* Paper funded by OERI under a contract to Center for Applied Linguistics, Washington, DC.

Zeichner, K. (1999, December). The new scholarship in teacher education. *Educational Researcher*, 4–15.

Zeichner, K., & Tabachnick, B. (1985). The development of teacher perspectives: Social strategies and institutional control in the socialization of beginning teachers. *Journal of Education for Teachers, 11*, 1–25.

Part II

TEACHER TRAINING AND SCHOOL REFORM

CHAPTER 5

TRENDS IN STAFF DEVELOPMENT FOR BILINGUAL TEACHERS

Margarita Calderón

ABSTRACT

This chapter addresses the type of staff development practices in a variety of school/district contexts. It illustrates the level of commitment, or lack of, to the ongoing professional development of teachers working with language minority students.

Methodology: As part of a five-year study, this national survey focuses on beliefs, experiences and professional needs of teachers on the job. One hundred teachers participated in written and telephone surveys. The questions centered on 5 themes: type of staff development experiences and their value to the teachers; teachers use, confidence, and appropriation of linguistic and cross-cultural skills for bilingual instruction; teachers' knowledge of research-based instruction; the status of primary language and bilingual program at their school; the type of collegial practices, relationships, and support systems at the school/district.

Results: The range of professional development opportunities is presented, as well as their perceived value. Patterns indicate that certain comprehensive school reform models, two-way whole-school programs, and trainer of trainers' institutes provide more comprehensive approaches and follow-up support systems to help teachers transfer new knowledge and skills into the classroom, and satisfy individual needs. Implications for program developers will be discussed.

INTRODUCTION

Latino student populations in public schools are steadily increasing. In order to help teachers better respond to the strengths and challenges of all Latino students, it is critically important to reform teacher preparation programs and in-service professional development approaches. Universities and school districts simply assume teachers' bilingual proficiency because the teacher went through a bilingual program. While much of the lack of preparation of bilingual teachers stems from their university experiences, staff development practices in school districts are often no more helpful. Essentially, universities and school districts disempower bilingual teachers, forcing them to struggle on their own to find ways of closing the gaps left by their preparation programs. If students are to succeed in bilingual programs, their teachers must first succeed. Appropriate professional development practices, adequate time commitments, and supportive funding are critical to ensure this success.

Without changing the traditional forms of 'doing staff development,' education reform in schools with language minority students will rarely be successful. The level of a teacher's bilingual skills, and use of those skills, improves, stagnates, or diminishes in the context of staff development. Staff development practices in a school or school district either perpetuate inequalities or create contexts for effective practice. August and Hakuta (1997) found that while various studies indicated the need for well-trained teachers for English language learners, we have not studied how best to train these teachers. Although numerous articles are written on bilingual teacher preparation each year, fewer studies have been conducted to identify the professional needs and wants of bilingual teachers. We know little about what they think about their ongoing staff development programs. We know less about the collective quality of their yearly professional development activities. This chapter reports on the preliminary findings from a longitudinal study on bilingual/ESL teacher development. This portion of the study examined beliefs, experiences, and professional needs of bilingual/ESL teachers in various school settings and working with different instructional models.

METHODOLOGY

The data collected for this update on staff development was conducted over an 18-month period, as part of a larger five-year study. The data for the first stage consisted of surveys, interviews, informal conversations at staff development events, and observations as participants-observers-trainers in various regions. Workshop agendas, evaluations, training materials, and similar artifacts were also analyzed.

Participants in the Study

One hundred elementary bilingual certified teachers participated in the study. Sixty-five bilingual teachers completed the formal surveys and 35 were interviewed. This is a sample from the states of New York, Massachusetts, Virginia, District of Columbia, Philadelphia, Illinois, Texas, New Mexico, Arizona, California, and Hawaii. Ten of the teachers were currently teaching only in English due to program mandates, but all others were teaching in either transitional, developmental/dual language, or two-way bilingual programs. Their instructional models ranged from a district prescribed basal reader, reading programs only in the primary grades such as Open Court or Reading Recovery, to comprehensive school reform (CSR) models such as Accelerated Schools, Success for All/Éxito Para Todos, and five other emerging comprehensive school designs that were still in development.

Context of the Study

The context of the school and type of bilingual program were considered in order to see where and how context might impact on the responses of the teachers. Cohorts 1 and 2 comprised one-fourth of the teachers in either ESL, transitional bilingual, or programs that were loosely structured, or schools that had bilingual teachers in only two-to-three classrooms. Cohorts 3–5 comprised three fourths of the teachers who were participating in comprehensive whole-school reform programs. The comprehensive school reform schools had either two-way immersion, transitional, and developmental bilingual programs. There were 8 teachers from two-way bilingual charter schools. The rest were from public schools. There were 10 trainer of trainers participants from transitional and two-way immersion programs/schools. The trainer of trainers group comprised 10 exemplary teachers who were selected by their county offices of education as trainers of teachers of English Language Learners (ELL).

Typology of School Contexts for the Teachers in the Study

Type of Bilingual Program in the Teacher's School	Number of Teachers in the Study
1. ESL only program	10
2. Transitional bilingual program; undefined program; small number of bilingual classrooms	14
3. Whole-school comprehensive reform model	45
4. Whole-school two-way bilingual programs	21
5. Trainer of trainers program to adapt standards	10
Total Participants	100

Data Collection

The questions in the surveys and interviews focused on five categories or themes:

A. Teachers use, confidence, and appropriation of linguistic and cross-cultural skills for bilingual instruction.
    1. How teachers use Spanish and English; for what content; amount of time for each language; separately or at the same time; preview-review; translation, etc.
    2. How teachers perceived their oral, reading, writing, and teaching skills in general, in Spanish and English.
B. Teachers' views and experiences with staff development programs.
    1. The types of staff development experiences (content and process) that teachers had encountered in the past two years;
    2. What they found as the most useful learning experiences; and
    3. What they found as the least useful learning experiences.
C. Their knowledge of research-based instruction.
    1. What theories, methods, approaches they used for teaching English as a Second Language, reading, writing, and content in English.
    2. What theories, methods, approaches they used for teaching oral language development, literacy and content in Spanish.
D. The status of their students' primary language and beliefs about the bilingual program at the school.
    1. How teachers perceived the students' primary language and its place in the curriculum.
    2. How teachers advocated or acquiesced to institutional demands on language use.
    3. How teachers perceived their own identity, cultural heritage and cultural experiences.

E. The type of collegial practices, relationships, and support systems at the school.
  1. How teachers worked and related with teachers in the bilingual program.
  2. How teachers worked and related with teachers outside the bilingual program.
  3. Opportunities for collegial activities in the school.
  4. Opportunities for teachers' learning communities.
  5. Type of support systems.

Data from the surveys and the transcription of the interviews were analyzed using qualitative analysis techniques described by Silverman (1997) and Holstein and Gubrium (1997). The techniques involved systematic data coding, grouping or summarizing the descriptions provided by the teachers, and providing a framework for explaining aspects of the social world of bilingual teachers across multiple school contexts.

The participation of some of the researchers as trainers in several of these regions enabled them to add a broader perspective to the teachers' situations. During the training, comments from teachers that related to staff development were recorded, and evaluation forms were carefully analyzed for relevant commentaries. While setting up the training sessions and dealing with the schools' and districts' administrators, the researchers were able to learn more about the support or lack of support systems for the teachers. In one fourth of the cases, we were also able to observe the teachers in their classrooms, thus adding a third dimension to the data. In one fourth of the cases, data on student achievement were also available. This chapter reports on the main themes that were found for the 5 categories of questions.

RESULTS

The results were clustered around the themes (1) Appropriation of Bilingual Skills; (2) Bilingual/ESL Teachers' Staff Development Experiences; (3) Bilingual/ESL Teachers' Knowledge of Research-Based Instruction; (4) Bilingual Teachers' Advocacy or Acquiescence to Bilingual Issues; and (5) Opportunities for Collegial Practices and Support Systems for Bilingual/ESL teachers.

Major Themes About Teachers' Appropriation of Bilingual Skills

Bilingual Skills

Bilingual teachers recognize the need to continue to upgrade their bilingual skills. The teachers were asked to list and prioritize what they perceived as their greatest staff development needs dealing with their bilingual skills. The most frequently mentioned needs are listed in Table 2.

Response categories	*% of teachers*
1. How to improve my skills in Spanish	90%
2. Knowledge and teaching strategies for reading in Spanish	85%
3. Knowledge and teaching strategies for reading in English.	80%
4. Knowledge and teaching strategies for writing in English.	65%
5. Proficiency in Spanish for teaching grammar and content.	60%
6. How to deal with the low status of the bilingual program in the school.	55%
7. When and how to use Spanish effectively (time frames, when to translate, etc.)	50%
8. How to help students transition from Spanish into English.	45%
9. How to diagnose and assess students.	30%
10. How to teach math more effectively in Spanish and English.	25%

The typology of schools did not have any bearing on these responses. Even teachers in whole-school reform or in two-way bilingual programs expressed the same concerns in basically the same order of priority. For example, all teachers said they would welcome more workshops in Spanish, even if once in a while. More than 90% of the teachers checked "needs improvement in Spanish" on their survey. During the interviews, most teachers avoided the issue at first, but gradually began to offer examples of their limitations with the students' primary language. For example: "I'm afraid to elicit higher order discussions in Spanish because I don't know enough vocabulary." "If it's not in the manual, I'm afraid to ask questions in Spanish." "We don't have math books in Spanish, so we use key terms in English and I let the students explain to the other students."

The observations in more than one third of the participants' classrooms overwhelmingly revealed a gamut of spelling and grammatical errors in the teachers' and students' work that was posted, and in the teachers' delivery. Simple phrases on the board or charts with instructions for the students contained spelling errors and lacked accents for the most part.

Thirty-five percent of the bilingual teachers expressed that they still prefer teachers' manuals, basals, and materials that are in both English and

Spanish for their own benefit. Some still need to resort to the English portion of the manual to understand the Spanish, and need to have the Spanish scripted in order to use the "appropriate Spanish." Sixty-five percent preferred materials/teachers' manuals all in Spanish. In five-day sessions that we have offered on teaching reading in Spanish, teachers overwhelmingly mention that what they learned and liked best was using "correct Spanish" for an extended period of time.

The national controversy about which is the 'appropriate Spanish' is quite prevalent (e.g., Puerto Rican, Mexican, South American, TexMex, and other regional versions were mentioned as not being appropriate). Each region is still quite ethnocentric about its dialect, and complains about improper examples in their texts or their trainers' dialects. As classrooms become more heterogeneous in Spanish variations, teachers will need to learn, accept and acknowledge those variations. Teachers must also learn the variations with their students. Several teachers said they would welcome glossaries of dialectical differences and regionalisms.

Time on Each Language of Instruction

Time spent on Spanish instruction varied considerably. Responses ranged from 5% to 90% of the day. The average was 30%. Most teachers reported that they were not certain, but they offered a percentage anyway. However, it is difficult to ascertain that these percentages reflect the actual amount, except where we visited their classrooms for systematic observations. In an earlier study, observations confirmed that bilingual teachers in two-way bilingual programs were off by at least 15–20%. In a 50–50% program, the actual total for a week averaged 65–35% (65% English and 35% Spanish) (Calderón & Carreón, 2000). The issue of time on language will be examined further in years 3 and 4 of this study.

Strategies for Dual Language Instruction

There was no clear tendency toward strategies for dual language use, and findings were similar to those reported previously by other researchers and practitioners. Teachers reported using the following strategies:

1. Preview-review methods for introducing a story, content lessons and/or content texts.
2. Translation when introducing new concepts, when it's faster than trying to explain in English, or when a new student joins the class for the first week or so.
3. Kept two languages separate by team teaching, or by teaching in one language in the morning and the other in the afternoon, and/ or teaching certain content area such as science in one language and another subject in the other language.

English was used mostly for reading, writing, and oral language development. Oral language development in Spanish was not mentioned except by the Success for All/Éxito Para Todos teachers. Cohorts 1–2 mainly taught math in English and social studies in Spanish. Cohorts 3–5 mainly taught math in Spanish ("because there is a lot of problem solving and reading") and science and social studies in English ("because it is more hands-on and I usually read the text to the students"). More classroom observations will be conducted to study these trends further.

Major Themes About Bilingual Teachers' Staff Development Experiences

The Prevalent Content of Staff Development Practices

Prevalent types of staff development for bilingual teachers were basically the same across schools and across the country in both content and process. The prevalent content for in-service workshops fell into six categories, with number 1 being the one most frequently mentioned (see Table 3).

Most frequent responses	*% of teachers*
1. Teaching reading in English and Spanish.	95%
2. Adapting ESL techniques with the current school reform model.	65%
3. Adapting/translating into Spanish the current school reform curriculum.	60%
4. Teaching math in English and Spanish.	55%
5. Teaching writing in English and Spanish.	30%
6. Adapting standards to ESL or bilingual instruction.	25%

The fifty-five teachers involved in comprehensive school reform models reported items #1, #2, #3, and #4 as the staff development content for the year. The twenty-one teachers involved in adapting state standards for ESL or Spanish instruction and training other teachers mentioned mainly #6, #1, and #5.

The remainder of the twenty-four teachers were participating in district programs that offered a variety of topics through two-hour, four-hour, or one-day workshops. These teachers were from schools with transitional, ESL or undefined bilingual programs. The number of bilingual teachers in the school was usually small. The categories listed in Table 4 were the most frequently cited by these teachers.

Topics on one-time workshops	*Percent of teachers participating in those workshops*
Test-taking strategies for reading.	50%
Test-taking strategies for math.	49%
How to use a recently adopted basal reader.	15%
Strategies for teaching sheltered English content areas.	15%
Teaching reading in Spanish (however, all workshops were conducted in English).	10%
Classroom management.	10%
Discipline techniques.	9%
Strategies for teaching reading.	5%

Thus, the teachers from cohorts 1–2, and about 25% from cohorts 3–5 mentioned test-taking as one of the yearly workshop topics. The lower the ranking of the school, the more staff development days that were spent on test-taking preparation. Does this mean that instead of upgrading the skills of teachers, some schools would rather invest in ways to pass the test?

The comparison of trends for these 2 cohorts of teachers begins to show a tendency toward polarization of staff development practices. At one end of the spectrum, more than 75% of the teachers mentioned topics relevant to whole-school reform and that lend themselves to profound study or at least continuous learning. At the other end, the teachers mentioned topics that do not necessarily lend themselves to ongoing learning. As the trend toward whole-school reform continues, the content of bilingual teacher training practices will need to keep up with such demands rather than focus on superficial topics.

The Prevalent Process of Staff Development

The process for staff development also seemed divided between the staff development programs for teachers participating in reform models and adaptation of standards with traditional bilingual schools. The staff development program for the twenty-four teachers in cohorts 1 and 2 consisted mainly of one-day workshops spread throughout the year on different topics. The topics were selected by a cross-section of teachers, or a teacher staff development committee, which had to try to please all the teachers in the school as they filled those 5 days with topics. Teachers were not afforded the opportunity to follow a line of study or inquiry such as "reading in English and Spanish" throughout the whole year.

At the positive end of the continuum, the teachers who were being trained as trainers on topics such as Standards for English Language Development participated in one or two-week summer institutes, followed by 5 or more days of training throughout the year, with collegial activities between the training sessions. Sessions on peer coaching and teachers' learning communities were interspersed throughout the year, and they were asked to keep logs of their collegial activities and present their successes and challenges three to four times a year to their regional learning community.

The teachers involved in school-wide reform models had similar intensive opportunities for professional development. Bilingual teachers participating in Success for All/Éxito Para Todos schools reported the most days of staff development, follow-up activities, implementation visits by trainers, and collegial structures than those participating in any of the other reform models. SFA teachers reported more differentiated types of staff development. The kindergarten teachers received training and materials relevant to their grade level; first grade teachers for theirs, tutors for their tutoring, and so on. Some schools provided training in Spanish for the bilingual teachers. Others did not and the teachers expressed dissatisfaction for this omission. In contrast, non-SFA teachers participated in workshops where K-5th grade teachers received the same generic training and materials. SFA principals and school facilitators attended the teachers' as well as their own one-week institute. Three yearly one-week SFA conferences convened schools across the nation for updates, reviews, and networking.

Teachers' Likes and Dislikes About Staff Development

In general, all 100 bilingual teachers in the study found the following experiences most useful:

1. Modeling/demonstrations by experts. (95%)
2. Materials appropriate to each grade level. (95%)
3. Opportunity to observe other teachers using the same model. (80%)
4. Feedback from experts on the strategy/model. (70%)
5. Opportunity to work with peers to adapt the strategies to their students. (60%)
6. Implementation visits ("kept us on our toes"). (35%)

The least useful experiences were:

1. The two-hour workshops on different topics. (100%)
2. Having to adapt presentations to ESL or translate into Spanish for classroom use. (90%)
3. No opportunity to share with colleagues (80%)
4. No follow-up visits or more training. (60%)
5. The workshops were not in Spanish. (60%)
6. Content of workshops selected by someone else. (25%)

Some teachers particularly disliked the disjointed workshop offerings. They complained that a speaker would be brought in to present a particular approach to reading one month, only to be followed by another presenter who expounded opposite views, and discounted everything they had attempted to do up to that time. Some teachers found ways to subvert attending workshops, staying in their classrooms to plan their own lessons. If they had to attend, they brought papers to grade or mentally prepared their lessons or dealt with other personal concerns.

There seemed to be two prevalent extremes of staff development opportunities for the 100 teachers of English Language Learners. At one end of the extreme, there are still many schools, districts, CSR model developers, and even state departments that offer workshops in what we will call the "traditional" way. At the other extreme, there are emergent teacher-relevant practices that need more study to determine their effectiveness. Table 5 contrasts some of the basic elements that were synthesized from this preliminary study.

Summary of Staff Development Practices

Traditional Staff Development	Teacher-Centered Staff Development
1. A series of one-shot workshops on "the fad of the moment" or the "guru of the day."	1. A series of workshops on connected research-based practices.
2. Professional development that separates bilingual from mainstream teachers.	2. Professional development that includes bilingual and mainstream teachers.
3. No learning communities after the workshops for reflection and adaptation.	3. Teachers create contexts for self-analyses of own teaching, adaptation to students, and their impact on student success.
4. Focus on "bag of tricks" for Monday morning.	4. Focus on profound learning of a topic (e.g. reading) through theory, demonstrations, practice, and feedback.
5. Typically transmission models rather than constructivist	5. Teachers co-construct knowledge in collegial learning communities.
6. Ignore diversity of teachers' needs.	6. Incorporates a differentiated approach to meet individual teachers' needs.
7. Ignore context and diversity of classrooms.	7. The social context, languages, culture, and diversity of the classrooms are part of any workshop content.
8. Offer minimal support to teachers.	8. Teachers work with program trainers, facilitators, expert coaches, peer coaches, and researchers.
9. The impact of staff development on teachers and students is not measured.	9. Quantitative and qualitative data is used to measure the transfer from training into the classrooms and the impact on students and teachers.

Major Themes about Teachers' Knowledge of Research-Based Instruction

Research-based Instructional Repertoire

Although more research is currently being conduced on various aspects of bilingual instruction (August & Hakuta, 1997; August, Carlo & Calderón, 2000; Center for Research on Education, Diversity, and Excellence [CREDE] publications; Center for Research on the Education of Students Placed at Risk [CRESPAR] publications; Center for Applied Linguistics [CAL] publications) and on Latino students in particular (Slavin & Calderón, 2001), more than 65% of the teachers representing all the school typologies felt that researchers' work rarely filters into their staff development programs. However, the majority of the teachers involved in the trainer of trainers' institutes rated themselves on the high end of this category. They were able to cite and allude to a variety of approaches, name researchers in each field, and their work. Teachers involved in comprehensive school reform (CSR) models were able to cite few references outside the model they were currently implementing. Most were not able to cite the research undergirding their particular CSR model nor why this model was more effective than others.

Teachers in cohorts 1 and 2 described their programs as archaic. They still taught in a separate sequential order: listening first, then speaking, and once there was sufficient oral language, students began reading, and eventually writing. This long linear sequence was felt to be neither efficient nor effective. Students were "kept too long" on "isolated insignificant activities" that "wasted their valuable time."

Diagnosis, Assessment and Placement of Students

Teachers in cohorts 1 and 2 felt that diagnosis and assessments were not being used appropriately. Although their school districts complied with state mandates for assessing language proficiency through popular assessment instruments, they never finished this process on time for placing students into appropriate instruction. Assessment was rarely used to mediate and improve instruction, much less to assess each student on a systematic basis.

The majority of teachers in the SFA schools were satisfied with the assessment and placement of students. They also liked the fact that the issue of time and language use had been determined by the program. Only two teachers disliked "being dictated to" but "were willing to put up with that" because they could see "the benefits for the students."

The majority of teachers in the less structured CSR models liked their freedom to teach the way they wanted. However, they voiced more complaints about the following:

- too much work (100%)
- ineffective assessments and student tracking (90%),
- the lack of materials in both languages (60%),
- lack of direction for the bilingual program (60%), and too much accountability (90%).

Student progress was mainly measured by the state standardized tests or the language proficiency tests. Teachers were very concerned with the uncertainty of their students' ability to succeed in middle and high school levels.

Major Themes about Teachers' Advocacy or Acquiescence to Bilingual Issues

Views About Bilingual Education

There was a range of philosophies on bilingualism reported by the teachers. Their views about bilingual education were usually accompanied by emotional incidents from their own past experiences. Teachers whose first language was Spanish related the traumas they faced in schools as they were learning English or when they were forbidden to use their mother tongue. Some teachers said that these experiences helped to make them more sensitive to their students' ordeals. Others said that they lost their "pride in speaking Spanish" and never recuperated.

Seventy-five percent of native English speakers from Hispanic and non-Hispanic backgrounds expressed more frequently the issue of "placing ELLs into English as quickly as possible." They also felt uncomfortable expressing their views about bilingual education. Most had opted to teach in ESL/sheltered English programs even though they spoke "some" or "sufficient" Spanish to teach in bilingual programs.

Sense of Disempowerment

Teachers also felt that status quo staff development practices perpetuated their disempowerment. Staff development also defined the limited roles of bilingual teachers in the schools. This was particularly evident by the absence of the language of school change and collaborative learning in the teachers' responses. The teachers decision-making power, or lack thereof, was also evident in the type of bilingual program their school implemented.

- The teachers participating in two-way bilingual programs rated themselves high on the advocacy end of the continuum.
- Teachers in undefined bilingual programs or in schools with few ESL or bilingual teachers felt they had no power to advocate for bilingualism, and limited power to advocate for their students.

Sixty teachers believed that the sooner their students transitioned into English, the better they could be prepared to pass the state tests. If a school had selected a bilingual version of a comprehensive model, the teachers felt comfortable letting their students progress in both languages. These teachers also felt that their students were benefitting from bilingual education, even if they didn't like that model. When the schools selected a model that was available only in English, bilingual teachers felt relegated to a passive and hopeless role. They "knew that there was no way to change things." When the program was missing materials in Spanish, teachers felt as "second-class citizens" in the school and were looking for ways to subvert the implementation of that model.

Major Themes about Teachers' Opportunities for Collegial Practices and Support Systems

Not surprisingly, the themes around collegial opportunities and support systems also went hand-in-hand with the typology of schools. Teachers in the ESL, undefined and transitional programs reported fewer opportunities for collegial activities than the other cohorts.

Separate and Not Equal

Some of the comments on the issues of collegiality and support systems reflected the abyss that is created between bilingual and mainstream teachers. Except for school-wide meetings and test-taking sessions, bilingual teachers were usually separated from the mainstream for most staff development activities. This separation generated negative consequences, as voiced by the bilingual teachers:

1. Mainstream teachers developed misconceptions about the bilingual program.
2. Bilingual teachers are treated as second-class citizens.
3. The transition of students from bilingual to mainstream classrooms is too abrupt and detrimental.
4. There are few opportunities for bilingual and mainstream teachers to discuss, plan, and address the needs of individual students after their transition.
5. Mainstream teachers always blame the bilingual teachers if a student does not do well after transition.
6. Each year there are "silent and not so silent battles" over resources between bilingual and mainstream teachers.

7. Mainstream and bilingual teachers are rarely satisfied with the compromises they have to make on obligatory staff development selections.
8. The Title VII office offers workshops that teachers feel they do not need.
9. There are no funds for teachers to construct their own staff development programs.
10. Teachers enjoy going to conferences, but feel that they are not learning anything new; that it is always the same presenters giving the same speeches.

Learning Communities

Only two ESL teachers discussed the concept of teachers' learning communities, but added that they missed their former relationships with bilingual teachers. When we probed further, the two teachers admitted that while the district espoused a philosophy of collegial work, the concept did not materialize at the school level.

Collegiality

Teachers in whole school two-way bilingual programs were more satisfied with their collegial opportunities than teachers in schools with only some classes with two-way bilingual instruction. Whole-school two-way bilingual programs engendered more collegial relationships simply because of the nature of the innovation and the whole-school effort. The teachers acknowledged that they did not know everything there was to know, and had a need to collectively make their program work. There was also a sense of pride in their efforts. They felt that their program was "better than the one down the road" or the ones they had visited. Unfortunately, this pride can also lead to blind love. When researchers suggested in two schools that their students could be reading at a higher level in their third grade classrooms, the teachers were not willing to accept recommendations. The principals later verified that their students' reading scores were below the norm in the district.

Two-way bilingual charter school teachers are particularly bound by collegial norms and joint activity. The relationships are tighter and they spread out to the community and the parents. The teacher-parent partnership becomes more of a peer relationship that is often missing in the traditional public schools. Two-way bilingual programs in charter schools reach out to the Latino culture with more genuine involvement and relationship-building.

Conflict and Tension

Seventy-two teachers mentioned that tensions or conflicts existed in their schools because of language, culture, and racial issues. These ranged from minor squabbles to racial tension and prejudice at the teacher level. Teachers expressed a lack of leadership and direction to solve these workplace tensions. None of the staff development programs set out to deliberately address these issues.

DISCUSSION AND IMPLICATIONS

This preliminary phase of the study has raised questions about the interface of staff development and bilingual programs that require further study. It also seems clear that the trends toward whole-school reform, and whole-school programs that address the needs of the ever-growing Latino population, require a different approach to staff development. It became apparent that the professional development of bilingual teachers is definitely impacted by the context of the school and the type of bilingual program in the school.

Bilingual Proficiency and Teaching Efficacy

The teachers overwhelmingly reported the need for staff development to improve their skills in Spanish and English for delivering instruction in all subject areas. They also wanted guidance from research-based practices on how and when to use each language in the context of their specific programs.

"Bilingual education can be defined generically as education involving two languages as media of instruction. As with many such labels, however, the literal meaning of the component words tells only part of the story" (Christian & Genesee, 2001, p. 1). The term "bilingual teachers" also fails to capture the variety of bilingual and biliterate proficiencies of each teacher. In terms of practice, a bilingual teacher's or bilingual instructional assistant's use of Spanish and English is also a reflection of the school community's beliefs about bilingual education and Latino students. If reductionist bilingual programs exist even in schools with large numbers of bilingual teachers, are bilingual teachers prepared to exert influence and change such a context? Can bilingual teachers take a more active role in changing beliefs and orchestrating bilingual school reform? Without the school administrators', the district's, and state department's support, it is very doubtful.

The diversity of bilingual teacher background and preparation affects the continuity of effective programs in all grade levels. Research informs us that if a student does not learn to read in the first grade, she or he may experience a downward spiral effect the rest of his/her elementary grades (Slavin, 1993). While there can be excellent speakers of Spanish as role models for students in kindergarten and second grade, a limited Spanish-speaking teacher in first grade can delay the students' reading progress for a whole year. If the kindergarten teacher is not comfortable teaching in Spanish, that will certainly impact the pre-literacy and oral language development that is so critical to reading success in the first grade. If fourth and fifth grade teachers do not feel competent to teach higher level literature pieces or science and social studies concepts in Spanish, will that continue to be the deciding factor to stop bilingual programs at third grade?

Bilingual teaching is a craft. This implies that successful bilingual teaching is where bilingual students are achieving successfully in school and becoming proficient in two languages. Bilingual teaching is also the process of building communities of learners for their students. Because bilingual instruction is such a young science, bilingual teachers must continuously read and integrate research-based instructional strategies into their teaching repertoire. They need to form collegial teams to support and learn from each other. The must practice together, solve problems, analyze their teaching in the context of individual student success, and inspire one another. Schools with English Language Learners are now expected not only to offer equal education but also to ensure learning. Teachers are expected not only to 'cover curriculum' but also to create a bridge between the linguistic and sociocultural needs of each learner, and most of all to ensure that ELL students do well on state tests in either English or Spanish. Ironically, in Texas, where the test used for accountability can be offered in either English or Spanish, the ELL students often cannot pass the tests in Spanish. Is this a reflection of the lack of practice and preparation of their teachers?

Research-Based Teaching and Learning

Teachers report a dire need to enhance their knowledge-base with research and effective practice. A growing body of research is clarifying the true nature of teaching and learning, and how best to accomplish this for adults and children. Teaching well means helping students learn well. Teaching can make a big difference to students when there is evidence that the instructional models work. One of the most important contributions by research is the attempt to learn how much difference it makes to personal, social, and academic growth if we use one teaching strategy rather than another (Joyce et al., 1992). By repeatedly computing the sizes of differences in effect sizes between control and experimental groups, one can determine the effectiveness of various teaching and curricular procedures (Glass, 1982; Joyce et al., 1992; Slavin, 1999). However, these types of studies in bilingual schools are very rare. In fact, only 3 such studies were found to exist, after an extensive review by the National Research Institute (August & Hakuta, 1997) and other researchers (Fashola et al., 1996, 2001). The lack of research-proven instructional approaches for bilingual settings clearly implies that the content of bilingual staff development all these years has lacked evidence of effectiveness. Empirical research and evidence of the relationship between proposed attributes of effective bilingual teaching and student learning also needs further research (August & Hakuta, 1997; Grant & Secada, 1990; Minaya-Rowe, 1990).

The wide gap in achievement between language minority and non-language minority students attests to the fact that bilingual/ESL instructional practices are not having much of an impact. Clearly school reform must change the routine practices that are not working. As schools, teachers, and administrators select instructional models, they must first ask for the evidence that a model works. Then, the whole school must set out to train all teachers extensively on that model, and ensure fidelity in its implementation.

Transfer from Training

Over half of the teachers reported that their professional development activities were not facilitating transfer. Transfer refers to the effect of learning instructional skill(s) in a training setting and the ability to apply or adapt that skill to improve the learning of a teacher's students. The transfer of training into the actual classroom and its impact on the students has also been studied and documented (Joyce & Showers, 1982; Sharan & Hertz-Lazarowitz, 1982; Calderón, 1984; Hertz-Lazarowitz & Calderón, 1994; Calderón, Hertz-Lazarowitz & Slavin, 1998; Calderón & Carreón, 2001; Slavin & Madden, 2001).

Transfer and mastery of new bilingual instructional skills consists of understanding the purpose and rationale of an instructional model or approach, knowing how to adapt it to students, applying it to subject matter; modifying or creating correlated instructional materials; organizing and teaching students how to use it; integrating cultural adaptations, and being proficient in both languages to impart content and process. Transfer can be an easy or a difficult endeavor depending on the prior knowledge and skills of a teacher. The greater the degree to which a new skill fits into already familiar patterns, the less adjustment is needed. However, when a teacher has more skills to develop and more adjustments to make in order to be able to use the skill effectively, more time and support will be needed. That teacher will also experience a greater level of discomfort. The discomfort might manifest as opposition to the new instructional model or a quiet subversion of it behind closed doors.

In earlier empirical studies on teacher transfer, a group of 50 bilingual teachers attended year-long training sessions on complex models of teaching (Inquiry Model, Group Investigation, and other complex models that were adapted to English language learners or conducted in Spanish). During the training sessions bilingual teachers learned theory and watched experts demonstrate the models while they experienced them as students. After 5 days of training, the 50 teachers were randomly assigned to an experimental and control group. As follow up to the training, the experimental teachers saw the demonstrations 15 to 20 additional times, took home videos to study them further, and practiced about 10 times with expert feedback. They also observed their peers and reflected and debriefed their observations. They met in their learning communities once every two weeks for 90 minutes, and later in the year began teaching new teachers the models. Part of the researchers' role was to work with administrators to ensure that the experimental teachers were adequately supported during the follow-up implementation phase. In contrast, the control teachers were left on their own device after the training sessions. They took the videotapes home, but they did not attend the follow-up demonstrations, practice sessions, learning communities, nor participated in the peer-coaching observations. While both experimental and control teachers felt high levels of discomfort during the first four months, only the experimental teachers continued using the new strategies effectively throughout the year. The control teachers went back to their "old way of teaching" giving many reasons such as: it was much more comfortable, their students liked it better, there were no materials for that, it didn't teach to the test. The effect sizes between students in the experimental and control were between .75 and 1.2 in all these studies (Calderon, 1984; Hertz-Lazarowitz & Calderón, 1994; Calderon & Carreón, 2001).

In essence, what we learned from the studies of teacher transfer is that in order to help a teacher become a competent learner, one must carefully orchestrate a comprehensive staff development program, teachers' learning communities, and help administrators create a support system for teachers. The training content must be research-based and the process must involve extensive time commitment. The context of the training must be one where learning is exciting, and where the needs of individual teachers are addressed. Some teachers needed assistance with classroom management, others needed the "language of inquiry" in Spanish, still others only needed constant reassurance that they were doing it right. A differentiated approach is necessary for adult learners just as it is for children. A variety of staff development strategies and techniques emerged from those studies. Those have been widely disseminated through journal publications, newsletters, conference presentations, and trainer of trainers institutes. Nevertheless, most staff development programs throughout the country still consist of 3–5 days of in-service workshops on disjointed topics or attendance at conferences where teachers are exposed to new ideas without follow-up implementation support. When funds are scarce, the staff development funds are the first to be cut. Time is rarely allocated during the workday for teachers' learning communities. When it is, many other agendas are dealt with instead of genuine collegial learning.

The existence of well-researched and well-evaluated programs creates an unprecedented opportunity to have direct impact on bilingual education, as long as teachers are provided with quality professional development programs.

Staff Development, School Reform, and Collegial Relationships

Most policymakers and school change experts consider teachers to be the centerpiece of educational change. Therefore, not surprisingly, many current reform efforts target teachers, and the involvement of teachers in school reform is seen as critical (Datnow & Castellano, 2001). However, in our studies, we find that *bilingual* teachers are not taking an active role in school reform; nor are current reform efforts directed to *bilingual* teachers (Calderón, 1999). The literature on school reform does not address the issue of teachers' linguistic proficiency nor their bilingual preparation. Nevertheless, there are some powerful messages from the traditional literature that have implications for building on the few studies that apply to bilingual teacher development.

For instance, Roland Barth finds that when schools are serious about reform, they first establish "learning communities." A community of learners works from assumptions fundamentally different from those of traditional staff development practices:

- Schools have the capacity to improve themselves if the conditions are right for learning communities.
- When the conditions are right, adults *and* students learn and each energizes and contributes to the learning of the other.
- What needs to be improved about schools is their culture, the quality of interpersonal relationships, and the nature and quality of learning experiences.

- School improvement is an effort to determine and provide, from without and within, conditions under which the adults and youngsters will promote and sustain learning among themselves (Barth, 1990).

When bilingual teachers become involved in establishing school-wide learning communities, all adults and children benefit from those communities (Calderón & Carreón, 1999). When teachers are enlisted and empowered as school leaders, everyone wins. Important issues about English language learners receive more care and attention. The principal appreciates the shared leadership on issues she or he might not have been prepared to discuss, much less handle. More important, the needs of the bilingual teachers are met. Today, the conditions in schools in the U.S. are becoming more conducive to collegiality and learning communities. Title I, Title III, Comprehensive School Reform Demonstration grants and such types of funding call for these new approaches. It behooves all bilingual teachers to avail themselves of this knowledge and institute their learning communities. Unfortunately, teachers learning communities are not typically in schools, including bilingual schools.

Effecting fundamental change is the mission of staff collegial efforts in bilingual schools. Professional development must now be viewed as a collegial structure that facilitates the implementation of a dynamic bilingual program constantly under review and improvement. Increased diversity among school faculties makes collegial processes quite complex and at times superficial. Nevertheless, without the appropriate collegial relationships, nothing moves forward in a school. If children from diverse backgrounds are to succeed in schools, teachers from diverse backgrounds need to learn to work together (Calderon, 1999). When teachers in a faculty come from different social, cultural or linguistic backgrounds, it becomes very difficult to get to the heart of equity in reform. When a school's faculty and administration reflect polarized beliefs or philosophies about bilingual education or an instructional practice, change is avoided or subverted.

Most schools with ELL have an infrastructure of conflict. They do not address, head on, issues of race, language and bias. They avoid dealing with tensions between majority and minority teachers, between bilingual and mainstream teachers. Avoidance usually exacerbates tension and discord. It is also evident that current staff development practices (including Title VII funded practices) do not want to deal with these issues either.

As this study continues in the next four years, a new series of questions will guide the collegial relations component:

- How can staff development practices help diverse faculties learn to work collaboratively?

- How can fundamental change be brought about in schools where Latino student populations have increased dramatically?
- How can CSR models address these issues as part of their transformation process?
- How do ELL-oriented CSR models deal with politics, power, influential teachers who seek to maintain the status quo?
- Can environments of turbulence (Simons, 2001) be transformed through staff development practices focusing on ELL/diversity issues?

While this study provides a strong support for the emerging staff development practices through comprehensive models of school reform, it is also noteworthy to point out recent findings by the Northeast and Islands Laboratory at Brown University (2001). They examined the degree to which the needs of ELL were being considered and accommodated in states' guidelines for CSR planning, development, and implementation of models. They found no incentive for model developers to address the needs of ELL. Only two states, Rhode Island and Massachusetts included concrete references to ELL. They offer the following recommendations to low-performing schools that are using or plan to use externally developed models:

- Can state education agencies identify an inventory of models with demonstrated effectiveness with ELL?
- How can state education agency staff such as Title VII, Title 1, and Migrant Education coordinators contribute more substantively to the CSR process?
- Do those who review proposals for program aimed at low-performing schools pay specific attention to the need of ELL? Or do they allow promises of "including all students" to suffice?
- Can state education agency staff, especially those overseeing CSR programs, develop greater expertise with regard to ELL issues through effective professional development?

Sam Stringfield, Amanda Datnow, and associates (1998, 2001) have documented ELL's historic exclusion from overt consideration in the comprehensive school reform movement. This study begins to point to CSR as effective vehicles to reconstruct powerful staff development practices. It also points to the urgent need for bilingual educators to take more active roles in the design and implementation of comprehensive school reform and transformation of professional development practices.

FUTURE DIRECTIONS

The implications from this and former studies are that staff development practices for bilingual/ESL teachers have not changed very much for the past 20 years. However, from the comprehensive school reform models, we can see emerging and valid efforts. These efforts show that the content and process of staff development can be changed and can set out to address all the teachers' needs in a school through the following recommendations.

First, a school's staff development program for all teachers should include the following, so that bilingual and mainstream teachers can first reflect on their own attitudes, beliefs and skills:

- profound knowledge of research-based instruction;
- the linguistic skills to impart effective bilingual instruction;
- the status of the students' primary language and beliefs about the bilingual program at the school;
- the type of collegial practices and relationships in the school; and
- the tools to create change where change is needed.

After an analysis of the five components, a plan for differentiated professional development activities can be drawn.

Second, even schools with structured models such as Success for All and Open Court need to go through this reflective process. It would certainly enhance the teacher's contribution to the model, fidelity of implementation, student success rate, the teachers' linguistic skills, as well as meet the needs of teachers indecisive about what and how they are asked to teach.

Third, the ultimate responsibility for improved teaching lies at the school level, where the most pressing needs can be addressed in an intensive manner. District and bilingual funding sources should provide the advocacy, support, and flexibility to address teacher diversity.

Fourth, there are many positive lessons to learn from whole-school two-way bilingual programs, effective comprehensive models, and Latino charter schools in terms of collegial relationships. Positive relationships among mainstream and bilingual teachers are key to advocacy and effective implementation of ELL programs.

Finally, the transfer from training must be measured all along, and the voices of the teachers heard so that effective professional development meets its goals. Cuban (2001) likes to remind model developers that teachers are the gatekeepers, that they are a paradox—they are the problem or the solution. However, if we listen to their voices, we find that they have the solutions—it is the context and infrastructure of the school, and the commitment from the district that stifles or enriches professional development.

ACKNOWLEDGMENTS

This study was conducted as part of a grant from the U.S. Department of Education/OERI. The opinions expressed in this article do not necessarily reflect the policy of OERI.

The author would like to thank Saul López, Lupe Espino, Randi Suppe, and the many SFA/EPT trainers that assisted in the data collection, the National Council of La Raza charter schools, Kay Taggart and Elena Tovar.

REFERENCES

August, D., Carlo, M., & Calderón, M. (2000, March/April). The transfer of skills from Spanish to English. *NABE News, 24*(4).

August, D., & Hakuta, K. (Eds.). (1997). *Improving schooling for language minority children: A research agenda.* Washington, DC: National Academy Press.

Barth, R. (1990). *Improving schools from within: Teachers, parents, and principals can make the difference.* San Francisco: Jossey-Bass.

Barth, R. (1980). *Run, school, run.* Cambridge, MA:Harvard University Press.

Calderón, M. (1984). *Application of Innovation Configurations of a Trainer of Trainers.* Program-Bilingual Education Selected Papers Series. Los Angeles, CA: Evaluation Dissemination and Assessment Center.

Calderón, M. (1994). *Cumulative Reports: 1. Bilingual teacher development within school learning communities: A synthesis of the staff development model. 2. The impact of the bilingual cooperative integrated reading composition model on bilingual programs.* El Paso, TX: Department of Educational Leadership.

Calderón, M. (1997a). *Staff development in multilingual multicultural schools.* ERIC Digest EDO-UD-97-5. New York: ERIC Clearinghouse on Urban Education.

Calderón, M. (1997b). *Preparing teachers and administrators to better serve the needs of Latino students.* Proceedings from the 1996 ETS Invitational Conference. Princeton, NJ: Educational Testing Service.

Calderón, M. (1999a). School reform and alignment of standards. In *Including culturally and linguistically diverse students in standards-based reform: A report on McRel's Diversity Roundtable I* (pp. 23–46). Aurora, CO: Mid-continent Regional Educational Laboratory.

Calderón, M. (1999b). Teachers Learning Communities for cooperation in diverse settings. In M. Calderón & R.E.Slavin (Eds.). *Building community through cooperative learning.* [Special Issue of *Theory into Practice Journal, 38*(2).] Columbus: Ohio State University.

Calderón, M., & Carreón, A. (2001). A two-way bilingual program: Promise, practice and precautions. In R.E. Slavin & M. Calderón (Eds.), *Effective programs for Latino students* (pp. 125–170). Mahwah, NJ: Erlbaum.

Calderón, M., & Carreón, A. (2000, September). *A two-way bilingual program: Promise, practice and precautions* (Report No. 47). CRESPAR, (OERI), U.S. Department of Education (R-117-D40005).

Calderon, M., & Carreon, A. (1999). In search of a new border pedagogy: Sociocultural conflicts facing teachers and students along the U.S.-Mexico border. In C.J. Ovando & P. McLearn (Eds.), *The politics of multiculturalism and bilingual education: Students and teachers caught in the cross-fire.* New York: McGraw-Hill.

Calderón, M., Hertz-Lazarowitz, R., & Slavin, R.E. (1998). Effects of bilingual cooperative integrated reading and composition on students making the transition from Spanish to English reading. *The Elementary School Journal, 99*(2), 153–165.

Christian, D., & Genesee, F. (2001). *Bilingual education.* Case in Studies TESOL Practice Series, Alexandria, VA. Teachers of English to Speakers of Other Languages, Inc.

Darling-Hammond, L. (1993). Reframing the school reform agenda: Developing capacity for school transformation. *Phi Delata Kappan, 74,* 752–761.

Datnow, A. & Castellano, M. (fall 2001). Teachers' responses to Success for All: How beliefs, experiences, and adaptations shape implementation. *American Educational Research Journal, 37*(3), 775–599.

Fashola , O.S., Slavin, R.E., Calderón, M., & Durán, R. (1996). *Effective programs for Latino students in elementary and middle schools. Hispanic Dropout Project.* Washington, DC: U.S. Department of Education, Office of Educational Research and Improvement.

Fullan, M., & Hargreaves, A. (1996). *What's worth fighting for in your school?* New York: Teachers College Press.

Glass, G.V. (1982). Meta-analysis: An approach to the synthesis of research results. *Journal of Research in Science Teaching, 19*(2), 93–112.

Grant, C.A., & Secada, W.G. (1990). Preparing teachers for diversity. In W.R. Houston (Ed.), *Handbook of research on teacher education* (pp. 403–422). New York: Macmillian.

Hargreaves, A. (1994). *Changing teachers, changing times: Teachers' work and culture in the postmodern age.* New York: Teachers College Press.

Hertz-Lazarowitz, R., & Calderón, M. (1994). Implementing cooperative learning in the elementary schools: The facilitative voice for collaborative power. In S. Sharan (Ed.), *Handbook of cooperative learning.* New York: Praeger.

Holstein, J.A., & Gubrium, J.F. (1997). Active interviewing. In *Qualitative research: Theory, method and practice* (pp. 113–129). Thousand Oaks, CA: Sage.

Huberman, M. (1990). *The social context of instruction in schools.* Paper presented at American Educational Research Association annual meeting, Boston, MA.

Joyce, B., Weil, M., & Showers, B. (1992). *Models of teaching.* Boston: Allyn and Bacon.

Joyce, B., Weil, M., & Showers, B. (1982, October). The coaching of teaching. *Educational Leadership, 40*(1), 4–10.

Joyce, B., Weil, M., & Showers, B. (1980). Improving in-service training: The messages of research. *Educational Leadership, 37*(5), 379–385.

Joyce, B., Weil, M., & Showers, B. (1981). *Models of teaching* (4th ed.). Englewood Cliffs, NJ: Prentice-Hall.

Lieberman, A., & Miller, L. (Eds.). (1991). *Staff development for education in the 90's.* New York: Teachers College Press.

Little, J. (1982). Norms of collegiality and experimentation: Workplace conditions of school success. *American Educational Research Journal, 5*(19), 325–340.

Little, J.W. (1981, April). *School success and staff development in urban desgregated schools: A summary of recently completed research.* Boulder, CO: Center for Action Research.

Lortie, D. (1975). *School teacher: A sociological study.* Chicago: University of Chicago Press.

Minaya-Rowe. L. (1990). Teacher training in bilingual education and English as a second language: Recent research developments. In A. N. Ambert (Ed.), *Bilingual education as a second language: A research handbook* (pp. 259–297). New York: Garland Publishing, Inc.

Ross, S.M., Hauser, B.A., & Workman, K. (2001, July 18–20). *Regional Educational Laboratories' studies on race/ethnicity, language, and cultural diversity: A synthesis of findings from CSRD Research and Evaluation.* Paper presented at the OERI Symposium on Comprehensive School Reform Research and Evaluation, Denver, CO.

Sharan, S., & Hertz-Lazarowitz, R. (1982). Effects of an instructional change program on teachers' behavior, attitudes, and preceptions. *The Journal of Applied Behavioral Science, 18*(2), 185–201.

Silverman, D. (Ed.). (1997). *Qualitative research: Theory, method and practice.* Thousand Oaks, CA: Sage.

Slavin, R.E. (1993a). Students differ: So what? *Educational Researcher, 22*(9), 13–14.

Slavin, R.E. (1993b). Ability grouping in the middle grades: Achievement effects and alternatives. *The Elementary School Journal, 93* (5), 535–552.

Slavin, R.E., & Calderón, M. (2001). *Effective programs for Latino students.* Hillsdale, NJ: Lawrence Erlbaum Associates.

Slavin, R.E. & Madden, N. (2001). Effects of bilingual and English as a second language: Adaptations of Success for All on the reading achievement of English language learners. In R.E. Slavin & M. Calderón (Eds.), *Effective programs for Latino students* (pp. 207–230). Mahwah, NJ: Erlbaum.

Slavin, R.E., & Madden, N.A. (1999). Effects of bilingual and second language adaptations of Success for All on the reading achievement of students acquiring English. *Journal of Education for Students Placed At Risk, 4*(1), 393–416.

Stringfield, S., Datnow, A., Ross, S., & Snively, F. (1998). Scaling up school restructuring in multicultural, multilingual contexts: Early observations from Sunland county. *Education and Urban Society, 30*(3), 326–57.

CHAPTER 6

RETHINKING SCHOOL REFORM IN THE CONTEXT OF CULTURAL AND LINGUISTIC DIVERSITY:

CREATING A RESPONSIVE LEARNING COMMUNITY

Eugene E. Garcia, Marco A. Bravo, Laurie M. Dickey, Katherine Chun, and Xiaoqin Sun-Irminger

ABSTRACT

This contribution presents an overview and results from the Responsive Learning Communities (RLC) project, a multi-year school reform effort in two multilingual urban elementary schools. RLC is a collaboration between teachers, district personnel, and university researchers. Through our work, we aim to reform language arts instruction and assessment practices in bilingual and English Language Development classrooms serving culturally and linguistically diverse (CLD) students. The paper provides (a) the theoretical framework guiding our school reform activities, (b) our research methodology, and (c) our interim findings. In presenting our findings, we will focus on students' bilingual writing development in English, Spanish, and Chinese. In understanding the interrelationship between linguistic and cultural diversity,

147

and educational endeavors, educators continue to integrate diverse theories of language, learning, thinking, teaching, and culture (Garcia & McLaughlin, 1995). The growing study of linguistic, psychological, and social-cultural domains with regard to effective instructions for CLD students. It is this complex set of understanding that educators must depend upon when addressing teaching and learning in today's diverse classrooms. Through Responsive Learning Communities, we have turned to an in-depth research agenda designed to pursue the challenge of addressing CLD students' needs, with a focus on effective literacy instruction and assessment in two elementary schools with large concentrations of language minority (Spanish-English and Chinese-English bilingual) students.

INTRODUCTION

Our understanding of linguistic and cultural diversity as it relates to educational endeavors continues to expand in its utilization of diverse theories of language, learning, thinking, teaching, social structures and culture (Anyon, 1995; Garcia, 1999, 2001; Garcia & McLaughlin, 1995; Wong Fillmore, 1991). The growing ethnic and linguistic diversity of our students has led educators to become more interested in an interlocking study of linguistic, psychological, and social domains, each independently significant, but converging in a singular attempt to reconstruct the nature of schooling for these students. It is this complex set of understandings upon which an educator must depend when addressing teaching and learning in today's classrooms. For the educator of culturally and linguistically diverse students as a constituency, the issue of culture—what it is and how it directly and indirectly influences academic learning—becomes particularly important. Recently developed foundations as implemented at two school sites over time for culturally and linguistically diverse students will be the focus of this chapter. We include an expanded discussion of the issues that bring together research, theory, and educational policy and practice of significance to these students. Even more specifically, the present work addresses educationally related conceptual/theoretical pursuits which attempt to "explain," and, therefore, lay the foundation for educational "action" toward improved educational conditions for culturally and linguistically diverse students.

Our research specifically recognizes the United States is a country of incredible cultural and linguistic diversity. This trend of ethnic and racial population diversification continues most rapidly among its young and school age children. California has already been transformed into a minority/majority state; 52% of California's students come from "minority" categories and 25% are identified as non-English proficient, and, in less than twenty years, 70% of California's students will be non-White and one-half will speak a language other than English on their first day of school. Nationwide, White, non-Hispanic student enrollment has decreased since 1976 by 13%, or a total of 5 million students (National Center for Educational Statistics, 1996).

A portrait of educational vulnerability has been a historical reality for culturally and linguistically diverse (CLD) children in the United States. This population is a relatively new educationally related term. Of course it has little appreciation for the diversity among such identified U.S. populations. That is, it is quite evident that such identified populations (African Americans, Mexicans, Mexican-Americans, Puerto Ricans, Cubans, Chicanos, Latinos, Southeast Asians, Pacific Islanders, Filipino, Chinese, etc.) are quite heterogeneous linguistically and culturally both within and between such identified categories. However, educational interest spawned by a significant record of educational underachievement has generated educational programs, educational research and a wide range of intellectual discussion regarding the "at risk" educational circumstances of these populations (Barona & Garcia, 1990). The contemporary educational "zeitgeist" embraces excellence and equity for all students, best reflected in the National Commission on Excellence in Education 1983 report, *A Nation at Risk*, and the national goals legislation, *Goals 2000* (1994), reauthorization of The Elementary and Secondary Education Act—now known as the Improving America's School Act of 1994—and, the most recent Bush administration initiative of "Leave No Child Behind" (2001). Each of these policy articulations pays particular attention to the underachievement of linguistically and culturally diverse students. The major thrust of any such educational effort aimed at these populations has been centered on identifying why such populations are not achieving, and, how schools can be "reformed" or "restructured" to meet this educational challenge (Comer, 1986; Garcia, 2001; Garcia & Gonzalez, 1995). It is evident that the nation cares about these students, recognizes their historic and present profile of educational underachievement, and, is acting to enhance this achievement at national, state and local levels. The present longitudinal study provides an empirical investigation of how schooling for a diverse population of students can be enhanced in the context of recent delineations of school reform (Garcia & Gonzalez, 1995: Garcia, 1999).

BACKGROUND

U.S. Educational Response to Linguistic and Cultural Diversity

Within the last five decades, research and practice in language, culture and education has ranged from a focus on "Americanization" (Gonzalez,

1990), educational equity (Ramirez & Castaneda, 1974), to multicultural education (Banks, 1982; Banks & Banks, 1995; Grant & Sleeter, 1988), and, more recently to the "responsive" relevant (Garcia, 1994, 2001). Educational responses to cultural diversity are examined here briefly to set the stage for the development of the conceptual framework we propose for addressing cultural and linguistic diversity through a more robust view of its central role in establishing Responsive Learning Communities (RLC) that serve all students optimally. For the most part, educational approaches addressing linguistic and cultural diversity have lacked strong theoretical foundations, addressed only curriculum, produced many single case studies of ethnic groups, and produced little empirical data to substantiate the positive effects of implementation. Equal educational opportunity activity has and continues to generate legislative and legal policy along with concomitant resources to address this core societal value. But such action has not addressed, in any comprehensive manner, how educational equity should be achieved. Moreover, educational inertia in and around multicultural education has similarly espoused important societal values but has led to advances in a number of educational fronts. It has not produced a set of comprehensive strategies that address the educational concerns it has raised (Grant, 1999; Sleeter, 1995; Sleeter & Grant, 1999). Therefore the result of these educational equity and multicultural reform initiatives has been to raise and articulate important value. They have accomplished that outcome superbly and they have been assisted by the demographic reality of a changing culturally diverse society.

The legacy of an equal educational opportunity and multicultural education era has left us with some clearly identifiable results. First, educational endeavors related to linguistically and culturally diverse students have been pragmatically oriented. That is, they have focused on a set of problems—discrimination, desegregation, underachievement, low self-esteem, non-English proficiency, etc.—and have forwarded programs to address these problems. In doing so, these efforts tended to lack any substantive theoretical underpinnings. The proposed solutions were driven by the social values associated with educational equity and pluralism.

Another legacy of the last three decades of educational activity centered on linguistically and culturally diverse populations, particularly the result of multicultural education endeavors, has been the extended case study approach to cultural diversity. The educational community has produced an extensive literature of the characteristics of different racial, ethnic and ethnolinguistic groups. The goal of this work was to document the cultural and linguistic attributes of different groups in this country such that these attributes could be understood and utilized to better serve these populations. It was not uncommon to learn that American Indian children were nonverbal (Appleton, 1983), Asian American children were shy (Sue &

Okazaki, 1990), Mexican American children were cooperative (Garcia, 1983), African American children were aggressive (Boykin, 1983) and Anglo children were competitive (Kagan, 1983). Although this case study work was meant to further advance our understanding of culturally diverse students, it often had the effect of promoting stereotypes. Moreover, it did not recognize the broader, well-understood axiom of social scientists who study culture: there is as much heterogeneity within any cultural group as there is between cultural groups. If all Mexican Americans are not alike, if all African Americans are not alike, if all Asians are not alike, etc., then what set of knowledge about those groups is important educationally? What overarching conceptualization of their language, cultural and their schooling is important to provide optimal learning opportunities and results? The following is a brief over view of recent research and conceptualizations that address these questions and that have guided our work.

August and Hakuta (1997) provide a comprehensive review of optimal learning conditions which serve linguistically and culturally diverse student populations-conditions leading to high academic performance. Their reviews of some 33 studies indicate that the following attributes were identified by this case study research strategy:

> A supportive school-wide climate, school leadership, a customized learning environment, articulation and coordination within and between schools, use of native language and culture in instruction, a balanced curriculum that includes both basic and higher-order skills, explicit skill instruction, opportunities for student-directed instruction, use of instructional strategies that enhance understanding, opportunities for practice, systematic student assessment, staff development, and home and parent involvement. (August & Hakuta, 1997, p. 171)

A more recent report by the National Research Council in March 1999, *Starting Out Right: A Guide to Promoting Children's Success in Reading,* summarizes a large body of research over the last two decades regarding reading and effective reading instruction for students who come to school speaking Spanish as their primary language. That report makes clear that both phonetic analysis and meaning making are important in the beginning stages of reading development. Of significance, the report makes very clear that the body of research available regarding the reading development of English by nonnative English speakers whose first language is Spanish is most effective by instruction in reading in the child's native language.

A series of case studies of exemplary schools throughout the United States serving highly diverse and poor student populations also illustrates what can be done to promote academic excellence (McLeod, 1996). In these studies, selected schools with demonstrated academic success records were subjected to intensive site by site study with the goal of identifying specific attributes at each site related to the functioning of the school as well as a more ambitious effort to identify common attributes across the sites. Schools in four states (Texas, Illinois, California, Massachusetts) were particularly successful in achieving high academic outcomes with a diverse set of students and utilized these common goals for ensuring high quality teaching.

Foster English acquisition and the development of mature literacy. Schools utilized native language abilities to develop literacy that promoted English literacy development. Programs in these schools were more interested in this mature development than transitioning students quickly into English language instruction. This approach paid off in English language development at levels that allowed students to be successful in English instruction.

Deliver grade-level content. Challenging work in the academic disciplines was perceived and acted on simultaneously with the goals of English language learning. Teachers organized lessons to deliver grade-level instruction through a variety of native language, sheltered English, and ESL activities.

Organize instruction in innovative ways. Examples of innovations included: (a) "schools-within-schools" to more responsively deal with diverse language needs of the students; (b) "families" of students who stayed together for major parts of the school day; (c) "continuum classes" in which teachers remained with their students for two to three years, helping teachers become more familiar with and respond to the diversity in the students; and (d) grouping of students more flexibly on a continuous basis so as to respond to the developmental differences between their native language and second language.

Protect and extend instructional time. Schools utilized after-school programs, supportive computer-based instruction, and voluntary Saturday schools and summer academies. These school activities multiplied the opportunities for students to engage in academic learning. Regular teachers or trained tutors were utilized to extend this learning time. Not surprisingly, a majority of students took advantage of these voluntary extensions. Care was taken not to erode the daily instructional time that was available—erosion often related to auxiliary responsibilities by teachers that take valuable time away from instruction.

Expand teachers' roles and responsibilities. Teachers were given much greater roles in curricular and instructional decision making. This decision making was much more collective in nature to ensure cross-grade articulation and coordination. Teachers in these schools became full copartners. They devised more "authentic" assessments that could inform instruction, developing assessment tools and scoring rubrics in reading and mathematics.

Address students' social and emotional needs. Schools were located in low-income neighborhoods serving poor families. Therefore, a proactive stance with regard to issues in these communities was adopted. An after-school activity that was aimed at families, particularly dealing with issues of alcohol and drug abuse, family violence, health care, and related social service needs, brought the school staff together with social service agencies at one school site. Similar examples of actual family counseling and direct medical care were arranged at other sites.

Involve parents in their children's education. Some of the schools were magnet schools. Parents had chosen to send their children there. In such schools, parent involvement was part of the magnet school contract. This included involvement in school committees, school festivals and celebrations, student field trips, and other activities. In non-magnet schools, parent outreach services were an integral part of the school operation. In all cases, communication was accomplished on a regular basis in various home languages. Parent participation in governance of the school was a common attribute, although levels of parent participation were highly variable (adapted from McLeod, 1996, pp. 13–33).

In a more intensive case study of two elementary schools and one middle school, Miramontes, Nadeau, and Commins (1997) describe in detail the development of exemplary school attributes with an emphasis on linking decision making to effective programs. These schools, serving a majority of Hispanic students over a period of several years, developed local, state and national recognition for their academic success with very linguistically and culturally diverse student bodies—schools with as many as five languages represented in significant proportion. They conclude that a set of premises were key in guiding the development and reform of the schools' effective programs.

CHART 1
Basic Premises of Effective School Reform

Premise 1—Active Learning. Knowledge is best acquired when learners actively participate in meaningful activities that are constructive in nature and appropriate to their level of development.

Premise 2—The primary language foundation. The more comprehensive the use of the primary language, the greater the potential for linguistically diverse students' to be academically successful. There are always ways to nurture the primary language regardless of school resources.

Premises 3—The quality of primary language use. There is a difference between a token use of the primary language in instruction and its full development as a foundation for thinking and learning.

Premise 4—Strategies for second language development. Second language development creates an added dimension to instructional decision-making. Instruction must reflect specific strategies designed to meet the needs of second language learners.

Premise 5—Contexts for second language development. Second language instruction must be organized to provide student the time, experiences and opportunities they need to fully develop language proficiency. This requires a range of social and academic contexts in which both language and content are emphasized.

Premise 6—First and second language environments. Bilingual academic proficiency requires that clear, distinct, and meaning enriched contexts for each language be created during instructional time.

Premise 7—Transitions and redesignations. Decisions regarding transition to formal second language reading and redesignations that exit students from programs cannot be made arbitrarily.

Premise 8—Instructional assessment. Instructional assessment must be based on students' first and second language development, rather than on grade level or predetermined criteria. An appropriate assessment plan should address language and literacy development, as well as content knowledge.

Premise 9—Parents and community. Parents and community need to play a major role in the learning and schooling of their children.

Premise 10—Planning for cross-cultural interactions. Instruction must be organized to help students understand and respect themselves and their own culture as well as the cultures of the broader society. Planned cross-cultural interactions are an essential component of programs for all students.

Premise 11—Socio-cultural and political implications. Socio-cultural factors and political context must be considered in

> making decisions regarding every aspect of program planning.
>
> **Premise 12—Teachers as decision makers.** Teachers are decision-makers. As part of a learning community they are all equally responsible for decisions regarding the instructional program for linguistically diverse students.
>
> *Source:* Miramontes, Nadeau, and Commins (1997, pp. 37–38).

In conclusion, information derived from recent research indicates that linguistically and culturally diverse students can be served effectively (Lockwood & Secada, 1999; Romo, 1999; Tashakorri & Ochoa, 1999). These students can achieve academically at levels at or above the national norm. Instructional strategies that serve these students best acknowledge, respect, and build upon the language and culture of the home. Teachers play the most critical role in students' academic success, and students become important partners with teachers in the teaching and learning enterprise. Although much more research is required, we are not without a knowledge base that can make a difference.

A RESPONSIVE PEDAGOGY AND DEVELOPING RESPONSIVE LEARNING COMMUNITIES

We frame this discussion in a broad educationally relevant theoretical continuum. At one end of this continuum, it is argued that addressing linguistically and culturally diverse populations call for a deeper understanding of the interaction of a student's language and culture and the prevailing school language and culture (Cole, 1996; Garcia, 1999). This cultural significance position is supported by a rich contribution of research which suggests that the educational failure of "diverse" student populations is related to this culture clash between home and school. Evidence for such a position comes from Boykin (1986) for African American students, Heath (1983) for poor white students, Wiesner, Gallimore, and Jordan (1988) for Hawaiian students, Vogt, Jordan, and Tharp (1987) for Navaho students, Romo and Falbo (1996) for Mexican American students and Rodriguez (1989) for Puerto Rican students. In essence, these researchers have suggested that without attending to the distinctiveness of the contribution of culture, educational endeavors for these culturally distinct students are likely to fail.

Table 1.   Addressing Cultural & Linguistic Diversity A Continuum of Theoretical Perspectives

| School Culture– <———> Reponsive Pedagogy <———> "What we know works" |
| Home Culture | | General Principles for |
| | | Teaching & Learning |

To facilitate the discussion of how considerations of cultural diversity can be integrated into the development of a pedagogy and practices that improve the educational conditions of diverse students, Table 1 provides a depiction of the continuum of approaches suggested by the literature reviewed briefly here. Theoretically, students do not succeed because the difference between school culture and home culture lead to an educationally harmful dissonance. The challenge for educators is to identify critical differences between and within ethnic minority groups and individuals within those groups and to incorporate this information into classroom practice. In this manner, the individual and the cultural milieu in which that individual resides receives educational attention.

At the other extreme of this theoretical continuum lies the position that instructional programs must insure the implementation of appropriate general principles of teaching and learning. The academic failure of any student rests on the failure of instructional personnel to implement what we know "works." Using the now common educational analytical tool known as meta-analysis, Walberg (1986) suggests that educational research synthesis has identified robust indicators of instructional conditions which have academically significant effects across various conditions, and student groups. Other reviews (Baden & Maehr, 1986; Bloom, 1984; Slavin, 1989, 1995) have articulated this same position. In this vein, a number of specific instructional strategies including direct instruction (Rosenshine, 1986), tutoring (Bloom, 1984), frequent evaluation of academic progress (Slavin, Karweit, & Madden, 1989) and cooperative learning (Slavin, 1989, 1995) have been particular candidates for the "what works" category. Expectations play an important role in other formulations of this underachievement dilemma. Levin (1989) and Snow (1990) have suggested that students, teachers and school professionals in general have low academic expectations of culturally and linguistically diverse students. Raising student motivation in conjunction with enhancing academic expectations with challenging curriculum is a prescribed solution. Implied in this "general principle" position is that the educational failure of "diverse" populations can be eradicated by the systemic and effective implementation of these understood general principles of instruction which work with "all" students.

Interspersed within this continuum are other significant conceptual contributions which attempt to explain the academic underachievement of culturally and linguistically diverse students. Paulo Freire (1970) has argued that educational initiatives cannot expect academic or intellectual success under social circumstances which are oppressive. He and others (Cummins, 1986; Pearl, 1991) suggest that such oppression taints any curriculum or pedagogy and only a pedagogy of empowerment can fulfill the lofty goals of educational equity and achievement. Similarly, Bernstein (1971), Laosa (1982), and Wilson (1987) point to socioeconomic factors which influence the organization of schools and instruction. Extensive exposure, over generations, to poverty and related disparaging socioeconomic conditions, significantly influence the teaching/learning process at home, in the community and in schools. The result is disastrous, long-term educational failure and social disruption of family and community. Ogbu (1999) offers an alternative, macro-sociological perspective with regard to the academic failure of culturally and linguistically diverse students. Such a conceptualization interprets this country's present social approach to several immigrant and minority populations as "caste-like." In this theoretical attempt to explain underachievement, theorists argue that these populations form a layer of our society that are not expected to excel academically or economically and are therefore treated as a "caste-like population." As the result, these expectations are transformed into parallel self-perceptions by these populations with academic under-achievement and social withdrawal.

Clearly, the above conceptualizations are not presented here in any comprehensive manner. Moreover, the "cultural dissonance" to "general principles" continuum need not be interpreted as a set of incompatible approaches in the attempt to understand the educational circumstances of culturally diverse students. Instead, this short introduction should make evident that a wide variety of scholars have seriously dealt with this topic of attempting to understand why so many culturally and linguistically diverse students are not well served by today's educational institutions. These conceptual contributions have attempted to address the issues surrounding the challenges of educating a linguistically and culturally diverse population by searching for explanations for those conditions.

These contributions take into consideration the work of Anyon (1975), Bernstein (1971), Cummins (1979, 1986), Heath (1986), Freire (1970), Levin (1988), Ogbu (1991), Rose (1995), Trueba (1987), and Tharp and Gallimore (1989) who have suggested that the schooling vulnerability of culturally diverse students must be understood within the broader contexts of this society's circumstances for students in and out of schools. That is, no quick fix is likely under social and schooling conditions which mark the student for special treatment of his/her cultural difference without consideration for the psychological and social circumstances in which that student resides. This approach warns us against the isolation of any single attribute (poverty, language difference, learning potential, etc.) as the only variable of importance.

This more comprehensive view of the schooling process includes an understanding of the relationship between home and school, the psycho-socio-cultural incongruities between the two and the resulting effects on learning and achievement (Brown & Campione, 1998; Cole, 1996).

Imbedded in this perspective is the understanding that language, culture, and their accompanying values, are acquired in the home and community environment (Cummins, 1986; Goldman & Trueba, 1987; Heath, 1981), that children come to school with some knowledge about what language is, how it works, and what it is used for (Goodman, 1980; Hall, 1987; Smith, 1971), that children learn higher level cognitive and communicative skills as they engage in socially meaningful activities (Duran, 1987), and that children's development and learning is best understood as the interaction of linguistic, sociocultural, and cognitive knowledge and experiences (Trueba, 1988). A more appropriate perspective of learning, then, is one which recognizes that learning is enhanced when it occurs in contexts that are both socioculturally and linguistically meaningful for the learner (Cole, 1996; Diaz, Moll, & Mehan, 1986; Heath, 1986; Moll, 2001; Scribner & Cole, 1981; Wertsch, 1985). Covington (1996) further emphasizes that students learn best and teachers feel most satisfied when both are encouraged to become allies in the learning process and encouraging the cooperation and sharing.

How do we as educators begin to understand such a complex set of interactions? One framework for understanding is founded on the concept of "act psychology." First formulated at the end of the nineteenth century, the notion of act psychology proposes a model for human cognitive processes, or how we come to know. It focuses on the assertion that the mental functions of perceiving, remembering, and organizing-ultimately, knowing-are all acts of construction. It also asserts that what we know is closely related to the circumstances in which we come to know it.

The term "constructivist" really is an apt one. The constructivist perspective is rooted in the notion that for humans, knowing is a result of continual building and rebuilding. Our "construction materials" consist of give and take between the organization and content of old information and new information, processes of organizing that information, and the specific physical and social circumstances in which this all occurs. We come to understand a new concept by applying knowledge of previous concepts to the new information we are given. For example, in order to teach negative numbers, a math teacher can use the analogy of digging a hole—the more dirt you take out of the hole, the greater the hole becomes; the more one subtracts from a negative number, the greater the negative number becomes. But a math teacher cannot use this example with children who have no experience digging holes. It won't work. As you can see, this theory of how the mind works imply that continual revisions (or "renovations," as an architect might say) are to be expected. Therefore, when we organize teaching and learning environments, we must recognize the nature of those environments. As educators, we "build" teaching and learning environments out of what we know and how we come to know it. And we must continue to build. To ignore that is to discount the relevance of previous educational environments to the ones we are considering now. They got us to here, but that does not mean they will get us to tomorrow.

Embedded in the constructivist approach to education is the understanding that language and culture, and the values that accompany them, are constructed in both home and community environments (Cummins, 1986; Goldman & Trueba, 1987; Heath, 1981). This approach acknowledges that children come to school with some constructed knowledge about many things (Goodman, 1980; Hall, 1987; Smith, 1971) and points out that children's development and learning is best understood as the interaction of past and present linguistic, sociocultural, and cognitive constructions (Cole & Cole, 2001). A more appropriate perspective of development and learning, then, is one that recognizes that development and learning is enhanced when it occurs in contexts that are socioculturally, linguistically, and cognitively meaningful for the learner. These meaningful contexts bridge previous "constructions" to present "constructions" (Cole & Cole, 2001; Diaz, Moll, & Mehan, 1986; Heath, 1986; Ladson-Billings & Grant, 1997; Scribner & Cole, 1981; Wertsch, 1985, 1991).

Such meaningful contexts have been notoriously inaccessible to linguistically and culturally diverse children. On the contrary, schooling practices often contribute to their educational vulnerability. The monolithic culture transmitted by the U.S. schools in the form of pedagogy, curricula, instruction, classroom configuration, and language (Walker, 1987) dramatizes the lack of fit between the culturally diverse student and the school experience. The culture of the U.S. schools is reflected in such practices as:

- The systematic exclusion of the histories, languages, experiences, and values of these students from classroom curricula and activities (Banks & Banks, 1995).
- "Tracking," which limits access to academic courses and which justifies learning environments that do not foster academic development and socialization (Noguera, 1999; Oakes, 1990) or perception of self as a competent learner and language user.
- A lack of opportunities to engage in developmentally and culturally appropriate learning in ways other than by teacher-led instruction (García, 1999; Ladson Billings & Grant, 1997).

Responsive pedagogy and learning communities. The implication of this rethinking has profound effects for the teaching/learning enterprise related to culturally diverse students (Garcia, 1994). This new pedagogy is one that redefines the classroom as a community of learners in which speakers, readers, and writers come together to define and redefine the meaning of the academic experience. It might be described by some as a pedagogy of empowerment (Cummins, 1986), by others as cultural learning (Heath, 1986; Trueba, 1987), and others as a cultural view of providing instructional assistance/guidance (Tharp & Gallimore, 1989). In any case, it argues for the respect and integration of the students' values, beliefs, histories, and experiences and recognizes the active role that students must play in the learning process. It is therefore a *responsive pedagogy,* one that encompasses practical, contextual, and empirical knowledge and a "world view" of education that evolves through meaningful interactions among teachers, students, and other school community members. This responsive set of strategies expands students' knowledge beyond their own immediate experiences while using those experiences as a sound foundation for appropriating new knowledge.

Of course, a teaching and learning community that is responsive to the dynamics of social, cultural, and linguistic diversity within the broader concerns for high academic achievement both requires and emerges from a particular schooling environment. While considerable work has been devoted to restructure schools and change the fundamental relationships that exist among school personnel, students, families, and community members, seldom have these efforts included attention to the unique influences of the linguistic and sociocultural dimensions of these same relationships and structures. The environments that potentially support and nurture the development of responsive learning communities are not unlike those promoted by leading school reform and restructuring advocates; however, we further suggest that the incorporation of social, cultural, and linguistic diversity concerns creates a set of educational principles and dimensions that are more likely to address the challenges faced by schools that must attend to the needs of growing populations of diverse students.

Responsive learning communities.   The learning environments that we consider essential to the development of a responsive pedagogy are referred to as "Effective Schooling" (Garcia, 1994, 1999, 2001) and "High Performance Learning Communities" (Berman, 1996). The focus on the social, cultural, and linguistic diversity represented by students in today's public schools further challenges us to consider the theoretical and practical concerns relative to ensuring educational success for diverse students. That is, responsive learning communities must necessarily address issues of diversity in order to maximize their potential and to sustain educational improvement over time. To further examine this challenge, Table 2 summarizes the conceptual dimensions for high performing responsive learning communities.

Table 2.   Conceptual Dimensions of Addressing Cultural and Linguistic Diversity in Responsive Learning Communities

School-wide Practices

- A vision defined by the acceptance and valuing of diversity—Americanization is *not* the goal.
- Treatment of classroom practitioners as professionals, colleagues in school development decisions.
- Characterized by collaboration, flexibility, enhanced professional development.
- Elimination (gradual or immediate) of policies that seek to categorize diverse students thereby rendering their educational experiences as inferior or limiting for further academic learning.
- Reflection of and connection to surrounding community—particularly with the families of the students attending the school

Teacher/Instructional Practices

- Bilingual/bicultural skills and awareness.
- High expectations of diverse students.
- Treatment of diversity as an asset to the classroom.
- Ongoing professional development on issues of cultural and linguistic diversity and practices that are most effective.
- Basis of curriculum development to address cultural and linguistic diversity:
  1. Attention to and integration of home culture/practices.
  2. Focus on maximizing student interactions across categories of English proficiency, academic performance, schooling prior to immigration to the United States, etc.
  3. Regular and consistent attempts to illicit ideas from students for planning units, themes, activities.
  4. Thematic approach to learning activities—with the integration of various skills, events, learning opportunities.
  5. Focus on language development through meaningful interactions and communications versus on grammatical skill-building that is removed from its appropriate context.

Conclusion

In summary, a Responsive Learning Community recognizes that academic learning has its roots in processes both out-of-school and in-school. Such a conceptual framework rejects the "Americanization" strategy, extends beyond the policy and practice frameworks of "Equal Educational Opportunity" and concludes that a focus on broader issues of culture, like those represented in the "Multicultural Education" movement is useful but not enough for serving, effectively, culturally diverse students in today's schools. Instead, a focus on responsive instructional engagement encourages students to construct and reconstruct meaning and to seek reinterpretations and augmentations to past knowledge within compatible and nurturing schooling contexts. Diversity is perceived and acted on as a resource for teaching and learning instead of a problem. A focus on what students bring to the schooling process generates a more asset/resource oriented approach versus a deficit/needs assessment approach. Within this knowledge-driven, responsive and engaging learning environment, skills are tools for acquiring knowledge, not a fundamental target of teaching events (Cole, 1996; Garcia, 1994; Tharp & Gallimore, 1989).

In addition, the search for general principles of learning that work for all students must be redirected. This redirection considers a search for and documentation of particular implementations of "general" and "non-general" principles of teaching and learning which serve a diverse set of environments, in and out of school. This mission requires an understanding of how individuals with diverse sets of experiences, packaged individually into cultures, "make meaning," communicate that meaning and extend that meaning, particularly in social contexts we call schools. Such a mission requires in-depth treatment of the processes associated with producing diversity, issues of socialization in and out of schools, coupled with a clear examination of how such understanding is actually transformed into pedagogy and curriculum which results in high academic performance for all students.

THE STUDY: RESEARCH QUESTIONS

We turn now to outlining a research agenda designed to pursue the challenge of addressing cultural and linguistic diversity with a focus on improved teaching and learning. Just as there are certain elements of school wide and teaching practices that increase the likelihood that culturally and linguistically diverse students can be academically successful, the literature reviewed thus far provides considerable guidance in the particular research questions that can serve as a starting point for developing useful strategies for schools.

Beginning with the core issue of student engagement in the classroom, we are reminded by the literature on language acquisition and effective instruction for language minority students that students are much more likely to be engaged learners in environments in which the curriculum and teaching approaches build on the diversity of the students and teachers (Pease-Alvarez et al., 1991; Wong Fillmore 1991). This also requires of teachers a familiarity with, or ideally a close connection to, the home communities that the students represent in the schools in order to begin to develop practices that reflect the kinds of experiences that serve as a basis upon which students can build an understanding of complex ideas and new concepts (Pease-Alvarez et al., 1991). In addition, as discussed previously, engaged learning for culturally and linguistically diverse students necessitates considerable time devoted to interactions with each other and with the adults in the school community that can help to develop improved social and communication skills, as well as create a "safe" environment in which to learn. Finally, assessments of the progress that students are making in learning various subjects, developing conceptual understandings of subjects, and acquiring particular skills, need to be aligned with the curricular and instructional goals set forth, and, assessments have to involve all students as a means of truly gauging the quality of the learning environment. In other words, if linguistically and/or culturally diverse students are systematically left out of regular school wide or classroom assessments, the results of such efforts cannot begin to address all of the learning that goes on in a school—or, more important, the areas in which further attention should be devoted.

With these elements in mind, the following have served as a set of critical questions to help guide a systematic assessment of the existence of responsive learning communities at the school site level:

- What is the school vision and mission(s); how are issues of language, culture and diversity addressed in these; and, how are these articulated for/to teachers, students, district and school administrators and policy bodies, and parents?
- What are the prevailing norms and underlying beliefs that shape the roles, expectations and standards; how do these change as schools create and implement new policies and practices aimed at developing responsive performance learning communities?
- How are language, culture and student diversity incorporated into the instruction, curriculum and assessment practices?
- What are the resources, experiences, and structures that contribute to the professional development of the school community; how are these related to student achievement?

Specifically, this chapter will deal with our effort to collaborative address issues of establishing a responsive learning community with a particular emphasis on issues of literacy development in multilingual settings.

Over the past two decades, teachers of literacy influenced by a growing body of research about language and literacy learning and by their own observations of how children develop as writers, have shifted their practice from a product to a process orientation (Calkins, 1986; Graves, 1994). Most educators see this as positively impacting students' literacy skills, but problems abound in how to document student progress and program effectiveness due to inadequate assessment tools and over reliance on standardized achievement tests, including English and primary language tests (Wiggins, 1994). One problem is the perceived lack of validity between standardized tests and new, more process-oriented curricula. Many schools now implement authentic assessments, including portfolio assessment to supplement or replace these tests (Hewitt, 1995; Porter & Cleland, 1995). This description of an authentic assessment work-in-progress attempts to describe our recent efforts to deal with the co-development and implementation of an assessment process and tool that is of particular significance to multicultural and multilingual instructional setting.

To provide educators, particularly those serving multilingual/multicultural students, with meaningful and consistent writing assessment tools and methods of quantifying data from their classroom observations and students' portfolios, new assessments must be developed, field-tested, and researched to determine their validity and reliability. Assessment procedures must match classroom practices and current research in order to provide valid and reliable information (Williamson, 1993). According to Wiggins (1994), "an authentic and pedagogically-supportive writing assessment would educate students and teachers alike as to the qualities sought in finished products and the processes deemed likely to yield exemplary products," (p. 130). The Authentic Literacy Assessment System (ALAS) described here attempts to meet this goal in English, Spanish and Cantonese.

THE STUDY SCHOOLS

Sierra Madre Elementary School enrolls students from five different neighborhoods in the San Francisco Bay Area. The school houses eight General Education classes, nine Spanish bilingual immersion classrooms and two Special day classes serving about 375 students. The school offers a two-way Bilingual Program for grades kindergarten through grade five. The program focuses on language maintenance, cultural appreciation and ample opportunities for students to acquire both Spanish and English for academic and social purposes. Content-based units are used by the bilingual faculty to instruct and support students in becoming fully bilingual and biliterate. The program was designed to address the specific needs and abilities of the large number of limited English proficient students. Two thirds of the students at Sierra Madre are in the Two Way Spanish/English Bilingual Program. The other third of the students are enrolled in English Language Development (ELD)/General Education classes. Teachers in these classes are trained in ELD methodology for English language learners. The emphasis of this program is to develop English in the context of content area instruction. To avoid isolation, collaboration among teachers and across programs is accomplished by exchanging students during a set block of time for mathematics instruction.

Parent and community involvement is also a goal and a priority of the school. The parent and community involvement coordinator along with the staff have developed several programs at Sierra Madre which incorporate both parents and community. Among the programs is an integrated technology program which trains families on computer and internet use culminating with computers placed in the homes of students enrolled at Sierra Madre. Parent involvement also comes in the form of interactive journals. Teachers communicate with parents regarding school and the home life of students on a weekly basis to keep lines of communication open between parent and teacher. Saturday school for families is another outreach program established at Sierra Madre. The school offers Spanish and English language and literacy classes on Saturdays for families to enable them to better support their children in their literacy development.

This urban site also houses students who come from low socioeconomic background as evidenced by the 54.9 % of students who are receiving either free or reduced lunch. The linguistic make-up of the school is also highly limited and non English speaking, representing 34.7% of the school population. The ethnic and linguistic landscape of Sierra Madre is diverse. Nonetheless, the Latino student population still represents the majority with an increase from the previous 1998–1999 school year from 48.2% to 51.3% during the 1999–2000 school year (see Table 3).

Table 3.   Sierra Madre Student Profile (1999–2000)

Student Category	Number	Percent
Student Enrollment	357	100.0%
LEP/NEP	124	34.7%
Special Education	35	9.8%
EDY	124	34.7%
GATE	2	.6%
Free Lunch	167	46.8%
Reduced Lunch	29	8.1%
Latino	183	55.4%
Chinese-American	13	3.6%
African-American	69	23.4%
Other White	34	9.5%
Other Non-White	29	8.1%

Chang Ching Elementary School is a pre-kindergarten through fifth grade school also located in the San Francisco Bay Area. Chang Ching is a magnet school with an emphasis on Science, Technology, and Foreign Language Development. The school provides Chinese, Spanish, and American Sign Language bilingual classes as well as African-centered and Multicultural classes. Some classes are multi-age such as kindergarten-grade1, grade 2–3, grade 4–5.

The student profile of the school under study is diverse. During the fall of 1998, at the inception of the longitudinal study, Chang Ching had a population of 548 students (according to SFUSD school profile, 1998). There were 354 limited English proficient (LEP) and non English proficient (NEP) students (total 65%), 44 special education students (9%), 185 educationally disadvantaged youth (EDY) students (29.9%), and 447 students (82%) come from low socioeconomic backgrounds and are on free or reduced lunch. In addition, Chang Ching provides other support services through its school-wide Title I, Title VII, and Healthy Start funding.

Latino students made up the largest ethnic student population at Chang Ching at 45% (245 students). Chinese-American students represented 27.3% of the student population (150 students). African-American at 9.9% (54 students), White students at 5.7% (31 students) while there were two Japanese-American students, five Native American students, and 18 Filipino students. Finally, 8% of the students are categorized as Other Non-White (41 students): this would include students from the Middle East (see Table 4).

Table 4.   Chang Ching Student Profile (1998–1999)

Student Category	Number	Percent
Student Enrollment	548	100.0%
LEP/NEP	354	65.0%
Special Education	44	9.0%
EDY	185	30.0%
GATE	5	.9%
Free Lunch	382	70.5%
Reduced Lunch	45	12.1%
Latino	245	45.0%
Chinese-American	150	27.3%
African-American	54	9.9%
Other White	31	5.7%
Other Non-White	68	12.0%

English-plus-primary language programs. The English-plus-Chinese and English-plus-Spanish programs at this school are enrichment/maintenance programs with the purpose of enhancing students' bilingual and multicultural abilities, as stated by one Chinese bilingual teacher:

Our program is a maintenance bilingual program. That means we try to maintain Chinese as they (the students) are learning English. So, we don't really see that you have to give up your Chinese in order to learn English. We really believe you can develop both languages equally well. In fact, if you develop your Chinese, which is your child's native language, and we help them to develop Chinese as well, it's going to help them to learn English much faster . . .

At our school, by fifth grade, we really want our kids to have a very solid foundation in reading and writing (in Chinese) so that by the end of fifth grade, our goal is for them to pick up a Chinese newspaper and be able to understand some of the articles. In Chinese, we expect our kids to be able to write a simple Chinese composition that will communicate what they are trying to say. In English, we have the same expectations as everybody else in the district because we have standards. (Taken from a teacher interview on 3-21-2000)

For the English-Plus-Chinese Program, there are 150 students in six self-contained K-5 classes. The teachers and most students speak Cantonese, and the Chinese language arts instruction is conducted in Cantonese. In this program, all teachers are from Chinese descent whether they were born here or they immigrated; as are all students. For the English-Plus-Spanish program, which is an immersion bilingual program, 250 students from various backgrounds, including African-American and Asian-Americans, are enrolled in 13 classes from pre-kindergarten to fifth grade.

Parent meetings are conducted in English, Spanish, and Chinese. A Parent Newsletter is published every week in the same three languages. A Parent Liaison helps involve parents. Currently, through a Healthy Start grant, parents are conducting a needs assessment to help develop programs to meet the needs of families. Parents also work on special activities such as Black History, Chinese New Year, Festival de las Americas, Women's History, and Deaf Culture. A variety of after-school programs provide computer and homework tutoring, sport, and theater.

ALAS design. Along with teachers and administrators, researchers planned and implemented the ALAS with the understanding that it (a) would allow students to explore writing as a process and in the context of the curriculum; (b) would not be constrained by traditional standardized assessment tools; (c) would take place in the different languages of instruction; and (d) would occur at regular intervals during the school year, giving teachers periodic indicators of their students' strengths and needs. With these elements in mind, the ALAS cycle included: the ALAS administration, ALAS scoring and ALAS link to instruction, which would take place three times during the academic year.

Administration of the ALAS: Teachers are provided with instructions and scripts for the administration of the ALAS in the respective language in which literacy is being assessed. The purpose of these scripted instructions is to maintain consistency across grade levels and languages. These scripted instructions are provided for teachers during all 6 ALAS administrations that take place during the school year. The school decided upon the frequency of the administration of the ALAS and decided that the ALAS should be administered quarterly and in both Spanish and English. The quarterly administration of the ALAS in turn allowed for teachers and literacy coaches to reflect and augment instruction to fit the needs of students. The literacy activity involved in the administration of the ALAS is organized in a two-day procedure, which resembles the writing process approach:

1. Teachers prepare for the ALAS administration by reading a grade-level appropriate literature selection to the students on the initial day. Purposefully, the literature selections are from the school's adopted language arts textbooks.

2. Students engage in comprehension discussions regarding the reading with the assistance of a graphic organizer.

3. Students are then given a second graphic organizer for brainstorming the writing prompt which is thematically related to the reading selection.

4. On the second day, students utilize their graphic organizer and write in response to the prompt provided for them. Students are given 30–60 minutes (depending on grade level) to complete their composition.

Scoring process.   Teachers meet shortly after each ALAS administration to probe students' needs and strengths as measured by the rubric in each language. The rubric developed by teachers, administrators and the UC Berkeley Responsive Learning Community research team includes four domains of strategies and skills that children are measured against: *Topic, Organization, Style/Voice, and Conventions.*

At Sierra Madre Elementary School, the rubric is used to assess the literacy development within each of four domain categories in English (see Table 5) and in Spanish (see Table 6). Each student's writing sample receives a score for each of the four domains. Two grade levels are included in each rubric with a benchmark score for each, based on district standards. The rubric has a scale of one to six where a score of 3 is the benchmark score for the lower grade and a score of 4 would reach the benchmark score for the higher grade. Special modifications were made to the Spanish rubric because it needed specific inclusions due to the nature of the Spanish language in comparison to English. For example, the Conventions domain obligated incorporating punctuation marks such as (¿?, ¡!) as well as accent marks.

Table 5. 2nd/3rd Grade Writing Rubric Sierra Madre Elementary

	Topic	Organization	Style/Voice	Conventions
6	• addresses topic coherently • develops central idea, incident, or problem with supporting details	• organizes ideas into at least 2 paragraphs • includes topic sentence, supporting sentences, and conclusion • writes paragraphs in correct sequence	• uses varied sentence structure • writes complex sentences • may incorporate sense of audience through vocabulary, description	• *spells* most irregular words in an understandable way and almost all high frequency words correctly • *punctuation:* few errors in use of (, ') • uses dialogue with appropriate *punctuation* • *grammar:* uses correct plurals for irregular nouns and correct comparisons (good, better, best) • *grammar:* few significant errors in use of pronouns, adjectives, conjunctions, and adverbial forms
5	• expands on topic with several details, mostly relevant to the topic • writes detailed descriptions that support the topic	• organizes ideas into at least one paragraph • includes topic sentence, supporting sentence, and conclusion • uses some transition words	• uses varied sentence structure • may write complex sentences • uses adjectives and may use adverbs • uses varied word choice	• uses conventional *spelling* for almost all high frequency words • applies varied strategies to *spell* blends, orthographic patterns, contractions, compounds, homophones & irregular words • almost always uses appropriate *punctuation & capitalization* at beginning/end of sentences
4	• expands on topic with some details, mostly relevant to the topic	• organizes ideas into at least one paragraph • may include a topic sentence and closing sentence • writes in a simple sequence	• uses varied sentence structure • writes detailed descriptions of familiar persons, objects, or places • writes as to not confuse the reader	• uses conventional *spelling* for most high frequency words • applies varied strategies to *spell* some blends, orthographic patterns, contractions, compounds, homophones • applies varied strategies to *spell* irregular words • few errors in use of *capitalization* • *punctuation:* uses (,) and few errors in use of (? . !) • *grammar:* pays some attention to nouns, pronouns, adjectives, irregular verbs, and adverbial forms

Table 5. 2nd/3rd Grade Writing Rubric Sierra Madre Elementary (Cont.)

	Topic	Organization	Style/Voice	Conventions
3	• expands on topic with some details, mostly relevant • develops topic with 3 or more sentences	• combines at least 3 sentences to develop one topic in a paragraph • shows some evidence of organizational plan (beginning, middle, and end)	• may move beyond simple sentence structure • writes detailed descriptions of familiar persons, places, or objects	• demonstrates exceptional command of *spacing* between words, sentences • uses conventional *spelling* for most high frequency words • applies varied strategies to *spell* some irregular words • few errors in *capitalization* (beginning sentence, proper nouns) • *punctuation:* few errors in the use of (? . !) at the end of sentences • *punctuation:* may use commas in a series and in dates • *grammar:* pays some attention to proper use of nouns, pronouns, adjectives • few run on sentences, due to content • indents paragraphs
2	• expands on topic with few details • develops topic with a few sentences	• writes at least 1 topic sentence and 2 supporting sentences • may demonstrate a logical sequence	• may use varied sentence structure • uses a variety of adjectives • integrates personal interests & experiences • illustrations extend writing	• almost always uses *spaces* between words, sentences • uses conventional *spelling* for most high frequency words and words with regular spelling patterns • uses common phonics rules to attempt *spelling* of irregular words • few significant errors in the use of *capitalization* at beginning of sentences, proper nouns • *punctuation:* uses (? . !) at the end of a sentence with few errors • some run on sentences, due to content
1	• expands on topic with a couple of details • communicates main idea in a sentence	• organizes ideas around one topic • produces more than one sentence about main idea, line of thought may wander • uses some supporting details	• uses simple sentence structure • may use adjectives • uses simple language (nouns, verbs) • uses repetitious, pattern-like vocabulary • may integrate personal interests & experiences • illustrations extend writing	• uses *spaces* between most words • uses conventional *spelling* for some high frequency words & words with regular spelling patterns • uses common phonics rules to attempt *spelling* of some irregular words • few significant errors in the use of *capitalization* (beginning of sentences, proper nouns) • *punctuation:* uses (? !) at the end of a sentence • *punctuation:* uses a period at the end of a sentence • *grammar:* uses verb tense, plurals, s/v agreement

Table 6. Segundo/Tercer Grado Pauta de Escritura

	Tema	*Organización*	*Estilo/Expresión*	*Reglas de Gramática*
6	• se dirige al tema en una manera coherente con varios detalles • incluye una oración que introduce al tema	• organiza ideas en por lo menos 2 párrafos • incluye una oración principal, oraciones de detalle y una oración final • incluye algunas palabras de transición • escribe párrafos según la secuencia correcta	• usa varias estructuras para formar oraciones • escribe oraciones complejas • puede que incorpore sentido del autor con vocabulario, descripción	• usa *deletreo* correcto para casi todas las palabras irregulares y casi todas las palabras comunes • *puntuación*: pocos errores en el uso de (, ") • utiliza diálogo con *puntuación* apropiada • *grámatica*: pocos errores importantes en el uso de pronombres, adjetivos, conjunciones y formas adverbiales • puede que use los *acentos* según las reglas de acentuación
5	• detalla sobre el tema con varios detalles, por la mayor parte son pertinentes • escribe descripciones detalladas según el tema	• organiza ideas en por lo menos un párrafo • incluye una oración principal, oraciones de detalle y una oración final	• usa varias estructuras para formar oraciones • puede que escriba oraciones complejas • usa adjetivos, puede que use adverbios • usa un vocabulario variado	• usa *deletreo* correcto para casi todas las palabras comunes • utiliza una variedad de estrategias para *deletrear* diptongos, patrones ortográficos • pocos errores en el uso de *acentos* en palabras comunes • casi siempre usa *puntuación y mayúsculas* al principio/final de la oración
4	• detalla sobre el tema con algunos detalles, por la mayor parte son pertinentes	• organiza ideas en por lo menos un párrafo • puede que incluya una oración principal y una oración final • escribe en una secuencia básica	• usa varias estructuras para formar oraciones • escribe descripciones detalladas de personas conocidas o lugares o objetos conocidos • escribe para no confundir el lector	• usa *deletreo* correcto para la mayoría de las palabras comunes • utiliza una variedad de estrategias para deletrear las palabras irregulares • pocos errores en el uso de mayúsculas • puntuación: usa (,) y pocos errores en el uso de (¿ ? ¡ .) • grámatica: pone atención al uso de nombres, pronombres, adjetivos, verbos irregulares y formas adverbiales

Table 6. Segundo/Tercer Grado Pauta de Escritura (Cont.)

	Tema	Organización	Estilo/Expresión	Reglas de Gramática
3	• desarrolla el tema con algunos detalles, casi todos pertinentes al tema • desarrolla el tema con tres o más oraciones	• junta por lo menos 3 oraciones para desarrollar la idea central en un párrafo • muestra un plan organizado (principio, contexto, final)	• puede que use varias estructuras para formar oraciones • escribe descripciones detalladas sobre personas conocidas o lugares o objetos conocidos	• demuestra conocimiento excepcional del uso de *espacios* entre palabras, oraciones • usa *deletreo* correcto para la mayoría de las palabras comunes • usa varias estrategias para *deletrear* algunas palabras irregulares • usa *acentos* en palabras comunes • pocos errores en el uso de *mayúsculas* (principio de la oración, sustantivos propios) • *puntuación:* pocos errores en el uso de (¿ ? . ¡ !) al principio/ final de la oración • *gramática:* pone un poco de atención al uso propio de sustantivos, pronombres y adjetivos • de vez en cuando comunica ideas en seguido en una oración • empieza el párrafo más adentro del margen
2	• desarrolla el tema con pocos detalles • desarrolla el tema con pocas oraciones	• escribe por lo menos una oración principal y 2 oraciones que detallan sobre el tema • puede que muestre una secuencia lógica	• puede que use varias estructuras para formar oraciones • usa una variedad de adjetivos • comunica sus intereses personales y experiencias • los dibujos y el escrito se complementan	• casi siempre *usa espacios* entre palabras • usa *deletreo* correcto para casi todas las palabras comunes y las palabras con patrones regulares de deletreo • usa las reglas de fonética para intentar a *deletrear* palabras irregulares • pocos errores importantes en el uso de *mayúsculas* (principio de la oración, sustantivos propios) • *puntuación:* usa (¿ ? . ¡ !) al principio/ final de la oración • a veces comunica ideas en seguido en una oración
1	• desarrolla el tema con dos detalles • describe la idea central en una oración	• organiza ideas sobre un tema • produce más de una oración sobre el tema, pero no es muy claro • detalla sobre el tema	• usa una estructura básica de la oración • puede que use adjetivos • usa un lenguaje básico (sustantivos, verbos) • usa un vocabulario repetidor • puede que comunique sus intereses personales y experiencias • los dibujos y lo escrito se complementan	• usa *espacios* entre palabras • usa *deletreo* correcto para algunas palabras comunes y palabras con patrones regulares de deletreo • usa las reglas de fonética para intentar a *deletrear* algunas palabras irregulares • empieza a usar *acentos* en palabras comunes • pocos errores importantes en el uso de *mayúsculas* (principio de la oración, sustantivos propios) • *puntuación:* puede que use (¿ ? . ¡ !) al principio/ final de la oración • *puntuación:* usa un punto al final de la oración • *gramática:* conjuga los verbos, usa la forma plural y singular

At Chang Ching Elementary School, in addition to receiving scores in the four domains, each student's writing sample also receives an overall holistic score which reflects the writing's overall strength. The teachers develop a rubric with a scale of 1–14 scores which cover writing performance indicators for PreK-5th grade, and include benchmarks for each grade level in both English (see Table 8 and 9 in Appendix) and Chinese (see Table 9 and 10 in Appendix).

The goal for developing the Spanish and Chinese rubrics is to provide an authentic and reliable assessment tool that measures the literacy skills of diverse students against high expectations in their primary languages. Consequently, those primary language rubrics in Chinese and Spanish are to empower children of diverse backgrounds, to make sure that the Chinese and Spanish language arts instruction is of high quality, and to specify that the content of the primary language rubrics reflect Vygotsky's notion of "zone of proximal development" and incorporate what children should be able to do in Chinese and Spanish at each grade level.

Each scoring session commenced with a calibration where teachers score a single student paper. Following, analyses of the strengths and needs of the student paper is conducted and shared with reference to the rubric. Strategies used in the scoring process are also discussed. This initial scoring allows teachers to become acquainted with the scoring procedure and to assure students papers are scored in a similar fashion.

After calibration, teachers score students' papers in grade level teams. Each teacher scores one third of their own class and one third of each of the other classes at their grade level. The scoring is done together where questions and discussions during the scoring can take place. Once the scoring is complete, teachers outline the strengths and needs of students' writing and share those observations with the grade level team. Cross grade conversations about the needs and strengths of students writing take place during the following faculty meeting. Teachers are given additional assistance in scoring student papers with anchor papers that were chosen by teachers as representing benchmark level scores.

Links to instruction.   After the teachers have administered the ALAS, as an integral part of the "academic thermostat," there are analytical discussions of students' needs and strengths. The examination of students' writing is then utilized to guide and inform classroom instruction. Literacy coaches then provide professional development in Spanish and English during the *ALAS Link to Instruction* session that take place after every ALAS administration. In these workshops, teachers explore practical teaching strategies to address specific students' needs as evidenced from students' writing samples. Keenan (1975) advocates that tests should be used to better understand children's current knowledge manifested in students' written products and then reflect back to instructional issues, such as (a) different performance in different classes, (b) instructional problem or learning problem when students somehow do not match our expectations, and (c) how to keep scoring consistent across teachers.

Sierra Madre Findings

The data collected for the 2nd/3rd grade cohort included scores for the four domains of the rubric (Topic, Organization, Style/Voice, Conventions) and analysis on their performance in both Spanish and English. Students were given a score between one and six on each domain according to the level of development demonstrated in their writing samples. Scores for students in the 2nd grade cohort (1998–1999 school year) were analyzed as were their scores the following year when they entered the third grade (1999–2000 school year) using the 2nd/3rd grade rubric.

The rubrics' alignment with the school district's standards facilitated establishing benchmark scores representing grade level performance. When students were in the 2nd grade, they were measured against a score of 3 within each domain, the benchmark goal. When these students entered the 3rd grade, they were measured up against a score of 4 on the six point rubric. The following results are organized around one central related questions: *Is there equivalent literacy development in Spanish and English when students are taught in both languages?*

The longitudinal data collected on this cohort over the course of two years illustrates students' growth in Spanish and English writing. This is evident when we compare the initial ALAS scores attained by students during the 1998–1999 school year to the final scores recorded at the end of the second year (1999–2000). Students' writing maturity in both languages became apparent when we analyzed their performance in each individual domain for both Spanish and English.

Topic. The *Topic* category in the ALAS rubric deals with the student's ability to address and support the writing prompt given. The prompt is directly related to the piece of literature read by or to students the previous day.

At the time of the initial Spanish and English ALAS administration during the 1998–1999 school year the bilingual 2nd grade children were able to expand their writing by providing a couple of details related to and in support of the topic in their Spanish and English writing. These characteristics drew a score of one on the six-point rubric scale for Spanish and English ALAS #1 (see Figure 1).

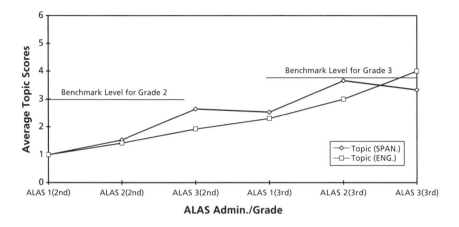

Figure 1.   1998–2000 Longitudinal Bilingual Spanish Topic Scores (Sierra Madre Grade 2 to Grade 3 cohort: n = 14)

An increase was noted by the second and final ALAS administration in both languages where students demonstrated the ability to expand on the topic of the writing with more than two details as well as communicated the main idea with more than one sentence. A similar trend in development of topic emerged the following year (1999–2000) as ALAS scores were collected, scores in both Spanish and English made steady gains through out the year, culminating with higher scores than where they began (Spanish Topic Score = 2.64, English Topic Score = 1.92).

At the end of third grade, students were able to strengthen their use of details in support of the topic in both Spanish and English. This was evident by the benchmark score of 4 in English and similar score in Spanish (3.33), which neared the benchmark score. The final ALAS administration further cemented the students understanding in dealing with the topic in both languages. The longitudinal data presented delineates this biliteracy development.

Organization.   The second category in the ALAS rubric outlines specific criteria that gauges the organization of the students' writing. The criteria includes a logical sequence to the paper, a topic sentence at the beginning of the paper with a concluding sentence toward the end of the paper and represents ideas in paragraph form with internal organization as well. The average English and Spanish scores for the students during the 1998–1999 school year began with a score of one (see Figure 2).

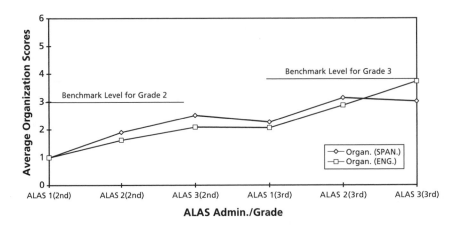

Figure 2. 1998–2000 Longitudinal Bilingual Spanish Organization Scores (Sierra Madre Grade 2 to Grade 3 cohort: n = 14)

Students' writing increased by ALAS #2 (English = 1.62, Spanish = 1.9) and #3 (English = 2.08, Spanish = 2.5). A similar trend was visible during the 1999–2000 school year when the students entered the 3rd grade. Scores went from an initial English score of 2.06 and Spanish score of 2.26 to an English ALAS #3 score of 3.71 and Spanish ALAS#3 score of 3. These scores made clear that from grade 2 to grade 3, students were developing an understanding of the need to pay particular attention to the organization of their writing. When students wrote in English the Organization domain score hovered near the benchmark score in the 3rd grade with a score of 3.71 followed close behind by a Spanish Organization score of 3.

Style & Voice.   This domain of the rubric is shaped with three characteristics in mind: 1. sentence structure (varied v. simple) 2. Detailed descriptions of familiar persons, places or objects 3. Incorporates a sense of audience. Initial scores for the cohort revealed a lack of control over this domain with an equivalent ALAS#1 score of 1 in both English and Spanish. Their average score of one meant their sentence structure was simple, using simple language (e.g., mostly nouns and verbs). Scores in both languages with respect to this domain followed a similar developmental pattern with ALAS#2 scores of 1.19 for English and 1.51 for Spanish (see Figure 3).

The students heightened their awareness of varying their sentence structure when promoting their experiences in their writing by the final ALAS administration in the 2nd grade with an average English score of 1.75 and average Spanish score of 2.43. ALAS scores for this cohort of students were collected the following year and recorded a drop from what the students had achieved the previous year. Recall student papers are scored on the

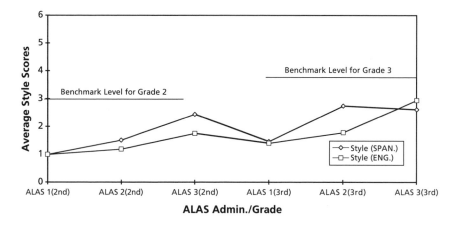

Figure 3.   1998–2000 Longitudinal Bilingual Spanish Style Scores (Sierra Madre Grade 2 to Grade 3 cohort: n = 14)

same rubric. Students quickly rebounded by the fifth ALAS administration exhibiting an English mean score of 1.78 and mean Spanish score of 2.73. An additional increase was noted at the final ALAS administration (English ALAS #6: 2.93, Spanish ALAS #6: 2.6). Students affirmed their developing command of the style and voice domain when writing in both languages.

Conventions.   The traits in the conventions domain clearly was the most difficult for students to fully grasp. The characteristics of the conventions domain include: 1. Spelling 2. Grammar 3. Punctuation. Students' ALAS #1 score of 1 in both languages depicted the students difficulties with these three traits (see Figure 4).

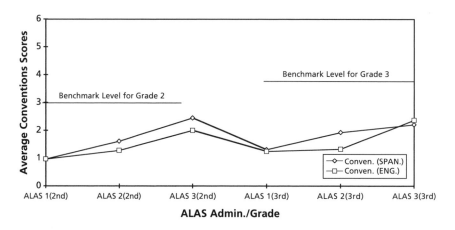

Figure 4.   1998–2000 Longitudinal Bilingual Spanish Conventions Scores (Sierra Madre Grade 2 to Grade 3 cohort: n = 14)

Students made some gains in succeeding ALAS administrations posting gains of .62 in Spanish and .3 by ALAS #2 (score: 1.3). ALAS #3 also showed a parallel development that reached an average English score of 2 for the students' writing with regard to the conventions domain and 2.43 Spanish Conventions. These gains demonstrated the students' slow but progressive understanding of the spelling, grammar, punctuation, and conventions.

Scores recorded for students the following year (1999–2000), while they were enrolled as 3rd graders followed a similar trend as the other three domains explained above. A drop from the previous year can be clearly seen, and can be attributed to the long summer vacation. ALAS #4 average scores of 1.33 in Spanish and 1.27 in English improved during ALAS#5 (English Score: 1.35, Spanish Score: 1.93) and the final ALAS administration for the year (English Score: 2.35, Spanish Score: 2.2). The improved scores over subsequent data points illustrates the students' better understanding of the various spelling strategies to spell blends, orthographic patterns, contractions, compounds, homophones and irregular words as well as the role of correct punctuation to make their writing more cohesive. The Conventions domain fell short of the benchmark scores when we measured the final ALAS administered in the 3rd grade to the benchmark. Conventions score of 2.35 in English and 2.2 in Spanish translated into a distance away from the district standard of 1.8 (Spanish) and 1.65 (English).

These findings reveal that in both languages, students demonstrated a stronger grasp of the Topic and Organization domains than the Style/ Voice and Conventions categories, but growth toward the bench mark standard was observable in each language.

Chang Ching Findings

The data collected was based on teachers evaluating student writing samples and creating quantitative data by scoring according to the ALAS rubric. The longitudinal data set consisted of ALAS writing sample scores from 43 students, 22 in the 2nd to 3rd grade cohort and 21 in the 4th to 5th grade cohort who had completed at least six ALAS writing prompts in English and Chinese during 1998–2000 school years.

The results of 1998–2000 ALAS performance score analysis of both cohorts demonstrate three clear trends:

1. Consistent parallel writing progression in both English and Chinese as evident in all the writing domains (topic, organization, style/ voice, and conventions).

2. Writing scores in both languages reaching or at slightly above grade level writing benchmark, with the fourth and fifth grade cohort

showing higher average gains in both languages than the second and third grade cohort.

3. The quality of the students' writing showed progression and development in both content as well as form with observed systematic patterns of "invented" spelling and grammatical errors in their strive for meaning making in their writing. Limited English-speaking students in the two cohorts are acquiring English writing proficiency at grade level while at the same time also developing and maintaining proficiency in their own native language.

Analysis of Findings for Grade 2 and Grade 3 Cohort

Holistic. The average mean score for the first ALAS in second grade was 5.14 for Chinese as compared to 5.73 for English (see Figure 5). The average mean score for the last ALAS in third grade was 8.43 for Chinese and 8.87 for English. There was an increase of 3.29 in English and 3.14 in Chinese. The *difference* in increase is 0.15. In the rubrics, Score 6 is benchmark for Grade 1, Score 8 for 2nd grade, and Score 9 for 3rd grade. In other words, this cohort of 22 students started out with writing at approximately 1st grade level, and almost reached the 3rd grade level benchmark, which is aligned with the district and state standards.

Topic. The second grade benchmark of 8 in the Topic domain requires students to develop the main idea with one or more examples, including details which go beyond answering Who, What, and When. The average mean score for the first ALAS in second grade was 5.32 for Chinese as compared to 5.82 for English (see Figure 6). The average mean score for the last ALAS in third grade was 8.75 for Chinese as compared to 8.77 for

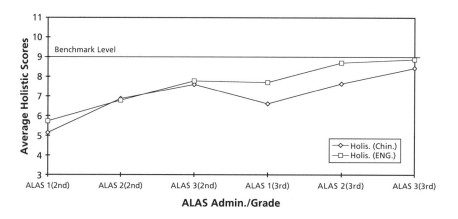

Figure 5.   1998–2000 Longitudinal Bilingual Chinese Holistic Scores (Chang Ching Grade 2 to Grade 3 cohort: n = 22)

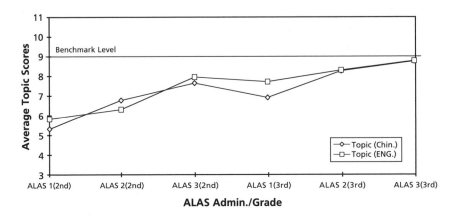

Figure 6.   1998–2000 Longitudinal Bilingual Chinese Topic Scores (Chang Ching Grade 2 to Grade 3 cohort: n = 22)

English. There was an increase of 3.43 for Chinese and an increase of 2.95 for English. The *difference* in increase between the two languages was 0.48. Although students initially scored below the second grade benchmark, they approached the third grade benchmark of 9 by the six ALAS administration. This would indicate students were increasing the amount of details and examples used to support the main idea.

Organization.   In the Organization domain, a second grade benchmark score reflects the student's ability to develop the writing piece sequentially with a beginning, middle, and end. The student is beginning to write paragraphs at this stage and attempting to use transitional words in sentences to assist the fluidity of the piece. In the Chinese rubric, the emphasis is also on the importance of topic description and the story sequence, however, the thesis statement is de-emphasized. Because Chinese narratives commonly have a spiral composition pattern (Kaplan, 1967), this de-emphasis encourages the Chinese way of composing. That is, it allows for the circular spiraling in the narrative as long as the writing still achieves sound organization of the whole composition.

The average mean score for the first ALAS in second grade was 5.32 for Chinese as compared to 6.05 for English (see Figure 7). The average mean score for the last ALAS in third grade was 8.47 for Chinese and 9.28 for English. There was an increase of 3.15 for Chinese and an increase of 3.23 for English. The *difference* in increase between the two languages is 0.08. Students reached the benchmark in English, writing at least two paragraphs on average and transitional words to organize their ideas. The similar increase over the two years in Chinese and English indicates students made comparable progress in achieving the Chinese writing goals in this domain despite the differences in the use of topic sentences.

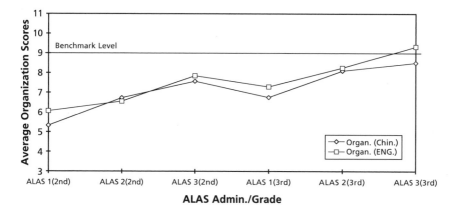

Figure 7.   1998–2000 Longitudinal Bilingual Chinese Organization Scores (Chang Ching Grade 2 to Grade 3 cohort: n = 22)

Style/Voice.   To reach the second grade benchmark in this domain, students should begin to employ more descriptive vocabulary, including adjectives and adverbs, and demonstrate an awareness of appropriate word choice. They may experiment with dialogue as well as more complex sentences. While the overuse of fixed phrases is discouraged in English writing, in Chinese, extensive and creative use of fixed proverbs is considered an indicator or mature writing. This is reflected in the Chinese rubric.

The average mean score for the first ALAS in second grade was 5.14 for Chinese as compared to 5.86 for English (see Figure 8). The average mean score for the last ALAS in third grade was 8.32 for Chinese and 8.59 for

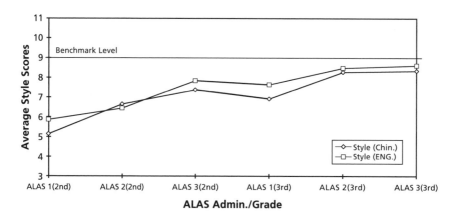

Figure 8.   1998–2000 Longitudinal Bilingual Chinese Style/Voice Scores (Chang Ching Grade 2 to Grade 3 cohort: n = 22)

English. There was an increase of 3.18 for Chinese and 2.73 for English. The *difference* in increase between the two languages is 0.45. While not reaching the third grade benchmark, students increased at a similar pace in both Chinese and English in a domain that has traditionally been overlooked in the focus of writing instruction. The 8.32 for Chinese and 8.59 for English are evidence that students are demonstrating the skills articulated by the second grade benchmark and are continuing to develop their own voice in writing, not just in one, but two different styles.

Conventions. Reaching the second grade benchmark in Conventions indicates students' writing is comprehensible with few usage errors and more consistent use of punctuation. Students are more consistent in writing high frequency words correctly and employ strategies to spell unfamiliar words. In Chinese, characters consist of radicals (which carry meaning) and phonetic compounds (which signify pronunciation). The Chinese rubric reflects this important distinction by placing emphasis on students' mastery of radicals.

The average mean score for the first ALAS in second grade was 5.27 for Chinese as compared to 6.23 for English (see Figure 9). The average mean score for the last ALAS in third grade was 8 for Chinese and 9.1 for English. There was an increase of 2.73 for Chinese and 2.87 for English. The *difference* in increase between the two languages is 0.14. Students reached the second grade benchmark in Chinese and the third grade benchmark in English. We continue to note the seemingly parallel progress in the two languages.

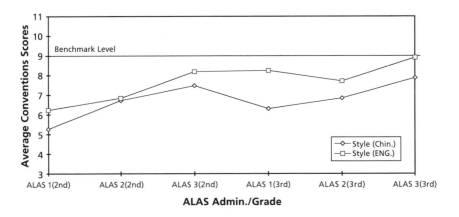

Figure 9.   1998–2000 Longitudinal Bilingual Chinese Conventions Scores (Chang Ching Grade 2 to Grade 3 cohort: n = 22)

Findings for Grade 4 to Grade 5 Cohort

The results from the 4th and 5th grade cohort are similar to that of the 2nd and 3rd in that students' scores increased in each domain at a rather consistent rate. The difference between the increase in Chinese and English was slightly higher however. We will summarize the holistic score here and then discuss trends in the domains in Chinese and English.

Holistic. The average mean score for the first ALAS in fourth grade was 6.7 for Chinese as compared to 7.12 for English. The average mean score for the last ALAS in fifth grade was 12 for Chinese and 11.56 for English. There was an increase of 5.3 for Chinese and 4.44 for English. The *difference* in increase between the two languages is 0.86 (see Figure 10). In the rubrics, Score 9 is benchmark for Grade 3, Score 11 is benchmark for grade 4, and Score 12 is benchmark for grade 5. In other words, this cohort of 21 students started out with writing skills at approximately 2nd grade level, and almost reached the 5th grade level benchmark, which is aligned with the district and state standards.

There seemed to be strong indications of parallel bi-literacy development for this cohort as evident by similar change patterns of growth in both languages. The difference in total increase after two years showed a consistent strong increase in academic English writing and academic Chinese writing catching up with an impressive gain in the two years of ALAS.

Comparing the increase rate for the domain and holistic scores between the two languages, the area showing the least difference was in Topic (0.75) and the area showing the greatest differences was in organization (1.45) favoring Chinese composition. Part of the explanation might be contributed to the many discussions (during links-to-instruction sessions) that Chinese

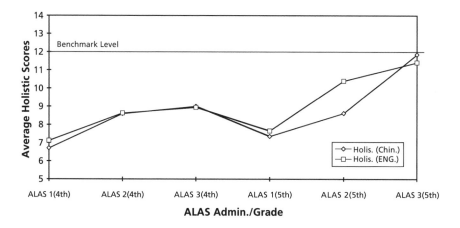

Figure 10.   1998–2000 Longitudinal Bilingual Chinese Holistic Scores (Chang Ching Grade 4 to Grade 5 cohort: n = 22)

bilingual teachers devoted to understanding the organizational characteristics of the Chinese narrative text and the type of strategies to help Chinese-English bilingual students develop their writing effectively. This might contribute to greater emphasis in instruction and greater awareness of organization by the students during their writing sessions in Chinese.

It is interesting to note that there was a slight drop in the ALAS score in the fourth ALAS administration for both languages. This could be due to four factors: (1) a summer break where no writing might be occurring, (2) greater reading and writing demand in a higher grade, (3) a change in teacher raters, and (4) possible topic effects.

For English writing, the cohort writing scores are approximately at grade level writing benchmark (set at 12) across all categories (average scores ranged from 11.08 to 11.56). In comparing the four domain score increases for the English ALAS, the gains were also parallel with little difference in average scores (see Figure 11). The increase rate was in the following order: Conventions (4.06), Topic (3.85), Style/Voice (3.81) and organization (3.48). The difference in increase rate among domain categories was also small (less than 1.0) suggesting that all domain categories increased at a similar rate. This finding suggests student can develop writing proficiency in both content (Topic, Style/Voice) and form (Organization, Conventions) simultaneously when the writing task is authentic and engaging to them.

For Chinese writing, the average student in this cohort are approximately at grade level benchmark (set at 12) in the categories of Organization (11.83), Style/Voice (11.67) and Conventions (11.83). The scores for the last ALAS administered also showed the average student at benchmark in the categories of Topic and Holistic (both 12.0).

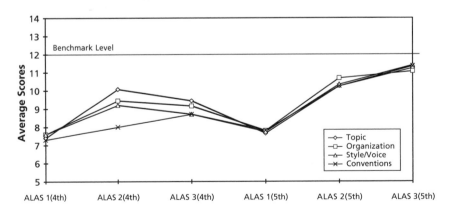

Figure 11.   1998–2000 Longitudinal Bilingual Chinese ALAS Domain Scores (English Writing for Grade 4 to Grade 5 cohort: n = 21)

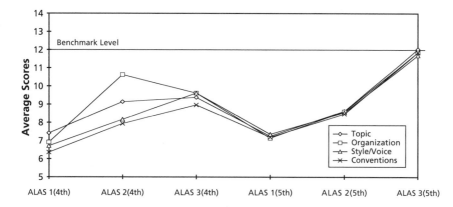

Figure 12.   1998–2000 Longitudinal Bilingual Chinese ALAS Domain Scores (Chinese Writing for Grade 4 to Grade 5 cohort: n = 21)

In comparing the four domain score increases for the Chinese ALAS, the average gains were parallel with very little differences among them. The increase rate was in the following order: Style/Voice (5.47), Organization (5.39), Conventions (5.1) and topic (5.06) (see Figure 12). Over the two-year period, teachers and the research team discussed extensively how to best articulate the characteristics of Chinese narrative styles, and how to instruct students to learn and use them. With this robust increase in style/voice score, it seems that students are developing writing in the Chinese in the Chinese style.

Student Writing Samples

The best way to look at the quality of the writing over time is to look at individual writing samples closely. Here are two ALAS Chinese and two ALAS English writing samples of the same student (we will call him Tim) who was part of this 2nd and 3rd grade cohort.

Tim was born in San Francisco. His primary language is Cantonese. He is 8 years and 8 months old at the start of the study in the fall of 1998. He entered Chang Ching Elementary school in Kindergarten and was designated to be Non English Proficiency (NEP) based on the evaluation of his low oral (level one) and reading skills. Evaluation of primary language at entering kindergarten shows Tim to be fluent in oral Chinese and limited in reading and non-proficient in writing.

Tim's Two Chinese Writing Samples

Chinese ALAS #2 (Second Grade) Writing Prompt. Please write a story about a pet. Describe what you and your pet like to do together and how does it make you feel?

Sample 1.   Chinese ALAS #2 (Second Grade) 12/10/1998

(English translation) *I have a little red kitten. Her name is "Siu Ying."* *Already 5 years old. No sharp teeth. I read books to her (drawing of cat). I draw books for her to read. She and I are very happy.*

This writing sample was produced on 12/10/1998. Topic was scored at 6, organization at 6, style/voice at 6, conventions at 6, and overall holistic at 6. This puts Tim's overall writing for this piece at first grade level (benchmark of 6). This piece contains 7 sentences and 36 words. Tim addresses the topic directly and gives good descriptions of the pet (i.e., red, little, sharp teeth, five years old) as well as the activities they do together. Tim also expresses his personal feelings. This piece is well organized with a clear beginning, middle and an ending. Some phrasing and sentence structure are not conventional but they do not interfere with the overall meaning.

Chinese ALAS #3 (third grade) Writing Prompt. Please write a story on how you solve a problem. What was the problem and who was involved? How did you go about solving the problem? After you solve the problem, how did you feel?

個	帶	妹	∞	進	拿	叫	在		請你寫一個故事，描寫你是如何解決了一個問題的？出現了什麼問題？發生在誰的身上？你是如何解決這個問題的？解決了以後，你有什麼感想呢？
膠	她	妹	。	。	個	我	小		
布	去	的	然	然	球	的	息		
。	拿	手	我	後	給	妹	的		
然	膠	流	不	她	她	妹	時	我	
後	布	血	小	拿	。	來	候	的	
我	。	。	心	個	她	玩	我	妹	
帶	她	我	推	王求	球	球	拿	妹	
她	「	扶	她	給	去	。	王球	摔	
出	手	她	摔	我	球	她	出	倒	
去	。	起	隻	。	倒	來	去		
。	然	來	手	她	。	王元	王元		
	後	我	。	∞	她	。	。		
	拿	我	我	玩	不	我	我		

Sample 2.   Chinese ALAS #3 (Third Grade) 5/11/2000

(English translation) *My Sister Fell Down*

During recess, I took a ball out to play. I called out to my sister to play ball and she came to play. I gave her the ball. She (drawing of a ball) to play (drawing of four square). She did not enter. Then she gave the ball to me. She (drawing of figure eights and circles). Then I was careless and tripped her hand. My sister's hand was bleeding. I helped her up. I took her to get bandage. Then I took her back.

This writing sample was produced on 5/11/2000. Topic was scored at 9, organization at 8, style/voice at 6, conventions at 7, and holistic score at 8 which puts her overall writing for this piece at second grade level (benchmark of 8). This piece contains twelve sentences and a total of 71 words which is almost three times as much as the last piece. Tim gives his story a title and addresses the topic directly and answers the questions of what, who, how, and when. When he lacks the words, he draws them and some of the drawings such as the picture of four square do provide meaning. The only question not addressed was how he felt afterwards. There is a clear beginning, middle and ending with the use of transitional words. Tim shows his knowledge of storytelling and describing parallel actions between two characters. Sentences are short but the word choices are conventional with few grammatical and punctuation errors.

In looking at the two Chinese compositions written over the course of two years, Tim consistently demonstrates that he is a thoughtful and attentive writer who addresses the topic and provides personal examples. He also shows strengths in his story organization and creating parallel actions. Tim shows his growing ability to describe a scene with careful attention to details of characters, action, setting and mood. As Tim composes more Chinese narratives and essays, the areas that seemed to be the most challenging for him is in making smoother transitions between sentences, developing paragraphs, using more dialogues and conventional sentence structure and phrasing as well as variety of punctuation marks besides periods. Promoting his writing through grade level literature and writing practices in different genre seems to be useful instructional support to promote and maintain Tim's Chinese writing proficiency. Comparing Tim's earlier Chinese writing samples to the later ones provides us with a very vivid picture of development in Chinese writing proficiency.

Tim's Two English Writing Samples

English ALAS #1 (Second grade) Writing Prompt: Who is your best friend? What do you like to do together? Draw a picture and write about it.

English ALAS # — Second Grade

"Tim"

‒Benjamin‒ I Play basket ball ‒ ‒ ‒ ‒ ‒ ‒

‒I‒ read ‒book‒ with best ‒friend's‒ ‒ ‒ ‒

‒MY‒best friend's at MY house to cleanqup

Sample 3.   English ALAS #1 (Second Grade) 9/17/1998

This writing sample was completed on 9/17/98. Across all the categories (topic, organization, style/voice, conventions, holistic), Tim's was given the score of 5 which puts Tim's writing competence below first grade level (benchmark of 6). There are three sentences and 18 words to this composition. Tim is able to address the topic briefly but with little development in his ideas. For organization, he is able to produce short sentences but they are mainly a list without transitional words to connect the ideas. In conventions, he has difficulty with grammatical structure and punctuation.

English ALAS #3 (Third grade) Writing Prompt: Write a first person narrative about a big event that has happened to you.

Writing Prompt: *Write a first person narrative about a big event that has happened to you.*

> Things to Remember:
> - Make sure you understand the writing prompt.
> - Use your graphic organizer to plan your written response.
> - Leave time to proofread your writing at the end. Review punctuation spelling, and grammar.

Once upon a time my dad took me and my sister to the park. We bring my bike. My sister bring a bike too. But my dad is not bring it. My dad play with me too.

My dad sometime play my bike too. But he can4 sit on it. He is so strong. He is not playing anymore. He try my blue bike.

I had bring my basketball. We are playing over there. My dad can use one hand to throw on the basket. My basketball is little. But we can4. My sisters hand is small and me too. We use two hand to throw on the basket. My sister can4 throw on it. because she is little.

Sample 4.   English ALAS #3 (Third Grade) 5/4/2000

We are playing swills.
My dad teach me hond to
play. He push me first. And
then I shek me feet. He
help my sister too. My dad
push my sister too. And than she
shek her feet. I had little
bit hid.

I play slid with my
sister. The slid is long. Sometime
my sister push me down. And
than I hit on the floor.
My legs are hurt. I can
climb up to the slid.

Sometimes the slid had
so much sand we are put
it back on the floor. The sand
Some had hard. I throw it
on the wall. The sand is
break. The slid had water because
the sand is wet than we
go home.

The
End

Sample 4 (cont.).   English ALAS #3 (Third Grade) 5/4/2000

This writing sample was produced on 5/4/2000, the last ALAS administration in this study. Topic was scored at 9, organization at 9, style/voice at 8, Conventions at 8 and holistic score at 9 which puts Tim's overall writing at the third grade level (benchmark of 9). This composition contains twice as many words and sentence than the last one (255 words with 38 sentences ranging from 4 to 15 words). There is a main topic sentence and four supporting paragraphs containing details of who, where, what and how. There is a clear beginning, middle and an ending is there but again not as well developed. Tim is using more pronouns, verbs, prepositions and a few adjectives to describe the scene and action. There is a marked progress in correct sentence structure but still some difficulties with correct verb tenses and syntax but they do not interfere with the overall meaning. In spelling, he is using mostly conventional spelling and attempting to spell more difficult words by sounding them out (i.e., shek for shake, swills for swings).

In this particular writing sample, it is interesting to point out that a teacher rating this paper might question why a day in the park would be considered a "big" event and whether the student is "off topic" since all the activities described can be considered "typical" things one do at the park. This example illustrates how critical it is for a teacher to understand the student's background and social environment. For example, going to the park and spending time with family is a "big" deal for some of the students who are from low SES households. They live in a world where going to a safe park in the neighborhood and spending time with your parents are not something a young person can take for granted due to many economic pressures on the parents. It is in this context that we understand how a day in the park with family was chosen as the big event in Tim's world.

In comparing this piece to Tim's composition produced at the beginning of second grade (9/1998), this is a impressive development from one which consists of three short sentences with under-developed ideas and incorrect syntax and punctuation to writing personal narratives where there is a clear focus following a line of thought and paragraphs containing rich details, personal voice and mostly conventional sentence structure and spelling. The author shows his growing ability to describe a scene with careful attention to details of characters, action, setting and mood. As Tim composes more narratives and essays, the areas that seemed to be the most challenging for him is in making smoother transitions between sentences and paragraphs and paying more attention to audience and developing the middle and ending of a piece. Another area is in creating dialogues between characters to develop the story, and lastly, attention to verb tense agreements and correct syntax, punctuation and using more conventional spelling. Promoting his writing and building of his vocabulary through literature-based reading and writing practices in many different genre seems to be useful instructional support for Tim's English writing development. Comparing Tim's earlier English writing samples to the later ones provides us with a very vivid picture of development in English writing proficiency.

It is from such ongoing individual assessment that we understand what the student can do and also where the difficulties are. While it is useful to

look at cohort trends in this study, the effectiveness of authentic litera\
assessment lies in teachers being able to evaluate on the individual level coi
sistently. Furthermore, the assessment should not be restricted to just thı
text itself. It is very critical for teacher to have ongoing writing conferences
with each student. This interactive assessment of writing allows teachers to
understand the context of a student's writing as well as identify with greater
accuracy where the strengths and needs are for each particular student.

CONCLUSION

In this chapter, we have attempted to articulate the importance of developing and implementing a more responsive pedagogy and establishing a
responsive learning community with particular attention to authentic
assessment of literacy for multilingual and multicultural student populations. From this work, we have demonstrated that the language of the student can be developed and assessed utilizing a set of important principles
to guide this effort.

> **The assessment process and instrument must be aligned with
> instructional activity existent in the classroom, including the lan-
> guage in which instruction is taking place.**

In the schools in which we are working, we found little student assessment in the primary languages of the students even though instruction in
the primary language was a preeminent aspect of the instructional program. For example, we found no informal or formal student assessments in
Chinese in a program that was very clear about instructing and achieving
literacy goals in that language. Moreover, the only Spanish student assessments took place utilizing a standardized test in math and reading given to
students in the Spring of each year. Results of that test were not distributed
or discussed until the following Fall. Discussion of this test by instructional
staff was often problematic since they were unfamiliar with the test terminology (NCE's) and indicated a concern that the test did not measure what
they were teaching.

> **The assessment must maximize the student's experience and ability
> to demonstrate literacy competencies in several domains.**

Student assessments that were available also suffered form their standardized approaches to the material that was included in the actual assessment. For example, students were asked to write about vacations or travel,
when many of the students in these urban and poor schools were not likely

to vacation or travel. Therefore, in the ALAS integrated assessment, teachers discussed and chose reading material and prompts which they felt would be more intrinsically interesting, motivating and likely to maximize common experiences for the students. In addition, the rubrics that were developed took into consideration four distinct but interlocking areas of literacy. In doing so, teachers recognized that a writer must be able to make clear and keep to the topic, organize her/his writing, develop a sense of audience or style/voice, and attend to proper writing conventions. The multiple "skilled" assessment recognizes the complexity of the domains of literacy. The scoring of the assessment produces a score for each domain as well as a holistic score.

The assessment must be ongoing and able to demonstrate development/learning over the entire academic year.

If student assessment is to benefit instruction, it is imperative that such assessment occur at strategic times during the year. In the present work, the ALAS was/will be given to students once every two months. By doing so, teachers have access to information regarding students literacy on a continuous basis. Moreover, instructional modification can be aligned to what this assessment coupled with other students generated information may be available. Of significance as well is the development and growth information that becomes available. The rubrics were constructed in a way that reflects our theoretical and empirical understanding of literacy development. Such an understanding makes clear that such development is not linear, can be unique to each student and is related to the opportunity structure created by literacy instruction. Therefore, for example, in the development of writing conventions, we would expect that the development of these conventions would be directly related to the types of conventions that have been emphasized during instruction. Growth and development can be linked directly to those instructional opportunities. If we see students are not developing these conventions, we do not look to the student as a primary source of non-development, we look to the instructional opportunities.

The assessment must be tied to a theoretical and empirical knowledge base, high standards and coupled with teacher practice expertise.

The uses of authentic assessments strategies are their promise are not new to the field of education (Garcia, 1999). In most cases the promise has been more than the realized product (Bauer, 1999). For these reasons, as authentic literacy assessments were emerging in these schools, it was important to recognize previous work in the field and build upon that work while at the same time recognizing the expertise of the individual teachers that were utilizing the ALA. Moreover, the school district and state in which the school and classrooms resided were in the process of articulating a set of language arts standards in English, Spanish and Chinese (only at the district level). The intent of these standards was to make clear the expectations for student's skill level at each grade. Therefore, the rubrics developed for the ALA reflected and were aligned with these standards. They also went one step further. The rubrics also indicated grade level benchmarks. That is, these identified levels were identified as a minimum level of development expected by that particular grade level associated with the benchmark.

The results and analyses of the assessment must be usable by teachers to inform, adapt and maximize literacy instruction.

In what became to be known as "literacy digs," teachers worked in groups with scoring sheets and actual student writing products from the ALAS to:

1. Verify the writing they were seeing on the ALAS and what they might know of the students writing on other writing activities;
2. Explore particular trends in the ALAS artifacts in single students and groups of students; and,
3. Identify specific instructional strategies that might assist students to develop in areas that were identified as weaknesses, and, likewise to share instructional strategies that may have led to the observed strengths.

These "digs" and related efforts attempted to utilize assessment results to understand how instruction might be influencing literacy development as well as what new strategies might be beneficial.

Wherever possible, students should be able to participate in the development and utilization of the assessment process.

One of the strategies identified early in this process of utilizing the ALAS, was to provide for the students a sample of the rubric their work would be evaluated on and examples of student work that had already been evaluated by teachers using the rubric. Teachers felt that it was important to let the students know of the expectations and to provide them with numerous examples of student work. In one classroom, the rubric used by teachers was "translated/adapted" to a more friendly format by students.

In another classroom, students used the rubric to score their own and other student's writing. In this manner, a serious attempt was made to bring students into the process and to realize their own potential in assuming a role in assessing their learning.

The present study of schooling in multilingual/multicultural sites is based a conceptual framework we have identified as a responsive learning community. The framework recognizes the primary linguistic assets that each child brings to the schooling process and utilizes those assets in constructing instruction. Moreover, it provides for the authentic assessment of the effects of that assessment within well-articulated primary and English literacy standards, and, utilizes those assessments on an ongoing bases to modify instruction to benefit student learning. By doing so, the data in this study make clear that students from distinct primary language experiences in Spanish and Chinese can develop sophisticated literacy expertise in their primary languages and in English. We wish to conclude that the framework of the study, its principles and its implementation at two specific schools add an important ingredient to our continuing challenge of effectively serving all students in the present effort to reform U.S. schools.

APPENDIX

Table 7. Kindergarten–5th Grade English Writing Rubric (Chang Ching)

	Topic	Organization	Style/Voice	Conventions
14	• **Developing Main Idea:** Develops the main idea with engaging details/examples. • **Clarity:** Line of thought is clear and coherent with *maturing* reflection/insight. • **Focus:** Focus is consistent with no digression at all.	• **Logic:** Sequence of narrative is effective and may include risk-taking or experimentation that achieve higher level of effectiveness. **Fluidity:** • Text flows in a natural manner • Paragraphs provide clear details of events/ideas/observations **Format:** • Paragraphs are used effectively to indicate changes in narrative • Writes 3 or more paragraphs using topic sentences with supporting sentences	• Personal Info./Audience: Engages the audience **Word Choice:** • Masters the use of descriptive/expressive vocabulary • Uses expanded and varied vocabulary (e.g., synonyms) **Sentence Use:** • Uses varied sentence structures throughout text • Point of view is consistent • **Dialogue:** Masters the use of dialogue as a narrative technique (where applicable)	• **Grammar:** Demonstrates control of varied grammatical forms • **Punctuation:** Demonstrates mastery in use of periods, commas and capital letters; proficient in using less common punctuation (e.g., ?"!) • **Spelling:** Demonstrates mastery of frequently-spelled words, spells infrequent words with increasing accuracy
13		**Logic:** • Sequence of narrative is well-defined • May attempt to use advanced techniques (e.g. flashbacks) to advance the narrative • Fluidity: Transitional sentences are used between paragraphs and achieve increased fluidity among sections of the text **Format:** • Each paragraph is fully developed, providing events/ideas/observations • Writes 3 or more paragraphs using topic sentences with supporting sentences	• Personal Info./Audience: Demonstrates clear awareness of audience **Word Choice:** • Uses expanded vocabulary (e.g., synonyms) • Uses descriptive/expressive vocabulary effectively (e.g., simile, metaphor and personification) **Sentence Use:** • Uses varied sentence structures effectively • Shows point of view effectively • **Dialogue:** Uses dialogue to achieve a stylistic effect within the narrative (where applicable)	• **Grammar:** Proficient in use of varied grammatical structures • **Punctuation:** Uses correct punctuation • **Spelling:** Uses conventional spelling for frequently spelled words; spells infrequent words with increasing accuracy

Table 7. Kindergarten–5th Grade English Writing Rubric (Chang Ching) (Cont.)

	Topic	Organization	Style/Voice	Conventions
12 (5)	• **Developing Main Idea**: Main idea is fully developed with expanded details/examples • **Clarity**: Line of thought is clear and coherent with some reflection/insight. • **Focus**: Focus is consistent with no digression	• **Logic**: Sequence of narrative is well-defined • **Fluidity**: Transitions between sections of text are logical and begin to flow naturally **Format:** • Text is clearly organized, with an introduction, body, and conclusion or a beginning, middle and end. • Writes 3 or more paragraphs using topic sentences with supporting sentences	• **Personal Info./Audience:** Shows awareness of audience **Word Choice:** • Begins to use expanded vocabulary (e.g., synonyms) • Uses descriptive/expressive vocabulary (e.g., simile and metaphor) • **Sentence Use:** Uses varied sentence structures effectively • **Dialogue:** Uses dialogue effectively to attempt to achieve a stylistic effect within the narrative (where applicable)	**Grammar:** • Separates different ideas into different sentences • Uses varied grammatical forms conventionally, may have minor errors that do not detract from meaning (i.e. few significant errors in use of pronouns, adjectives, conjunctions, and adverbs) • **Punctuation**: The use of punctuation is largely correct, including apostrophes to show possession and contractions • **Spelling**: high-frequency words are spelled conventionally; low frequency words are spelled approximately and are identifiable
11	• **Developing Main Idea**: Supports main idea with 3 or more reasons and/or examples with rich details • **Clarity**: Answers questions Who What When Where Why How with supporting details • **Focus**: Details support topic more consistently and do not distract from main idea. Focus may shift near end.	**Logic:** • Paragraphs are organized in a logical manner • Sequencing is largely clear to reader; details do not confuse the narrative **Fluidity:** • Uses a variety of transitional words to organize the narrative (e.g. "two months later," or "At the end of the day.") • Transitions between different sections of text may not yet flow naturally **Format:** • Text may include introduction, body, and conclusion, or beginning, middle and end • Paragraphs are indented • Writes 3 or more paragraphs using topic sentences with supporting sentences	**Personal Info./Audience:** Begins to show awareness of audience **Word Choice:** Begins to use common descriptive/expressive vocabulary (e.g., simile and metaphor) **Sentence Use:** Uses varied sentence structures **Dialogue:** Uses dialogue to develop the narrative with increasing skill (where applicable)	**Grammar:** • Uses plurals, pronouns and verb tenses appropriately most of the time • Uses conventional sentence structures with ease **Punctuation:** • Mostly correct use of periods, commas, capital letters • Begins to experiment with less common punctuation (e.g., ! ": ; -) • **Spelling:** High frequency words spelled conventionally most of the time

Table 7. Kindergarten–5th Grade English Writing Rubric (Chang Ching) (Cont.)

Topic	Organization	Style/Voice	Conventions
10	**Logic:** • Paragraphs are organized in a logical manner • Excessive details may confuse the narrative • **Fluidity:** Uses basic transitional words to add fluidity to text (e.g., then, next, first, later, finally) and between paragraphs • **Format:** Paragraphs are indented	• **Personal Info./Audience:** Conveys personal information and feeling with increasing depth • **Word Choice:** Experiments with less common descriptive/expressive vocabulary (e.g., adverbs) • **Sentence Use:** Uses varied sentence structure • **Dialogue:** Uses dialogue conventionally most of the time (where applicable)	**Grammar:** • Uses conventional sentence structures with ease • Effective use of plurals, pronouns, and verb tenses • **Punctuation:** Uses quotation marks and apostrophese more accurately • **Spelling:** Uses conventional spelling for high frequency words most of the time
9 (3)	• **Developing Main Idea:** Supports main idea with 2 or more reasons/examples with details • **Clarity:** Answers questions: Who, What, When, Where, Why, How—provides some supporting details • **Focus:** Details may cause lack of focus from main idea	• **Logic:** Uses 2 or more paragraphs to organize ideas • **Fluidity:** attempts to use transitional words to begin a new paragraph or organize ideas • **Format:** Begins to indent	• **Personal Info./Audience:** Conveys personal information and feeling with increasing depth • **Word Choice:** Uses descriptive/expressive vocabulary effectively • **Sentence Use:** Begins to use varied sentence structures (e.g., uses conjunctions to create complex sentences) • **Dialogue:** Uses dialogue conventionally some of the time (where applicable); dialogue use does not interfer with comprehension	• **Grammar:** Uses subject-verb-object word order with little lack of agreement (tense, number, gender) that does not interfere with comprehension at all **Punctuation:** • Uses correctly a variety of punctuation (e.g., . , ?) and capitalization (e.g., proper nouns, beginning of sentences) • Begins to use quotation marks and apostrophes • **Spelling:** Uses conventional spelling for high frequency words some of the time

Table 7. Kindergarten–5th Grade English Writing Rubric (Chang Ching) (Cont.)

	Topic	Organization	Style/Voice	Conventions
8	• **Developing Main Idea:** Supports main idea by 1 or more reasons/examples, including limited details • **Clarity:** Answers questions: Who, What, When, Where, Why, How. Attempts to provide some details • **Focus:** Text may not be focused on one idea. Details may confuse main idea	• **Logic:** Central idea developed sequentially (beginning, middle, end); end of piece needs to be developed • **Format:** Begins to write paragraphs • **Fluidity:** Attempts to use transitional words to connect sentences so that text flows smoothly	• **Personal Info./Audience:** Conveys personal information and feeling with increasing detail • **Word Choice:** Begins to use descriptive/expressive vocabulary (i.e., simple adjectives) **Sentence Use:** • Uses simple sentences effectively • Attempts to use varied sentence structures (e.g., experiments with conjunctions to create complex sentences) • **Dialogue:** Begins to use dialogue (where applicable) with some success	**Grammar:** • Begins to develop understanding of plurals, pronouns, and verb tense • Uses subject-verb-object word order with some lack of agreement (tense, number, gender) that does not significantly affect comprehension • **Punctuation:** Spacing and punctuation become more consistent (capitals, periods) • **Spelling:** Uses strategies to spell unfamiliar words; may self-correct approximated spelling
7		**Logic:** • Sentences are largely connected and include some details and facts • Central idea is introduced. The middle and end of the piece need to be developed • **Format:** May mix lists with fluent narratives • **Fluidity:** Moves away from lists; text does not flow smoothly	• **Personal Info./Audience:** Conveys personal information and feelings with simple details • **Word Choice:** Attempts to use descriptive/expressive vocabulary (i.e., simple adjectives) • **Sentence Use:** Uses understandable simple sentences • **Dialogue:** Experiments with the use of dialogue (where applicable) with limited success; dialogue use may interfere with reader's comprehension of text	**Grammar:** • Uses subject-verb-object word order with some lack of agreement (tense, number, gender) that may interfere with comprehension • Uses commonplace vocabulary conventionally • Uses common parts of speech with increasing fluidity (pronouns, nouns, verbs, adjectives) • **Punctuation:** Begins to use capitals and other punctuation (e.g., . , ?) **Spelling:** • Begins to use more conventional spelling • Attempts to spell unknown words

Table 7. Kindergarten–5th Grade English Writing Rubric (Chang Ching) (Cont.)

	Topic	Organization	Style/Voice	Conventions
6 (1)	• **Developing Main Idea**: Supports main topic with 1 or more reasons, events, or ideas • **Clarity:** Answers questions: Who? What? When? attempts to give some details • **Focus:** Text may deal with several ideas in unfocused manner	• **Fluidity:** Begins to use lists to develop ideas but may be unconnected • **Logic:** Writes two or more *related* sentences	• **Personal Info./Audience:** Conveys personal information and feelings using limited vocabulary • **Word Choice:** Attempts to use adjectives • **Sentence Use:** Uses simple sentences with some efficacy; many sentences may not be comprehensible • **Dialogue:** Does not attempt to use dialogue (where applicable)	**Grammar:** • Uses subject-verb-object word order with some lack of agreement (tense, number, gender) that interferes with comprehension • Uses pronouns, nouns, and verbs; may begin to use adjectives **Punctuation:** • Begins to use capitals and common letters conventionally • Writing is legible • **Spelling:** Begins to use approximated spelling of high frequency words and words with regular spelling patterns
5	• **Developing Main Idea:** Addresses topic briefly but with no development • **Clarity:** Answers questions: Who? What? with little detail • **Focus:** May stray from main idea	• **Fluidity:** Produces one or more sentences • **Logic:** Attempts to sequence ideas	• **Personal Info./Audience; Word Choice:** Attempts to convey personal information and feelings using limited vocabulary • **Sentence Use:** Attempts to use simple sentences to give literal account of topic	**Grammar:** • Attempts to use nound and verbs; may begin to use pronouns • Begins to use subject-verb-object word order **Punctuation:** • Begins to use lower case letters • Begins to use spacing • **Spelling:** Writes invented spelling words
4	**Developing Main Idea:** • Touches on topic • Text matches illustration • **Clarity:** Briefly answers questions: Who? What?	**Format; Logic:** • Uses words or short phrases to develop ideas	• **Personal Info./Audience; Word Choice:** Begins to convey personal information and feelings with pictures and a few words • May begin to show personal interest or experiences	• **Grammar:** May not use pronouns with nouns • **Punctuation:** Often writes words without spacing **Spelling:** • Begins to write invented spelling words; uses letter/sound correspondence for beginning and ending sound • May begin to use vowels

Table 7. Kindergarten–5th Grade English Writing Rubric (Chang Ching) (Cont.)

	Topic	Organization	Style/Voice	Conventions
3	**Developing Main Idea:** • Addresses a topic briefly • May copy environmental print that is related to topic	**Format:** • Groups invented words or letter strings to resemble words or phrases • Invented words are oriented from left to right and top to bottom	**Personal Info./Audience; Word Choice:** • Communicates personality through pictures • Personality not yet apparent in writing • Uses few details in text/illustration	**Spelling:** • Can give meaning to invented words • May copy related environmental print • Writes strings of letter-forms or invented words that begin to show letter/sound correspondence (beginning and ending sounds) • Writes own name
2	**Developing Main Idea:** • Illustration attempts to suggest a central idea • May copy environmental print that is unrelated to topic • May label pictures	**Format:** • Differentiates between text and illustrations • Attempts to copy environmental print or write *invented* words; words are disorganized on the page	**Personal Info./Audience; Word Choice:** • Identifies persons, places, things, ideas, without details or descriptions • May use incomplete oral phrases to describe text	**Mechanics:** • May copy environmental print unrelated to illustration • Writes strings of letters and letter forms that do not display letter/sound correspondence • Attempts to write own name
1	• **Developing Main Idea:** Illustrations have no connection to a central idea	• **Format:** Text and illustrations are not differentiated	**Personal Info./Audience; Word Choice:** • Doesn't yet identify or label • May not use oral language	**Mechanics:** • May make random markings and scribbles • Makes controlled markings (e.g., circles, arcs, lines) • Begins to make letter-like marks • Letter-like marks are not grouped to resemble words

Table 8.   Chinese Writing Rubric for K–5th grades (draft) 7-2000

中 文 作 文 評 分 標 準 （幼 稚 園 - 五年級 ）（草稿）

Chinese Writing Rubric for K-5th grades (DRAFT) 7-2000

	Topic 主題	Organization 組織	Style/Voice 文風/個性	Conventions 文法
14	主題 □ 深入有效地描述主題 思題 □ 思路清晰並包含深思熟感的反思 中心 □ 沒有任何離題的地方	邏輯 □ 作文邏輯次序清楚，勇于創新使作文內容更豐富有趣味。 流暢 □ 作文發展自然流暢，細節提高清楚有效。 組織 □ 段落發展順序有效，前後關聯清楚 □ 整篇作文至少有三個段落以上，並每段落都含有主題句。	個人感覺/讀者意識 □ 作文吸引讀者，文風獨特 選詞用字 □ 詞匯豐富有變化，包括豐富地成語使用 句型選擇 □ 句型多變化，使用得當 □ 敘述角度統一有效 對話使用 □ 能有效地使用對話	文法 □ 各種語法用達掌握正確 標點符號 □ 所有標點符號使用正確 單字書寫 □ 所有常用字和詞拼寫正確，不常用詞也正確
13	主題 □ 描述主題有說服力 思題 □ 清晰，有連貫性，且表達清楚反思和感想 中心 □ 符合主題	邏輯 □ 作文邏輯次序清楚 □ 試圖使用比較題的敘述方法，例如回憶。 流暢 □ 作文發展有連貫性 組織 □ 每個段落都發展有效，包含細節 □ 至少三個段落，並包括主題句	個人感覺/讀者意識 □ 作者清楚顯示讀者意識。 選詞用字 □ 詞匯豐富，包括同義詞，成語運用 句型選擇 □ 句型多變化，使用適當 □ 敘述角度統一 對話使用 □ 能有效使用對話，且顯示個人風格	文法 □ 各種語法使用掌握正確 標點符號 □ 所有標點符號使用正確 單字書寫 □ 正確寫出字和詞，非常用字詞可能會有一些小錯誤，但不影響文章意思
12	主題 • 主題發展充分。 思題 □ 思路清晰並包含一些反思感想 中心 • 沒有任何離題的地方。	邏輯 □ 作文邏輯次序清楚 流暢 □ 各段落之間發展通順 組織 □ 文章結構清楚，包括開端，中間，和結尾 □ 至少三個段落並包括主題句	個人感覺/讀者意識 □ 顯示有明顯意識 選詞用字 □ 使用各種詞匯量，包括成語，同義詞，明喻，暗喻，和擬人用法 句型選擇 □ 句型多變化，使用適當 對話使用 □ 有效使用對話且顯示個人風格	文法 □ 文法正確 □ 能正確使用各種常用句型，雖有差錯，但不影響大意思 標點符號 □ 所有標點符號使用正確 單字書寫 □ 常用詞書寫正確，不常用詞大致正確
11	主題 □ 使用三個或更多的細節來支持主題，且細節豐富 思題 □ 對時間，地點，人物，原因和怎樣都交待清楚 中心 □ 細節貫持主題，沒有許多不支題的細節 □ 作文結尾可能會有一點離題	邏輯 □ 作文各段落組織有邏輯 □ 先后次序清楚 流暢 □ 能使用各種不同的轉折句和詞但段落與段落發展差不一定很 組織 □ 文章包括開端，中間，和結尾 □ 每段落開頭句都空開兩格 □ 至少有三個段落	個人感覺/讀者意識 □ 開始顯示有讀者意識 選詞用字 □ 開始使用非常用字和詞，包括成語，同義詞，明喻，暗喻，和擬人用法 句型選擇 □ 能使用不同和不常用的句型 對話使用 □ 能使用對話來發展作文	文法 □ 常用句型使用正確和恰當 標點符號 □ 能正確使用大部分的常用標點符號，開始使用不大常用的標點符號 單字書寫 □ 用字恰當，能正確書寫常用詞
10	主題 □ 用兩個以上文思來發展主題，細節解釋 思題 □ 具體交待時間，地點，人物，原因，如何發生 中心 □ 用連貫性的細節來發展主題	邏輯 □ 段落發展有邏輯 □ 過多的細節可能會使作文太不大清楚 流暢 □ 使用過渡詞匯 組織 □ 每段落開頭句都空開兩格	個人感覺/讀者意識 □ 深入地表達個人感覺和想法 選詞用字 □ 開始使用非常用形容詞，副詞，和成語 句型選擇 □ 能使用不同的句型 對話使用 □ 使用基本對話	文法 □ 常用句型使用正確 □ 能正確描寫使用連詞 標點符號 □ 正確使用引號與大多數常用標點符號 單字書寫 □ 能正確寫出常用字和詞
9	主題 □ 用二個以上的細節來支持主題 思題 □ 對時間，地點，人物，原因，和怎樣大致交待清楚 中心 □ 有些細節可能會使作文不夠清楚	邏輯 □ 使用二個以上段落來組織文思 流暢 □ 試圖在每個段落開端使用過渡詞，例如，但是，然后，假如 組織 □ 段落開頭空開兩格	個人感覺/讀者意識 □ 比較深入地表達個人感覺和想法 選詞用字 □ 有效使用簡單的形容詞來提高文章的描述性 句型選擇 □ 開始使用多種句型，並開始使用關聯詞和複合句 對話使用 □ 比較正確地使用對話	文法 □ 能正確使用主語，謂語結構 □ 文法問題不影響作文意思 □ 常用連詞使用正確 標點符號 □ 能正確使用大多數常用標點符號，例如：句號，逗號，引號，感嘆號，和問號 單字書寫 □ 大多數時間能正確寫出常用字和詞

Table 8.   Chinese Writing Rubric for K–5th grades (draft) 7-2000 (Cont.)

	Topic 主題	Organization 組織	Style/Voice 語氣／語調	Conventions 文法
8	主題 □ 用兩個文思來支持主題，並加細節 □ 對時間，地點，人物，原因，和怎樣有交待，但不夠具體 中心 □ 作文可能並不集中在一個主題上 □ 有些細節會令主題模糊不清	邏輯 □ 主題發展有順序，結尾需要加強 流暢 □ 開始使用過渡詞彙 組織 □ 開始寫段落	個人感覺／讀者意識 □ 開始比較深入地表達個人感覺和想法 選詞用字 □ 開始使用不同的選詞，試圖使用成語 句型選擇 □ 使用簡單句型 □ 試圖使用不同的句型對話使用 □ 使用對話而不影響作文意思	文法 □ 開始瞭解代名詞和點詞 □ 能使用量詞 標點符號 □ 基本能正確使用簡單的標點符號 □ 正確使用書名號 單字書寫 □ 能用筆畫和部首寫出不熟悉的字和詞
7	主題 □ 用一個或以上文思來發展主題，並加一個細節 思路 □ 提及時間，地點，人物，並加以解釋	邏輯 □ 大多句子有關聯，並有一些細節和事實 □ 已有中心思想、但中間和結尾需要發展 流暢 □ 開始不用單法，但作文不流暢 組織 □ 開始把列舉法和敘述混合使用	個人感覺／讀者意識 □ 用簡單的細節來達個人感覺和想法 選詞用字 □ 試圖使用不同的選詞，試圖使用成語 句型選擇 □ 句型簡單，但能類 對話使用 □ 試圖使用對話，但可能會影響作文意思	文法 □ 常用詞使用常規，開始使用各類詞 標點符號 □ 基本能正確使用簡單的標點符號 □ 開始使用書名號 單字書寫 □ 開始基本正確寫出常用字和詞 □ 能用簡單的筆畫和／或部首寫出可以辨認的非常用字和詞
6	主題 □ 用一個文思來發展主題 思路 □ 提及時間，地點	邏輯 □ 能使用二個以上相關的句子 流暢 □ 開始用列舉式來敘述，但思想之間可能不大相關	個人感覺／讀者意識 □ 使用簡單的詞匯來表達個人的想法 選詞用字 □ 試圖使用形容詞 句型選擇 □ 使用基本句型來字面描述題目，但一些句子可能雜亂	文法 □ 常用詞使用常規，開始使用各類詞，試圖使用形容詞和量詞 標點符號 □ 開始使用簡單的標點符號 單字書寫 □ 可以正確寫出熟悉的單字 □ 試圖使用簡單的筆畫，部首寫出可以辨認的非常用字和詞 □ 用插畫，羅馬拼音，或英語單詞來代替不知道的字
5	主題 □ 簡單描述主題，沒有發展思路 □ 交待時間，地點，但欠細節	組織和邏輯 □ 試圖組織思想 流暢 □ 能使用一個以上的句子	個人感覺／讀者意識 □ 試圖使用有限的詞匯來表達個人的想法 句型選擇 □ 試圖使用簡單句型來表達主題	文法 □ 試圖使用名詞，代詞，和點詞 □ 句子結構有主語之分 標點符號 □ 開始使用常用的標點符號 單字書寫 □ 開始用簡單的筆畫和／或部首寫出能辨認的字和詞 □ 試圖用插畫，羅馬拼音，或英語單詞來代替不知道的字和詞
4	主題 □ 插圖和文字含有中心思想 □ 字，詞與圖畫有關系	組織和邏輯 □ 能寫出與插圖有關聯的字和詞	個人感覺和詞匯使用 □ 使用有限的字和圖畫來表達個人的情況和思想 □ 試圖表達個人的興趣和經歷	文法 □ 可能不會開始使用名詞和代名詞 標點符號 □ 開始使用很簡單的標點符號 單字書寫 □ 能區分文字和插圖 □ 開始一個格子寫一個字，開始使用句號 □ 抄寫周圍環境的文字 □ 能寫自己姓名
3	主題 □ 以插圖和塗鴉來表達主題意思。	組織和邏輯 □ 字、詞寫在一起，近句子形式 □ 由右至左，上至下寫字	個人感覺和詞匯使用 □ 用圖畫來表達個人思想和經歷 □ 不一定能表達風格 □ 在文字或插圖裏表達一點細節	單字書寫 □ 塗鴉或寫簡單的文字 □ 抄寫周圍環境的文字

REFERENCES

Anyon, J. (1995). Race, social class, and educational reform in an inner-city school. *Teachers College Record, 97*(1), 69–94.

Appleton, C. (1983). *Cultural pluralism in education: Theoretical foundations.* New York: Longman.

August, D., & Hakuta, K. (1997). *Improving schooling for language-minority children: Research agenda.* Washington, DC: National Council Research.

Baden, B., & Maehr, M. (1986). Conforming culture with culture: A perspective for designing schools for children of diverse sociocultural backgrounds. In R. Feldman (Ed.), *The social psychology of education* (pp. 289–309). Cambridge, MA: Harvard University Press.

Banks, J. (1982). Educating minority youths: An inventory of current theory. *Education and Urban Society, 15*(1), 88–103.

Banks, C.A., & Banks, J. (1995). Equity pedagogy: An essential component of multicultural educaiton. *Theory into Practice, 34* (3), 152–158.

Barona, A., & Garcia, E. (1990). *Children at risk: Poverty, minority status and other issues in educational equity.* Washington, DC: National Association of School Psychologists.

Berman, P. (1996). *High performance learning communities: Proposal to the U.S. Department of Education.* Emeryville, CA: Research, Policy, and Practice Associates.

Bernstein, B. (1971). A sociolinguistic approach to socialization with some reference to educability. In B. Bernstein (Ed.), *Class, codes and control: Theoretical studies towards a sociology of language* (pp. 146–171). London: Routledge and Kegan Paul.

Bloom, B. (1984). The search for methods of group instruction as effective as one-to-one tutoring. *Educational Leadership, 41*(8), 4–17.

Boykin, A. W. (1983). The academic performance of Afro-American. In J. T. Spence (Ed.), *Achievement and achievement motives: Psychological and sociological approaches.* San Francisco: W. H. Freeman and Co.

Brown, A., & Campione, J. (1998). Designing a community of young learners. Theoretical and practical lessons. In N.M. Lambert & B. L. McCombs (Eds.), *How students learn: Reforming schools through learner-centered education* (pp. 153–186). Washington, DC: American Psychological Association.

Calkins, L. M. (1986). *The art of teaching writing.* Portsmouth, NH : Heinemann.

Cole, M. (1996). *Cultural psychology: A once and future discipline.* Cambridge, MA: Belknap Press of Harvard University Press.

Cole, M., & Cole, S. R. (2000). *The development of children.* New York: Worth Publishers.

Comer, J. (1986). Home-school relations as they affect the academic success of children. *Education and Urban Society, 16*, 323–337.

Covington, M. V. (1996). The myth of intensification. *Educational Researcher, 25*(8), 1–3.

Cummins, J. (1979). Linguistic interdependence and the educational development of bilingual children. *Review of Educational Research, 19*, 222–251.

Cummins, J. (1986). Empowering minority students: A framework for intervention. *Harvard Educational Review, 56*(1), 18–35.

Diaz, S., Moll, L.C., & Mehan, H. (1986). Sociocultural resources in instruction: A context-specific approach. In Bilingual Education Office (Ed.), *Beyond language: Social and cultural factors in schooling language minority students* (pp. 197–230). Los Angeles: Evaluation, Dissemination, and Assessment Center, California State University.

Duran, R. (1987). Metacognition in second language behavior. In J.A. Langer (Ed.), *Language, literacy, and culture: Issues of society and schooling* (pp. 49–63). Norwood, NJ: Ablex Corporation.

Freire, P. (1970). *Pedagogy of the oppressed.* New York: Seabury Press.

Garcia, E. (1983). *The Mexican-American child: Language, cognition, and socialization.* Tempe: Arizona State University.

Garcia, E. (1994). Addressing the challenges of diversity. In S.L. Kagan & B. Weissbourd (Eds.), *Putting families first* (pp. 243–275). San Francisco: Jossey-Bass.

Garcia, E. (1999) *Student cultural diversity: Understanding and meeting the challenge* (2nd ed.). Boston : Houghton Mifflin.

Garcia, E. (2001). *The education of Hispanics in the United States: Raíces y alas.* Boulder, CO: Rowen and Littlefield Publishers.

Garcia, E., & Gonzalez, R. (1995). Issues in systemic reform for culturally and linguistically diverse students. *Teachers College Record, 96*(3), 418–31.

Garcia, E., & Mclaughlin, B. (1995). *Meeting the challenges of linguistic and cultural diversity in early childhood.* New York: Teachers College Press.

Goals 2000: Educate America Act. Pub. No. L. (103–227), 108 Stats. 125 (1994).

Goldman, S., & Trueba, H. (Eds.) (1987). *Becoming literate in English as a second language: Advances in research and theory.* Norwood, NJ: Ablex Corporation.

Goldman, S., & Trueba, H. (Eds.). (1987). *Becoming literate in English as a second language: Advances in research and theory.* Norwood, NJ: Ablex Corporation.

Gonzalez, G (1990). *Chicano education in the segregation era: 1915–1945.* Philadelphia: The Balch Institute.

Goodman, Y. (1980). The roots of literacy. In M.P. Douglass (Ed.), *Reading: A humanizing experience* (pp. 286–301). Claremont, CA: Claremont Graduate School.

Grant, C.A. (Ed.). (1999). *Multicultural research : A reflective engagement with race, class, gender and, sexual orientation.* London/Philadelphia : Falmer Press.

Grant, C.A., & Sleeter, C. (1988). Race, class, and gender and abandoned dreams. *Teachers College Record, 90*(1), 19–40.

Graves, D.H. (1994). Writing workshop. Be a better writing teacher. *Instructor, 104*(4), 43–45, 71.

Hall, N. (1987). *The emergence of literacy.* Portsmouth, NH: Heinemann Educational Books, Inc.

Heath, S. B. (1981). Towards an ethnohistory of writing in American education. In M. Farr-Whitman (Ed.), *Variation in writing: Functional and linguistic cultural differences* (Vol. 1, pp. 225–246). Hillsdale, NJ: Lawrence Erlbaum.

Heath, S.B. (1983). *Ways with words: Language, life, and work in communities and classrooms.* Cambridge: Cambridge University Press.

Heath, S.B. (1986). Sociocultural contexts of language development. In California Department of Education, *Beyond language: Social and cultural factors in schooling language minority students* (pp.143–186). Los Angeles: Evaluation, Dissemination, and Assessment Center, California State University.

Hewitt, G. (1995). *A portfolio primer : Teaching, collecting, and assessing student writing.* Portsmouth, NH: Heinemann.

Improving America's Schools Act, 20, Sec. 6301-8962, (1994).

Kagan, S. (1983). Social orientation among Mexican-American children: A challenge to traditional classroom structures. In E. Garcia (Ed.), *The Mexican-American child.* Tempe: Arizona State University.

Keenan, E. (1975). Variation in universal grammar. In R. Fasold & R. Shuy (Eds.), *Analyzing variation in language* (pp. 136–148). Washington, DC: Georgetown University Press.

Ladson Billings, G., & Grant, C. (1997). *Dictionary of multicultural education.* Phoenix, AZ: Oryx Press.

Laosa, L.M. (1982). School, occupation, culture and family: The impact of parental schooling on the parent-child relationship. *Journal of Educational Psychology, 74*(6), 791–827.

Levin, I. (1988). *Accelerated schools for at-risk students.* (CPRE Research Report Series RR-010). New Brunswick, NJ: Rutgers University Center for Policy Research in Education.

Lockwood, A.T., & Secada, W. (1999). *Transforming education for Hispanic youth: Exemplary practices, programs, and schools.* NCBE Resource Collection Series No. 12. National Clearinghouse for Bilingual Education, Washington, DC. 1999-01-00.

Moll, L (2001, May). *Funds of knowledge: Bilingualism and culture as specific assets in schooling.* Language Minority Research Institute Conference, University of California, Los Angesles.

McLeod, B. (1996). *School reform and student diversity: Exemplary schooling for language minority students.* Washington, DC: George Washington University, Institute for the Study of Language and Education.

Miramontes, O., Nadeau, A., & Commins, N. (1997). *Linguistic diversity and effective school reform: A process for decision making.* New York: Teachers College Press.

National Center for Education Statistics. 1996). *The condition of education* (Vols. 1 and 2). Washington, DC: U.S. Department of Education.

National Commission on Excellence in Education. (1983). *A nation at risk: The imperative for education reform.* Washington, DC: U.S. Department of Education.

National Research Council. (1997). *Starting out right: A guide to promoting children's success in reading.* Washington, DC: National Academy Press.

Noguera, P.A. (1999). Confronting the challenge of diversity. *School Administrator, 56*(6), 16–18.

Oakes, J. (1990). *Multiplying inequalities: The effects of race, social class, and tracking on opportunities to learn mathematics and science.* Santa Monica, CA: Rand Corp.

Ogbu, J. (1991). *Cultural models and educational strategies of non-dominant peoples.* New York: City College Workshop Center.

Ogbu, J. (1999). *Collective identity and schooling.* Paper presented at the meeting of the Japan Society of Educational Sociology, Tokyo, Japan.

Pearl, A. (1991). Democratic education: Myth or reality. In R. Valencia (Ed.), *Chicano school failure and success* (pp. 101–118). New York: Falmer Press.

Pease-Alvarez, L., Garcia, E., & Espinoza, P. (1991). Effective instruction for language minority students: An early childhood case study. *Early Childhood Research Quarterly, 6*(3), 347–363.

Porter, C., & Cleland, J. (1995). *The portfolio as a learning strategy.* Portsmouth, NH: Boynton/Cook Publishers.

Ramirez, M., & Castaneda, A. (1974). *Cultural democracy, bi-cognitive development and education.* New York: Academic Press.

Rodriguez, C.E. (1989). *Puerto Ricans born in the U.S.A.* Winchester, MA: Unwin Hyman, Inc.

Romo, H. (1999). *Reaching out: Best practices for educating Mexican-origin children and youth.* Charleston, WV: Clearinghouse on Rural Education and Small Schools.

Romo, H., & Falbo, T. (1996). *Latino high school graduation: Defying the odds.* Austin: University of Texas Press.

Rose, M. (1995). *Possible lives: The promise of public education in America.* New York: Penguin Books.

Rosenshine, B. (1986). Synthesis of research on explicit teaching. *Educational Leadership, 43*(3), 60–69.

Scribner, S., & Cole, M. (1981). *The psychology of literacy.* Cambridge, MA: Harvard University Press.

Slavin, R.E. (1989). The pet and the pendulum. Fadism in education and how to stop it. *Phi Delta Kappan, 70.*

Slavin, R.E. (1995). *Cooperative learning : Theory, research, and practice* (2nd ed.). Boston : Allyn and Bacon.

Slavin, R., Karweit, N., & Madden, N. (1989). *Effective programs for students at risk.* Needham Heights, MA: Allyn and Bacon.

Sleeter, C. (1995). An analysis of the critiques of multicultural education. In J. Banks & C.A. Banks (Eds.), *Handbook of research on multicultural education* (pp. 81–94). New York: Macmillan.

Sleeter, C., & Grant, C. (1999). *Making choices for multicultural education : five approaches to race, class, and gender* (3rd ed.) Upper Saddle River, NJ: Merrill.

Smith, F. (1971). *Understanding reading.* New York: Holt, Rinehart and Winston.

Snow, C. E. (1990). The development of definitional skill. *Journal of Child Language, 17*(3), 697–710.

Sue, S., & Okazaki, S. (1990). Asian-American educationalachievements: A phenomenon in search of an explanation. *American Psychologist, 45*(8), 913–920.

Tashakkori, A., & Ochoa, S.H. (Eds.). (1999). *Education of Hispanics in the United States : politics, policies, and outcomes.* New York: AMS Press.

Tharp, R.G., & Gallimore, R. (1989). *Challenging cultural minds.* London: Cambridge University Press.

Trueba, H.T. (1988). Peer socialization among minority students: A high school dropout prevention program. In H. Trueba & C. Delgado-Gaitan (Eds.), *Schools and society: Learning content through culture.* New York: Praeger Publishers.

Trueba, H.T. (1987). *Success or failure? Learning and the language minority student.* Scranton, PA: Harper and Row.

Vogt, L., Jordan, C., & Tharp, R. (1987). Explaining school failure, producing school success: Two cases. *Anthropology and Education Quarterly, 18*(4), 276–286.

Walberg, H. (1986). Synthesis of research on teaching. In M. Wittrock (Ed.), *Handbook of research on teaching* (3rd ed., pp. 15–32). New York: Macmillan.

Walker, C.L. (1987). Hispanic achievements: Old views and new perspectives. In H. Trueba (Ed.), *Success or Failure? Learning and the language minority student* (pp. 15–32). Cambridge, MA: Newbury House.

Wertsch, J.V. (1985). *Vygotsky and the social formation of the mind.* Cambridge, MA: Harvard University Press.

Wertsch, J. V. (1991). *Voices of the mind : A sociocultural approach to mediated action.* Cambridge, MA: Harvard University Press.

Wiesner, T.S., Gallimore, R., & Jordan, C. (1988). Unpackaging cultural effects on classroom learning. Native Hawaiian peer assistance and child-generated activity. *Anthropology and Education Quarterly, 19*(4), 327–353.

Wiggins, G. (1994). The constant danger of sacrificing validity to reliability: Making writing assessment serve writers. *Assessing Writing, 1*(1), 129–39.

Williamson, M. (1993). An introduction to holistic scoring: The social, historical and theoretical context for writing assessment. In M. Williamson & B. Hout, (Eds.), *Validating holistic scoring for writing assessment: Theoretical and empirical foundations* (pp. 1–14). Cresskill, NJ: Hampton Press, Inc.

Wilson, W.J. (1987). *The truly disadvantaged: The inner city, the underclass, and public policy.* Chicago: University of Chicago Press.

Wong-Fillmore, L. (1991). When learning a second language means losing a first. *Early Childhood Research Quarterly, 6*(3), 323–347.

CHAPTER 7

EVALUATING THE EFFECTS OF THE PEDAGOGY FOR IMPROVING RESILIENCY PROGRAM:

THE CHALLENGES OF SCHOOL REFORM IN A HIGH STAKES TESTING CLIMATE

Yolanda N. Padrón, Hersh C. Waxman, Robert A. Powers, and Ann P. Brown

ABSTRACT

This chapter reports the results of the Pedagogy for Improving Resiliency Program (PIRP) that was implemented in six fourth- and fifth-grade classrooms in an urban elementary school serving predominantly Hispanic English Language Learners (ELLs) from low-socioeconomic backgrounds. The year-long PIRP consisted of training that incorporated several components designed to help classroom teachers improve their instruction and the learning of resilient and non-resilient ELLs. The findings from the present study are both promising and discouraging. The promising aspects are: (a) the treatment teachers' classroom instruction was better than the comparison teachers on some important aspects of teaching (e.g., more explanations, more encouragement of extended student responses, more encouraging students to succeed, more focus on the task's process), (b) students in the treatment classes reported a more positive classroom learning environment than students in the comparison classes (e.g., higher Cohesion, Satisfaction, and Teacher Support and less Friction), and (c) students in the treatment classrooms had significantly higher reading achievement gains than students in the comparison classrooms. The discouraging aspects of the PIRP relate to issues that impacted teachers' implementation of the PIRP program, such as the district's emphasis on high-stakes testing.

INTRODUCTION

Many school reforms in the past decade have not been successful because they have assumed that curricular or instructional innovations that improve the education of English monolingual students will work equally well for English Language Learners (ELLs) such as Latino students who are learning a new language (LeCelle-Peterson & Rivera, 1994; Reyes & Paredes Scribner, 1995). ELLs, however, have to face "double demands" of schooling, which include acquiring a second language while learning traditional academic content (Gersten & Jiménez, 1998). This academic challenge may explain why the deleterious conditions of underachievement, student alienation, and high dropout rates are very prevalent for Latino ELLs.

One approach that may help us improve the education of ELLs is to examine students who have done well in school and have begun to effectively use English. The present case study examines the effectiveness of a teacher training resiliency program that was designed to help teachers improve: (a) their classroom instruction, (b) student's resiliency behaviors, and (c) student's academic achievement. This case study is the second phase of the project, Improving Classroom Instruction and Student Learning for Resilient and Non-Resilient English Language Learners, which is a part of the Center for Research on Education, Diversity and Excellence (CREDE) and funded by the U. S. Department of Education, Office of Educational Research and Improvement. This two-phase project examines resilient (i.e., academically successful) and non-resilient (i.e., academically unsuccessful) Latino English language learners (ELLs) in order to determine factors that foster educational resilience. In Phase I, four categories or clusters of variables (i.e., individual attributes of learners, school and classroom factors, family factors, and out-of-school factors) were examined to provide information to help understand why some Latino ELLs have been successful in school despite coming from similar disadvantaged backgrounds and settings as their less-successful classmates. Drawing upon Phase I findings, Phase II developed, implemented, and tested an instructional intervention for improving the reading instruction in English of fourth- and fifth-grade Latino ELLs. The present article focuses on the results of the intervention project.

BACKGROUND

The term "English language learner" has recently been used to describe those students whose first language is not English and they are either beginning to learn English or have demonstrated some proficiency in English (LeCelle-Peterson & Rivera, 1994). Although Latinos constitute the largest group of ELLs, they have the lowest levels of education and the highest dropout rate of any other ethnic group (U.S. Department of Education, 2000). In fact, approximately 40% of Latino students are one grade level or more below expected achievement levels by the eighth grade and only about 50% graduate "on time" (U.S. Department of Education, 1999). To address these problems, educators need to focus on new instructional approaches for improving the education of ELLs (Padrón & Knight, 1989; Padrón & Waxman, 1993; Waxman & Padrón, 1995). These instructional programs need to specifically address the concerns of Latino students who are trying to learn a new language.

One approach that may be useful for helping language minority students is studying ELLs who may be classified as "at risk," but are resilient and doing well in school (Alva, 1991; Garmezy, 1991; Gordon & Song, 1994; McMillan & Reed, 1994; Wang & Gordon, 1994; Winfield, 1991). Educational resilience has been defined as "the heightened likelihood of success in school and in other life accomplishments, despite environmental adversities, brought about by early traits, conditions, and experiences" (Wang, Haertel, & Walberg, 1994, p. 46). This approach differs from those approaches taken in the past in that it focuses on predictors of academic success rather than on academic failure and identifies "alterable" factors that distinguish resilient and non-resilient students.

The Phase I results from the project revealed that there were dramatic differences between resilient and non-resilient students in several areas. We found, for example, that resilient elementary school students perceive a more positive instructional learning environment and they are more satisfied with their English reading and language arts classrooms than non-resilient students (Padrón, Waxman, & Huang, 1999). In addition, non-resilient ELLs reported that they have more difficulty in their class work than both average and resilient ELLs. The magnitude of these differences is both statistically and educationally significant. These findings provide a great challenge for classroom teachers who need to provide optimal learning environments for all their students.

Other results from Phase I indicate that there are several classroom behavioral differences between resilient and non-resilient elementary school students (Padrón, Waxman, & Huang, 1999; Padrón, Waxman, Read, Persall, & Huang, 1999). Some of the differences related to the amount and type of interaction that were found in the classroom processes. Resilient ELLs spent significantly more time interacting with teachers for instructional purposes, whereas non-resilient ELLs spent more time interacting with other students for social or personal purposes. The observational results from our project are extremely important given that the amount and quality of teacher and student academic interactions are two of the most influential variables that promote student outcomes (Wang, Haertel, & Walberg, 1993).

The student, teacher, and parent interview data from Phase I corroborate many of the quantitative findings. The student interview results, for example, reveal several distinctive differences between the attitudes of resilient and non-resilient students (Brown & Padrón, 2001). These findings strongly suggest that resilient and non-resilient students are experiencing very different school and classroom learning environments and that they have very different future aspirations. The results examining the cognitive reading strategies used by students while reading in English indicate that non-resilient students use significantly fewer "strong" reading strategies and significantly more "weak" strategies than resilient students. The results from the teacher interview data revealed several distinctive patterns of behaviors that teachers thought distinguished resilient from non-resilient students (Read, 1999). Most teachers, for example, indicated that the lack of parental involvement and low student motivation and self-esteem were the major factors contributing to the lack of success of non-resilient students, and the teachers similarly reported that these were the same factors that contributed to the success of resilient students. The teachers did not mention any school, program, or classroom factor (e.g., teaching practices) that contributed to the academic success or failure of ELLs. In addition, teachers reported that many instructional strategies were effective for resilient students. When later asked about effective teaching strategies for resilient students, the teachers generally responded that most strategies worked well for them. They could, however, only mention a few instructional strategies that they thought were effective for non-resilient students.

The findings from the parent interview data revealed several gaps between parents' literacy practices as compared to practices found to be effective in prior research (McEnery, 1999). The findings also revealed some tension between parents and the school personnel.

In Phase II of the project, which is the focus in the present article, the Phase I findings were used to develop an instructional intervention for improving the resiliency of Latino ELLs. The intervention included areas such as: (a) enhancing teachers' knowledge base in literacy; (b) training teachers to use cognitive reading strategies; (c) developing teachers' ability to evaluate and diagnose ELLs' learning strategies related to literacy; (d) providing teachers with effective strategies for promoting students' resiliency skills; and (e) providing teachers with skills to develop appropriate instructional materials. The intervention focused on promoting students' higher-level thinking, rather than merely increasing mastery of basic skills (Waxman, Padrón, & Knight, 1991). The intervention program drew upon the previous work of Tharp (1989) and Tharp and Gallimore (1988), as well as our own work that has specifically focused on instructional interventions for ELLs in elementary schools (Padrón, 1993, 1994; Waxman, Walker de Felix, Martinez, Knight, & Padrón, 1994).

DESCRIPTION OF THE PEDAGOGY TO IMPROVE RESILIENCY PROGRAM

The eight-month Pedagogy to Improve Resiliency Program (PIRP), which was examined in the present study, consisted of about 32 hours of training. Two university professors from a nearby large comprehensive, research university typically met with the five teachers after school for two hours, twice a month for eight months. The sessions were held in one of the teachers' classrooms in their school. The teachers received a modest stipend for participating in the program.

As indicated previously, the PIRP was developed as a result of two years of data collection on resilient and nonresilient students in the district. In addition, input was actively sought from the PIRP teachers. As a result, we identified seven instructional components that seemed most effective in serving the needs of the ELLs in the district. A brief description of each of the components follows.

Improving Classroom Instruction

This component provided an overview and context for effective teaching by focusing on some of the major current national issues related to teaching. A videotape produced by CREDE (1998), *Pedagogy, Practice, and Research,* was viewed and discussed. In addition, teachers were provided with a recent review of the research that described effective instructional practices for ELLs (i.e., Padrón & Waxman, 1999b). Other handouts on effective instruction also were provided to the teachers and discussed (Stigler & Hiebert, 1999; Tharp & Gallimore, 1988). Both the materials provided and the discussion were placed into a framework that described issues related to: (a) the quality of classroom instruction, (b) school-based reform issues, (c) alternative types of schools, (d) teacher qualifications and shortages, (e) school curriculum, and (f) accountability and statewide assessments.

Reciprocal Teaching

This component provided an overview of Reciprocal Teaching, which was explained as an instructional procedure that engages students and teachers in a dialogue in order for the students to comprehend text. The reciprocal teaching strategies of: (a) predicting, (b) generating questions, (c) summarizing, and (d) clarifying with an overarching goal of having students apply the strategies independently were demonstrated and teachers were provided with opportunities to use these strategies. A sample procedure from Palincsar and Brown (1984) was given to the teachers as an example followed by a reciprocal teaching simulation. Several articles also were provided to teachers and the group discussion addressed issues of how to implement reciprocal teaching in the classroom.

Culturally Relevant Instruction

This component provided an opportunity for teachers to share their knowledge of culturally relevant teaching and discuss the qualities of instruction that are included and excluded in culturally relevant instruction. The main focus of this component came from Gloria Ladson-Billings' (1994) book *The Dreamkeepers: Successful Teachers of African American Children.* Wlodkowski and Ginsberg's (1995) framework for culturally responsive teaching was explored with the teachers using the authors' four conditions necessary for culturally responsive teaching: (a) establish inclusion, (b) develop positive attitudes, (c) enhance meaning, and (d) engender competence. Several readings were provided and discussed with the teachers. Diagrams for principles for building a learning community and a culturally-responsive environment were presented and discussed with the teachers. A reading/language arts, three-day lesson plan was presented to the teachers using folk and fairy tales with traditional teaching techniques and using an example of culturally relevant teaching of folk and fairy tales.

The Five Standards of Effective Teaching

This component provided a detailed overview of CREDE's Five Standards of Effective Pedagogy (Tharp, 1997). The CREDE developed CD-Rom, *Teaching Alive* (Dalton, 1998b) was viewed and discussed. Handouts on each of the five standards ("Teacher and Student Producing Together," "Developing Language Across the Curriculum," "Making Meaning: Connecting School to Students' Lives," "Teaching Complex Thinking," and "Teaching Through Conversation") were distributed and discussed (Dalton, 1998a; Padrón & Waxman, 1999a; Tharp, 1997, 1989). One of the major goals of this component was examining how the five standards could be applied in each of the teachers' classrooms.

Educational Resiliency

This component focused on how classroom teachers could help improve the learning of non-resilient as well as resilient students. Case studies of resilient and non-resilient students (Barone, 1999; Strother, 1991) were provided to the teachers and discussed. In addition, handouts focusing on ways to improve the education of non-resilient students were provided and later discussed (Benard, 1997; Bickart & Wollin, 1997; Henderson, 1997; Krovetz, 1999). Furthermore, teachers completed and then discussed their responses on the instrument developed by Henderson and Milstein (1996) that assesses the school's overall capacity for building resiliency.

Feedback from Data Collection

This component focused on the observation and learning environment results from the data we collected near the beginning of the school year. Instead of providing individual teacher data, we shared overall, school-wide results from the 11 classrooms we observed and surveyed in the school. This provided a less-threatening situation for the teachers and allowed us to openly discuss strengths and weaknesses in instructional practices as well as resilient and non-resilient students' perceptions of their classroom environment. The teachers viewed the feedback process quite seriously, and many mentioned specific changes they would try to implement in their classroom.

Implementation of Learning Centers

One of the components that the PIRP teachers expressed interest in after viewing, *Pedagogy, Practice, and Research* (CREDE, 1998), was the development of learning centers. After studying and discussing the value of learning centers, each PIRP teacher designed, constructed, and implemented their individual learning centers into their classrooms. Examples of some of the learning centers constructed by the teachers were reading comprehension, fluency in reading, and multicultural education. Teachers decided to construct learning centers in a variety of areas so that they would be able to exchange ideas as well as centers.

METHODS

Participants

The elementary school where the study was conducted is located in a major metropolitan area in the south-central region of the United States. Students in the school are predominately Latino (>90%) and most of them receive free or reduced-cost lunches. The academic achievement of students in the school is lower than others in the same school district and lower than the state average.

The five teachers who participated in the PIRP were recommended by their principal. When we asked the principal to explain his rationale for selecting these teachers, he indicated that these were the teachers he thought would agree to be part of the project. He did not think that they were necessarily better or more effective than other fourth- or fifth-grade teachers in the school, but merely more likely to cooperate with us. There were three fourth-grade teachers and two fifth-grade teachers. Two of the teachers were Latino and bilingual. Another teacher was white, but bilingual in English and Spanish. The other two teachers were white, but had a few years of teaching experience working with ELLs. All the teachers received a modest stipend for participating in the project. A comparison group of six classrooms was chosen from all the remaining fourth- and fifth-grade teachers in the school.

Near the beginning of the school year, both teachers in the treatment and comparison groups were asked to identify their population of students at risk of academic failure (e.g., students from families of low socioeconomic status, living with either a single parent, relative, or guardian). Students identified as gifted, talented, or special education were excluded from the population to avoid potential effects related to ability difference. From this pool of students at risk, teachers were then told to select up to three resilient (i.e., high-achieving students on both standardized achievement tests and daily school work, very motivated, with excellent attendance) and three non-resilient students (i.e., low-achieving students on both standardized achievement tests and daily school work, not motivated, with poor attendance).

Sample sizes varied by instrument. A total of 115 students were observed using the Classroom Observation Schedule (COS). There were 210 students who completed the My Class Inventory. The final sample for the achievement component of the study consisted of 29 students of teachers in the PIRP training and 89 students of teachers in the comparison group. These numbers of participants were determined by the availability of specific English reading achievement scores reported from the 1998–1999 and 1999–2000 school years.

Instruments

Several different instruments were used in this study. A learning environment instrument was used to assess students' perceptions of their classroom learning environment. Two classroom observation instruments were used to observe teacher and student behaviors in the classroom. Student achievement data were collected by the statewide assessment tests. Ethnographic observations of the classroom and school were conducted throughout the year. Finally, both formal and informal interviews were conducted with teachers and students.

Learning Environment Instrument

An adapted version of the My Class Inventory (Dryden & Fraser, 1996; Fraser, Anderson, & Walberg, 1982) was used to collect data on students' perceptions of their classroom learning environment near the end of the school year. The inventory is a 50-item questionnaire read to students in Spanish or English by researchers. Students circle either "Yes" or "No" in response to statements about their reading class. The questionnaire contains eight scales that assess students' perceptions in the following areas: (a) Satisfaction, (b) Friction, (c) Competition, (d) Difficulty, (e) Cohesion, (f) Self-Esteem in Reading, (g) Teacher Support, and (h) Equity. A brief description of the scales and a sample item from each follows:

- *Satisfaction:*   The extent of students' enjoyment of class work (e.g., I enjoy the schoolwork in my reading class).
- *Friction:*   The amount of tension and quarreling among students (e.g., Some students in my reading class pick on me).

- *Competition:*   The emphasis on students competing with each other (e.g., I try to be first to finish the class work in reading).
- *Difficulty:*   The extent to which students find difficulty with the work of the class (e.g., In my reading class, the work is hard for me to do).
- *Cohesion:*   The extent to which students know, help, and are friendly toward each other (e.g., In my class, I often work with other students).
- *Self-Esteem in Reading:*   The extent to which students think that they are good at reading (e.g., I am a very good reader).
- *Teacher Support:*   The extent to which students think that their teachers are supportive (e.g., My reading teacher really cares about me).
- *Equity:*   The extent to which students are treated equally as their classmates (e.g., I am treated the same way as other students in my reading class).

The instrument has been found to be reliable and valid in many different school settings and it is especially applicable for elementary school students (Fraser, Anderson, & Walberg, 1982; Waxman, Walker de Felix, Martinez, Knight, & Padrón, 1994; Padrón, Waxman, & Huang, 1999). The internal consistency reliability coefficients of the eight scales in the present study: Satisfaction, Friction, Competition, Difficulty, Cohesion, Self-Esteem in Reading, Teacher Support, and Equity are .80, .66, .63, .66, .76, .64, .79, and .62 respectively, with an average of .70. In other words, the revised survey questionnaire has adequate internal consistency reliability. Discriminant validity statistics for the sample indicates that the mean correlation coefficient of a scale with each of the other scales ranged from .01 to .59, with an average of .22, suggesting that there is adequate scale discriminant validity, although a few scales overlap to a certain degree.

Classroom Observation Schedule

The Classroom Observation Schedule (COS) (Waxman, Wang, Lindvall, & Anderson, 1990) was used to systematically obtain information on students' classroom behaviors. It documents observed student behaviors in the context of ongoing classroom instructional-learning processes. The COS was modified for the present study to include a Language Used section. Students are observed with reference to (a) their interactions with the teacher or other students, (b) the selection of activity, (c) the type of activity on which they are working, (d) the setting in which the observed behavior occurs, (e) their classroom manner, and (f) the language used (i.e., Spanish or English). Each student was observed for 10 30-second intervals during each class period. This observation schedule has been found to be valid and reliable in previous studies (Waxman & Huang, 1999). In the present study, the inter-observer agreement (Cohen's kappa) was found to be excellent, with an inter-observer reliability coefficient of .96.

Teacher Roles Observation Schedule

The Teacher Roles Observation Schedule (TROS) (Waxman, Wang, Lindvall, & Anderson, 1990) was used in the present study to systematically obtain information on teachers and behaviors. Similar to the COS, it is a systematic observation schedule designed to document observed teacher behaviors in the context of ongoing classroom instructional-learning processes. Teachers are observed with reference to (a) their interactions with students, other teachers, or aides, (b) the settings in which observed behaviors occur, (c) the types of content with which they are working, and (d) the specific types of behaviors they are using. Each teacher was observed for 10 30-second intervals during each data collection period. This observation schedule has been found to be valid and reliable in previous studies (Waxman & Huang, 1999). In the present study, the inter-observer agreement (Cohen's kappa) was found to be excellent, with an inter-observer reliability coefficient of .94.

Achievement Data

Student achievement was measured using the reading portion of the Texas Assessment of Academic Skills (TAAS) examination. The TAAS is a state-mandated test given to all students in grades 3–8 at the end of the academic year (TEA, 2001). Student scores on the TAAS are reported in three formats: raw scores, the Texas Learning Index (TLI), and the Scale Scores. A raw score is the number of items that a student answers correctly on a test. For example, if a student answers 48 questions correctly on a test with 53 items, the raw score is 48. The Texas Learning Index (TLI) is a score that measures how far a student's performance is above or below the passing standard. The TLI was developed to assess student performance in a single subject across time. For example, if a student's reading TLI score is 70 in grade 4, he or she is right at grade level. If the same student has a reading TLI score of 75 in grade 5, the student is above grade level and has demonstrated more than one year's normal progress in reading. The scale scores, like the TLI scores, are a mathematical transformation of the raw score and were developed to ensure that the same level of difficulty and passing standard is maintained across administrations. The scale score is applicable for the Spanish versions of TAAS (Grades 3–6 reading and mathematics and Grade 4 writing).

Student academic achievement was measured by the 2000 administration of the TAAS English reading exam. Specifically, TAAS 2000 TLI scores in reading were used. Since the methods of the present study included intact groups of students, a measure of prior student achievement was necessary to measure any differences in student English reading skills that may have resulted from the PIRP training. Prior achievement in English reading was measured by the prior year's TAAS examination. Specifically, the TAAS 1999 TLI scores in English reading were used.

The reliability of the TAAS test is based on internal consistency measures. In particular, the Kuder-Richardson Formula 20 (KR-20) continues to be used to demonstrate the reliability of the instrument. According to TEA (2001), most KR-20 measures of reliability are in the high .80 to low .90 range. Content and construct validity of the reading portion of the TAAS test is based on the statewide curriculum in the course. According to TEA (2001), the TAAS tests contain test items that conform to the requirements of the courses through educator and test developer input.

Procedures

All the fourth- and fifth-grade students in the treatment and comparison classrooms completed the learning environment survey near the beginning (September) and near the end of the school year (May). Trained researchers read survey items to all students and told the students that the survey questionnaire was not a test and their responses would not be seen by any school personnel. Trained researchers observed the resilient, average, and non-resilient students identified by teachers during regular reading classes.

A stratified random sample of students (stratified by resiliency classification) from each of the 11 classrooms were observed using the COS near the beginning and near the end of the school year. All experimental and comparison teachers were observed using the TROS near the beginning and near the end of the school year.

RESULTS

The results are reported separately for each of the instruments. The pretest data for the classroom observation data (TROS and COS) and the learning environment data are not reported here because there were few meaningful initial differences between the treatment and comparison groups. For example, on the TROS, there was only one statistically significant difference on task's content focus (90% for the treatment group and 47% for the comparison group). Additionally, on the COS, there was no statistically significant difference between the treatment and comparison groups on most pretest measures, including teacher assigned activities (100% of the time for both groups), rarely used activities designed for students to interact for instructional purposes (approximately 6% for both groups), working with manipulatives (never for both groups), and whole class setting (100% for both groups). There were, however, statistically significant pretest differences on the use of English only (79% for the treatment group and 100% for the comparison group) and the use of both English and Spanish (2% for the treatment group and 0% for the comparison group), which need to be considered when interpreting the results of the present study.

TROS Results

Table 1 reports the means and standard deviations of the teacher end-of-year observations by treatment group. Each mean value represents the average percentage of time that the teachers were observed to be involved in the activity. Both groups of teachers spent the majority of time interacting with students in an instructional manner: 93.3% of the time in the experimental group and 73.8% of the time in the comparison group. Nearly all instruction time (92.7%) in the comparison classrooms took place in a whole class setting. In the experimental classrooms, while the majority of instruction time (61.7%) took place in a whole class setting, 16.7% of the time teachers interacted with students in small groups and 11.7% of the time was spent at the students' desks. All communication in the comparison classroom was in English, while teachers in the experimental classrooms communicated with students in English 73% of the time and in both English and Spanish 27% of the time. The purposes of interaction were much more varied and extensive in the experimental classrooms than in the comparison classrooms. Teachers in the experimental classroom engaged in interaction more than 20% of the time for eight different reasons (i.e., praise student performance, task's product focus, check student work, task's content focus, task's process focus, show interest in student work, encourage extended student responses, and encourage students to succeed) compared to three reasons for the comparison group (i.e., task's content focus, communicate procedures, and correct student behavior). Finally, the nature of the interaction for teachers in both groups was mainly explaining but included commenting, listening, and questioning. Standard deviations of the activities in the experimental group ranged from 0.0 to 49.2 and in the comparison group from 0.0 to 36.0, indicating substantial variability in several observed behaviors of teachers in both groups.

Table 1.   Independent *t*-Test Results of Teacher Observations on the TROS by Treatment Group

	Experimental (*n* = 5)		Comparison (*n* = 6)		
	M	*SD*	*M*	*SD*	*t*
INTERACTION					
None	3.33	8.17	15.67	13.82	−1.88
With Student—Instructional	93.33	16.33	73.83	14.39	2.19**
With Student—Managerial	1.67	4.08	8.83	14.29	−1.18
With Student—Social	.00	.00	1.67	4.08	−1.00
SETTING					
Whole Class	61.67	49.16	92.67	17.96	−1.45
Small Group	16.67	40.83	.00	.00	1.00
Teacher's Desk	6.67	16.33	3.67	8.98	.39
Student's Desk	11.67	24.01	.00	.00	1.19
Traveling	3.33	8.17	3.67	8.98	−.07
LANGUAGE USED					
English	73.33	43.21	100.00	.00	−1.51
Both English and Spanish	26.67	43.21	.00	.00	1.51
PURPOSE OF INTERACTION					
Task's Content Focus	28.67	28.93	27.33	31.33	.08
Task's Product Focus	32.50	21.85	9.83	8.16	2.38**
Task's Process Focus	27.83	36.44	7.33	9.00	1.34
Communicate Procedures	.00	.00	21.33	19.61	−2.66*
Communicate Criteria	.00	.00	7.67	9.25	−2.03
Restructure Learning Task	2.83	6.94	.00	0.00	1.00
Redirect Student's Thinking	8.83	14.29	4.83	11.84	.53
Discuss Student's Work Plans	8.33	20.41	1.67	4.08	.78
Help Student Complete Work	10.00	15.49	3.67	8.98	.87
Check Student Work	32.17	26.39	12.50	17.30	1.53
Respond to Student Signal	.00	.00	4.00	6.33	−1.55
Show Interest in Student Work	26.67	29.70	9.50	17.34	1.22
Show Student Personal Regard	10.00	24.50	2.33	5.72	.75
Encourage Students to Succeed	22.83	25.93	3.33	8.17	1.76
Encourage Extended Student Responses	23.33	30.37	8.83	11.57	1.09

Table 1. Independent *t*-Test Results of Teacher Observations on the TROS by Treatment Group (Cont.)

	Experimental (n = 5)		Comparison (n = 6)		
	M	SD	M	SD	t
Praise Student Performance	36.67	27.61	5.67	8.98	2.62*
Correct Student Behavior	15.33	8.98	21.17	30.45	−.45
Correct Student Performance	10.33	20.02	3.67	5.72	.78
Provide Comprehensible Input	.00	.00	1.67	4.08	−1.00
Correct Language Errors	.00	.00	3.33	8.17	−1.00
NATURE OF INTERACTION					
Questioning	28.17	23.12	30.00	27.20	−.13
Explaining	61.00	23.88	29.00	26.49	2.20**
Commenting	34.50	19.52	22.00	31.55	.83
Listening	28.83	23.24	21.50	35.98	.42
Cueing or Prompting	.00	.00	6.83	7.81	−2.14
Demonstrating (visual aids)	1.67	4.08	5.33	8.64	−.94
Modeling	.00	.00	5.33	8.64	−1.51
Other	.00	.00	2.33	5.72	−1.00

Notes: * $p < .05$; ** $p < .10$

A *t*-test for independent samples was used to compare the experimental and comparison groups on observed behaviors. The results of these tests are presented in Table 1. Based on Levene's test for equality of variances, several of the activities were determined to have significantly different variability in most observed activities. All *t*-tests took the results of the Levene's test into account when determining significance.

The results indicated two significantly different purposes of activities between the experimental and comparison groups. First, teachers in the comparison group spent significantly more time (21.3%) communicating procedures to their students than teachers in the experimental group (0%). Second, teachers in the experimental group spent significantly more time (36.7%) praising their students' performance compared to the teachers in the comparison group (5.7%). Although significance levels were not obtained, three activities approached significance ($p < 0.10$). The teachers in the experimental group spent more time interacting with students for instructional reasons, focusing on the task's product, and explaining compared to their counterparts in the comparison group.

Classroom Observation Schedule Results

Table 2 reports the means and standard deviations of the student observations by treatment group. Each mean value represents the average percentage of time that the students were observed to be involved in the activity. The results from the COS revealed that students in both groups spend more than 80% of their time doing independent work (no interaction with other students or the teacher). All of the comparison classrooms and more than 90% of the experimental classrooms used teacher-selected activities. The predominant activity types in both types of classrooms were watching or listening, working on written work, reading, or not attending to task. More than 80% of class time was spent in a whole class setting, however, the experimental group did utilize small group and individual settings. Most of the time (more than 70%) students were on-task. Finally, comparison classroom communication was found to be English only, while teachers in the experimental classrooms communicated predominately in English, but also some in both English and Spanish.

Table 2. Independent *t*-Test Results of Student Observations on COS by Treatment Group

	Experimental ($n = 60$)		Comparison ($n = 55$)		
	M	SD	M	SD	t
Interactions					
No interaction/independence	82.10	25.89	85.75	22.51	−.80
With teacher—Instructional	6.05	10.90	6.00	12.48	.02
With teacher—Managerial	.52	2.82	1.16	6.97	−.66
With teacher—Social	.00	.00	.18	1.35	−1.00
With students—Instructional	9.20	18.31	1.55	5.00	3.11**
With students—Social	1.22	5.77	5.36	14.41	−1.99*
Selection of Activity					
Teacher assigned activity	92.92	23.71	100.00	.00	−2.31*
Student selected activity	7.08	23.71	.00	.00	2.31*
Activity Types					
Working on written work	24.88	30.97	21.49	25.89	.06
Interacting—Instructional	14.12	20.73	6.15	12.11	2.54*
Interacting—Social	1.45	6.00	4.25	10.58	−1.73
Watching or listening	42.60	35.42	38.20	29.17	.73

Table 2. Independent *t*-Test Results of Student Observations on COS by Treatment Group (Cont.)

	Experimental (n = 60)		Comparison (n = 55)		
	M	SD	M	SD	t
Reading	13.92	23.22	19.56	25.59	−1.24
Getting/Returning materials	1.10	5.97	1.24	4.10	−.14
Drawing, creating graphics	.00	.00	.55	2.99	−1.35
Working with manipulatives	.00	.00	3.56	9.04	−2.92**
Presenting/acting	.00	.00	.67	2.93	−1.70
Not attending to task	16.88	22.77	17.98	23.38	−.26
No activity/transition	1.33	5.87	2.40	8.65	−.78
Other	.00	.00	.53	3.91	−1.00
Setting					
Whole class	86.00	34.41	98.96	4.37	−2.89**
Small group	8.05	24.51	.36	1.89	2.42*
Pairs	.00	.00	.00	.00	
Individual	5.95	21.40	.67	2.93	1.89
Manner					
On task	80.33	22.45	73.22	29.64	1.46
Waiting for teacher	1.38	6.54	3.62	9.48	−1.48
Distracted	17.28	21.46	19.49	23.93	−.52
Disruptive	1.02	4.50	3.29	9.92	−1.56
Language Used					
English	79.07	37.48	100.00	.00	−4.33***
Spanish	1.35	6.47	.00	.00	1.62
Both English and Spanish	20.00	36.90	.00	.00	4.20***

Notes: $p < .05$; ** $p < .01$; *** $p < .001$

In addition, Table 2 presents the results of the independent *t*-tests of the student observations by treatment group. Several significant differences between the students of teachers who attended the PIRP training and their counterparts were apparent. The students in the experimental group spent significantly more time (9.2%) than the students in the comparison group (1.6%) interacting with students for instructional reasons, whereas students in the comparison group spent significantly more time (5.4%) than student in the experimental group (1.2%) interacting with students for social reasons. Students in the experimental group engaged in student-selected activities (7.0%), while students in the comparison group spent significantly more time in teacher assigned activities (100%). There were significant differences on two activity types. Students in the experimental group spent significantly more time (14.1%) than their comparison counterparts (6.2%) engaged in activities that involved instructional interaction. Students in the comparison group, however, were involved with working with manipulatives (3.6%) significantly more than experimental students (0.0%). There were significant differences between groups on the two activity settings as well. Students in the comparison group spent almost all their time (99.0%) in a whole class setting, while students in the experimental group spent significantly more time in small group (8.0%) settings. Finally, there were significant differences between the groups on two of the communication techniques. The students in the comparison group spent all their time speaking English; whereas students of teachers who were trained in PIRP spent 20.0% of the time speaking both English and Spanish.

Learning Environment Results

Table 3 reports the means and standard deviations of the learning environment constructs by treatment group. A mean value close to three for each variable indicates that the students perceived that the particular construct was very prevalent (i.e., responded that all of the items on the scale were "true"), while a mean value close to one indicates that the students perceived that the particular construct was not prevalent (i.e., responded that all of the items on the scales were "false"). The descriptive results suggested that, with the possible exception of Difficulty, students perceived to some degree that each construct did exist in their classrooms. The experimental group perceived Cohesion, Teacher Support, and Satisfaction as the most prevalent environmental characteristics, while the comparison group sensed Teacher Support, Cohesion, and Competition the most. Both groups perceived Difficulty and Friction the least.

The results of independent t-tests of the learning environment by treatment group also are presented in Table 3. There were statistically significant differences between the students whose teachers participated in the PIRP training and students whose teachers did not have special training on several constructs. Students in the experimental classrooms scored significantly higher on their perceptions of Cohesion ($M = 2.67$), Satisfaction ($M = 2.42$), and Difficulty ($M = 1.65$) than their counterparts ($M = 2.42$, $M = 2.15$, and $M = 1.43$, respectively). Additionally, students in the experimental group ($M = 1.84$) scored significantly lower on their perceptions of Friction than the students in the comparison group ($M = 2.04$). No differences

Table 3.   Independent t-Test Results of Learning Environment by Treatment Group

	Experimental ($n = 100$)		Comparison ($n = 110$)		
	M	SD	M	SD	t
Cohesion	2.67	.42	2.42	.65	3.31**
Competition	2.38	.62	2.41	.64	−.36
Difficulty	1.65	.49	1.43	.53	3.17**
Friction	1.84	.57	2.04	.59	−2.53*
Satisfaction	2.42	.68	2.15	.71	2.75**
Reading Self-Esteem	2.26	.56	2.32	.58	−.80
Equity	2.26	.59	2.31	.59	−.65
Teacher Support	2.46	.60	2.45	.68	.17

Notes: * $p < 0.05$; ** $p < 0.01$

between the two groups were found for Competition, Self-esteem in reading, Equity, and Teacher Support.

To measure the educational significance of the PIRP training on student perceptions of their learning environment, effect sizes for the variables were calculated. The effect size was calculated as the difference in the mean scores between the experimental and comparison groups divided by the standard deviation of the comparison group. The effect sizes with the largest magnitude were 0.42 for Difficulty, 0.38 for Cohesion, 0.38 for Satisfaction, and -0.34 for Friction. These values might be interpreted in the context of how the experimental group ranks with respect to the comparison group. For the positive effect sizes, if the comparison group were placed at the 50th percentile regarding their perceptions of the learning environment scales, then the experimental group would be at the 66th percentile in Difficulty and at the 64th percentile in both Cohesion and Satisfaction. Alternatively, if the comparison group were placed at the 50th percentile regarding their perception of Friction, then the students in the experimental group would be at the 36th percentile.

Reading Achievement Results

An analysis of covariate (ANCOVA) was performed to determine whether or not measurable differences existed in students' English reading achievement of the teachers who received PIRP training and those who did not. The results of the analysis are presented in Table 4. There is a significant difference ($F = 122.6$, $p < .001$) between the two treatment groups on the student reading TLI scores. Table 5 presents the means and standard deviations of the 1999 Reading TLI scores (pretest) and the 2000 Reading TLI scores (posttest) as well as the adjusted means of the treatment groups. The results indicate that, after controlling for prior achievement, students whose teachers were in the PIRP training program (87) scored significantly higher on the TAAS achievement test in reading than students of teachers who did not participate in the PIRP training (82). These findings should be viewed cautiously, however, because of the small number of students that had both pretest and posttest reading achievement scores.

Table 4. Analysis of Covariance Results of 2000 Reading Scale Scores Controlling for 1999 Reading TLI Scores

	SS	DF	MS	F	p
Treatment Group	475.422	1	475.422	7.276	.000
1999 Reading TLI	8008.628	1	8008.628	122.568	.000
Error	6468.693	102	65.340		

Table 5. Mean 1999 and 2000 Reading TLI Scores and Adjusted Mean Scores by Treatment Group

		1999 Reading TLI		2000 Reading TLI		Adjusted
Group	n	M	SD	M	SD	M
Experimental	29	87.24	9.80	91.38	9.02	86.98
Comparison	89	78.37	13.94	80.22	13.02	81.97

DISCUSSION

The findings from the present study are both promising and discouraging. The promising aspects are: (a) the treatment teachers' classroom instruction was better than the comparison teachers on some important aspects of teaching (e.g., more explanations, more encouragement of extended student responses, more encouraging students to succeed, more focus on the task's process), (b) students in the treatment classes reported a more positive classroom learning environment than students in the comparison classes (e.g., higher Cohesion, Satisfaction, and Teacher Support and less Friction), and (c) students in the treatment classrooms had significantly higher reading achievement gains than students in the comparison classrooms. While these results need to be viewed cautiously due to the selection validity threat and the small sample sizes, they still suggest that the program was relatively effective.

The discouraging aspects of this study are highlighted in the following sections and they relate to prevalent themes that impacted the implementation of the PIRP program. First, the primary concern that all of the PIRP teachers continually raised throughout the year is how will the PIRP program impact their students' achievement on the statewide assessment test. The former principal of this school was removed at the end of the last school year due to low test scores on the statewide assessment, and the current principal made it explicitly clear that teachers were expected to improve students' test scores. The teachers frequently told us that they were aware that the various components of the PIRP were important, but they also knew that they only were going to be held accountable for increased test scores on the statewide assessment tests. As Merrow (2001) puts it, "this constant focus on high-stakes tests creates intense pressures on teachers and administrators and unfortunate decisions are being made as pressure for 'accountability' overwhelms common sense" (p. 655).

A second predominant concern was that instruction in this school and throughout the district reflects a direct instructional, drill approach where teachers predominantly use whole-group instruction to emphasize basic skill acquisition (Padrón, Waxman, & Huang, 1999). Most of the PIRP teachers, for example, stated that they understood and valued the importance of the Five Standards of Effective Pedagogy, but they indicated that the District in-service training sessions only stressed the need for explicitly focusing (i.e., directly teaching) on the statewide assessment standards. Those teachers who began to implement/use more effective pedagogy did so only after the statewide assessment tests were completed for the year.

A third concern that became apparent to us was that the teachers thought that non-resilient students were unsuccessful because the students and/or their parents lacked the motivation and commitment to do well in school. This finding especially surprised us since every PIRP teacher could easily identify at least one non-resilient student they had taught that had significantly improved enough to be considered resilient. When the PIRP teachers were presented with the feedback about differences between resilient and non-resilient students in their classes, they were not surprised, but no one mentioned any specific actions they would take to help a non-resilient student.

During one of the PIRP training sessions, we read and discussed a chapter from Diane Barone's (1999) book on resiliency. This particular chapter focused on an African American child, Laquisha, who had a terrible home life, yet became resilient because of the caring and support of a few of her elementary school teachers. This is a compelling, true-life account that we thought would inspire every teacher into believing that they could similarly make a dramatic difference in the lives of some of their students. Unfortunately, the PIRP teachers did not think that they could make an impact in the lives of their students. This finding is similar to our prior Phase I research where we also found that teachers thought that low parental involvement and low student motivation and self-esteem contributed to non-resilient students' lack of academic success.

Another major concern that was constantly apparent was the school-level environment factors that impacted the PIRP teachers and other teachers in the school. Several structural or physical factors impacted teachers in this school. Although the school was recently remodeled and all the PIRP teachers were in newly constructed classrooms, there were several structural factors that teachers constantly complained about. These included: (a) poor air quality, (b) power outages, (c) infestation of classrooms by rodents, and (d) inoperable bathrooms. Other concerns that were raised throughout the school year by the teachers were that there was a lack of adequate instructional materials for their students and that computers in their classroom did not work. Teachers mentioned that there were no monies available to purchase any instructional materials because the entire school budget had been used to purchase test preparation (i.e., TAAS) materials. Consequently, teachers had to use their own monies if they needed something for the classroom. The teachers also indicated that there were no professional resources (e.g., academic books or journals) in the school that they could use as references.

Finally, it was apparent that the school was not a learning community for the teachers. While the PIRP program provided a learning community (i.e., continuous supported professional development) for the teachers where they could interact with colleagues about education, it was apparent that such a learning community did not exist throughout the school. In fact, PIRP teachers often talked in derogatory terms about many of the other teachers in the school. Part of this friction may be in part due to the large number of new teachers who were alternatively certified (~20%) and recently hired to teach in the fourth and fifth grades. The other plausible explanation for the lack of learning community stems from the fact that the principal was newly appointed. He had replaced the previous principal who was very popular with the teachers and the community and who had grown up in this community and had worked in the school district for many years.

A final noteworthy implication centers on the basic premise of the PIRP, namely focusing on the strengths of students who have managed to succeed despite coming from economically disadvantaged circumstances. The PIRP focused on both instructional strategies for promoting student learning and affective strategies for promoting resiliency in students. Teachers had more difficulty discussing issues related to promoting resiliency than they did talking about methods to improve classroom instruction. One plausible explanation is that teachers are unfamiliar with issues that are student-centered. As Darling-Hammond (1997) puts it, the teacher's job is to get into the hearts and minds of their students. It was apparent that the PIRP teachers knew some basic demographic or background information about their students (e.g., number of siblings, employment status of parents), but the teachers did not know very much about the goals and aspirations of their students. We rarely observed teachers discussing social or personal issues with students. This school, like others in urban school districts we have previously examined (Waxman, Huang, & Padrón, 1995; Waxman & Huang, 1998), was very depersonalized and teachers appeared to spend little time learning about their students.

If there was one component that we thought was more effective than others in the PIRP, it would probably be the specific feedback from the classroom observation and learning environment measures we provided to the teachers. This approach has been found to be very effective to help teachers understand their current instructional strengths and weaknesses (Fraser, 1991; Fraser & Fisher, 1986; Stallings, & Mohlman, 1988; Waxman, 1995; Waxman, Huang, & Padrón, 1995). The feedback profiles we provided to the PIRP teachers contained the teachers' individual data and a summary of the aggregated data across the elementary school. The class means for each of the indicators on both of the observation and survey instruments were presented along with the overall school mean value. This allowed each teacher to compare their class means to the school's average. Feedback from these profiles was used to stimulate dialogue and discussion about instructional strengths and weaknesses in the school. The profiles also helped initiate discussion about specific instructional areas that needed to be improved in the school.

The feedback profiles provided some guidelines for practice; they were not attempts to tell teachers what to do. These profiles provided teachers with concepts and criteria that they could use to reflect about their own teaching (Nuthall & Alton-Lee, 1990). We did not view the feedback session as one where we would apply our research findings into specific rules or guidelines for teachers to follow. Rather, the observational and survey feedback was intended to be used as guides for teachers where they and their colleagues could reflect about their practices on their own and decide what action to take. Quality staff development is one of the keys to successful school reform, and feedback from classroom observation and survey data can be the catalyst for this process.

The professional development of teachers needs to be seriously addressed in order to improve the education of ELLs (Jiménez & Barrera, 2000). As Jackson and Davis (2000) put it, "teachers cannot come to expect more of their students until they come to expect more of their own capacity to teach them, and until they seize the opportunity to witness their power to elicit dramatically better work from those groups of students who are today failing" (p. 14). The findings from the present case study suggest that much more emphasis must be placed in providing high-quality professional learning experiences and opportunities for teachers serving ELLs. While the PIRP provided a collaborative culture for the teachers involved in the program, it was still not enough to help them overcome some of the state, district, and school policies that limited their capacity for helping students in their classroom. The high-stakes testing context contributed to teachers' feelings of powerlessness and alienation which results in a weak sense of teacher self-efficacy and self-belief. When teachers have a strong sense of their own efficacy, they can make a real difference in the lives of their students (Ashton & Webb, 1986). On the other hand, when teachers lack hope, optimism, and self-belief, schools and classrooms will "become barren wastelands of boredom and routine" (Hargreaves & Fullan, 1998, p. 1).

Schools need to provide continuous, quality professional learning experiences for all teachers. These learning experiences need to help teachers become optimistic, hopeful, and empowered so that they believe they can help improve the education of all children. While the PIRP provided meaningful, learning experiences for the teachers involved, other projects need to be developed, implemented, and tested that focus on reculturing or changing the entire school climate so that teachers and administrators create more collaborative, supportive work cultures that enable them to be "out there" in ways that make a difference for all students (Hargreaves & Fullan, 1998).

ACKNOWLEDGMENTS

This research was supported in part by a Department of Education, Office of Educational Research and Improvement grant from the National Center for Research on Education, Diversity, and Excellence. The opinions expressed in this article do not necessarily reflect the position, policy, or endorsement of the granting agency.

A previous version of this paper was presented at the annual meeting of the American Educational Research Association, Seattle, WA.

Correspondence concerning this article should be addressed to Yolanda Padrón, College of Education, University of Houston, Houston, TX, 77204-5872. Electronic mail may be sent via Internet to [YPadron@UH.EDU].

REFERENCES

Alva, S.A. (1991). Academic invulnerability among Mexican-American students: The importance of protective and resources and appraisals. *Hispanic Journal of Behavioral Sciences, 13,* 18–34.

Ashton, P., & Webb, R. (1986). *Making a difference: Teacher's sense of efficacy.* New York: Longman.

Barone, D. (1999). *Resilient children: Stories of poverty, drug exposure, and literacy development.* Newark, DE: & Chicago: International Reading Association and National Reading Conference.

Benard, B. (1997). *Turning it around for all youth: From risk to resilience* (ERIC/CUE Digest No. 126). New York: ERIC Clearninghouse on Urban Education.

Bickart, T.S., & Wolin, S. (1997). Practicing resiliency in the elementary classroom. *Principal, 77*(2), 21–24.

Brown, A.P., & Padron, Y.N. (2001, April). *Portraits of fourth- and fifth-grade resilient and non-resilient Latino students.* Paper presented at the annual meeting of the American Educational Research Association, Seattle, WA.

Center for Research on Education, Diversity, and Excelllence. (1998). *Pedagogy, practice, and research* (Videotape). Santa Cruz, CA; author.

Darling-Hammond, L. (1997). *The right to learn: A blueprint for creating schools that work.* San Francisco: Jossey-Bass.

Dalton, S.S. (1998a). *Pedagogy matters: Standards for effective teaching practice* (Rsch. Rpt. No. 4). Santa Cruz, CA: Center for Research on Education, Diversity, and Excellence, University of California.

Dalton, S. (1998b). *Teaching Alive!* (CD-Rom). Santa Cruz, CA; California Consortium for Teacher Development and the Center for Research on Education, Diversity, and Excellence.

Dryden, M., & Fraser, B.J. (1996, April). *Evaluating urban systematic reform using classroom learning environment instruments.* Paper presented at the annual meeting of the American Educational Research Association, New York.

Fraser, B.J. (1991). Two decades of classroom environment research. In B.J. Fraser & H.J. Walberg (Eds.), *Educational environments: Evaluation, antecedents and consequences* (pp. 3–27). Oxford, England: Pergamon.

Fraser, B.J., Anderson, G.J., & Walberg, H.J. (1982). *Assessment of learning environments: Manual for Learning Environment Inventory (LEI) and My Class Inventory (MCI)* (3rd ed.). Perth, Australia: Western Australian Institute of Technology.

Fraser, B.J., & Fisher, D.L. (1986). Using short forms of classroom climate instruments to assess and improve classroom psychosocial environment. *Journal of Research in Science Teaching, 5,* 387–413.

Garmezy, N. (1991). Resilience and vulnerability to adverse developmental outcomes associated with poverty. *American Behavioral Scientist, 34,* 416–430.

Gersten, R., & Jiménez, R. (1998). Modulating instruction for language minority students. In E.J. Kameenui & D.W. Carnine (Eds.), *Effective teaching strategies that accommodate diverse learners.* Columbus, OH: Merrill.

Gordon, E.W., & Song, L.D. (1994). Variations in the experience of resilience. In M.C. Wang & E.W. Gordon (Eds.). *Educational resilience in inner-city America: Challenges and prospects* (pp. 27–43). Hillsdale, NJ: Lawrence Erlbaum.

Hargreaves, A., & Fullan, M. (1998). *What's worth fighting for out there.* New York: Teachers College.

Henderson, N. (1997). Resiliency in schools: Making it happen. *Principal, 77*(2), 10–17.

Henderson, N., & Milstein, M.M. (1996). *Resiliency in schools: Making it happen for students and educators.* Thousand Oaks, CA: Corwin.

Jackson, A.W., & Davis, G.A. (2000). *Turning points 2000: Educating adolescents in the 21st century.* New York: Teachers College.

Jiménez, R.T., & Barrera, R. (2000). How will bilingual/ESL programs in literacy change in the next millennium? *Reading Research Quarterly, 35,* 522–523.

Krovetz, M.L. (1999). *Fostering resiliency: Expecting all students to use their minds and hearts well.* Thousand Oaks, CA: Corwin.

Ladson-Billings, G. (1994). *The dreamkeepers: Successful teachers of African American children.* San Francisco: Jossey-Bass.

Le Celle-Peterson, M., & Rivera, C. (1994). Is it real for all kids? A framework for equitable assessment policies for English language learners. *Harvard Educational Review, 64,* 55–75.

McEnery, L.B. (1999, January). *Parents' perceptions of school and home literacy development.* Paper presented at the annual meeting of the Southwest Educational Research Association, San Antonio, TX.

McMillan, J.H., & Reed, D.F. (1994). At risk students and resiliency: Factors contributing to academic success. *The Clearing House, 67,* 137–140.

Merrow, J. (2001). Undermining standards. *Phi Delta Kappan, 82,* 653–659.

Nuthall, G., & Alton-Lee, A. (1990). Research on teaching and learning: Thirty years of change. *The Elementary School Journal, 90,* 546–570.

Padrón, Y.N. (1993). The effect of strategy instruction on bilingual students' cognitive strategy use in reading. *Bilingual Research Quarterly Journal, 16*(3 & 4), 35–51.

Padrón, Y.N. (1994). Comparing reading instruction in Hispanic/limited English-Proficient schools and other inner-city schools. *Bilingual Research Journal, 16*(3/4), 35–51.

Padrón, Y.N., & Knight, S.L. (1989). Linguistic and cultural influences on classroom instruction. In H.P. Baptiste, J. Anderson, J. Walker de Felix, & H.C. Waxman (Eds.), *Leadership, equity, and school effectiveness* (pp. 173–185). Newbury Park, CA: Sage.

Padrón, Y.N., & Waxman, H.C. (1993). Teaching and learning risks associated with limited cognitive mastery in science and mathematics for limited-English proficient students. In Office of Bilingual Education and Minority Language Affairs (Eds.), *Proceedings of the Third National Research Symposium on Limited English Proficient Students: Focus on middle and high school issues* (Vol. 2, pp. 511–547). Washington, DC: National Clearinghouse for Bilingual Education.

Padrón, Y.N., & Waxman, H.C. (1999a). Classroom observations of the Five Standards of Effective Teaching in urban classrooms with ELLs. *Teaching and Change, 7*(1), 79–100.

Padrón, Y.N., & Waxman, H.C. (1999b). Effective instructional practices for English language learners. In H.C. Waxman & H.J. Walberg (Eds.), *New directions for teaching practice and research* (pp. 171–203). Berkeley, CA: McCutchan.

Padrón, Y.N., Waxman, H.C., & Huang, S.L. (1999). Classroom and instructional learning environment differences between resilient and non-resilient elementary school students. *Journal of Education for Students Placed at Risk of Failure, 4*(1), 63–81.

Padrón, Y.N., Waxman, H.C., Read, L., Persall, F.C., & Huang, S.L. (1999, April). *Examining classroom and instructional learning environment differences between resilient and non-resilient English language learners.* Paper presented at the annual meeting of the American Educational Research Association, Montreal, Quebec.

Palincsar, A., & Brown, A. (1984). Reciprocal teaching of comprehension-fostering and comprehension-monitoring activities. *Cognition and Instruction, 1,* 117–175.

Read, L. (1999). Teachers' perceptions of effective instructional strategies for resilient and non-resilient students. *Teaching and Change, 7*(1), 33–52.

Reyes, P., & Paredes Scribner, A. (1995). Educational reform, students of color, and potential outcomes. *The High School Journal, 78,* 215–225.

Stallings, J.A., & Mohlman, G.G. (1988). Classroom observation techniques. In J.P. Keeves (Ed.), *Educational research, methodology, and measurement: An International handbook* (pp. 469–474). Oxford: Pergamon.

Stigler, J.W., & Hiebert, J. (1999). *The teaching gap: Best ideas from the world's teachers for improving education in the classroom.* New York: Free Press.

Strother, D.B. (Ed.). (1991). *Learning to fail: Case studies of students at risk.* Bloomington, IN: Phi Delta Kappa.

Texas Education Agency. (2001). *Texas student assessment program. Technical digest for the academic year 1999–2000.* Austin, TX: author. Available online: http://www.tea.state.tx.us/student.assessment/

Tharp, R.G. (1989). Psychocultural variables and constants: Effects on teaching and learning in schools. *American Psychologist, 44,* 1–11.

Tharp, R.G. (1997). *From at-risk to excellence: Research, theory, and principles for practice.* Santa Cruz, CA: Center for Research on Education, Diversity, and Excellence.

Tharp, R.G., & Gallimore, R. (1988). *Rousing minds to life: Teaching, learning, and schooling in social context.* Cambridge: Cambridge University Press.

U.S. Department of Education (1999). *The condition of education 1999.* Washington, DC: U.S. Department of Education, National Center for Education Statistics.

U.S. Department of Education (2000). *Key indicators of Hispanic student achievement: National goals and benchmarks for the next decade.* Washington, DC: U.S. Department of Education, National Center for Education Statistics.

Wang, M.C., & Gordon, E.W. (Eds.). (1994). *Educational resilience in inner-city America: Challenges and prospects.* Hillsdale, NJ: Lawrence Erlbaum.

Wang, M.C., Haertel, G.D., & Walberg, H.J. (1993). Toward a knowledge base for school learning. *Review of Educational Research, 63,* 249–294.

Wang, M.C., Haertel, G.D., & Walberg, H.J. (1994). Educational resilience in inner cities. In M.C. Wang & E.W. Gordon (Eds.), *Educational resilience in inner-city America: Challenges and prospects* (pp. 45–72). Hillsdale, NJ: Lawrence Erlbaum.

Waxman, H.C. (1995). Classroom observations of effective teaching. In A.C. Ornstein (Ed.), *Teaching: Theory into practice* (pp. 76–93). Needham Heights, MA: Allyn & Bacon.

Waxman, H.C., & Huang, S.L. (1997). Classroom instruction and learning environment differences between effective and ineffective urban elementary schools for African American students. *Urban Education, 32*(1), 7–44.

Waxman, H.C., & Huang, S.L. (1998). Classroom learning environments in urban elementary, middle, and high schools. *Learning Environments Research: An International Journal, 1,* 95–113.

Waxman, H.C., & Huang, S.L. (1999). Classroom observation research and the improvement of teaching. In H.C. Waxman & H.J. Walberg (Eds.), *New directions for teaching practice and research* (pp. 107–129). Berkeley, CA: McCutchan.

Waxman, H.C., & Huang, S.L., Anderson, L., & Weinstein, T. (1997). Investigating classroom processes in effective/efficient and ineffective/inefficient urban elementary schools. *Journal of Educational Research, 91,* 49–59.

Waxman, H.C., Huang, S.L., & Padrón, Y.N. (1995). Investigating the pedagogy of poverty in inner-city middle level schools. *Research in Middle Level Education, 18*(2), 1–22.

Waxman, H.C., & Padrón, Y.P. (1995). Improving the quality of classroom instruction for students at risk of failure in urban schools. *Peabody Journal of Education, 70*(2), 44–65.

Waxman, H.C., Padrón, Y.N., & Knight, S.L. (1991). Risks associated with students' limited cognitive mastery. In M.C. Wang, M.C. Reynolds, & H.J. Walberg (Eds.), *Handbook of special education: Emerging programs* (Vol. 4, pp. 235–254). Oxford: Pergamon.

Waxman, H.C., Walker de Felix, J., Martinez, A., Knight, S.L., & Padrón, Y.N. (1994). Effects of implementing classroom instructional models on English language learners' cognitive and affective outcomes. *Bilingual Research Journal, 18*(3/4), 1–22.

Waxman, H.C., Wang, M.C., Lindvall, C.M., & Anderson, K.A. (1990). *Classroom observation schedule technical manual* (rev. ed.). Philadelphia: Temple University, Center for Research in Human Development and Education.

Winfield, L.F. (1991). Resilience, schooling, and development in African-American youth: A conceptual framework. *Education and Urban Society, 24,* 5–14.

Wlodkowski, R.J., & Ginsberg, M.B. (1995). *Diversity and motivation: Culturally responsive teaching.* San Francisco: Jossey-Bass.

Part III

EFFECTIVE TEACHER TRAINING MODELS

CHAPTER 8

MODELS OF BILINGUAL TEACHER PREPARATION:

WHAT HAS WORKED AT THE UNIVERSITY OF TEXAS AT EL PASO

Josefina V. Tinajero and Dee Ann Spencer

ABSTRACT

This chapter presents a profile of two highly successful programs at the University of Texas at El Paso focused on improving the preparation of teachers: a pre-service program for paraprofessionals and other undergraduate students interested in bilingual teacher certification, Project BECMS—Bilingual Education with a Concentration in Mathematics and Science—and an in-service program for bilingual teachers, Project BEEMS—Bilingual Education with Emphasis in Mathematics and Science. The chapter discusses (1) the needs in the El Paso area that led to the request of federal funds; and (2) effective new structures and practices for professional development inherent in the two projects. An examination of participants' surveys is discussed in terms of program sustainability. The chapter then offers practical advice to educational professionals at various levels: school districts, university professors and students of all teacher preparation programs, and policy makers. The chapter concludes with a discussion of a number of interconnected factors to which the success and sustainability of two complementary teacher preparation projects can be attributed.

241

INTRODUCTION

All teachers bring strengths to the profession and ... are capable of both excellence and improvement. Teachers want their students to achieve and feel good about themselves, and they will attempt new ways of teaching when they are convinced that their students will benefit.
—*Green and del Bosque (1994, p. 11).*

Despite the dedication of many teachers, English Language Learners (ELLS) are not faring well in U.S. public schools. As documented in the introduction to this book, a major problem related to ELL students' academic underperformance is the lack of certified teachers prepared to meet their social, linguistic, cultural, and academic needs. In addition, pre-service and in-service teachers lack knowledge in methodology, content, and pedagogy appropriate for ELLs (De la Cruz, 1998; Mullis & Jenkins, 1998; Secada, 1992; Secada & De la Cruz, 1996; Suter, 1996). In particular, both novice and veteran teachers report being unprepared to teach math and science (Mather & Chiodo, 1994). An alarming number of teachers in self-contained classrooms (including bilingual classrooms) are performing inadequately in the teaching of math and science, citing as a major factor their lack of preparation for teaching these two subject areas (Garfunkel, & Young, 1992; Oakes, 1990a, b; NSF, 1990; O'Malley, 1992).

To address this complex of problems, the College of Education at the University of Texas at El Paso (UTEP) mounted the following major, two-fold, complementary initiative: to increase the number of bilingual teachers and to transform bilingual teacher preparation in mathematics and science. Working in conjunction with several school districts in the El Paso area, the College of Education revamped its bilingual program to incorporate creative new coursework, hands-on field experiences, specialized workshops focused on ELL issues and advocacy, and intensive mentoring by professors for the duration of students' undergraduate and graduate years.

In June of 1993, the College of Education secured a five-year Title VII grant to enable the University to extend and refine its efforts to address both the shortage of bilingual education teachers and their lack of preparation in teaching mathematics and science. A similar grant was secured in 1994. The overall goal of these grants was to enhance the capacity of local schools to provide excellent educational experiences for ELLs in mathematics and science by supporting the professional development of teachers and pre-service development of undergraduate students interested in becoming bilingual teachers. Both grants were focused on preparing and supporting educators to help ELLs achieve high academic performance within instructional contexts characterized by rigorous standards of learning and development. The grants enabled paraprofessionals (i.e., instructional aides) to enroll at UTEP and join other undergraduate students in pursuing and completing their undergraduate degree in bilingual education with a concentration in mathematics and science (Project BECMS). In addition, in-service teachers were able to pursue and complete a Master's degree in bilingual education with emphasis in mathematics and science (Project BEEMS). During their coursework, all participants—undergraduates and graduates alike—received training in leadership and mentoring strategies coupled with career-development advisement.

An extended goal common to these two Projects was that the UTEP model would influence other university-based teacher education programs by demonstrating the benefits of cross-district and school-university collaboration and reform. Toward this end, both projects collaborated with teachers and administrators in urban and rural districts in the design and implementation of the projects, and recruited teachers and instructional aides from these areas to participate in BEEMS and BECMS. Over the five-year period presented here, 1993–1998, more than 110 new and existing teachers upgraded their skills in the designated areas. All completed either the BIS (Bachelor of Interdisciplinary Science) or M.Ed. degree with a specialization in bilingual education and an emphasis in both math and science.

This chapter presents a profile of these two highly successful programs at the University of Texas at El Paso. The authors first discuss the needs in the El Paso area that led to the request for federal funds. They also discuss effective new structures and practices for professional development inherent in these two projects. The chapter then offers practical advice to educational professionals at various levels: for school districts—including teachers, administrators, curriculum specialists and staff development specialists; for university professors and students of all teacher preparation programs; and for policy makers at all levels of schooling. The chapter concludes with a discussion of a number of interconnected factors to which the success of these two complementary projects can be attributed.

NEED FOR PROJECTS BECMS AND BEEMS IN THE EL PASO AREA

The El Paso/Juárez complex of more than 2 million residents represents the largest metropolitan area along the 2,000 miles of international border separating the United States and Mexico. El Paso's metropolitan area, a designated Empowerment Zone, is the fifth poorest in the United States, and El Paso's school districts (two of the eight largest in Texas) have a history of severe under-funding. Thus, El Paso is marked by great disparities and challenges, including high levels of poverty, high unemployment, and in general, poor academic achievement. A significant factor in El Paso's population growth is the migration of residents from Mexico. Almost a quarter of El Paso's population is foreign born, more than 70% of El Pasoans are of Mexican descent, over 75% are Hispanic, and over 50% of El Paso's households speak Spanish as the language of preference.

The University of Texas at El Paso (UTEP) prepares teachers for the nine school districts in the region. The vast majority of the 15,000 students at UTEP are from area schools and more than 40% are the first in their families to attend college. More than 70% of UTEP's students are Mexican-American and most are from low-income families. They represent a promising pool of potential teachers and need to be introduced early to careers in teaching. UTEP, the only state university which offers bilingual education training within a 350-mile radius in Texas, graduates approximately 600 teachers a year. They constitute 70% of the new teachers hired by the local public schools. Seventy percent of these graduates are Mexican-American and 3% are African American. However, even these six hundred new teachers each year do not meet the staffing needs of the area's schools, particularly in the critical specializations of bilingual education, mathematics and science. In 1993, when federal funds were first secured, the University was graduating approximately 500 teachers per year.

In 1993 and 1994 when proposals for Projects BECMS and BEEMS were written, data showed that about 18.8% of ELLs (6,000) in the El Paso area were not being served by bilingual education or ESL programs. These figures represented a shortage of about 240 trained bilingual teachers to serve ELLs in the UTEP area (25:1 student–teacher ratio). The shortage of bilingual teachers had compelled some of the large districts in the metropolitan area to offer "salary supplements" for bilingual teachers in order to attract sufficient numbers. The smaller school districts in the area were even harder hit because they were small and more rural. The smaller school districts were even harder hit, partly because their social environments and geographic distance from urban areas offered little to attract new teacher prospects.

The teacher shortage was being filled in part by special permit and regular teachers who were not trained to work with ELLs, much less trained in the current, innovative teaching and learning methodologies in mathematics and science. There were, at this time, 101 teachers on special permits working in bilingual education classrooms and 22 teachers on special permits working in ESL classrooms.

Thus, the shortage of bilingual teachers had resulted in thousands of ELL students neither being served through a bilingual education program nor being taught by teachers who had appropriate training in bilingual/ESL methodologies. The ultimate result was lower achievement and performance scores earned by ELLs on standardized achievement tests and, most important, the Texas Assessment of Academic Skills test (TAAS), the State basic skills test used to determine eligibility to graduate from high school.

In addition to the critical shortage of teachers, data showed that bilingual teachers, in general, had little formal training in mathematics or science content and methods, and that the need existed for improved instructional capabilities in these two subject areas. The results of two surveys conducted with bilingual teachers prior to the request of federal funds found dramatic deficiencies in the number of credit hours teachers had earned in science and mathematics content courses and pedagogy. Teachers were found to have averaged only one course in the areas of chemistry, physics, biology and geology. Teachers averaged 1.5 courses in mathematics. The average number of courses taken in teaching mathematics and science in Spanish was .35, that is, less than 1 course. It also became clear from the results of the Non-Referenced Assessment Program in Texas (NAPT) test administered to all students in Texas that teachers did a relatively poor job of imparting the essential elements in mathematics and science to their students. These data clearly demonstrated the need for mathematics and science content and methods instruction among teachers in general, and, particularly for areas such as the El Paso region, among bilingual elementary teachers. To achieve even to normative academic expectations, as well as to excel, ELLs needed teachers who could convey basic knowledge in science and mathematics in both the native language and English, while developing their English proficiency. Projects BEEMS and BECMS addressed these needs.

COMPREHENSIVE PROFESSIONAL DEVELOPMENT THROUGH PROJECTS BECMS AND BEEMS

Professional development refers to processes and practices that improve the job-related knowledge, skills, and attitudes of school employees (Loucks-Horsely, 1987, as cited by IASA Professional Development Planning Subgroups, 1995). In planning the professional development activities for the participants of both Project BECMS and BEEMS, we followed the fundamental belief of Green and de Bosque that all teachers: "bring strengths to the profession and ... are capable of both excellence and improvement. Teachers want their students to achieve and feel good about themselves, and they will attempt new ways of teaching when they are convinced that their students will benefit" (1994, p. 11). The following five principles, suggested by Wilde (1996), guided the planning of the professional development activities for Projects BEEMS and BECMS:

1. Professional development must build upon practitioners' current foundation of basic skills, knowledge, and areas of expertise. It will link new knowledge and activities with what they already know and are able to do, and extend their thinking.
2. Professional development should include rich and varied opportunities that engage practitioners as learners and offer the opportunity to apply new skills and knowledge.
3. Professional development should offer practitioners opportunities for practicing the new skills, strategies, and techniques; providing feedback on performance; and continuing follow-up activities.
4. Successful and effective professional development should be manifested by measurable increases in teacher knowledge and skills.
5. Professional development should be linked to measurable outcomes in student performance, behavior, or achievement, and, more important, to all three.

In addition, for teachers of ELLs, professional development should also include an understanding of the basics of language (its nature and how it operates), language acquisition (first and second, and literacy) and how language works in written form to communicate (Krashen & Biber 1988; Snow & Tabors 1993). These understandings, and their effective articulation and integration in applied classroom practice, are critical to ELLs becoming literate in standard, academic English and maximizing their academic achievement across the curriculum—especially in mathematics and science. Teachers, regardless of their content areas and specializations, must possess basic conceptual and skill-based knowledge concerning language, language acquisition, and literacy to enable ELLs to move fluidly and with increasing success within general literacy and academic contexts, in school and in their wider community.

Thus, major components incorporated into both Projects BECMS and BEEMS were: concepts of language, language acquisition, and content and teaching of mathematics and science. In addition, both projects incorporated (1) mentoring of participants by university faculty, (2) intensive preparation in ELLs issues and advocacy, (3) leadership development, (4) parental involvement, and (5) intensive field-based experiences (particularly for undergraduate students) that were designed and implemented in collaboration with the schools. In short, a major aim of both projects was to infuse the curriculum with the knowledge, skills, and strategies—with special emphasis in mathematics and science instruction—with which all school personnel need to be equipped when working with ELLs. Both projects, therefore, focused on undertaking curricular revisions and enhancing the core courses required of all pre-service and practicing classroom teachers. New courses and special workshops were also developed, and will be elaborated upon later in this text

Program Recruitment and Enrollment

The administrators—who shared the responsibility for both projects—actively recruited undergraduate students already enrolled at UTEP, as well as paraprofessionals and teachers from the seven school districts in the El Paso area. The selection of participants was done collaboratively and involved university project administrators and school district personnel. All undergraduate students were required to enroll as a cohort for twelve credit hours each semester, and six during the summers. Teachers in BEEMS—all of whom were pursuing Master's degrees—were required to enroll as a cohort for six credit hours each semester, including summers. The cohort model proved to be extremely important for all project participants, providing them with the opportunity to support each other, to work with teachers outside their district and to work collaboratively in numerous projects and activities. During the five-year period under discussion, a total of 35 paraprofessionals and other undergraduate students completed their degrees through Project BECMS, and seventy-seven (77) bilingual teachers completed their master's degrees through Project BEEMS.

Curriculum Development and Enhancement and Instruction

From the beginning of both projects, program administrators and their university and school district partners were in common accord relative to their vision regarding curriculum and instruction: the character, quality, and nature of what is taught to ELLs, particularly in mathematics and science, and how it is taught needed to be altered dramatically. University and school district personnel agreed that mathematics and science content and teaching had to engage project participants (and, ultimately ELLs) in (1) active, hands-on discovery learning and experimentation; (2) project-based activities that are interdisciplinary and stress the relationship and connections among subject-matter skill and knowledge; (3) learning of concepts and gaining of knowledge within the context of application to real-world problems; (4) experiences rooted in the realities of our community—a binational, bilingual border; (5) exploring, observing, reasoning, and problem-solving in their environment using mathematics and science; and (6) working in teams.

Program administrators also recognized the need for teachers of mathematics and science to serve as facilitators of student learning rather than as dispensers of knowledge. They understood that teachers need to guide and assist students as they engage in exploration, questioning, analyzing and problem solving across all learning contexts, and particularly in developing powerful mathematical reasoning skills. These three needs, once realized and integrated in instructional practice, would enable ELL students to become successful, independent learners and critical thinkers, and thus, increasingly reliant on their own authority, rather than that of the teacher.

During the first two years of the dual projects, new courses were developed and others were revised or enhanced, or both, to improve the teaching of mathematics and science. As the two projects were designed with an interdisciplinary, collaborative focus, the course revisions and enhancements were realized with faculty from the College of Science and administrators of an Eisenhower grant which focused on improving mathematics and science instruction. This collaboration had the additional benefit of enabling students in Project BEEMS to enroll in courses offered through the Eisenhower grant, including Chemistry for Teachers and Physics for Teachers. This experience allowed students to capitalize on the exceptional opportunity to work directly with professors in the departments of mathematics and science who shared an interest in teacher preparation.

Project BEEMS and BECMS administrators also sought to broaden its support base by collaborating with the Sandia National Laboratories (SNL) of Albuquerque, New Mexico. The Laboratories provided a chemist with an interest in the preparation of bilingual teachers. In his consulting capacity, he taught a special course for both graduate and undergraduate students: "Teaching Content in Spanish," in which the GANAS (Gaining Access to Natural Abilities in Science) model was integrated. This two-week institute focused on innovative ways of teaching mathematics and science in bilingual settings. Additional broadening of the program's support base was made possible by the program administrators' practice of employing several consultants, who were experts in mathematics and science instruction. The consultants conducted workshops and also provided faculty members in UTEP's Department of Teacher Education the opportunity for capacity building, an experience which ultimately served as the basis for the department's curriculum and course revisions.

In addition to their course work and field experiences, BEEMS students also participated in numerous workshops on integrating mathematics and science effectively in classroom practice. Workshop themes included "Experience Mathematics Through Manipulatives," "Workshop on Teaching Mathematics and Science in Whole Language," and "How to Use Manipulatives in the Teaching of Mathematics and Science." Workshops focused on exemplary and integrative teacher qualities, such as (1) "hands-on" manipulation of concrete objects for specific learning objectives in mathematics and science; (2) the development of appropriate questions for assessing students' understanding of mathematics; and (3) techniques for helping students solve problems, reason, communicate, and become confident in their ability to do mathematics and science.

Mentoring Project Participants

Research on the importance of having someone counsel and guide one in a career began in the mid-1970s. Having a mentor and being a mentor are important developmental tasks for the career-oriented (Sheehy, 1981). Mentoring activities in most career programs have resulted in a positive influence on employees (Garfunkel & Young, 1992; Gibelhauf & Bowman, 2000).

Mentoring, as defined by Projects BEEMS' and BECMS' administrators and staff, provided for collegial interaction among program administrators, professors, and project participants. Project participants, for example, were mentored by their professors, and particularly by the program director and coordinator. The mentors and their students often presented together at local, state and national conferences and collaboratively organized the local BEEMS conference. Mentors and program participants presented together at least three times a year, including presentations at the TABE (Texas Association for Bilingual Education), NABE (National Association for Bilingual Education) and the local BEEMS (Bilingual Education with an Emphasis in Math and Science) conferences. Examples of presentations at conferences by mentors and BEEMS/BECMS participants included the following: "Strategies for Involving Parents in the Educational Process in Math and Science: Project BEEMS," presented in 1994 in Los Angeles at the OBEMLA National Professional Development Institute with three BEEMS participants; "Teacher Enhancement: Bilingual Education with Emphasis in Mathematics and Science (Project BEEMS)" presented in 1994 in Washington, D.C. at the third Annual Conference of the Quality Education for Minorities in Mathematics, Science and Engineering (MSE) Network with two BEEMS participants; "Interactive Strategies for Teaching Math and Science to LEP Students" presented in 1996 in Orlando, Florida at the NABE Conference in Orlando, Florida with 6 BEEMS and BECMS participants; and "Parent Involvement: The UTEP/Ysleta ISD Even Start Family Learning Center Project," presented in 1996 in El Paso, Texas at the TABE Conference with four BEEMS and BECMS participants. BEEMS and BECMS participants continue to present at local, state, and national conferences.

Leadership and Advocacy

Both Projects BEEMS and BECMS infused an ongoing education and leadership development component for all project participants, in which they engaged in dialogue- and activity-centered experiences regarding the phenomena of leaders and leadership. This curricular infusion culminated in a natural constituency of beginning and experienced teachers who were (1) knowledgeable and highly articulate about ELL social and academic issues, (2) steeped in research-based practices, and (3) strong and willing advocates for quality instruction and high academic attainment for ELLs. As will be evident in the following passages, these professional characteristics were put to effective use even during their tenure in the projects, as participants disseminated information to principals and other administrators, to other teachers, and to parents in their schools and communities, and became deeply involved in the home-school connection through direct and extended interactions with parents of students.

Parental Involvement Component

Parents are among the partners who are most critical to the success of ELLs. Unfortunately, parents of ELLs are, in too many cases, neither informed nor organized in ways that make it possible for them to significantly contribute to improving their children's academic experiences and ultimate academic success, particularly in mathematics and science courses. Parents of ELLs, moreover, generally look to the education system to provide their children with a better chance at success in life and do not see themselves as a significant formal partner with the teacher in their children's academic success.

In light of the above, the program administrators added a new component to the preparation of bilingual teachers beginning in the Spring of 1994. Specifically, all cohorts of new teacher candidates and candidates for the Master's degree would receive classroom and field-based instruction in teaching in urban schools and communities, with particular focus on collaborating with parents in the education of their children. This experience was as essential as it was innovative, particularly with respect to teacher retention. The Metropolitan Life Survey of Beginning Teachers, for example, indicates that a major reason for new teachers leaving the field is a lack of success at working with parents and the community.

During the first two years of the dual-project program, the course "Involving Parents in the Educational Process" was developed and field-tested at both undergraduate and graduate levels. Because of academic constraints related to poverty, lack of formal education, and limited

English skills, many parents do not know how to help their children learn math and science subject matter. This course, in its respective forms at the undergraduate and graduate levels, addressed the above-mentioned parental needs and provided opportunities for students, through field-based activities, to work directly with parents and their children. In the course, graduate (that is, in-service teachers) and undergraduate (that is, pre-service teachers) students planned and carried out mini-conferences in the schools where parents learned how to engage their children in mathematics and science activities at home. All students worked collaboratively with parents at the Even Start Literacy Center, located at the Housing Authority in one of the districts. Additionally, students prepared lessons integrating mathematics and science, and worked with children and their parents in highly motivational hands-on settings, in which they used manipulatives and materials readily available in the home. Prior to, and concurrent with, the miniconferences, graduate and undergraduate students prepared their lessons and presentations at UTEP for use in the mini-conferences and learned how to deliver the content in pedagogically exciting and motivating ways to parents in both English and Spanish.

The above-mentioned course, due to its effectiveness as an instructional and learning experience for both students and parents, became a required course for undergraduate students specializing in bilingual education and an elective at the graduate level. The focus of this multi-tiered course is to help teachers, both novice and veteran, develop the knowledge and skills of parents so that they can support more fully the home and school-related experiences of their children in order that they may attain high mathematics and science achievement.

EVALUATION OF THE PROJECTS

Several qualitative methods were used to gather data that, once analyzed, would identify, codify, and help explain students' perspectives, opinions, and first-hand descriptions of Projects BEEMS and BECMS. The effects of the projects on practicing teachers' and prospective teachers' perspectives, career aspirations and choices, and their work in classrooms were likewise assessed. Data were gathered from questionnaires sent to all participants during the period when they were in the program, and, for those in Project BEEMS, questionnaires were again sent out in February 2001. More than 50% of the participants responded to the February 2001 questionnaire. The purpose of the surveys and questionnaire was to assess the short- and long-term impact of both Projects.

In addition to the above mentioned data gathering strategies, during the five years of the implementation of the projects complementary data were gathered from focus group interviews. Teachers and prospective teachers in the focus groups were asked about their perspectives, opinions, and first-hand descriptions of the respective projects and the effects on their work and professional lives. Thirty (30) BECMS participants were interviewed in 3 focus groups—two in the winter of 1995 and one in the fall of 1995. Seventy-five BEEMS teachers were interviewed in 6 focus groups—two in the winter of 1994, two in the winter of 1995, and two in the fall of 1995. The interviews were transcribed and coded, then integrated with similar questions in the open-ended questions section asked on the survey questionnaires. Additional data were compiled from a review of undergraduate and graduate students' journals written while completing their course-work.

Focus Group Interviews and Survey Comments: 1994–1995

A summary of the participants' perspectives and experiences in the BEEMS and BECMS projects are reviewed in this section.

1. The program (in the form of both projects) exerted a major influence *on teachers' pedagogical practice and educational philosophy.* Many program graduates reported they had taken a totally different approach to their teaching, citing the inclusion of more effective pedagogical paradigms and methodologies. More specifically, participants reported a greater use of instruction involving a thematic approach, a whole language approach, cooperative learning, and hands-on projects.

    As a result of my participation in Project BEEMS, I now focus my instruction a lot more on math and science and in developing integrated thematic units that are highly motivational for my students. One such example is a unit entitled "Pockets, Pockets!" This unit includes a great many hand-on activities with a special emphasis on endangered species. I have also integrated strategies to encourage my second language learners to develop higher order thinking skills. My children learn more about math and science in this very fun way.

2. Teachers and prospective teachers reported they felt *more confident in mathematics and science.* The teachers agreed that previous to their participation in the program, they had a fear (in the form of anxiety or avoidance, or both) of mathematics and science stemming from their own experiences in school, as well as from not having had adequate training in their coursework. They said, however, that after having been in the BEEMS and BECMS projects—that is, going to

classes, undertaking filed experiences, and participating in conferences—their fears had dissipated and the world of mathematics and
science had opened up to them in a fun and exciting way. Now they
reported that they looked forward to conducting mathematics and
science projects in their classes, and in fact, had shifted their lesson
plans from a focus on language arts to an integrated focus where
mathematics and science played a salient pedagogical role.

> *I always felt very weak in science. My father was a surgeon and I
> always felt that, why couldn't I have been into science more? But I
> didn't like science a lot. And all this cooperative learning, hands-on,
> that is very foreign to me because I was born and raised in Mexico and
> we didn't have anything like that. But doing the actual experiments
> and hands-on in a class this summer helped me a lot with chemistry
> and how to bring it to the elementary level. And it's amazing how easy
> it has been for me to really bring it into the classroom and see the kids
> and their excitement. So all this is fun. I'm a little kid; the little kid in
> me is coming out. And I think that's what is really neat.*

3. Teachers reported they had taken on *different roles* in their class-
    rooms—from a less teacher-centered to a more student-centered
    approach, where they exercised a role of facilitator and monitor of
    learning. Program graduates also reported using more effective
    strategies for managing students' behavior and, in the case of the
    BEEMS graduates, reported being more analytical (that is, less emo-
    tional, less anxious, more thoughtful) toward establishing and
    maintaining classroom management, as a result of their experience
    in BEEMS.

    > *I now use a lot more hands-on activities, more strategies for developing
    > higher order thinking skills, my kids participate more actively in their
    > own learning. We use more family and community resources and we
    > have incorporated more technology—related activities.*

4. Program graduates emphasized they had experienced considerable
    professional and personal growth as a result of being in the program.
    Some said they felt "renewed" or "energized," and that teaching was
    more fun than in the past. Particularly impressive were comments
    from teachers having more than 20 years' experience and who had
    felt "burned out" previous to their entry into the program. They
    now reported having a tremendous sense of professional renewal, as
    if they were getting a chance to begin again their teaching career.

    > *Deep inside we're full of creativity and we slowly burn ourselves out.
    > We're now reviving ourselves. It's not just lecture [in the program];
    > there are a variety of activities that can be used immediately.*

In terms of *personal growth*, teachers reported feeling more self-confident, especially in presenting before an audience. Some mentioned they had always sat back and let others take leadership roles but now viewed themselves as better leaders, engaged in organizing other teachers and providing training in mathematics and science within their schools. In addition to presenting to teacher audiences within their schools, they also felt confident presenting in front of larger audiences in workshops and conferences locally, nationally, and even internationally (*"It has made me feel that I can conquer any obstacle that comes my way"*).

5. Within the BEEMS cohort, most participants mentioned the positive benefits of working on authentic instructional-related activities at different school sites because the experience fostered *interchange with peer professionals* across different school districts in El Paso, as well as with teachers in Mexico. Rather than working in isolated environments within schools or within school districts, as is typically the case, the boundaries and barriers of communication were broken down through the collaborative method that characterized the program design. Students noted that this networking reduced competition between districts and fostered a sense of collegiality.

    I continue to think that the major strength of Project BEEMS was the collaboration of ideas in math and science from educators in the different school districts. The networking with other professionals who have the same interest in math and science continues to be very important. This was a direct result of my participation in BEEMS. I felt that we were not competing against each other to see which district was better. Rather, we were working side by side with one common goal—the children!

6. BECMS students were appreciative of the *opportunity to work with experienced teachers* and gain the benefit of their expertise and knowledge. For example, one student commented:

    It's so incredible how things that were shared with us during the workshops could sink in so deep and all of a sudden pop out automatically as I started teaching in the classroom myself. It really feels good to be able to do that and have the confidence that more can be offered … It has allowed me to open a variety of doors in the field of education that will give me a better view of what not to become as I join the teaching force.

    A major goal of the BEEMS project was the dissemination of information to other teachers. This was accomplished, in part, through the development of an annual conference organized and conducted by the BEEMS' and BECMS' students. The first conference was held in April of 1994 at which 300 teachers from the seven school districts were present. By 2001, the BEEMS conference has grown to include 700 teachers. Participants of both Projects BEEMS and BECMS continue to present at each annual conference.

Teachers' comments about a trip to Guadalajara, where they attended the *Seminario de Actualizacion para Maestros Bilingues* and *La Feria Internacional del Libro*, as well as comments about their visits to schools in Juárez during the U.S.-Mexico Institute, were especially meaningful as the experiences left a deep impression on the teachers' views of cross cultural educational issues. The experiences not only affected their own teaching techniques, but also gave them an appreciation for Mexican teachers, and a much better understanding of the school experiences of students who come from Mexico.

Being able to spend a day in a low economic elementary school in Mexico opened my eyes to appreciate what I have in my classroom.

7. All teachers mentioned they had significantly better relationships with *parents* as a result of being in the BEEMS and BECMS projects and having taken the course "Involving Parents in the Educational Process." Teachers were asked to keep records of activities they organized or participated in which provided direct contact with parents. Data for the *first year* showed that teachers engaged in a wide variety of activities with parents. The total number of activities for the 34 teachers who provided these data was 109. The total number of parents participating in these activities was 3,190. Data for the *second year* demonstrated that of the 23 project teachers reported, 2,824 parents participated in activities. It should be noted that there was wide variation between the teachers and the number of parents with whom they had contact. For example, some teachers worked with several groups of small numbers of parents and others very large groups of 100 or more.

Examples of parent activities organized by the teachers were:

- mathematics and science nights (ways to help children with their homework);
- using computers;
- parent orientations and conferences;
- celebrations of Mexican culture.

All of the teachers commented on the improvement in communication they had with parents as the result of their course work and involvement in the BEEMS and BECMS projects. As their communication improved, parents became more involved, and in the process, teachers better understood that parents wanted the contact; that they were not "disinterested bystanders," but often did not know what to do to become more involved in their children's education. By taking the first step in bridging the communication gap with parents, teachers gained parents' support and a partnership was built which ultimately helped the children's progress in school. One teacher noted the appreciation of parents' and grandparents' contribution to the education of their children, regardless of its formal or informal nature:

> *I'm not only getting the parents involved in my projects, but the grandparents as well. And that has taught me to become humble because I see that not only the parents but the grandparents have a lot of knowledge they can share with me. They are very smart people and I need them as much as they need me.*

8. Teachers said that they had a *greater appreciation of bilingual education* and of bilingual teachers, and indicated that they had more compassionate attitudes toward their Spanish-speaking students.

    > *My BEEMS experience altered my view of bilingual education, which I used to regard simply as a bridge to the world of English. I am now convinced that first language cognitive development is key.*

    > *Even though I was always a bilingual teacher, I have now become more passionate toward the bilingual students' needs.*

    > *BEEMS helped me to be a better advocate for bilingual education.*

9. In addition to the above-mentioned factors, the students lauded the *leadership* of their professors, finding them to be instrumental to the success of the program. Students saw their professors as experts who could demonstrate direct application of philosophies and methods to classroom activities; as caring human beings; and as extremely positive role models. They expressed deep gratitude and respect for the Director and to the Program Coordinator and also recognized and appreciated the spirit of teamwork apparent among the program's staff.

    > *I am so blessed to be a part of this unique project. I am currently on an educational high! I am so thankful to [the Director] for being the brainchild of this project. I am learning so much!!*

    > *[The Director] is helpful on all issues; it's her support and leadership that makes the program what it is. She's helping us build a support system, a true community of learners. We're not just left out there, which is very rare in education. She doesn't do what professors usually do— just sit back and lecture on. She practices what she preaches. She even loans us her own personal materials.*

10. Last, it was not surprising that the *financial support* for BEEMS and BECMS participants was seen as a major strength of the program. It was not only a major factor in motivating teachers to apply for the project but was a primary factor in allowing students to remain in it. Many students were supporting families and, despite the home and work "juggling act" they performed, said they would not have been able to have gone to undergraduate or graduate school without the resources provided through the project.

I know that many of my friends could never afford to be full time students if they did not have BECMS. The program allows many of us to reach our goals faster and more smoothly than we would on our own, and this way we can look forward to improving our lives and the lives of our loved ones a lot sooner than without the aid we are receiving.

Another BECMS student commented:

The BECMS Program has been like a dream come true. I was a part-time student in a community college struggling to work and pay for college classes. When I was informed that I was chosen as one of the participants for the BEMCS program, I was very happy. I immediately gave my two weeks notice on my job and started going to school full time. This program has given me the opportunity to complete my degree as a bilingual educator.

Journals, 1993–1995

Additional data were gathered from journals kept by teachers while in the program that detailed how they implemented mathematics and science projects in their classrooms. An excerpt from one of them is included here to best illustrate the extent to which the program impacted teachers' classroom instruction and relationships with parents.

Mario Aguilar,[1] at that time, a second grade bilingual teacher at Lorenzo Primary School, San Elizario Independent School District, documented how he got parents involved in their children's progress in school as a direct result of taking the course, "Involving Parents in the Educational Process." One practice he used was to call every parent every week of the school year. A sample of his journal entries on parent involvement follow:

Sept. 23, 1993. *I am making an effort to contact each student's parents at least every week. Some of my students don't have telephones so with these I write notes. These same parents who don't have phones also communicate with me via notes or letters. It's a great feeling to know that I have their interest and support with their children. Report cards are out next week and I* *know that as a parent myself, I like to know what to expect from my children's report cards. This is why I have been in weekly contact with my students' parents. I gave my home phone number to my students and told them that they could call me at home if they had any questions or problems. I am getting at least two phone calls per day from my students but I have also had the opportunity to talk with some of the parents as well. Their reaction has been that seldom if ever has a teacher called them at home. If they called it has almost always been for problems their children are experiencing. Every one of the parents I have called at home has thanked me for taking the interest in their child. I have learned something from the experience. It is extremely important to make parent contacts and in fact, to solicit their help in making their children succeed.*

Oct. 12, 1993.   *Out of twenty students, I have kept pace with my commitment to contact parents weekly. My attendance has really improved as well. Anytime any of my students are not in class in the morning when class begins, I go to the office and call the parents of the missing student. If the parents have no phone, I'll call a neighbor...*

Nov. 5, 1993.   *The parents have been commenting to me about their children's attitude. They tell me they have seen remarkable change. The parents are commenting to me that their kids do not want to stay home, and even when they don't feel too well, they come to school.*

Nov. 17, 1993.   *Today was a really exciting, rewarding day! I gave my parental workshop (required of the BEEMS course) at Lorenzo Loya Primary. To my surprise instead of the 120 parents predicted to attend, there were over 500 people in attendance. I used my students who were in attendance to help me demonstrate how Touch Mathematics works. Five students helped me show the parents how they could help their children at home.*

Mario Aguilar was a bilingual teacher in San Elizario ISD, a small rural community of about 2,500 students when he was selected to participate in Project BEEMS. He taught there for several years before going on to Socorro ISD, another mostly rural district of about 20,000 students. He taught first grade for a few years and then went on to become a Lead Teacher. He is now an Assistant Superintendent in the district.

The following example of a science experiment with parents and children conducted at the Kennedy Housing Authority with Even Start participants was selected from the journal of a BECMS student.

May 2, 1995.   *Today is our last presentation at the Kennedy Housing Complex. Our presentation is in the form of a fair, where all the UTEP students put up a display of their project and give a short presentation to the parents as they come around to the tables. This was a different type of setting* *from our previous presentation because we waited until we had an audience to present. At our table there were two other presenters, so we took turns giving our presentation.*

My presentation consisted of glitter dough and play dough. The focus was to get children involved in helping Mom or Dad do the measurements so parents can learn to help their children learn the measuring concepts and how a substance changes from solid to liquid and to solid again . . . One of the parents was accompanied by her child, a young girl, and when I made my presentation of glittering dough she was fascinated by the outcome. I asked her to try the glittering dough by drawing two geometric figures, a triangle and a square. She drew the figures with the glue and she thought that was so neat. At the end of the class, the little girl stood next to me. I felt this was her way of saying, "Thank you, I enjoyed making the figures." I had some of the glitter dough left over. I got it from my bag and gave it to her. She looked at me with a big smile and said, "Thank you!" She gave me a hug and a kiss.

Before we left, we received compliments from the parents and their gratitude for sharing our presentations with them. This moment was very special because we received recognition from the parents, who took the time to be there.

This was a wonderful experience for me as a student. I had the opportunity to work with parents in a setting not otherwise provided in a classroom at the university. I hope other students have the opportunity to participate in a class under the same environment.

The perspectives of students could be summarized in the words of one student who said, "Being a BEEMER is like being a part of the bilingual teachers' Dream Team."

QUESTIONNAIRES: 2001

In the spring of 2001, former BEEMS participants were sent a questionnaire asking them about their careers and the long-term effects of having participated in the program. Of the 70 questionnaires sent out, 38 were returned, yielding a 54% response rate.

The former participants were asked to identify the positions they held in their school districts while in the project, as well as identify their current positions. When in the program, 100% of the participants were classroom teachers, but by 2001, only 58% were still classroom teachers. The remaining teachers had moved into a range of leadership roles including administrative positions (11%), positions as mentor or lead teachers or as specialists (24%), or were program coordinators (8%). It is important to note that none had left the profession.

Former participants were also asked if they were currently enrolled in or had completed other certification or degree programs since the completion of their Master's degrees in the BEEMS program. Seventy-one percent (27 respondents) reported that they had continued or were continuing their education. As shown in Table 1, most former BEEMS students who responded to the questionnaire were committed to continuing their education and a significant proportion (about 30%) were in doctoral programs.

Table 1.   Continued Education of BEEMS Students, Spring 2001

Program	Number	Percent
More Master's Degrees	6	15.8%
Doctoral Courses	3	7.9%
Dissertations	8	21.0%
Mid-management Credentials	7	18.4%
Other Certification Programs	3	7.9%
Not in a Program	11	29.0%
Total	38	100.0%

Participants were also asked to identify the long-term influence of the BEEMS program on their current work, the major strengths of the program, and specifically, the influence on their interest in mathematics and science. Responses were quite similar in some ways to the responses in 1994–95, especially those focused on professional and personal growth, exchange and collaboration with peer professionals, and changes in their roles in the classroom, particularly in regard to teaching mathematics and science. In view of the high number of participants who have continued their education, it is not surprising that most respondents mentioned that a major influence of the program was in giving them the confidence to advance their careers and education. Among their comments were:

> *The program influenced me to continue to further my education and I have since earned three Master's degrees.*

> *I have grown professionally and have been able to secure better positions with our district, thanks in large part, to Project BEEMS.*

> *BEEMS gave me the courage to apply for new positions.*

> *BEEMS has kept me abreast of the issues in the bilingual education arena— every year we are pumped and rejuvenated about what needs to happen or*

about what should continue to happen. My expertise has been instrumental in getting $1 million plus for our district.

The influence of the program on teachers' professional growth also extended to their increased confidence in making presentations as the result of opportunities given them while in the program. As mentioned earlier in the chapter, teachers were encouraged and supported to present to their own faculties and staffs, those of other schools and school districts, and at professional conferences. Representative examples from their comments include:

BEEMS has impacted my career because I feel very comfortable presenting and preparing presentations.

Being a presenter at different conferences gave me the security to become a presenter at the national level. The confidence that I received in being able to do math and science that was initiated in BEEMS, has continued to support me in the daily contacts with students, teachers, and administrators.

Moreover, the strong collaboration and camaraderie that was developed between the teachers during their participation in the project has had lasting effects on their views of professional relationships. There has also been continued contact and networking with former "BEEMERS," as the following comments demonstrate:

I think one of the major strengths of Project BEEMS was the integration of teachers from all the different districts brought together to work on one unified goal.

BEEMS allowed me to connect with people that have similar professional goals; the network that was created with the project is strengthened as years go by.

Collaboration comes to mind when thinking about the strengths of the program; we were teachers from many districts, yet our goals were the same.

Another area mentioned most often by the respondents was the positive impact their participation in the program continued to have on their teaching philosophies and practices, especially in mathematics and science. The following comments are indicative of respondents' assessments in this area:

I've learned to hear my students and be able to listen to what they are asking for.

I (now) try to break with the given and challenge my students and myself in ways that encourage more critical thinking, hope, commitment, and transformation.

Project BEEMS primarily influenced me in what I do in the classroom now (through) the realization that my students, particularly those of low income and racial/ethnic minority backgrounds, do not fail in school because their problems are rooted in cognitive and motivational deficits; instead, institutional structures and inequitable school practices are taken into consideration.

I remain true to the idea that equity in education is key to all future success; teaching reading to the children through science remains a priority. Math and success in math is what is going to allow the children to dream and pursue an education in scientific camps.

In summary, there were long-term positive effects on teachers who completed the BEEMS program. It not only introduced them to new knowledge, philosophies, and teaching strategies in mathematics and science, but also created durable professional support networks and increased personal confidence to continue to grow professionally.

SUMMARY AND CONCLUSIONS

The need for bilingual teachers in El Paso has always been particularly acute as the Hispanic student population in the county public schools ranges from 75 to 98%, and many of these students are designated as ELLs. The results of several surveys and those of the Norm-Referenced Assessment Program in Texas (NAPT) test administered to all students in Texas demonstrated a need to improve math and science instruction. To address this need, the University of Texas at El Paso submitted two proposals to the U.S. Department of Education in 1993 and 1994 to support its efforts to: (1) increase the number of bilingual teachers and (2) enhance the knowledge and skills of bilingual teachers in the areas of mathematics and science. The aim was to improve services for ELLs through an intensive professional development effort of both in-service and pre-service teachers with a focus on mathematics and science. Inherent in the preparation were opportunities for career development, advancement, and lateral mobility. Project administrators took to heart Fullan's (1991) thinking that "the ultimate goal [of professional development] is changing the culture of learning for both adults and students so that engagement and betterment is a way of life in the schools" (p. 344).

To determine the impact of these two projects on participants, data were gathered from three primary sources, namely, focus group interviews, open-ended questions on student questionnaires, and students' journals. Analysis of data show that program participants remained in the teaching profession and that their knowledge and skills in teaching mathematics and science were enhanced. More than 42% of the BEEMERs are now employed as science mentors, administrators, and program directors. Seventy-one percent have continued their education, and 29% of the respondents are enrolled in doctoral programs. The annual BEEMS Conference continues to be an opportunity for the University to prepare student leaders and to disseminate information concerning best practices in bilingual education. This two-day gathering, offered annually, initially brought participants of these two projects as the featured presenters. The 9th annual conference being planned for next year will draw approximately 900 participants. It continues to provide this same opportunity for other pre-sevice and in-service teachers working on degrees at UTEP.

At a broader level, UTEP is now engaged in a teacher preparation partnership to refine and strengthen teacher education in the El Paso region. The partnership—now initiating its eighth year—is composed of the Colleges of Education, Science, and Liberal Arts at UTEP; the El Paso Collaborative for Academic Excellence (which includes the three largest school districts in El Paso—El Paso ISD, Socorro ISD, and Ysleta ISD—that collectively serve 135,000 students); and El Paso Community College. Moreover, since 1992, UTEP has been a member of the National Network for Educational Renewal, a network of 34 universities in 14 states, who partner with 100 school districts and 500 Partner Schools for the simultaneous renewal of teacher education and the public schools. Our present endeavors draw on current research and best practices, are data-driven, and are designed with the primary purpose of improving the learning of all children through improving the quality of teachers.

Based on the results of the two projects discussed in this chapter and the continued teacher shortages, particularly in the areas of bilingual education, special education, and mathematics and science, the University applied for and received funds for two other grants in 1999. Projects CBTL (Cultivating Bilingual Teachers and Leaders) and BEEM (Bilingual Education Enhancement and Mentoring Project) focus on enhancing and expanding two-way dual language education in the El Paso area. These projects continue to build on the success and lessons learned from Projects BEEMS and BECMS and integrate important components of these two projects.

There are a number of interconnected factors to which the success of the dual-project program can be attributed.

1. **Strong leadership**. The leadership team at UTEP (director and coordinators) was the major factor to which the success of the program can be attributed. The program's direction, as well as the classroom instruction of the Project Director, support staff, faculty, and the College were instrumental to the project's successes. The creation of such a team involved considerable planning and foresight as well as a clear vision of how the team needed to work to fulfill the goals and

objectives of the program. The strategy of hiring people who were committed to bilingual education, and familiar with the program, or had been participants in it, was particularly effective. This team is best described as exemplary, strongly committed, and indefatigable.

2. **Focus on systemic change through networking.** A second factor which led to the success of these programs was the provision for and assurance of opportunities for collaboration within and between participating partners in the organizational systems involved in educational change: the university, local school districts, and school communities. At the University, the projects meshed their objectives with those of the mission of the College of Education through increased course offerings, the introduction of innovative teaching methods in courses, and by crosscutting, that is, integrating, content areas. The program's focus on mathematics and science also impacted course offerings in the mathematics and science departments at the University (e.g., university mathematics and science courses at public school sites during normal operating hours; team teaching with College of Education professors).

    Opportunities for exchange between members of these systems fostered reciprocity of interpersonal exchange and of information that directly affected children in area schools. Bilingual education was placed at the center of these exchanges. The ambience of professional teamwork also created a network that broke down barriers of isolation typically felt by teachers in their classrooms, between teachers in different school districts, between teachers and the university community, between teachers and parents, and between teachers in U.S.-Mexico border communities such as El Paso-Juárez. The cohort model, where program participants formed supportive cohorts across school districts, shared common experiences and moved together through their program, proved invaluable. The University has continued to use the concept of cohorts to prepare teachers in the use of technology, two-way dual language education, and rural education.

3. **Empowerment at all levels.** Power was distributed across the projects in such a way to ensure that teachers were treated as professionals. As opposed to innovative efforts which *claim*, but do not often ensure in practice, that members at all levels of the organizational structure are included in decision-making, these projects actually empowered their participants to full participation in decision-making. An inside look into the decision-making process, in turn, exemplified to students, strategies for replication of the process in their schools. The inclusion of teacher education students in this process was a particularly valuable experience as it provided a more realistic socialization experience into teaching than is typically the case in colleges of education.

4. **Demystification of barriers.** The program demystified several traditional barriers to teacher collaboration as well as to effective teaching, including:

    • Anxieties and fears teachers had about mathematics and science that keep them from spending significant time on activities in their classrooms. Science, particularly, was demystified for program participants, which allowed them to put it at the center of their lesson plans or classroom activities, or both.

    • Frequent interactions between professors who were experts in mathematics, science, and bilingual education, allowed students to demystify the typical status divisions found in university settings. Instead, professors and other professionals shared their knowledge and interacted with students on an egalitarian basis. The professional role models served as facilitators of learning in the same way as is recommended to teachers when working with students in their classrooms.

    • Requirements for the course "Involving Parents in the Educational Process," as well as other avenues provided in the projects for increased interaction with parents, demystified the traditional barriers created between schools, teachers, and parents— as separate spheres of influence on children's lives. The development of collaborative relationships between teachers and parents created partnerships to help children in ways that are frequently recommended, but are rarely seen, in schools. We note that although many parents in El Paso are among the nation's poorest families, they became willing partners in helping their children succeed in school.

    • Although many children in El Paso schools have transferred from Mexican schools, in the past, teachers have had little knowledge of these schools and of the Mexican educational system. The U.S.-Mexico Institute developed for the project included visits to and presentations in Mexican schools. The visits served to demystify teachers' perceptions of the schools. It gave teachers a realistic view of the Mexican schools and an appreciation of Mexican teachers and their working conditions. This, in turn, gave them a greater appreciation of their own working conditions in U.S. schools.

5. **Professional experiences.** The opportunities provided to participants for presenting in professional forums gave them self-confidence and a sense of professional expertise. They saw that speaking both Spanish and English were valuable assets in a multicultural environment. Over half of those completing their studies through Project BEEMS have been presenters at major national conferences

(International Reading Association [IRA]; National Association for Bilingual Education [NABE]; Texas Association for Bilingual Education [TABE]; Texas State Reading Association [TSRA] Teaching English to Speakers of Other Languages [TESOL] and others).

6. **Opportunities for career development, advancement, and lateral mobility.** The University preparation and degrees provided through Projects BEEMS and BECMS were innovative, comprehensive and current. The added specialty training in mathematics and science, in parental involvement, and in training of other teachers equipped them with the necessary tools to meet the needs of ELLs, to be knowledgeable and articulate about issues affecting ELLs, to willingly seek continued professional competence, and have a fulfilling sense of professional satisfaction. The results were leaders and advocates for ELLs who took on other responsibilities in their schools and districts where they now impact the education of students on a larger scale.

7. **Ongoing evaluation and change.**   Success of the projects was also attributed to the proactive view the leadership team took in regard to the centrality of ongoing evaluation as the impetus for continual change. Unlike many examples found of educational innovations where evaluation takes place well into, or even at the end of a multi-year cycle, evaluation and review of progress was central to the project to ensure that what worked continued or expanded and what didn't work was altered or eliminated.

8. **Institutionalization of change.**   Through the institutionalization of changes made as the result of Projects BEEMS and BECMS, capacity building was assured. By working within the general mission of the College of Education, the goals of the University, with local school districts, and with local school communities over the years of the project, teacher preparation in bilingual education has continued beyond the time lines of the projects. The above-cited factors will continue to shape the direction of current and future projects at the University.

NOTE

1.   Not a pseudonym. Permission was granted by Mario Aguilar to use his real name.

REFERENCES

De la Cruz, Y. (1998). Issues in the teaching of math and science to Latinos. In M.L. Gonzalez, A. Huerta-Macias, & J.V. Tinajero (Eds.), *Educating Latino students: A guide to successful practice* (pp. 143–160). Lancaster, PA: Technomic Publishing Co, Inc.

Fullan, M.G. (1991). *The new meaning of educational change* (2nd ed.). New York: Teachers College Press.

Garfunkel, S.A., & Young, G.S. (1992). *In the Beginning: Mathematical preparation for elementary school teachers.* Lexington, MA: COMPAP, Inc.

Gibelhauf, C., & Bowman, C. (2000). *Teaching mentors: Is it worth the effort?* Paper presented at the Association of Teacher Educators in Orlando, Florida. February. ERIC Document Reproduction Services No. ED 438277.

Green, C., & del Bosque, R.L. (1994). Making a difference through effective professional development. *IDRA (Intercultural Development Research Associates) Newsletter.* Teacher Retention and Renewal. Nov./Dec.

Holloway, J.H. (2001). The benefits of mentoring. In *Educational leadership.* Alexandria, VA: Association for Supervision and Curriculum Development.

Krashen, S., & Biber, D. (1988). *On course: Bilingual education's success in California.* Sacramento: California Association for Bilingual Education.

Loucks-Horsely, S. (1987). As cited by IASA Professional Development Planning Subgroups, (March 1995). *Professional growth and development for California educators: Fostering the learning community.* Working papers. Sacramento, CA: CA Department of Education.

Mather, J.R.C., & Chiodo, J.J. (1994, Spring). A mathematical problem: How do we teach mathematics to LEP elementary students? *The Journal of Educational Issues of Language Minority Students, 13,* 1–12.

Mullis, I., & Jenkins, L. (1998). *The Science report card: Elements of risk and recovery.* Princeton, NJ: National Assessment of Educational Progress, Educational Testing Service.

National Science Foundation. (1990). *Women and minorities in science and engineering.* Washington, DC: Author.

Oakes, J. (1990a). *Lost talent: The underparticipation of women, minorities, and disabled persons in science.* Santa Monica, CA: Rand.

Oakes, J. (1990b). Opportunities, achievement, and choice: Women and minority students in science and mathematics. In C.B. Cazden (Ed.). *Review of research in education* (Vol. 16, pp. 153–222). Washington, DC: American Educational Research Association.

O'Malley, J.M. (1992). *Project evaluation year 1, Project FAST Math.* Fairfax, VA: Fairfax County Public Schools.

Secada, W. (1992). Race, ethnicity, social class, language, and achievement in mathematics. In A. Douglas (Ed.), *Handbook on research on mathematics teaching and learning* (pp. 623–660). New York: Macmillan.

Secada, W., & De la Cruz, Y. (1996). Teaching mathematics for understanding to bilingual students. In J. Flores (Ed.), *Binational programs meeting the needs of migrant students: A handbook for teachers and administrators.* Washington, DC: ERIC Clearinghouse on Rural Education and Small Schools.

Sheehy, G. (1976). *Passages: Predictable crises of adult life.* New York: Dutton.

Snow, C.E., & Tabors, P.O. (1993). Language skills that relate to literacy development. In B. Spodek & O.N. Saracho, (Eds.) *Language and literacy in early childhood education* (pp. 1–20). New York: Teachers College Press.

Suter, L.E. (Ed.). (1996). *The learning curve: What we are discovering about U.S. science and mathematics education.* A prefatory report of the National Science Foundation's indicators of science and mathematics 1995. (NSF 96-63) Washington, DC.

Wilde, J. (1996). *Assessment strategies for professional development activities.* EAC West, Center for the Education and Study of Diverse Populations, New Mexico Highlands University, Albuquerque, New Mexico. Grant # TO 3H10004-94D.

CHAPTER 9

ADVANCING THE PROFESSIONAL DEVELOPMENT OF BEGINNING TEACHERS' THROUGH MENTORING AND ACTION RESEARCH

Jack Levy, Lynn Shafer, and Kristy Dunlap

ABSTRACT

The Language Minority Teacher Induction Project (LMTIP) at George Mason University seeks to increase achievement of bilingual students through a mentoring system for beginning teachers that features reflective practice and action research. It was developed after a careful analysis of relevant literature and discussions with K-12 partners. Incorporated in the model is a research design which addresses each of the project's main features. The questions which explore the role of action research are presented below, and are the main focus of this chapter.

1. How can action research contribute to the academic achievement of bilingual students?

2. How can action research contribute to an improvement of instruction for bilingual students?

3. How can mentoring, reflective practice and the formation of teacher support groups contribute to successful action research in multilingual settings?

The mentoring system, supported by reflective practice and teacher research, resulted in many examples of improved academic achievement and instruction for bilingual students. In addition, it contributed to the confidence and resiliency of the project's beginning teachers.

The project has been a benefit to the school in that it helps all of us better our teaching skills through the interactions of the teachers in the group. A lot of us discovered that we had mutual problems with the kids, and the group was able to come up with answers that no one teacher was able to come up with alone.

—Beginning high school teacher

INTRODUCTION

The Language Minority Teacher Induction Project (LMTIP) at George Mason University seeks to increase achievement of bilingual students through a mentoring system for beginning teachers that features reflective practice and action research. It was developed after a careful analysis of relevant literature and discussions with K-12 partners. Incorporated in the model is a research design which addresses each of the project's main features. The questions which explore the role of action research are presented below, and are the main focus of this chapter.

1. How can action research contribute to the academic achievement of bilingual students?
2. How can action research contribute to an improvement of instruction for bilingual students?
3. How can mentoring, reflective practice and the formation of teacher support groups contribute to successful action research in multilingual settings?

BACKGROUND

The LMTIP was developed to address critical needs in the areas of bilingual student achievement and personnel. More than 70% of the students in each of the 13 project schools are from linguistically diverse backgrounds. Most average two grade levels below expectations in academic skills and achievement. Due to impending teacher retirements they will be taught by an increasing number of new teachers in the near future. As a result of low minority enrollment in teacher education, these novices most often do not share the same ethnic and language backgrounds of their students.

In response, George Mason University developed an induction model based on the concepts of reflective practice and learning community. We felt that a project of this nature would have a short- and long-term impact by addressing the needs of current bilingual youngsters while also creating a model for future pre- and in-service teacher education. Thus, the project has two major goals: to facilitate achievement for English Language Learners (ELLs) by providing induction services for their beginning teachers, and to engage in significant reform of ELL education at the district and university levels. It is supported by a grant from the U.S. Department of Education.

Started in 1998, the model is simple in design, but has evolved in a wonderfully varied manner in each of the schools. Induction teams composed of 4–6 beginning teachers, a mentor and a university professor were formed in 5 high schools, 2 middle schools and 2 elementary schools in Northern Virginia and Washington, DC. Four more schools will be added in the next two years. Through regular meetings both inside and outside of school, each of the induction teams provides support through reflective discussions and dialogue, team planning and observations. Each teacher (both beginning and mentor) develops an action research project to address a particular challenge. The participants' action research activities are presented annually to colleague faculty in their schools and throughout the district, and also compiled in a book (to be published by the National Clearinghouse for Bilingual Education, see Levy, 2002). National dissemination of the beginning teachers' work is strongly encouraged and financially supported, and project presentations have been made at the annual meetings of the American Educational Research Association, International Reading Association, National Association for Bilingual Education and National Association for Multicultural Education. The teachers are provided with a stipend, tuition assistance and funds to support conference attendance and presentations of their work.

As of this writing (Spring 2001), 66 teachers have participated in the project, and another 36 are presently involved. By the time of its conclusion in 2004 the LMTIP will have served more than 200 beginning teachers and 4000 students.

As will be noted, results from the LMTIP have chronicled increased student achievement and improved instruction. The project has also helped improve GMU's teacher education program as well as the in-service offerings at the schools involved.

THEORETICAL FRAMEWORK

The LMTIP is based on the following principles of staff development and induction.

1. *Learning Team Approach to Development:* All teachers are LEARN-ERS. Through establishment of the induction teams, the project exemplifies a "learning community" philosophy. Each member of the team has something to contribute and something to learn from every other member. Each can grow individually, as can the group. The power of learning teams has been repeatedly demonstrated in the literature (Manning & Saddlemire, 1996).

One of the greatest challenges in teaching is overcoming the feeling of isolation. It has long been realized that individual teachers cannot accomplish as much alone as when they are members of teams. The problem is even more acute for beginning teachers. "In addition to learning how to effectively work with a variety of students, new teachers are in the throes of developing a professional identity and navigating a new school culture . . . New educators often progress through predictable, developmental stages of concern, gradually shifting from a primary focus on survival to a primary focus on student learning" (Halford, 1998, p. 34). By having induction teams composed of veteran teachers, beginning teachers and university faculty, the LMTIP model insures a variety of interactions, resource-sharing and perspectives that strengthen the project's outcomes.

In addition to sharing challenges and triumphs, teachers frequently work together on action research projects, since task collaboration also has been shown to be quite powerful in improvement of learning environments (Craig, Hull, & Haggart, 2000; Dufour, 2000; Hecht, Roberts & Schoon, 1996; Stiggins, 1999).

2. *Mentoring:* Naturally, coaching/mentoring should be at the center of any induction program. "In California, a state study found that among the many approaches to supporting new teachers, the most effective focused on the relationship between the new teacher and a support provider" (Halford, 1998, p. 35). The LMTIP group of mentors is quite experienced, with an average of 15+ successful years teaching in multilingual settings and extensive knowledge of teacher research. In order to be effective, however, mentors need time, rewards, a clear understanding of their roles and the skills to facilitate growth among themselves and their mentees. The LMTIP provides funds for release time for both mentors and beginning teachers. Such support is critical for encouraging consultation, cross-observations, reflection and collaborative planning. In addition to professional growth and contribution, mentors (and beginning teachers) receive a variety of rewards, including a stipend, funding for travel to professional conferences and tuition for advanced graduate study. It is felt,

however, that even without external motivators, most mentors would be sufficiently reinforced by their perception of making a significant contribution to the profession, as well as fostering their relationships with beginning teachers. To further contribute to their success, the project provides mentors with important resources to facilitate teacher growth, such as materials and consultants on effective instruction and assessment with bilingual students, adult learning and development, peer situational problem solving, conferencing skills, classroom observation, data collection and reflective analysis of practice.

3. *Results-Driven Action Research*: An outgrowth of the reflective practice and organizational learning movements popularized by Donald Schon (1983) and Chris Argyris (1993), action research has become a well-accepted strategy for addressing classroom problems and empowering teachers. Because they focus on real problems faced by beginning teachers, the LMTIP action research projects are the driving force behind the growth and improvement of ELL education for the schools and the university.

The project envisions the participating teacher as "...one who learns from teaching rather than as one who has finished learning how to teach, and the job of teacher education as developing the capacity to inquire systematically and sensitively into the nature of learning and the effects of teaching" (Darling-Hammond, 1998, p. 9). Along with the other members of their learning teams, the beginning teachers have conducted investigations of their practice in such areas as building literacy skills, understanding cultural influences on learning, increasing parent involvement in schools, understanding students' lives outside of school, evaluating student work, developing curriculum, and providing for individual student differences (including English proficiency and cross-cultural communication), among other topics. The project makes available some of the more helpful literature on teacher research, such as works by MacLean and Mohr (1999) and Schmuck (1997).

The LMTIP was thus developed after a critical analysis of the literature on staff development and the education of culturally and linguistically diverse (CLD) students, as well as a review of similar programs.

RESEARCH QUESTIONS—RESULTS

As outlined above, the LMTIP began in 1998, and is currently in its third year. Thus far, 66 beginning teachers have completed their one-year active participation (the following year they become "alumni," assisting the next group), and 36 are currently involved. Their research reports, compiled in a double volume entitled "From Concept to Practice" and presented at four national conferences in the past year, provide substantial documentation of qualitative improvements in student achievement and classroom instruction. These action research projects will be described below, according to the research questions. Excerpts from twenty of these reports will be presented in support. The action research reports represent a variety of secondary (6–12) fields: math, social studies, physics, chemistry, life science and literacy development/ESL (including reading and writing).

Research Question 1. How can action research contribute to the academic achievement of bilingual students?

Over half of the 66 projects completed thus far have reported significant cognitive improvement as measured by standardized tests and class assessments. Another 25–30% of the projects resulted in improvements in cross-cultural understanding, class behavior and a variety of attitudinal areas (e.g., toward schools, peers, etc.) as measured by survey and interview responses and teacher observation. Below are some examples of significant LMTIP outcomes in cognitive academic achievement, documented gains reported by pre and post data.

Cognitive Achievement—Standardized Assessment

Many of the action research projects were conducted within a 3–4 month period. Due in part to this short timeline, only four were able to use standardized tests as assessments of student growth. Nonetheless, after the new instructional treatments were introduced, the students in each of the four beginning teachers' classes registered significant improvement on the assessments. While the teachers' projects clearly had a positive effect, it should be noted that these gains cannot all be due to the treatments; a more rigorous research design would need to investigate all variables.

- *Middle school math teacher, a project to improve literacy skills through math.* **Pre:**   In order to meet the learning needs of a diverse student population, it is crucial that the material be as accessible as possible. The challenges that second language learners face are compounded by the need to master academic content, language connections, and social skills concurrently. "For students to learn to communicate mathematically, they need opportunities to hear math language and to speak and write mathematically" (Buchanan & Helman, 1993). This study is part of a larger focus on literacy development among language minority students, and its impact on achievement in content areas. Specifically: *How does an increased focus on content vocabulary development improve achievement in math?*

Post: In the EAME and POS assessments (both standardized tests), very few questions were left unanswered. Students struggling with a concept often try incorporating other math concepts and reasoning to get "partial credit." … The EAME results indicate that Math Eight students progressed between 1 and 1.5 years over the course of the school year … The greatest surprise, however, came with an analysis of the word problem portion of the POS (part III).… Students with the most limited language proficiency achieved the most progress in answering word problems, more than doubling their point scores in this portion of the assessment.

- *Middle school bilingual teacher, using "out-loud" reading to improve skills.*

  Pre: In my Reading class, the 6th grade students came to me at the beginning of the year with the following DRP (Degrees of Reading Power, a standardized test) reading levels. The reading levels from lowest to highest of the eight students in my class were: 3.4, 3.7, 4.0, 4.3, 4.4, 4.8, 4.8, 4.8. … I have always liked to read books out loud to my classes. I enjoy theater and acting out different characters in the book. I have tried to make the books come alive as I read them and the students have always seem to respond positively to this. … For my research project, I wanted to really find out if reading out loud to the students was beneficial. I wanted to find out if students really did as well as or even better overall on tests taken on books read out loud as opposed to books they have read silently on their own. I also wanted to find out about how students felt about silent reading as opposed to out loud reading. Did they really enjoy being read to? Would they rather not be read to and just read to themselves? Did they feel that they did better on tests for books read silently or read out loud? Why?

  Post: The results of the DRP test taken in February and May show that students continued to progress in their reading levels during the year. Some students progressed much more quickly than others. … The overall average of the class reading level at the beginning of the year was 4.28. By the end of the year, it was 5.22. As a class, scores went up a grade level which is definitely positive. Most students are still not up to their grade level, but have at least made a big jump in that direction. While it's not specifically clear that reading-out-loud was responsible for this, it does seem that it was beneficial.

- *High school ESL teacher, using audiobooks to improve reading achievement.*

  Pre: In the beginning of the year, the students were struggling to read on their own and be able to comprehend what they read in order to summarize or react to their reading. During Sustained Silent Reading, or SSR, the students would read silently for twenty minutes, then I would either ask them to write a reaction to what they had read or to summarize the story. Most students would turn in a word-for-word copy of the story. Needless to say, this was not what I had expected. I knew, at that point that I needed to provide a different means for my students to read and comprehend material. **(Post—in which the majority of students improved significantly on the DRP)**: This project turned out to be very successful. I was happy to see an improvement in my students' reading scores for the majority of the class. All of the students, with the exception of the three students mentioned earlier in this paper, will be moving to the next level of ESL next year. I am glad I was able to provide an alternative method for my students to not only improve their reading scores but also their pronunciation.

- *High school Social Studies teacher, project in vocabulary development.*
  Pre: Although I am officially a first-year teacher at XXX High School, I had the opportunity to spend the previous year in an internship in world history at the same school. It was there that I noticed that students had not acquired the vocabulary necessary to succeed on the standardized history tests. Some students could not understand what the questions were asking because of their lack of understanding of the vocabulary, let alone come up with the correct answer. I noticed that these tests were especially difficult for student whose first language was not English (approximately 40% of my students have English as their second language, although they have graduated from the ESL program). ... With this in mind, and the forum of the LMTIP to motivate me, I set about to focus on vocabulary acquisition for my students.
  Post: Seventy-two of my students took the DRP in the fall and again in the spring. A comparison of pre- and post-scores for the DRP indicated an overall increase in student scores of three points. Anything over two points is considered a significant gain.

In this final example the students register a modest gain on the standardized test and the teacher reflects on what is actually being measured—and if this type of measurement is comprehensive enough to indicate full student learning.

Pre: In addition to the self-assessment measures I administered in September, I began my research by gathering student information from my own extensive questionnaire. Finally, I gave fifth period a pretest in order to anchor their performance. This pretest involved the silent reading of a one-page Stars biography and answering a series of typical standardized questions. On average the students scored forty points out of a possible fifty points.

Post: Fifth period's standardized scores fluctuated initially. However, as the students continued to use art as a response mechanism these scores improved. This improvement was not marked, but rather in the amount of two or three points. Each set of standardized questions was worth a total of fifty points. What does this reveal? It may demonstrate that while engagement is critical for thoughtful literacy, it is not imperative for standardized success. I prefer to look at those two to three points and think about what I as the teacher can do better next time. How can I provide better supports and structure so that students can build on those two to three points? Additionally, I wonder about my original intention to explore alternative response mechanisms to reading. I was eager to create pathways that might lead to improved textual engagement. Do standardized questions supercede the pedagogical desire to generate a student-centered learning environment? Are standardized questions in direct and irreparable conflict with the *IRA and NCTE Guidelines for Assessment*? It appears that my students did have a positive response to the biography/visual arts unit. While they experienced initial frustrations with unfamiliar tasks, they did begin to assume an active agency, producing sensitive and sound readings. Do the minimal gains on standardized scores discount these more qualitative goals? I am happy that I implemented the Motivational CheckList as evidence to support fifth period's increased engagement. Furthermore, their illustrations document the significant gains made with textual involvement, along with the accurate ability to select main ideas and supporting details, define/modify reading goals, manipulate information and reflect upon themselves as readers.

Cognitive Achievement—Teacher Assessment

Skill Development: As illustrated above, most of the projects resulted in increased academic achievement of bilingual students. The teachers used a variety of traditional pencil/paper and oral measurements to assess these improvements. Their efforts resulted in gains in a large number of skill areas, a few of which are presented below:

Test taking	Vocabulary use
Organization/Study skills	Making inferences
Portfolio development	Sequencing information
Social interaction	Locate themes, apply to own lives
Group interaction, teamwork	Metacognitive evaluation of
Cross-cultural	own reading skills, processes
Reading comprehension	Problem solving

Teachers believed their own projects were critical to their students' development. The following excerpts from their end-of-year reflections give voice to those beliefs.

Organization/Study Skills: I have accepted the notion that as long as I teach this population, I am an organizational and study skills teacher in addition to being a content-area teacher, and an ESL teacher. With the teaching of such skills, especially in the area of reading, what I ask my students to accomplish has changed, as well. As a result, I have had an easier time reaching and managing my students because they are getting more of the essentials that they, unfortunately at the high school level, still desperately need.

Vocabulary Development: My research has convinced me that vocabulary is an important aspect of the world history curriculum. I will continue to focus my lessons on student acquisition of vocabulary. I have been able, through this project, to set up a vocabulary program that matches the county curriculum and the state standards. I have been, and will continue to share my findings and strategies with my colleagues. I will also keep searching for new and improved strategies that will maintain student interest and go beyond looking up the words. Next year I plan to work more with the English teacher to develop strategies and lessons. I also plan to introduce more technology into my curriculum. This project has been invaluable to me; I believe that having a focal point for my teaching helped in the planning and organization of the course. Although I have not, as of this writing, received my student's SOL scores, I am confident that they were prepared to read and understand the vocabulary on the exam.

Portfolio Development (1):   Because of the time that was put into organization during the semester, when the time arrived for course-end comprehensive portfolios and exams, my students did not have to spend nearly as much time reviewing and collecting pieces of work as they might have otherwise. Now, I have ideas, methods, and a system of organization to implement next year, leaving me with more time to focus on another issue or area.

Portfolio Development (2):   Specifically for the research study of Multiple Intelligences, "teacher X" used a portfolio as her final assessment. The portfolio had to contain a two-page typed report on any enjoyable activity done during the study, a career poster, a written dialogue and a recorded component. She was astonished at the differences between her control and experimental class. The portfolio grades for the experimental group were 20 points higher than the control group's average. She also noticed that there was a rising level of competitiveness between the two classes.

Portfolio Development (3): I can report that the finished portfolios are outstanding. They are bold and monumental. The students creatively placed photos and magazine clippings on artfully prepared backgrounds. The images used show the complexity and diversity of their individual lives. During the time fifth period was making their portfolios the classroom mood was collaborative and industrious. Through the portfolio construction, students became active agents in their own education. These portfolios are direct documentation that school environments can connect with the lives of students and do so in an authentic manner nurturing important academic competencies. These competencies include attention to detail, self-assessment, organization of information and synthesis of information. Most remarkably, fifth period was motivated by the portfolio assignment.

Cross-cultural: My interest in cross-cultural understanding, which was merely a strong curiosity at the outset, developed into a class project entitled, "Living in Two Cultures." First, I had my two beginning ESL classes reflect on ten questions related to: the differences between their home cultures and the culture as they see it here in the United States; what changes, if any, they experienced as they were adjusting to a new culture; and how they felt about such changes. The second step was for them to find two individuals who were from their own ethnic and religious communities and interview them with the same ten questions. The results of the interviews were to be reported in a five-paragraph composition. The total number of students who completed the project was 28. Of the 28, there were 9 Africans (5 Muslims, 4 Christians), 5 Latin Americans (all Christians), 6 West Asians (4 Muslims, 1 Sikh, 1 Edizy—a religion practiced by Kurdish people), and 8 East/Southeast Asians (3 Christians, 5 Buddhists). Some student comments:

> I enjoyed doing this project because I learned how Latin American people lived and what they do. I learned about the education of Latin American countries, I learned tourism and the sports they play. It was fun doing this project. I think we should do projects with partners because it is more fun. [A male from Thailand]

> The project allowed us to learn about other cultures and it broadened our view of the world. I think a similar project would help us learn even more. [A male from the United States]

Reading Comprehension: The students in my Transitional English classes are not the high-achieving students who adapt well to academics and are intrinsically motivated to do well in school. My students are in their last year of ESL, are still struggling to learn English, and more than likely come from cultures that do not put a high price on good grades or even education. Most of my students come from Central and South America where, they tell me, it would be unusual for them to continue school beyond the 8th grade.

In addition to improving the skills of my students, I wanted to sway their attitudes about school in general and about reading, specifically. This, truthfully, seemed a Herculean task. But if I could motivate them to read more, and if reading more would make them better readers, and if that, in turn, would increase their other skills, then it was worth the effort.

(After students' achievement had improved): Ultimately, any evidence of reading level or comprehension improvement must be anecdotal. The project only spanned about three months, not enough time to make a definitive claim about its cognitive effects on the students. Clearly, if we were able to extend this project over the entire school year, we would be in a better position to gauge the progress of the students and check ourselves against Krashen's gains in reading achievement. But that is missing the point. The affective changes brought about by a project of this nature outdistanced the cognitive changes. Reading scores may improve, but that is not necessarily the ultimate desired goal. When a child reads for pleasure, actually *enjoys* reading, she is more likely to continue reading and to continue learning. At the beginning of the project I asked the students to turn in lists of all the books they had read. One student gave me a list of more than 30 books. During the project he read another 4 or 5. This student tested at a 4.8 grade level on the Gates test, far below his grade level and far below many of his classmates. But I have never seen a child who enjoys reading as much as he does. On the last question of the student evaluation ("Will you continue reading on your own after the project is over?"), he answered, "Oh, yeah! I will, and always. That's my favorite." This should be our ultimate objective.

Group Interaction: The biggest success out of this lesson was the group work. I was very pleased with how much the students knew. For once, they were very comfortable and many relied more on one another and their notes than me. That may have been the first success I had with group work. I was able to see how the students work very differently when they feel more confident with the skills.

Social Interaction: The interaction between the academically strong NEPs [no English proficiency] and academically weak FEPs [full English proficiency] resulted in each group experiencing a greater degree of success, leading them to become more involved in the class. Their academic performance went up only slightly, but there was a significant increase in social interactions between students.

Inferences, Sequencing, Location/Application of Themes/Metacognition/ Problem Solving: Students began to notice the importance of making inferences and sequencing information. They began to relate to the characters in their reading, to find important themes and to relate these themes to their own experiences. Furthermore, they noticed textual significance and made steps in evaluating and reflecting on their own reading. They began to appreciate the importance of comprehension monitoring as it allowed them to better describe the reading. While fifth period did not make significant advancements on every dimension of response they did enjoy an increased ability to construct and reconstruct the world of the text, and to interpret and manipulate information. Again, this was evidenced through enhanced conversations around reading, the composition of the illustrations, the provocative questions asked by students regarding their reading and the students improved recall of textual information. Their critical and creative problem-solving skills improved as they selected information from reading, transferred information to their drawings and extended the information presented in the text by illustrating personal responses.

Test Taking: Example presented above, under standardized assessment.

Research Question 2. How can action research contribute to an improvement of instruction for bilingual students?

While a causal relationship cannot be established, the increased academic achievement cited above seems to correlate perfectly with a corresponding improvement in instruction. Teachers employed a huge number of instructional strategies in their quest to systematically upgrade learning levels. While these will be cited below, it's important to note the process by which these techniques were implemented.

After several meetings with the induction team, teachers began to formulate their research questions. As part of this process, they simultaneously consulted the literature and their colleagues about their area of focus. Although most of the questions changed often during the formative stage, once teachers settled on a question they designed an implementation strategy and shared it with the team.

The teachers carefully researched each strategy before using it. In addition to examining relevant literature and sharing her/his ideas with the induction team and other colleagues, teachers occasionally visited classrooms where the target technique was being employed. In some cases they learned about the approach at a conference.

As noted above, the implementation strategy often included some type of pre-assessment to determine baseline learning levels. The plans generally provided for formative and summative evaluation, and data-collection methods were continually checked to determine whether they addressed the research question. Team members shared instruments such as questionnaires and interview protocols among themselves. Thus, by developing basic skill in action research techniques, the teachers laid the groundwork for a career-long effort to improve instruction via systematic analysis.

As mentioned, the teachers improved their instructional approaches in a great many ways. Examples of dozens of techniques they used to achieve academic growth for their students are listed below. While the list may not include any particularly remarkable "innovations," each of the approaches represented an instructional change in its context.

Graphic organizers	Anticipation guides
Concept maps	Study guides
Reading road maps	Reading out loud
Peer tutoring	Lecture Bingo
Graffiti Wall	Index Card Match
Highlighters/Post-it notes	Directed reading-thinking
K-W-L	Audiobooks
Computer-assisted instruction (websites, Power Point, interactive software, etc.)	
Visual arts	Mnemonics
Autobiographical writing	Family research
Scaffolding	Self-assessment
Predicting, questioning, rereading, and tracking	Portfolio preparation
Journaling	Creating webs, organizers,
Peer editing	charts
Multiple intelligences	Simulations (e.g., "fishbowl")
Grouping students (coop lrning)	Assessment rubrics
Oral presentations-individual, group Games	
"Transfer of learning" techniques	In-depth openers

Rephrasing

Content vocabulary development

Culturally-responsive techniques

Independent reading

Field trips

Read-along tapes

Self-esteem activities

Reflecting, sharing, discussing

The instructional changes enumerated above reflect two overarching themes: making instruction relevant to students' real lives and cultural perspectives, and linking directly to the statewide assessment standards known as the Standards of Learning (SOL).

Here are a few of the teachers reflections on these approaches.

> *Relevant/Culturally Responsive Instruction:* (Middle school math teacher):   Activities that have been most helpful have been those that are of personal interest to the student, and allow greater access to the larger learning "picture." A combination of hands-on learning activities and real-life situations aid in conceptual development and problem-solving skills (Collier & Pateracki, 1998). Examples in statistics include the use of school and district data to "read" statistics for growth, suspensions, mobility, ethnic composition etc., and make predictions and comparisons about their schools, and those of their friends; and, the use of census data to learn about their community.

> *Standards of Learning:* (High school ESL teacher):   Regardless of the positive outcomes of this research project, my students would still need to master the course objectives of 9th grade English and be adequately prepared for 10th grade English (to say nothing of the SOLs looming in 11th grade English). Whether or not Krashen was correct in hypothesizing that reading, just reading, is enough to improve other reading and writing skills, I had an obligation to my students to cover certain comprehension, analysis, and writing skills. I decided to add a variety of assessment activities which would target the skills that the students needed to acquire.
>
> I was concerned about how my students would react to this change in tack, but I felt that it was a necessary improvement. The manner in which I introduced these assessments was, I felt, crucial to their success. First, I shared with the students the importance of these skills, and stressed that they were necessary to their survival throughout the rest of high school. I outlined certain goals that we needed to accomplish by the end of the year. Next, I asked them to help me create the assessments. The rationale for this, as with giving the students choice in reading materials, was to make the students

stakeholders in their learning. Under certain categories, which aligned with the SOLs, I asked the students to brainstorm on different activities/assessments that they could produce for each category using their current reading material. I compiled their ideas and added some of my own to create an assessment bank. From this assessment bank, I chose activities and products which would best fulfill our curricular goals. These assessments were accorded point values depending on their relative level of difficulty in Bloom's Taxonomy: Knowledge, Comprehension, Application, Analysis, and Synthesis. Students were to complete one assessment at each level, for a total of five. They could keep track of their assessments and points using a Scoring Sheet I had given them.

Standards of Learning.   (High school history teacher in "sheltered" class):   The goal of my project was to focus on vocabulary as a method of succeeding on standardized world history tests and ultimately the SOL exam. To achieve this goal I created vocabulary lists for every unit. These lists would contain not only the content words from the unit but also process words that would aid students in reading both questions and answers on tests. I also gathered strategies for teaching vocabulary to students. I sought to find strategies that would go beyond simply looking up a word and writing the definition.

(Results):   My research has convinced me that vocabulary is an important aspect of the world history curriculum. I will continue to focus my lessons on student acquisition of vocabulary. I have been able, through this project, to set up a vocabulary program that matches the county curriculum and the state standards.

A Mini Case—One Teacher's Story

Mark Wilson, a Physical Education teacher in a project middle school, became interested in motivating students to improve their fitness and strength. He decided to attempt a "language accommodation" approach. "After completing the first round of fitness tests," Mark wrote, "I needed to connect with the students in order to achieve better performance from them." Observing that students' efforts appeared half-hearted during daily exercise when they compared themselves to others in the class, he noted that "The students seemed to be more aware of the competition with other students than the goal of the test which is to compete with oneself to do the best that one can."

Focusing his efforts on one class in which 45% of the students were native Spanish speakers and another 21% were in the Spanish immersion program, he experimented with conducting workouts in Spanish. To distract the students from comparing themselves with others, Mark began counting repetitions in Spanish as he led work outs, using his somewhat broken Spanish that invited the students' correction of pronunciation or help with vocabulary. "That one decision turned the exercise portion of the class around," he wrote in his action research report. He related several examples of how he gradually introduced Spanish into the exercise repetitions, often intentionally miscounting in Spanish to prompt the students to count accurately. "The students had taken the focus off their perceived misery of exercise and began doing the exercises and focusing on the use of Spanish during that time." Mark cited the National Physical Fitness Standards pre- and posttest results as evidence of success of more effective exercise activities and motivation through incorporating Spanish language into his teaching. But, noting that most of his classes improved their fitness test scores to some degree, Mark believed the most significant changes were in the attitudes of his students in the Spanish-counting class:

> The most remarkable aspect was the vigor with which the students went about their daily routines. Discipline was less of a problem and participation was dramatically higher than other classes. The accommodation of language allowed me to connect with the students and empower them to overcome an obstacle that was preconceived in their minds about exercise.

Research Question 3: How can mentoring, reflective practice and the formation of teacher support groups contribute to successful action research in multilingual settings?

Over the course of the school year, the following key events (and the processes that accompanied them) seemed to have had the most influence on the final outcomes in the teachers' action research projects. In roughly chronological order, the events were:

1. The selection process used when teachers joined the LMTIP;
2. The support that the mentors offered to the teachers;
3. The definition and process of action research used in each school; and,
4. Other motivating events.

1. *The Selection Process Used When Teachers Joined the LMTIP.*   The first event that affected the final outcomes related to how the teachers were chosen for the LMTIP. At some schools, teachers were chosen by their principals; at others, by the mentors; and at still others, the teachers applied for a position on their school's team and then were selected by the mentor and the principal.

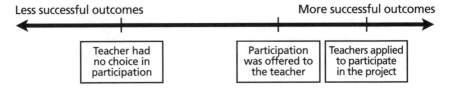

Figure 1.   Application process used by the schools

Based on the number of action research projects that were submitted at the end of the first year, it appears that, in the one school where teachers had little or no choice in the decision to participate in the LMTIP activities, teachers had the lowest submission rate of projects (two out of five teachers—and both projects were two months late). In the schools where teachers could choose to participate, four out of five teachers submitted action research projects by the end of the year deadline. In the school where teachers applied to participate in the project, five out of five teachers submitted projects well before the final due date.

At the beginning of the second year of the project, all of the schools involved with the LMTIP changed their selection process. All teachers were asked to apply in order to participate. At the end of the second year, submission rates of action research projects for all of the schools approached 100%.

2.   *The Support That the Mentors Offered to the Teachers.*   "Without quality coaching, guidance, and support, pilot groups [begin] to flounder" (Senge, Kleiner, Roberts, Ross, Roth, & Smith, 1999, p. 103). A key decision at the inception of the LMTIP was to designate the school-based mentor, rather than an outside consultant, as leader of that school's team. In this way, the mentor could provide immediate support to the teachers on a daily basis. Another key decision was that, rather than launching immediately into the action research projects, the mentors took the first half of the school year to focus on building and nurturing their teams.

One of the biggest challenges for the mentors was to help the beginning teachers move beyond survival mode. Many of the teachers seemed to be dealing more with staying alive in the classroom than with focusing on fine-tuning their instructional practices. One mentor commented that, "One problem is that new teachers are afraid to say no and so they get dumped on with extra tasks at schools." Another mentor added, "We have to be advocates for these teachers when they are getting overwhelmed. Be their voice and say it for them 'Sorry, they can't do this. They're booked already.'"

During the second year of the LMTIP, mentors feared that teachers might be overwhelmed if the action research projects became the focus too early during the group's formation. One mentor commented, "What I'm trying to do with my group is to bring the teachers along a little at a time.

At the beginning of the year, what I try to do is to focus on reflective writing each week at our meeting—because I think they first need to see what is going on in their classrooms before they actively start trying to change it."

As a result of this "go-slow" process, the foundation for the successful completion of action research projects was the bonding and support that the teachers found in their school-based team. One teacher commented, "A lot of us discovered that we had mutual problems with the kids, and the group was able to come up with answers that no one teacher was able to come up with alone." Another teacher told us, "This grant was especially beneficial in the beginning. The mentoring sessions provided me with a lot of insight and opportunities to reflect. This forced me to stop and think about my teaching strategies rather than plowing through till the end of the year."

At the end of the year, one mentor wrote, "I have learned that being there for the teachers is very important. I have been able to set aside time during the day to meet with individual members as needed and I have found that doing the little things (like administrative tasks) for them frees them up to focus on their own questions. They need to feel that when they need guidance that someone is there to at least point them in the right direction."

Appreciating the process, one of the beginning teachers wrote,

> Simply being part of and having access to a new teacher support group prob-
> ably contributed to the improvement and tightening of my teaching by
> decreasing my frustration and feelings of hopelessness. Because participation
> in the group was an aid to me, my teaching got better, my students did better,
> and I felt better about my job. The school now has a happily returning
> teacher (with more knowledge and confidence), which is a benefit to the
> school. It was also a support to the already overwhelmed and overworked
> administration who didn't have to worry about administering me.

3.   *The Definition and Process of Action Research Used in Each School.*   How the action research was explained to the teachers affected how they defined their problems, conducted their research project and wrote their reports. To support the mentors as they explained to their teachers what an action research process entailed, the LMTIP provided a graphical organizer and characteristics of action research that fit each level of performance (see Figure 2). The purpose of the graphical organizer was to show that even as the level of complexity increased, there were commonalities among different types of professional development. The models served as targets at which the teachers might aim.

The teachers gradually arrived at a preferred-LMTIP model that combined reflective practice and hypothesis-testing action research. At some of the schools, where more of an emphasis on reflective practice was used, the

General teacher professional development (i.e., workshops and inservices)	Reflective practice (i.e., journal writing and support group)	Hypothesis-testing research (i.e., traditional action research, often quasi-experimental in design)	Hypothesis-generating research (i.e., teacher research, more qualitative type of research)
• Teacher has received additional training to improve his/her teaching • Teacher thinks and talks about how to improve • Teacher uses and adapts new technique to fit his/her classroom	• Teacher thinks about why he/she "does something in a certain manner" and talks about how to improve • Teacher uses journal to write reflectively • Use thinking to organize and prioritize work and life needs • Begins to identify underlying assumptions and views that motivate how he/she teaches • Highly subjective view	• Teacher thinks about why he/she "does something in a certain manner" and talks about how to improve • Has a central question that is being explored; question remains static throughout project • Teacher uses journal to write reflectively and collects some data systematically • Teacher has gotten feedback from others to refine his/her inquiry. But generally does not systematically consult to get other perspectives • The subjectivity of the view is checked by only a few types of data • Researcher begins to show how research is tied to others' research	• Has a central question that is being explored. Uses cycle model: creates question; tests it; sees how it works and then recasts the question to do the whole cycle again (and again…) • Reaches some tentative conclusions during each phase of the project • Teacher uses journal to write reflectively, collects data systematically, and then triangulates that data 1. by reading the literature 2. with other forms of data/evidence 3. with other educators' perspectives • View is "systematically subjective" • Shows how research is tied to others' research

Figure 2.   Continuum of professional development practices

mentors emphasized the process of writing and sharing during their meetings. The teachers used the models provided to do journal writing about their projects. This direction led, in some cases, to their creating final reports that were essentially reflective essays on their year. However, in these projects the teachers gave little or no evidence that supported the views that were within them. As a result, it was difficult to obtain a clear measure as to whether their professional practice had actually changed.

At other schools, where the mentors took more of an action research approach to the research projects, it was possible for both these teachers and the readers of their projects to get a clearer sense of the kinds of change that had occurred in their professional practices. The action research model not only incorporates reflective practice, but also requires teachers to actively test their views as they put them into practice in their classroom.

The more successful action research projects demonstrated a greater amount of change and growth in the teachers' assumptions and corresponding actions regarding their professional practices. One teacher commented on this process of gathering evidence of students' responses to changes in instructional practices:

> I collected my evidence really from the reactions of my students. They were able to share with me adaptations they liked the most and felt helped them the most. I based the effects of how adaptations in the classroom help students succeed from the class average grade each semester.

Another teacher wrote about the effect of the LMTIP on her own commitment to improving instructional practice:

> I think participation in the grant was the most important part of this project because it forced me to stay on top of an issue, really look to see if the things I was doing were working and to see what could be improved if not for this year for next! That, in and of itself, is what has helped to improve my instructional practice! (i.e., as opposed to assuming what I do works I was forced to really look at it to see if it works! If it makes me a better more reflective teacher then it will be a benefit to my school).

Many of the teachers appreciated the opportunity to read action research examples from "alumni" LMTIP teachers. One commented about the significance of models written by colleagues:

> Reading the research of other teachers really helped me get started with my project. I tried some of their methods in the beginning. Then, I started to ask my students for ideas of techniques we could use in the classroom. I also asked other teachers to share their methods with me. All of these were very successful. One of the mentors reported that, "Teachers from previous years are coming before the team and sharing their previous presentations with the new teachers. It helps get this year's teachers very focused, very into their projects."

In addition one of the mentors reported that, "Teachers from previous years are coming before the team and sharing their previous presentations with the new teachers. It helps get this year's teachers very focused, very into their projects."

4.   *Other Motivating Events.*   Two other events motivated the teachers during the school year. At the midpoint in the year, most of the school teams scheduled a day to come to the university to work both with a university librarian and in the computer lab. One teacher later wrote about the benefits of availability of useful resources, "The information in the articles and books I read was most useful in the beginning when I was trying to formulate a question. I began with a vague idea of what I wanted to accomplish but the research really helped me to solidify my question and my goals for the project."

Another event that positively motivated the teachers was the end-of-year round table conference among all of the teachers in the LMTIP. Knowing that they would have to present their ideas in front of the peers was a strong motivator for the majority of the participating teachers.

CHANGE IN TEACHERS' ASSUMPTIONS

At the end of each year of the LMTIP we ask teachers and mentors to respond to a series of questions on their progress and ways we might improve the project. The following responses represent a typical cross-section from the teachers who highlighted the lasting effects of reflective practice, collaboration with colleagues, and the action research process.

- I feel now I have a multi-discipline resource group in our school. The research team has become a support group for academic and personal reasons.
- This grant helped me to reflect about my teaching strategies. As a result, my teaching methods improved. Now, I am more inclined to try different techniques and seek out alternative methods. It has enabled me to be mindful about my strategies and methods because I have to constantly reflect about my teaching style. I have shared my results with my colleagues and my group will present our findings to the faculty in September.
- I have gained a better sense of how to start with a concrete idea and develop it into an abstract idea. It has also allowed me to gain a view of the overall trends of teaching at my high school.
- This grant has benefitted my school in that all of the work that has been done by myself and my team members are currently being implemented in my school. Other teachers, not involved in the research, are asking about what we are doing and how they too can get involved.

The act of conducting an action research project seems to have helped teachers to question some of the basic assumptions that they held about their LM students. Moll, Velez-Ibanez, and Greenberg (1988) suggest that, through the action research process, teachers can learn more about the realities that shape their students' lives and the funds of knowledge students bring with them to school. Teachers wrote specifically about the impact of learning about their students' cultural background, prior knowledge, and the shift in their own assumptions:

- I have learned that my assumptions are not always in line with the reality of my classroom. I have learned that sometimes a super-structured environment is not a bad thing. This process has further solidified my belief in practitioner reflection.
- I now know that I NEED to know my students better to understand their prior knowledge and what may or may not help or hinder them in my classroom. The more we know about students the more prepared we can be to not make the learning process more difficult than it already is.
- We learned that the majority of our students have more positive influences than we expected. We also have learned that there is a great disparity between what students are doing outside of school and what teachers think they are doing.
- I have learned that using the cultural knowledge I have—in this case, about East Asian cultures—has helped to motivate my East Asian students in ways that they were not being motivated before, and helped them to improve their grades and their learning. This is, in essence, a means of learning a new language with which to speak. Having a teacher understand a little about where the students are "coming from" goes a long way toward helping them understand their teacher—and in the process, they end up learning the material that they need to learn to pass the course.

MINI-CASES

To gain a larger perspective on the process that the beginning teachers experienced as they sought to both expand their instructional repertoires and make them more relevant to ELL students, two mini-cases are presented below.

Lewis Middle School

Lewis Middle School's principal was enthusiastic about participating in the LMTIP, in part due to the diversity of the student population, but also for its potential to support teachers in the school's Spanish Partial Immersion Program. Lewis is the only middle school in the district offering an extension of the bilingual immersion program which is initially offered in three elementary schools. Students in the middle school Spanish Partial Immersion Program spend half of their academic day in classes taught in English (math and English) and half taught in Spanish (science and social studies), plus one period per day of Spanish language arts.

Kerri Colbert

Kerri Colbert is a first-year teacher of 8th grade World Geography who became interested in motivational strategies in reading. One of her most successful and engaging activities was a "graffiti wall" which required students to take sides on a relevant issue reported in a *Washington Post* article: school rules about the length of girls' shorts. The article included excerpts of interviews with the Lewis principal, girls who challenged the ruling, and their mothers.

Among the most responsive and involved in grant activities of the beginning teachers, Kerri regularly posted her questions and responses on the grant website. When asked what she had learned from examining her research question, Kerri posted the following explanation:

> I have learned that I do not have to lower my expectations of students or "water" down material to help them learn info. Instead I need to enhance and motivate them with materials that adapt to their levels.

When asked about research techniques that worked best and how she collected evidence, Kerri responded:

> I collected my evidence really from the reactions of my students. They were able to share with me adaptations they liked the most and felt helped them the most. I based the effects of how adaptations in the classroom help students succeed from the class average grade each semester.

She felt that her experience at a professional conference funded by the LMTIP grant was particularly valuable:

> During the course of my project I attended the VA middle school conference. Here I was able to pick up a lot of new great ideas to try in my classes. Communication among teachers is a key factor.

Kerri believed that the LMTIP activities and support improved her instructional practice and benefitted the school:

The grant provided allowed me to research some great techniques to not only motivate but enhance my students learning as well. The mentor/mentee program opened the doors to many opportunities. It allowed us to share with each other concerns and ideas.

Marie Soto-Bisset

Marie is herself a recent immigrant. Facing her first year of teaching in the United States with a Ph.D. and 14 years' experience teaching science in Costa Rica, she felt enormous "culture shock" in her Lewis classroom and pressure to adapt her teaching style and demeanor to her 8th grade students' expectations. Marie's final paper for the LMTIP grant, entitled "Reflections on the Impact of Culture in the Classroom," drew upon "my personal diary, conversations with colleagues and friends, evaluations of my administrators and copies of my disciplinary referrals of students to the principal's office." Her analysis of her year at Lewis focused on two major sources of cultural conflict, which she identified as "conceptual conflicts" and "behavioral conflicts," both of which "related to interpersonal interactions and had to do with general expectations, attitudes and behaviors."

Marie believed that conflicts arose in her classroom in part due to her approach to teaching science, which she believed was grounded in "cognitive patterns and generalities." Her Lewis 8th grade students appeared to be pragmatists who wanted "the bottom line," she wrote, and "complained that I talked 'too big.'" Another dimension of conceptual conflict that she identified was students' perception of learning and of the value of attending school. "I believe that the cultural conflict I felt was partly due to the fact that most American students view school principally as a means to getting a job and making money." As Marie reflected upon and tried to analyze the causes of "frequent class disruptions," she wrote of "great frustration for me and a general feeling of miscommunication and misunderstanding in the classroom."

Interested in the way she was being perceived by her students, Marie and two of her classes (Spanish Immersion and Physical Science) completed the Questionnaire on Teacher Interaction, a professional development instrument made available to the LMTIP teachers. She wrote about one of the differences that she expected to see reflected in the questionnaire responses, "I hypothesized that I was communicating more effectively with the immersion students because (a) I was teaching them in my native language and (b) I was developing my own curriculum and materials for the class." Results from the questionnaire, however, showed nearly identical perceptions of her by both classes. This is not an unusual outcome— while teachers frequently believe they are perceived differently in different classes (because they perceive their own behavior as different), the research is not supportive. Essentially, teachers develop a stable communication style which permeates all of their teaching (Wubbels & Levy, 1993).

Marie reflected upon the questionnaire results and speculated on the discrepancy that emerged as her own perception of herself as a teacher evolved during the school year:

> I began this year feeling I was a tough, yet amicable and organized teacher. Halfway into the year I was seeing myself much more softened (more willing to give breaks) and helpful than I used to be. My teaching and communication styles were not working at Lewis and I had to adapt quickly, but such adaptation brought feelings of uneasiness on my part that remained throughout the year.

Marie's understated "uneasiness" at the end of her first year suggests the enormity of adjustments necessary for teachers who are themselves recent immigrants. Among other factors, her commitment to being an effective teacher and her willingness to accept suggestions from the LMTIP mentor teachers enabled her to complete the school year.

Another "beginning" teacher in the Lewis induction group, who is highly educated, has teaching experience in Southeast Asia and speaks four languages fluently, requested a transfer out of her Lewis classroom midway through first semester. Despite support from her beginning teacher colleagues and the efforts of the mentor teachers to provide constructive feedback, the adjustment to the middle school classroom at Lewis proved to be overwhelmingly difficult.

CONCLUSION

At the time of this writing the LMTIP is completing its third successful year. Having worked out some of our early kinks (such as principals' requiring participation), and taking advantage of our alumni's experiences, the present group of teachers are engaging in more meaningful reflective practice and action research than ever before. The beneficiaries, of course, are the youngsters. By providing the beginning teachers with an opportunity to learn and improve their professional practice in a supportive setting the LMTIP has directly contributed to increased academic achievement, improved instruction and a higher quality educational experience for their bilingual students.

One of the most important goals of the project is to sustain itself after federal funds cease. The LMTIP has taken some significant steps to build capacity. First, the learning community aspect of the project has been extended by inviting alumni (e.g., teachers who have completed their year of active participation) to continue as "mini-mentors" to successive generations of beginning teachers. It is believed that these groups will continue to function in the future. Second, all project teachers have become members of a teacher research network in Northern Virginia which conducts regular activities and a yearly conference. Several project teachers have presented their work at the local teacher research conference. Finally, each year project teachers describe the LMTIP experience with their colleagues through formal and informal activities. They have aligned themselves with other mentoring, teacher-research activities in their schools and districts. It is believed that even though the LMTIP cannot function in exactly the same manner after federal funding ceases, the essential components—mentoring, learning community and action research—will live on.

As one of the teachers told us at the end of the year,

> This grant has improved my instructional practice by giving me time and support to examine one aspect of teaching. The grant also provided some of the resources I needed to have a successful project. [It] has been a benefit to my school because it allowed teachers from different disciplines to work as a team and it allowed us to try new techniques. . . . The resources we gained from being in this project will stay in our school.

REFERENCES

Argyris, C. (1993). *Knowledge for action: A guide to overcoming barriers to organizational change.* San Francisco: Jossey-Bass.

Collier, C.P., & Pateracki, T. (1998, March-April). Geometry in the middle school: An exchange of ideas and experiences. *Mathematics Teaching in the Middle School, 3,* 6.

Craig, S., Hull, K., & Haggart, A. (2000, January-February). Promoting cultural competence through teacher assistance teams. *Teaching Exceptional Children, 32*(3), 6–12.

Darling-Hammond, L. (1998, February). Teacher learning that supports student learning. *Educational Leadership, 55*(5), 6–11.

DuFour, R. (2000, Spring). School leaders as staff developers: the key to sustained school improvement. *Catalyst for Change, 29*(3), 13–15.

Halford, J. (1998, February). Easing the way for new teachers. *Educational Leadership, 55*(5), 33–36.

Hecht, J., Roberts, N., & Schoon, P. (1996, Spring). Teacher teams and computer technology: do combined strategies maximize student achievement? *Journal of Research on Computing in Education, 28,* 318–328.

Levy, J. (ed) (2002-projected). *From concept to practice: Improving bilingual students' academic achievement through mentoring and teacher research.* Washington, DC: National Clearinghouse for Bilingual Education.

Manning, M., & Saddlemire, R. (1996, December). Developing a sense of community in secondary schools. *NASSP Bulletin, 80,* 41–48.

MacLean, M., & Mohr, M. (1999). *Teacher researchers at work.* Berkeley, CA: National Writing Project.

Moll, L.C., Velez-Ibanez, C., & Greenberg, J. (1988). *Project implementation plan: Community knowledge and classroom practice: Combining resources for literacy instruction.* Tucson: University of Arizona.

Schon, D. (1983). *The reflective practitioner.* New York: Basic Books.

Schmuck, R. (1997). *Practical action research for change.* Arlington Heights, IL: IRI/ SkyLight Trng/Pub.

Stiggins, R. (1999, Summer). Teams. *Journal of Staff Development, 20*(3), 17–21.

Senge, P., Kleiner, A., Robert, C., Ross, R., Roth, G., & Smith, B. (1999). *The dance of change: The challenges to sustaining momentum in learning organizations.* New York: Doubleday.

Wubbels, Th., & Levy, J. (Eds). (1993). *Do you know what you look like? Interpersonal relationships in education.* London: Falmer Press.

CONCLUSION

Liliana Minaya-Rowe

A major theme threaded throughout all of the chapters in this volume is that to provide quality training for teachers of an increasing multilingual and multicultural student population. Volume contributors—teacher educators, researchers and practitioners—have described some of the complex, varied, and situated experiences of teachers and teachers-to-be in the context of schooling of ELLs. They have documented the foundations for effective new structures and practices for professional development as they need to be practiced, and in doing so, they have acknowledged how the contexts within which teaching occurs affect the processes of teaching or of learning to teach.

Clearly, there is a need for stronger research foci in teacher education in the context of student linguistic and cultural diversity. The authors in this volume provide a direction for continued research in a vein based upon diverse assumptions about training teachers of ELLs. Their quiet revolution has the potential to change the way teacher educators prepare teachers to teach ELLs and to learn alongside their students' needs and strengths. In this volume, Waxman and Padrón have used effective teaching practices in which students become active learners and teachers facilitate their learning. They contend that professional development programs need new ways to teach the standards-based curriculum so that ELLs can participate and benefit from classroom activities. Calderón has presented a range of professional development opportunities and follow-up support systems to help teachers transfer new teaching practices into their classrooms. In addition, she has asserted that teachers need to be retooled in areas of curriculum, teaching methodology, language and assessment that maximize learning potential. Garcia and his co-researchers have articulated the importance of a more responsive pedagogy with a focus on principles for authentic assessment to benefit student learning and have encouraged more research on teaching effective pedagogy to be conducted at all levels of instruction. Griego Jones has made it clear that professional development needs to be refocused for ELLs. She has shown how beliefs can affect change and how second language learning can influence how teachers learn to teach.

An important consideration is that the current U.S. teacher population is approximately 90% White American, and monolingual female and no significant changes in the percentage are predicted despite education reform efforts (Grant & Secada, 1990). Furthermore, teacher education programs, for the most part, reflect the monocultural and monolingual circumstances of teachers, especially in daily instructional practices (Valdés, 1998). For example, Goodland (1984) and Delpit (1995) describe the operation of schools (the textbooks, instructional practices, and the policies) as not substantially different from Anglo-American student teachers' own experience.

How can professional development for teachers and teachers-to-be be addressed to meet the needs of a linguistically and culturally diverse student population? The contributors to this volume have depicted teachers as sources of knowledge, as theorizers who, based on a combination of theoretical, personal, practical, and experiential knowledge, routinely enact theories of teaching and learning within the contexts of their own classrooms. For example, Dalton and Tharp have examined teachers' prior experience and knowledge and its utilization in their teacher education programs. Padrón and her co-researchers have examined the effectiveness of a teacher resiliency program for teachers of ELLs to improve their classroom instruction and their students' academic achievement. Contributors have given teachers the opportunity to theorize and to reflect about their work, their theories have become the basis of how they conceptualize, construct explanations, and respond to social interactions and shared meanings that exist within their classrooms. They have led teacher participants to become contributors to the substance and processes of their professional discourse communities. Their chapters have provided teachers for theorizing opportunities as they learn to teach ELLs. Some chapters have created structures that allow teachers to reflect on their experiences, share their evolving understandings with others, and jointly construct knowledge that is relevant to their teaching contexts. Minaya-Rowe and Olezza have presented an interactive professional development approach that uses both social and school factors which influence language and academic learning. Levy and his co-researchers have proposed a mentoring system that contributes to improvement of instruction and also academic achievement.

In this volume, the chapter authors have also framed structures that enable teachers to examine the theoretical knowledge in the course work within the familiar context of their own learning and teaching experiences, and have used their knowledge about teaching, learning, and students in situated and interpretative ways. They have provided for professional communities for teachers to present their professional understandings and teaching/learning experiences to others (Calderón, this volume).

Tinajero and Spencer have examined new structures and practices for teacher development and for program sustainability. Through these theorizing opportunities, teachers have come to see how their knowledge about themselves, their students, and the contexts in which they teach, shape what and how they teach.

The chapters also reflect agreement on basic principles for maximizing professional development and the practice of effective pedagogy and, also, for maximizing achievement of ELLs. Authors have enacted and studied professional development for effective teaching in widely diverse settings. They have provided program alternatives and models for teachers of ELLs with an understanding of the best conditions for achieving them. They have also added knowledge to design professional development programs based on their research findings.

All in all, this volume accounts for action research studies that bring together quantitative and qualitative research, that consider an interdisciplinary involvement, that are based on the constant interaction between pure and applied research. The research contributions presented in this book can provide answers to questions, and a clearer picture and insights about some of the following issues: (a) approaches to equity issues—e.g., how to empower teachers of ELLs and teachers-to-be in order to challenge the societal power structure of English-speaking America regarding bilingualism, bilingual instruction, and multiculturalism (Cummins, 2000); (b) approaches to policy practices—what are the implications of the authors' research contributions for teacher education in general; (c) considerations for the role of the federal government to build continuity in action research efforts, in addition to support with funding; (d) the significance of action research studies by researchers like the contributors to this volume who have constantly been at the heart of the problem, committed and doing a good job; and, (e) coordination of nationwide research efforts ensuring that research is not duplicated, but validated.

The contributors to this volume have also considered the theoretical principles that have been consistently supported in the literature. They have used this information in order to generate their own studies and for interpreting the data gathered for their own specific research purposes. Their research findings have told us something we did not know before they started. Their findings have acknowledged and strengthened issues in teacher education for which some valid answers already exist. Those issues have already been studied in other contexts based on theories that predict outcomes under a variety of different conditions. Furthermore, the contributors of this volume have based their studies on what we know in teacher education and, at the same time, have defended the principles underlying bilingual and bicultural education. Their research efforts reflect the concept that nothing is as practical as a good theory and they have unified facts for interpretation and general application of their research in professional development.

In recent years, critical pedagogy and bilingual bicultural education have led to a reexamination of curriculum and materials. This concept could be extended to professional development as applied by Dalton and Tharp, and Waxman and Padrón (this volume). The five standards for effective pedagogy are applicable across grade levels, student population and cultures, in teacher education. The standards reveal continuous interaction and activity in the ongoing social events of the classroom and beyond (Dalton, 1998). In defining the nation-state and its embodiment of knowledge, the nation-state's cultural, political, and educational hegemony becomes its democratic standard in the schooling process. Advocates of an "engaged pedagogy," Freire (1993) and Hooks (1994), consider this practice involving critical learning, action, and reflection for self-actualization and empowerment. Rather than opting for prepackaged teacher education that fails to acknowledge relearning as one teaches, Freire's writings, we may assume, address the challenges of teachers of ELLs who come into a new educational system, a new language, and a new culture toward the goals that they learn the language, the academics and observe and recognize the relationship between objects of the world. Giroux (1988) endorses empowerment when individuals move from being objects to subjects through a naming of their social reality. Through such learning, education becomes a practice of freedom as the student moves against and beyond social boundaries.

Ball (2000) acknowledges the cultural capital appropriated by teachers: "American public schools have had relatively little success in educating students who are poor, members of racially and ethnically marginalized groups, and speakers of first languages other than mainstream or academic English" (p. 227). Vygotsky's (1978) sociocultural theory emphasizes the social world where learning emerges, and that more knowledgeable members of a group engage in social mediation to bring others into the cultural practices.

Future studies need to consider the teacher education research put forth in this volume to conduct research in other settings with other ethnic groups and different languages. These theoretical frameworks can predict certain outcomes; the validity of the theories is precisely how well they can account for the data under different conditions. Further studies also need to be sensible to the kinds of changes that are occurring at the broader sociopolitical level. Research is needed to expand the potential of training teachers for bilingual instruction in dual language programs which include minority and majority students (Lindholm-Leary, 2001). There is a need to test and evaluate some of the programs' concepts and determine what principles are operating in the professional development of dual language program teachers. An ensuing task is then to deepen our analyses, synthesize our research and practice, and introduce professional development to teach linguistically and culturally diverse students in teacher education programs. Another activity would be to focus on a specific topic of professional development with researchers of professional development programs for teachers of ELLs with counterparts, including those mainstream, "non-diversity' teacher educators into joint work and dialogue to be able to influence the national policy and practice environment.

REFERENCES

Ball, A.F. (2000). Teachers' developing philosophies on literacy and their use in urban schools: A Vygotskian perspective on internal activity and teacher change. In C.D. Lee & P. Smagorinski (Eds.), *Vygotskian perspectives on literacy research: Constructing meaning through collaborative inquiry* (pp. 226-255). New York: Oxford University Press.

Cummins, J. (2000). *Language, power and pedagogy. Bilingual Children in the crossfire.* Clevedon, U.K.: Multilingual Matters.

Dalton, S.S. (1998). *Pedagogy matters: Standards for effective teaching practice.* Santa Cruz: CA: Center for Research on Education, Diversity, and Excellence.

Delpit, L. (1995). *Other people's children: Cultural conflict in the classroom.* New York: The Free Press.

Freire, P. (1993). *Pedagogy of the oppressed* (M.B. Ramos, Trans.). New York: Continuum (Original work published in 1970).

Giroux, H.A. (1988). *Teachers as intellectuals. Toward a critical pedagogy of learning.* Westport, CT: Begin and Harvey.

Grant, C.A., & Secada, W. (1990). Preparing teachers for diversity. In W.R. Houston (Ed.), *Handbook of research in teacher education* (pp. 403-422). New York: Macmillan.

Goodlad, J. (1984). *A place called school.* New York: McGraw-Hill.

Hooks, B. (1994). *Teaching to transgress: Education as the practice of freedom.* New York: Routledge.

Linholm-Leary, K. (2001). *Dual language education.* Clevedon, U.K.: Multilingual Matters.

Valdes, G. (1998). The world outside and inside schools: Language and immigrant children. *Educational Researcher, 27*(6), 4-18.

Vygotsky, L.S. (1978). *Mind in society: The development of higher psychological processes.* Cambridge, MA: Harvard University Press.

ABOUT THE EDITOR AND CONTRIBUTORS

Marco A. Bravo is a doctoral student in the Language, Literacy, and Culture Program at the University of California, Berkeley. For the past two years, he has worked with teachers at a K-5 dual (Spanish-English) language immersion program. His work focuses on assisting teachers in the use of the results of the Authentic Literacy Assessment System to augment or reinforce their practice to optimize instruction for culturally and linguistically diverse students. His dissertation research will focus on the trajectories taken by bilingual students in their learning to write in two languages and how teacher instruction influences these paths.

Ann P. Brown is a Research Associate in the U.S. Department of Education, National Center for Research on Education, Diversity, and Excellence at the University of Houston. Her areas of interest are culturally and linguistically diverse students and educational resilience.

Margarita Calderón is a Faculty/Research Scientist at the Center for Research on Education of Students Placed At Risk (CRESPAR), Johns Hopkins University, where she works in a number of projects: effective instruction for two-way immersion/dual language, ESL, and bilingual programs; teachers' learning communities; and, staff development practices in schools with language minority populations. Dr. Calderón also conducts research, training and curriculum development for the *Success for Al/lÉxito Para Todos* transitional, ESL, and two-way/dual language bilingual program components and directs the Leadership Enhancement Academy/Texas Teacher Recruitment, Retention and Assistance Program for bilingual teachers and binational education.

Donna Christian is President of the Center for Applied Linguistics (CAL) in Washington, DC, where she is active in research, program evaluation, policy analysis, and professional development. Dr. Christian's work focuses on language in education, including issues of second language learning and dialect diversity. Recent publications include *Bilingual Education* (co-edited with Fred Genesee, TESOL, 2001) and *Dialects in Schools and Communities* (co-authored with Walt Wolfram and Carolyn Adger, Lawrence Erlbaum, 1999).

Katherine Chun is a doctoral student in Education with an emphasis in the area of School Psychology at the University of California, Berkeley. Her dissertation addresses the challenge of student assessment reform and examines how educators can collaborate and use theory-based and research-driven authentic process assessment such as the Authentic Literacy Assessment System to understand and be responsive to the diverse and unique cognitive, cultural, linguistic, and social differences in students developing literacy in a second language.

Stephanie Stoll Dalton is a Senior Program Specialist with the Office of Educational Research and Improvement (OERI), U.S. Department of Education. Her federal work is informed by experiences as a K-12 teacher and teacher educator focusing on issues of diverse, immigrant, and at-risk students. Her research in teacher professional development for diversity has been supported through OERI-funded national research centers, Eisenhower Professional Development, and other grants. She served as Associate Director for the National Research Center on Cultural Diversity and Second Language Learning.

Laurie M. Dickey recently received a Master of Arts Degree in Education in the Language, Literacy, and Culture Program at the University of California, Berkeley. Previously, she taught in a Spanish bilingual program and served as a mentor teacher in an urban elementary school in the Los Angeles Unified School District. Her research interests include early literacy development among culturally and linguistically diverse students, the dynamics of multicultural classrooms, and dual language immersion programs.

Kristy Dunlap is Assistant Professor in the Graduate School of Education at George Mason University in the literacy and secondary education programs. She teaches courses related to effective literacy instruction in classrooms in both pre-service and advanced studies programs for teachers. She is conducting research related to the effects of student assessment on beginning teachers' experiences and in classroom discourse in middle and high schools. Her involvement in the Language Minority Teacher Induction Project as a university mentor offered an opportunity to support and study beginning teachers in a middle school as they experienced classroom challenges first-hand.

Eugene Garcia is Professor of Education at the University of California, Berkeley. He has published extensively in the area of language teaching and bilingual development. He served as a Senior Office and Director of the Office of Bilingual Education and Minority Languages Affairs in the U.S. Department of Education from 1993-1995 and he is conducting research in the areas of effective schooling for linguistically and culturally diverse student populations.

Toni Griego Jones is Associate Professor in the Department of Teaching and Teacher Education at the University of Arizona. Her research interests include pre-service teachers' beliefs about second language acquisition and Latino parent/community involvement in educational reform. She teaches courses in educational foundations, bilingual education, and equity issues. Prior to entering higher education in 1988 at the University of Wisconsin-Milwaukee, she was a teacher and administrator in the Denver area schools for fifteen years.

Jack Levy is a Professor of Multicultural/Multilingual Education at George Mason University in Fairfax, VA. Dr. Levy is the principal investigator for the Language Minority Teacher Induction Project, which provides support for beginning teachers in multilingual settings. He teaches courses in multicultural/multilingual education, and has consulted and presented workshops on diversity, intercultural communication and conflict resolution for more than two decades. In addition to his work with beginning teachers, he is currently conducting research on the cultural influences on students' perceptions of teachers.

Liliana Minaya-Rowe is Professor Emeritus of the Neag School of Education at the University of Connecticut. Her research interests, publications and teaching include teacher education, literacy, bilingual program development and implementation, standards-based curriculum in bilingual bicultural education, first and second language acquisition, assessment of bilingualism, second language teaching methodology, parent and community involvement in schooling, and discourse analysis. She is currently conducting research on the social contexts of dual language education.

Ana María Olezza is Director of Bilingual Bicultural Education at the Hartford Public Schools in Hartford, CT where she coordinates and supervises all initiatives of the Bilingual, Migratory, Dual Language and Foreign Language programs. She has taught college-level graduate and undergraduate courses in Bilingual, ESL and Foreign Language Education. Her research interests include standards-based instruction, literacy and effective pedagogy.

Yolanda N. Padrón is a Professor of Curriculum and Instruction in the College of Education at the University of Houston, and Co-Director of the U.S. Department of Education, National Center for Research on Education, Diversity, and Excellence. Her research focuses on bilingual education, students at risk of failure, and instruction for English language learners. She has recently published articles on those topics in journals such as *Bilingual Research Journal, TESOL Quarterly,* and *Journal of Education for Students Placed At Risk.*

Robert Powers is a Research Associate in the U. S. Department of Education, National Center for Research on Education, Diversity, and Excellence at the University of Houston. His area of research is mathematics education.

Lynn Shafer is a doctoral student in the Center for Multilingual/Multicultural Education in George Mason University. She served as the LMTIP Graduate Research Assistant for the first two years of the project. Prior to that, she was an ESL teacher in the Fairfax County (VA.) Public Schools and used teacher research as part of her professional practice. She has conducted numerous presentations on teacher research, cultural issues in second language acquisition, and assessing ELLs for learning disabilities. She currently works at PBS TeacherLine, an online staff development program. Her research interests include the spread of the English language worldwide and online staff development and training.

Xiaoqin Sun-Irminger has a bachelor and a master's degree in English and literature from Hangzhou University, China. She also has a master's degree in English as a second language (ESL) from the University of the Pacific, Stockton, California. Xiaoqin has taught English to Chinese college students for five years. The areas of her instruction include courses in linguistics, ESL and bilingual education, culture language and education, and methodologies in teaching minority students. She currently holds a teaching position at Portland State University.

Dee Ann Spencer is a Senior Research Specialist and the Director of the Office of School Improvement in the College of Education at Arizona State University. She has conducted research in schools for nearly 30 years and has published articles and chapters in the fields of sociology and education. The focus of many of these has been on teaching as an occupation and on teaching as women's work, including a book, *Contemporary Women*

Teachers: Balancing School and Home. She has continued this focus by comparing teachers' lives in Mexico and the United States. Her recent research, supported by federal, state, local, and foundation grants and contracts, is focused on evaluation of school programs and reform efforts, including the translation into practice of literacy, mathematics, science and technology initiatives, teacher training in bilingual education, and on teacher action research.

Roland G. Tharp won the Grawemeyer Award in 1993, for the book *Rousing Minds to Life,* based on work done while he was Principal Investigator of the Kamehameha Early Education Program (KEEP) in Honolulu for 20 years. He has also taught at the Universities of Hawaii and Arizona. His research and theory in the field of human development, education, culture, and linguistic diversity span publication dates of 40 years. Currently he is Director of the Center for Research on Education, Diversity & Excellence (known as CREDE) at the University of California, Santa Cruz, where he is also Professor of Education & Psychology. His latest book is a summary treatment, with CREDE coauthors, of "what we know" and "what we need to do," titled *Teaching Transformed.*

Josefina Villamil Tinajero is a Professor of Bilingual Education and Interim Dean of the College of Education at the University of Texas at El Paso, where she has also directed a number of Title VII Bilingual Education grant programs. Dr. Tinajero has presented numerous papers and keynote speeches at international, national and state conferences. Her most recent publications include *Literacy Assessment for Second Language Learners* (co-edited with S. Hurley), *The Power of Two Languages* (with R. DeVillar) and *Educating Latino Students: A Guide to Successful Practice* (with S. L. Gonzalez and A.Huerta-Macias). She is currently the Principal Investigator on two Title VII Grants: Projects CBTL (Cultivating Bilingual Teachers and Leaders) and Project BEEM (Bilingual Education Enhancement and Mentoring Project).

Hersh C. Waxman is a Professor of Curriculum and Instruction in the College of Education at the University of Houston, a Principal Researcher in the U.S. Department of Education, National Center for Research on Education, Diversity, and Excellence, and a Principal Investigator in the U.S. Department of Education, National Laboratory for Student Success, The Mid-Atlantic Regional Educational Laboratory. His research focuses on classroom learning environments, school and teacher effectiveness, urban education, and students at risk of failure. He has recently published articles on those topics in journals such as *Journal of Educational Research, Learning Environment Research: An International Journal,* and *Urban Education.*

INDEX

309